Santiago
de Chile

Wayne Bernhardson

LONELY PLANET PUBLICATIONS
Melbourne • Oakland • London • Paris

Santiago de Chile
1st edition – October 2000

Published by
Lonely Planet Publications Pty Ltd A.C.N. 005 607 983
192 Burwood Rd, Hawthorn, Victoria 3122, Australia

Lonely Planet Offices
Australia PO Box 617, Hawthorn, Victoria 3122
USA 150 Linden St, Oakland, CA 94607
UK 10a Spring Place, London NW5 3BH
France 1 rue du Dahomey, 75011 Paris

Photographs
All of the images in this guide are available for licensing from
Lonely Planet Images.
email: lpi@lonelyplanet.com.au

Front cover photograph
Moai statue with communications tower (Stone/William J. Hebert)

ISBN 0 86442 433 7

Printed by Colorcraft Ltd, Hong Kong

Contents

The Author

Wayne Bernhardson

Wayne Bernhardson was born in Fargo, North Dakota, grew up in Tacoma, Washington, and earned a PhD in geography from the University of California, Berkeley. He has traveled extensively in Mexico and Central and South America, and he has lived for long periods in Chile, Argentina and the Falkland (Malvinas) Islands. His other LP credits include *Buenos Aires, Chile & Easter Island, South America on a shoestring* and *Baja California*.

'The gringo who knows Chile best,' according to Santiago's principal daily newspaper *El Mercurio*, Wayne resides in Oakland, California, with María Laura Massolo, their daughter Clio and his Alaskan malamute Gardel.

FROM THE AUTHOR

Many friends and acquaintances in Santiago and elsewhere were helpful and hospitable in the process of pulling this all together. The list could go on forever, but special mention goes to Yerko Ivelic of Cascada Expediciones, for harboring my truck in San Alfonso while I returned to California to write up my Argentine material; and to customs agent Juan Alarcón Rojas for navigating through the Chilean bureaucracy. Javier López of Cascada introduced me to hikes I had never known were so close to the city.

Thanks also to Pablo Fernández of Hostelling International, for arranging long-term accommodations in Santiago; Eduardo Núñez of Conaf in Santiago, for easing access to national parks and other reserves; Steve Anderson of the Chile Information Project; Harold Beckett of the Guía Aérea Oficial; María Fernanda Daza of the Municipalidad de Santiago; Simon Hosking of the British embassy in Santiago; Douglas Koneff and Diana Page of the US embassy in Santiago; Víctor Maldonado and Marisa Blásquez; Hernán, Carmen, Marcela and Paula Torres; Pato Ovando and Marializ Maldonado; Claudio Parra of Los Jaivas and his agent Claudia Schlegel; and Mauricio Carmona.

Thanks also go to Veronique Arancet Rodríguez of the Municipalidad de Valparaíso and Paola Lara of Sernatur in Viña del Mar.

In Los Angeles (California), Iván Zika of LanChile was most helpful in arranging flight details, along with Alberto Cortés of LanChile in Miami. Cecilia Aguayo of Miami and Silber Editores also deserve mention. Thanks also to Chilean consul Alberto Yoacham of San Francisco, and Paul and Philip Garber of the Chilean consulate in Boston.

Thanks once again to Tony and Maureen Wheeler for keeping me employed for nearly a decade and to Eric Kettunen and other Oakland office editors, cartographers and staff. My apologies to anyone I've overlooked.

This Book

This 1st edition of *Santiago de Chile* was researched and written by Wayne Bernhardson.

FROM THE PUBLISHER

The *Santiago de Chile* guide was produced in Lonely Planet's Oakland office. Rebecca Northen edited the book, with help from Kevin Anglin. Senior editor Michele Posner oversaw the project. Besides help with editing, Kevin proofed most of the book, with Rachel Bernstein taking care of the rest. Ken DellaPenta indexed the book.

Lead cartographer Chris Gillis! drew and corrected the maps with little fuss. He reported to senior cartographer Tracey 'T-Rock' Croom, while Guphy and Connie 'Pugs' Lock lended a cartographic helping hand with map editing.

Designer Josh Schefers proved himself a layout master, guided by design manager Susan Rimerman. The illustrations were created by Justin Marler, Beca Lafore, Hannah Reineck, Hayden Foell, Hugh D'Andrade and Mark Butler, and Rini Keagy designed the cover.

Foreword

ABOUT LONELY PLANET GUIDEBOOKS

The story begins with a classic travel adventure: Tony and Maureen Wheeler's 1972 journey across Europe and Asia to Australia. Useful information about the overland trail did not exist at that time, so Tony and Maureen published the first Lonely Planet guidebook to meet a growing need.

From a kitchen table, then from a tiny office in Melbourne (Australia), Lonely Planet has become the largest independent travel publisher in the world, an international company with offices in Melbourne, Oakland (USA), London (UK) and Paris (France).

Today Lonely Planet guidebooks cover the globe. There is an ever-growing list of books, and there's information in a variety of forms and media. Some things haven't changed. The main aim is still to help make it possible for adventurous travelers to get out there – to explore and better understand the world.

At Lonely Planet we believe travelers can make a positive contribution to the countries they visit – if they respect their host communities and spend their money wisely. Since 1986 a percentage of the income from each book has been donated to aid projects and human-rights campaigns.

Updates Lonely Planet thoroughly updates each guidebook as often as possible. This usually means there are around two years between editions, although for more unusual or more stable destinations the gap can be longer. Check the imprint page at the beginning of the book for publication dates.

Between editions, up-to-date information is available in two free newsletters – the paper *Planet Talk* and email *Comet* (to subscribe, contact any Lonely Planet office) – and on our website at www.lonelyplanet.com. The *Upgrades* section of the website covers a number of important and volatile destinations and is regularly updated by Lonely Planet authors. *Scoop* covers news and current affairs relevant to travelers. And, lastly, the *Thorn Tree* bulletin board and *Postcards* section of the site carry unverified, but fascinating, reports from travelers.

Correspondence The process of creating new editions begins with the letters, postcards and emails received from travelers. This correspondence often includes suggestions, criticisms and comments about the current editions. Interesting excerpts are immediately passed on via newsletters and the website, and everything goes to our authors to be verified when they're researching on the road. We're keen to get more feedback from organizations or individuals who represent communities visited by travelers.

Lonely Planet gathers information for everyone who's curious about the planet – and especially for those who explore it firsthand. Through guidebooks, phrasebooks, activity guides, maps, literature, newsletters, image library, TV series and website, we act as an information exchange for a worldwide community of travelers.

Research Authors aim to gather sufficient practical information to enable travelers to make informed choices and to make the mechanics of a journey run smoothly. They also research historical and cultural background to help enrich the travel experience and allow travelers to understand and respond appropriately to cultural and environmental issues.

Authors don't stay in every hotel because that would mean spending a couple of months in each medium-size city and, no, they don't eat at every restaurant because that would mean stretching belts beyond capacity. They do visit hotels and restaurants to check standards and prices, but feedback based on readers' direct experiences can be very helpful.

Many of our authors work undercover; others aren't so secretive. None of them accept freebies in exchange for positive write-ups. And none of our guidebooks contain any advertising.

Production Authors submit their raw manuscripts and maps to offices in Australia, the USA, the UK or France. Editors and cartographers – all experienced travelers themselves – then begin the process of assembling the pieces. When the book finally hits the shops, some things are already out of date, we start getting feedback from readers and the process begins again....

WARNING & REQUEST

Things change – prices go up, schedules change, good places go bad and bad places go bankrupt – nothing stays the same. So, if you find things better or worse, recently opened or long since closed, please tell us and help make the next edition even more accurate and useful. We genuinely value all the feedback we receive. Julie Young coordinates a well-traveled team that reads and acknowledges every letter, postcard and email and ensures that every morsel of information finds its way to the appropriate authors, editors and cartographers for verification.

Everyone who writes to us will find their name in the next edition of the appropriate guidebook. They will also receive the latest issue of *Planet Talk*, our quarterly printed newsletter, or *Comet*, our monthly email newsletter. Subscriptions to both newsletters are free. The very best contributions will be rewarded with a free guidebook.

Excerpts from your correspondence may appear in new editions of Lonely Planet guidebooks, the Lonely Planet website, *Planet Talk* or *Comet*, so please let us know if you *don't* want your letter published or your name acknowledged.

Send all correspondence to the Lonely Planet office closest to you:

Australia: PO Box 617, Hawthorn, Victoria 3122
USA: 150 Linden St, Oakland, CA 94607
UK: 10A Spring Place, London NW5 3BH
France: 1 rue du Dahomey, 75011 Paris

Or email us at: talk2us@lonelyplanet.com.au

For news, views and updates, see our website: www.lonelyplanet.com

HOW TO USE A LONELY PLANET GUIDEBOOK

The best way to use a Lonely Planet guidebook is any way you choose. At Lonely Planet, we believe the most memorable travel experiences are often those that are unexpected, and the finest discoveries are those you make yourself. Guidebooks are not intended to be used as if they provided a detailed set of infallible instructions!

Contents All Lonely Planet guidebooks follow the same format. The Facts about the City chapters or sections give background information ranging from history to weather. Facts for the Visitor gives practical information on issues like visas and health. Getting There & Away gives a brief starting point for researching travel to and from the destination. Getting Around gives an overview of the transport options available when you arrive.

The peculiar demands of each destination determine how subsequent chapters are broken up, but some things remain constant. We always start with background, then proceed to sights, places to stay, places to eat, entertainment, getting there and away, and getting around information – in that order.

Heading Hierarchy Lonely Planet headings are used in a strict hierarchical structure that can be visualized as a set of Russian dolls. Each heading (and its following text) is encompassed by any preceding heading that is higher on the hierarchical ladder.

Entry Points We do not assume guidebooks will be read from beginning to end, but that people will dip into them. The traditional entry points are the list of contents and the index. In addition, however, some books have a complete list of maps and an index map illustrating map coverage.

There may also be a color map that shows highlights. These highlights are dealt with in greater detail later in the book, along with planning questions and suggested itineraries. Each chapter covering a geographical region usually begins with a locator map and another list of highlights. Once you find something of interest in a list of highlights, turn to the index.

Maps Maps play a crucial role in Lonely Planet guidebooks and include a huge amount of information. A legend is printed on the back page. We seek to have complete consistency between maps and text, and to have every important place in the text captured on a map. Map key numbers usually start in the top left corner.

Although inclusion in a guidebook usually implies a recommendation, we cannot list every good place. Exclusion does not necessarily imply criticism. In fact, there are a number of reasons why we might exclude a place – sometimes it is simply inappropriate to encourage an influx of travelers.

Introduction

Santiago de Chile is a city of contrasts, a modern metropolis whose shining international air terminal greets foreign bankers and franchises rushing to invest their money in one of South America's most dynamic economies. Prosperous professionals pack fine restaurants, and cell phones and car alarms have become status symbols to a burgeoning middle class – but at the same time, struggling street vendors board city buses to hawk everything from pins and needles to pens and ice cream, and housemaids ride for hours to scrub floors and change diapers in exclusive suburbs where gardeners lug rakes and push-mowers on the backs of their bicycles.

Santiago's skyline is unprepossessing, but its glitzy exterior reflects more than a decade of vigorous economic growth. Santiago's commercial importance is one of the main reasons for the existence of this guidebook, but ordinary tourists and any other open-minded visitors will find much to enjoy in the city and its surroundings.

Chile's sprawling capital is really many cities in one – Santiago proper, the former colonial core, is surrounded by another 31 *comunas* of greater or lesser antiquity that have coalesced to form the present megacity. Each comuna has its own separate municipal administration, including mayor and council, but the national government legislates and administers many urban services, such as public transportation, throughout the Región Metropolitana (Metropolitan Region).

Unfortunately, most streets are too narrow for the heavy rush-hour traffic, and a blanket of smog frequently lurks overhead as the phalanx of the Andes, rarely visible except immediately after a rain, blocks the dispersal of pollutants. Many beautifully landscaped parks provide refuge from air pollution, but it's sometimes hard to ignore the visual pollution from the billboards and neon signs that an increasingly consumerist society has inflicted on the cityscape.

Besides growing out, the city has grown up, as ever more skyscrapers dominate the landscape, both downtown and rising toward the Andes in comunas like Providencia and Las Condes, which have been usurping downtown's historical role as the city's commercial and financial center. Most areas of interest to visitors are between downtown Santiago and the Andes, along with the surrounding central comunas of Ñuñoa, Estación Central, Quinta Normal, Recoleta and Independencia.

Santiago may be one of the finest cities in the world for excursions – less than an hour from the central Plaza de Armas are world-class ski areas and white-water rafting, while only a little farther are the colorful port city of Valparaíso and famous beach resorts, making it feasible to ski and surf on the same day. For visiting businesspeople, few other world capitals can match Santiago's options for a free afternoon, day or weekend.

9

Facts about Santiago de Chile

HISTORY

Gazing west from the rocky overlook of Cerro Santa Lucía to the skyscrapers and apartment blocks of metropolitan Santiago, it's hard to imagine that just six months after Pedro de Valdivia founded Santiago in 1541, Mapuche warriors nearly obliterated it. Spanish troops regrouped on the fortified summit of Cerro Santa Lucía, and Valdivia made immediate plans to rebuild the precarious settlement.

Valdivia had laid out a regular grid from the present-day Plaza de Armas, but for two years 'Santiago del Nuevo Extremo' was little more than a besieged hillside camp. Its tile-roofed adobe houses survived fire, but colonists nearly starved under Araucanian pressure. Two years passed before assistance arrived from Peru. After returning to Peru himself for new troops and supplies, Valdivia pushed southward, founding Concepción in 1550 and Valdivia in 1552. But these early settlements were merely fortified villages.

In Santiago, most houses were built around central patios and enhanced with gardens and grape arbors, but open sewers ran down the middle of the streets. As the settlements became more secure, soldiers formed households with Araucanian women. Tradesmen from Spain, like shoemakers, blacksmiths, armorers and tanners, provided services for the colonists. In the beginning, the towns were almost exclusively administrative centers for the new colony and bases for sorties into Mapuche territory, while most of the population lived in the countryside.

By the late 16th century, Santiago was a settlement of just 200 houses, inhabited by not more than 700 Spaniards and mestizos, plus several thousand Indian laborers and servants. Occasionally flooded by the Río Mapocho, it nevertheless lacked a safe water supply, and communications between town and countryside were difficult. But despite their precarious position, wealthy *encomenderos* (Spaniards who held rights to indigenous labor in exchange for providing religious and language instruction) and other elite elements sought to emulate European nobility, with platoons of servants and imported products from Europe and China. Shortages of resources like weapons, ammunition and horses contributed to the Spaniards' expulsion by the Mapuche from the area south of the Río Biobío, but wealthy households still enjoyed luxuries like velvet and silk.

From Inauspicious Beginnings ...

Subject to the Viceroyalty of Peru, Chile remained a backwater of imperial Spain for nearly three centuries, yielding little exportable wealth. Nevertheless, by the late 18th century Santiago began to acquire the substance of a city proper. New *tajamares* (dikes) restrained the Mapocho, improved roads handled increased commerce between the capital and its port of Valparaíso, and authorities targeted various beautification projects to please the landowning aristocracy.

As colonial rule ended in the early 19th century, Chile's population – including 100,000 sovereign Mapuches south of the Biobío – was perhaps half a million, 90% of whom lived in the countryside. Santiago had barely 30,000 residents. City streets remained largely unpaved, and most country roads were still potholed tracks. There were few schools and libraries, and, although the Universidad de San Felipe (founded in 1758 as a law school) provided intellectual spark, cultural life was bleak.

Growth was to come, however, and by the mid-19th century the capital had more than 100,000 inhabitants. It was now solidly linked to the port of Valparaíso, which had become a bustling commercial center of 60,000 people, by a railway and telegraph line. The landed aristocracy built sumptuous houses, adorned them with imported luxuries, founded prestigious social clubs, and visited their *fundos* (rural estates) during the holidays. The social life revolved around clubs, the track, the opera and outings to exclusive Parque Cousiño. The

Pedro de Valdivia

The histories of Chile and Santiago in a sense begin with Pedro de Valdivia. In 1535, Diego de Almagro had led the first expedition from Perú into what is now Chile, but his ill-organized venture in search of gold cost the lives of 10,000 Indians and 500 Spaniards. His efforts left barely a trace, except for frozen horses on the high Puna de Atacama, where later expeditions devoured their preserved carcasses.

Born in the Spanish province of Extremadura in 1500, Valdivia arrived in Perú in 1535 and soon took conquistador Francisco Pizarro's side in a power struggle against Almagro, who had attempted to compensate for his Chilean failures by capturing the Peruvian town of Cuzco and its riches. After executing Almagro, Pizarro authorized Valdivia to conquer the lands to the south of Perú.

Almagro's disaster made recruitment difficult, but by 1540 Valdivia had gathered 150 Spaniards to accompany him, and his leadership skills proved superior to Almagro's. After crossing the northern deserts – simultaneously disarming mutineers – and fighting Araucanian resistance, he founded Santiago in February 1541, but the city remained under Araucanian siege for years.

Valdivia persisted, founding the city of La Serena and the port of Valparaíso, and finally got Peruvian reinforcements that let him expand southward. Beyond the Río Biobío, he founded Concepción, his own namesake Valdivia, and Villarrica in the early 1550s. A conqueror and governor, rather than merely an explorer, Valdivia was also a gambler – once, reportedly, he bet 14,000 pesos on a single card game.

Valdivia's luck ran out in December 1553, when Araucanian forces under Lautaro, a former scout of Valdivia's, captured the conquistador and most of his men in the battle of Tucapel. Later that month, on Christmas Day, an impetuous Araucanian chief clubbed him to death despite Lautaro's objections.

Historian James Lockhart favorably compares Valdivia's effectiveness with that of his Extremaduran compatriots Hernán Cortés (the conqueror of Mexico) and Francisco Pizarro, who 'singlemindedly overcame all obstacles and rivals to conquer a land and found a permanent Hispanic society.' Within 13 years, Valdivia had established Spanish authority through most of what is now Chile; it was three centuries later before an independent Chile could expand its power beyond the Biobío.

governing class fashioned themselves as ladies and gentlemen who valued civilized customs, tradition and breeding, sending their children to be educated in Europe. For the elite it's still true that, as British diplomat James Bryce remarked at the turn of the 19th century:

The leading landowners spend the summers in their country houses and the winter and spring in Santiago, which has thus a pleasant society, with plenty of talent and talk among the men, a society more enlightened and abreast of the modern world than are those of the more northern republics, and with a more stimulating atmosphere.

... to Modern Problems

Santiago has since become one of South America's largest cities – the Región

Metropolitana (Metropolitan Region) contains well over four million inhabitants. The Museo de Santiago, in the colonial Casa Colorada off the Plaza de Armas, documents the city's phenomenal growth, in large part a function of oppression in the countryside. Poverty, lack of opportunity and paternalistic fundos drove farm laborers and tenants north to the nitrate mines, and also into the cities. Between 1865 and 1875, Santiago's population increased from 115,000 to more than 150,000, mainly due to domestic migration. This trend continued in the 20th century, and by the 1970s, more than 70% of all Chileans lived in cities, mostly in the heartland.

After WWII, rapid industrialization created urban jobs, but never enough to satisfy demand. In the 1960s, continued rural turmoil fostered urban migration, resulting in squatter settlements known as *callampas* (mushrooms, so called because they sprang up virtually overnight) around the outskirts

Human Rights & the Pinochet Factor

Despite self-serving amnesty laws passed under the military dictatorship of 1973–89, Chilean human rights issues have not gone away. On this theme, the biggest news of 1998–99 was the London arrest, detention and requested extradition of former dictator Augusto Pinochet on torture charges, at the request of Spanish judge Baltazar Garzón. Fearful that Pinochet's possible extradition to Spain could destabilize Chile's ostensibly fragile democracy, and under pressure from the military, the timid Concertación por la Democracia (Consensus for Democracy) government pressed for the general's release, but most Chileans seemed to take the events in stride – if not gain satisfaction.

Related news included indictments of five army officers linked to the infamous 'Caravan of Death,' under the direction of General Sergio Arellano Stark, at Pinochet's instigation, that resulted in summary executions of political prisoners in the dictatorship's early months. Chilean judge Juan Guzmán sidestepped the amnesty law by ruling that, because many of the victims' fates were unknown, the disappearances constituted continuing offenses of 'aggravated kidnapping.'

But as things change it appears that, as in Argentina, the military's code of silence is eroding. Retired army colonel Olagier Benavente Bustos stated publicly that Pinochet's favorite helicopter pilot had admitted dumping bodies of the disappeared into the remote Andes and the Pacific Ocean during the dictatorship's early years (unlike their Argentine counterparts, however, the Chilean military apparently did not toss live victims from helicopters). In August 1999, the heads of the armed forces agreed to help 'reconstruct' the facts behind the disappearances, while simultaneously denying that they had any information. This was not, however, sufficient for human rights activists and victims' families who continue to seek justice through the courts.

The release of formerly confidential documents from US government archives may also shed light upon the dictatorship's abuses, and the Clinton Administration was reportedly even considering Pinochet's indictment in the 1976 Washington, DC assassination of former Chilean diplomat Orland Letelier. Former DINA (Dirección de Inteligencia Nacional, the military government's secret police) chief Manuel Contreras and his deputy Pedro Espinosa went to prison several years ago for their roles in the Letelier case. Critics, however, consider their incarceration in a custom-built facility near Santiago only a slap on the wrist (some defenders of Contreras and Espinosa consider them scapegoats for the rest of the military). It's worth mentioning that General Contreras' 'cell' sports custom furniture, a large personal library, outside phone lines and an Internet connection, plus his own cook, waiter and full-time nurse.

Another worry for the former military rulers is the Buenos Aires trial of ex-DINA agent Enrique Arancibia Clavel for the 1974 assassination of General Carlos Prats, since it could reveal details of of Santiago and other major cities. Planned decentralization has eased some pressure on Santiago, and regularization, including the granting of land titles, has transformed many callampas. They still contrast, however, with affluent eastern suburbs like El Golf, Vitacura, La Reina, Las Condes and Lo Curro.

Enter Pinochet

Chile's most dramatic 20th-century event was the violent military coup in which General Augusto Pinochet Ugarte overthrew the constitutional government of Socialist President Salvador Allende Gossens in September of 1973. It left its mark on the city, both literally and indirectly. Air attacks and other military actions left monuments like the presidential Palacio de la Moneda unusable for more than a decade, and only recently did city mayor Jaime Ravinet announce a 'Plan Alameda 2000' face-lift to repair the remaining damage on surrounding buildings.

Human Rights & the Pinochet Factor

covert operations, outside the shield of military courts and hand-picked judges. In April 1999, US attorney general Janet Reno decided to release details of testimony by former DINA agent Michael Townley, a US citizen who turned state's evidence in the Letelier case in return for a lighter sentence, to the Argentine courts. This move could implicate many Chilean military officials of the Pinochet period.

The Chilean government, for its part, has supported the Prats family in the murder trial of Arancibia Clavel, who has been held for two years in Buenos Aires, but has refused to cooperate on charges of 'illicit association,' which could lead to broader action against Pinochet and his associates.

In addition, while the Spanish government has dropped its demand for extradition and prosecution of the killers of Carmelo Soria (a Spanish diplomat working under UN auspices in 1978) because Chile's Supreme Court invoked the amnesty law, Soria's family continues to pursue the case in Spanish and international courts.

On the other hand, the government of Uruguay has closed an investigation of the mysterious death of Eugenio Berríos, a former Chilean intelligence agent who disappeared in 1992 after seeking police protection in that country against his former DINA colleagues. An Uruguayan judge ruled the case 'unsolved.'

Having avoided extradition to Spain because of alleged deteriorating health, Pinochet faces nearly a hundred lawsuits in Chilean courts, but his senatorial immunity and self-decreed amnesty laws continue to be obstacles to his prosecution. The more realistic of Pinochet's own conservative supporters acknowledge that their identification with the discredited dictator is a tar baby that damages their electoral options with centrist voters, and center-right candidate Joaquín Lavín's creditable showing in the 1999-2000 presidential election owed much to his distancing himself from Pinochet.

More enduring than pockmarked walls has been the legacy of the Pinochet dictatorship's economic program, which reduced state involvement and introduced an ethic of corporate consumerism. Whatever its achievements in the macroeconomic sphere – and Chile has had one of South America's most robust economies for over a decade – the regime's promotion of private automobile ownership has taken a toll. It has exacerbated urban sprawl, congested city streets, led to water and electricity shortages, and worsened Santiago's already critical air pollution problems.

The Pinochet regime, of course, has both its champions (who believe the general saved the country from political and economic ruin) and detractors (who claim he destroyed Chile's tradition of representative government and governed with a brutal disregard for human rights). The general's October 1998 arrest in London, at the request of Spanish judge Baltasar Garzón, has encouraged a new openness on human rights discussions in the capital and country. But most santiaguinos seemed to take the events in stride, except for Pinochet's most vociferous supporters, who demonstrated loudly outside the British and Spanish embassies.

New Blood

In the midst of Pinochet's detention, Chile held a presidential election, remarkable for its civility, in which Socialist Ricardo Lagos, candidate of the center-left Concertación por la Democracia (Consensus for Democracy) defeated center-right candidate Joaquín Lavín of the Alianza por Chile (Alliance for Chile). Lagos, who had openly defied Pinochet under the dictatorship and paved the way for the return to democracy in 1990, obtained only a slight edge over Lavín in the first round of the December 1999 election. But by the January 2000 runoff he had a clear majority, as most supporters of minor parties apparently switched their votes to the Concertación candidate.

British Home Secretary Jack Straw's release of Pinochet for ostensibly humanitarian reasons a few days before the runoff, however, may have given Lagos a boost among left-wing voters who distrusted Lavín's rightist connections. In any event, the Pinochet issue has moved to the Santiago courts and is hardly apparent in the streets.

GEOGRAPHY

Ringed by the high Andes to the east and lower ranges to the north and west, Santiago sits on a southwest-sloping piedmont in the valley of the Río Mapocho, which drains west and then south before uniting with the westward-flowing Río Maipo. The Maipo, in turn, reaches the Pacific Ocean just south of the port of San Antonio.

Most of Santiago is about 550m above sea level, but sediments deposited by the Mapocho and the Maipo have been unable to cover peaks such as 635m Cerro Santa Lucía and 869m Cerro San Cristóbal, which are prominent city landmarks. Urban sprawl is rapidly impinging on farmland areas between Santiago and the Cordillera de la Costa (Coast Range), and has even sneaked around Cerro San Cristóbal into Huechuraba and toward the higher Cordón del Manquehue.

Politically, Santiago proper is a relatively small area bounded by the Río Mapocho on the north, Avenida Vicuña Mackenna to the east, Avenida Exposición to the west and Avenida Centenario to the south. Gran Santiago (Greater Santiago), however, consists of another 31 comunas (municipalities) that sprawl in all directions from the colonial core. Only a handful of these, mainly between Santiago proper and the Andes, are of interest to most visitors.

CLIMATE

Like the rest of the country's heartland, which stretches from the Río Aconcagua south to the Río Biobío, Santiago enjoys a Mediterranean climate. High temperatures average 28°C (82°F) in January and 10°C (50°F) in July; the rainy season lasts from May to August. The Coast Range blocks the advance of fogs that often last into the afternoon in the seaside cities of Valparaíso and Viña del Mar.

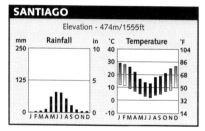

Because of Santiago's elevation, evenings and nights can be cool, even during summer. In the Andean heights east of the city, snow lasts into early summer, permitting excellent skiing much of the year.

ECOLOGY & ENVIRONMENT

For most santiaguinos, the single most palpable environmental issue is the cloud of smog that so often hangs over the city, which, like Los Angeles, sits in a basin between two mountain ranges and has a virtually identical climate. The air pollution stems from the growing number of private automobiles, the presence of diesel buses, the concentration of polluting industries and dust from unpaved streets. On some days it is so severe that schoolchildren may not take physical education and older citizens are advised not to leave home.

One approach to the problem has been urban afforestation projects. Some 700,000 trees are due to be planted by 2001, but nearly half of these will probably succumb to neglect and vandalism. Some effort has been made to improve the quality of public transportation vehicles, particularly through conversion of diesel buses to compressed natural gas. But the government has sent mixed signals by promoting automobile ownership through construction of new roads and highways, rather than restricting vehicular congestion in the crowded central city and clamping down on industrial polluters. There are usually weekday restrictions on private vehicles that lack catalytic converters, especially in the autumn months, but some have argued for restricting all vehicles.

Another serious environmental issue is the provision of water for a growing population and industry in this semiarid climate. When subnormal winter rains fail to fill reservoirs and recharge aquifers, there can be serious shortages. Paradoxically, heavy storms can overwhelm the city's antiquated drainage system, often causing flooding in low-lying areas.

Despite large parks like Cerro San Cristóbal's Parque Metropolitano, a lack of open space plagues some parts of the city. According to the environmental nonprofit Fundación Terram, Santiago's average of 2.5 sq meters of green space per resident falls short of the World Health Organization's recommended standard of 9 sq meters. Terram attributes part of this insufficiency to Pinochet's 1973–89 military dictatorship, which used urban development to restrict public spaces where its opponents might congregate. Some newly developed areas, dependent on the automobile for transportation, even lack sidewalks.

Trash disposal is yet another problem. In the northern suburb of Lampa, for instance, prime alluvial farmland is disappearing beneath mountains of garbage, and there is clandestine dumping. The unauthorized burning of garbage also contributes to air pollution.

FLORA & FAUNA

Sprawling Santiago's continuing growth has impacted the Metropolitan Region's plant and animal life, but in outer comunas like Las Condes, Lo Barnechea and La Reina there's still a fair amount of wild country. Even central Santiago has islands of biogeographical diversity – a recent inventory of the popular Parque Metropolitano, less than 10 minutes from the Plaza de Armas, discovered a variety of uncommon plants, including 52 different herbs, 20 bushes and 14 tree species, as well as falcons and eagles. A new environmental education center is under construction at the park, which also includes the city's aging zoo.

National Parks & Reserves

Since the mid-1920s, Chile's national parks have become a major international attraction. Most of the best-known units are in the Andean desert north, the southern mainland lake district and Chilean Patagonia, but a surprising number are in or just beyond the Región Metropolitana. The Corporación Nacional Forestal (Conaf, the state forestry agency) administers these as part of the state's 'Sistema Nacional de Areas Silvestres Protegidas del Estado' (Snaspe, or National System of State-Protected Wild Areas).

Travelers should visit Conaf's central information office (☎ 390 0282), Bulnes 291, for inexpensive maps and brochures that may be in short supply in the parks themselves. Regional Conaf offices, listed in the appropriate sections in the Excursions chapter, will sometimes assist in transportation to more isolated areas.

Chilean protected areas are of five main types: *parques nacionales* (national parks), *reservas nacionales* (national reserves), *monumentos naturales* (natural monuments), *áreas de protección turística* (tourist protection areas) and *santuarios de la naturaleza* (nature sanctuaries). Chilean law also permits the creation of private nature reserves, of which there are a handful.

National parks are generally extensive areas with a variety of natural ecosystems, while national reserves are open to economic exploitation on a sustainable basis and may include some relatively pristine areas. Natural monuments are smaller but more strictly protected, usually with a single outstanding natural feature. Tourist protection areas are usually private lands where management practices limit economic exploitation in the interest of scenic resources, while nature sanctuaries are primarily intended for research.

Now difficult to find and outdated in its coverage, the beautifully illustrated but expensive *Chile: Sus Parques Nacionales y Otras Areas Protegidas* (Incafo, Madrid, 1982) is still a good introduction to Chile's environmental diversity. See the Excursions chapter for further details about parks and reserves close enough to Santiago and/or Valparaíso/Viña del Mar for day trips. Many also offer camping and fishing.

GOVERNMENT & POLITICS

Despite its status as the capital of a highly centralized Chilean state, Santiago's political geography is more complex than might be expected. The national government consists of an executive branch based in Santiago and headed by the popularly elected president, a bicameral legislature (some of whose members are ex officio appointees under a constitution inherited from the dictatorship of General Pinochet) and an ostensibly independent judiciary still stacked with Pinochet appointees.

The Región Metropolitana that encompasses Santiago is one of the national government's 13 administrative entities; the other 12 are numbered ordinally, north to south, from I to XII. Several of the excursions in this book take place in Regions V (Valparaíso) and VI (Rancagua).

The highest administrative authority in each region, including the Metropolitana, is the *intendencia*, whose *intendente* is a presidential appointee; some services, such as transportation, fall under its authority. Within Gran Santiago, each comuna (municipality) has its own government responsible for standard services such as trash collection, but the more prosperous ones, like Providencia and Las Condes, have a broader tax base and provide greater amenities.

Each comuna has its own elected officials, including council and mayor, some of whom have acquired national prominence. Santiago's Jaime Ravinet is a prominent Christian Democrat often mentioned as a future presidential candidate, while Las Condes' Joaquín Lavín used his office as a springboard to the 1999 presidential nomination of the right-wing Unión Demócrata Independiente (UDI) and its more moderate ally Renovación Nacional (RN). Lavín resigned his mayorship after gaining the nomination.

Chilean presidential and congressional elections took place in December of 1999;

the winning presidential candidate, Ricardo Lagos, will occupy the presidential Palacio de la Moneda until March of 2006. Although Santiago is Chile's capital, the Congreso Nacional (Congress) meets in the port city of Valparaíso. Municipal elections took place in June 2000, while additional congressional elections are scheduled for December 2001.

ECONOMY

Until very recently, Chile's economy had improved greatly on a macro scale, enjoying a decade of uninterrupted growth at rates of 6% or higher. But close economic ties across the Pacific made the country vulnerable to the Asian meltdown of 1998, when the growth rate slipped to 3.4%. In the first half of 1999, Chile's gross domestic product actually fell to a figure of -2.9%, signifying the country's first serious recession in recent memory. Before showing a modest growth figure in October 1999, the economy had been in recession for 10 consecutive months. On the positive side, but perhaps predictably, inflation fell to 2.5% per annum.

The elite have benefited more from economic growth than the poor, and unemployment remains distressingly high, exceeding 10% in mid-1999. In the Región Metropolitana, the official government figure was 11.5%, but a Universidad de Chile study suggested the figure had reached 15.4%, causing regional intendente Eduardo Velasco to announce an ambitious US$1.5-billion program to create 24,000 new jobs. At one point the comuna of Quinta Normal hired 180 jobless fathers to act as schoolyard security, while even prosperous Las Condes contracted 47 local residents as minimum-wage street sweepers. Countless city dwellers earn a precarious subsistence as street vendors of ice cream, candy, cigarettes and cheap manufactured goods like audio cassettes.

The minimum wage, for those fortunate enough to have regular employment, is only about US$206 per month, and the gap between rich and poor is widening. According to a mid-1990s report by the United Nations' Santiago-based Economic Commission for Latin America and the Caribbean (Comisión Económica para América Latina y el Caribe, Cepal), the wealthiest 10% of Chileans receive more than 40% of the national income, while the poorest 40% earn just 13%. While these figures were among the region's worst, the number of Chileans living in poverty fell by half, from 46% to 23%, between 1987 and 1996.

Since the return to representative government in 1990, there has been an influx of foreign capital from companies that were clearly reluctant to invest in the dictatorship, but the recent economic slump has diminished hopes that vigorous economic growth would further reduce poverty. Since 1987, Chile has enjoyed an increasing trade surplus; its most important trading partners are the USA, Japan, Germany, Brazil and Argentina.

Santiago is the financial as well as political center of the country, but minerals are the most important single sector of the economy. Probably the single most important economic institution is the Corporación Nacional del Cobre (Codelco), the nationalized copper company. The world's largest subsurface copper mine is at El Teniente, in the Andes east of the regional capital of Rancagua.

POPULATION & PEOPLE

Chile's population of about 15 million is unevenly distributed. About a third, perhaps 4.5 million, reside in Gran Santiago, which includes the capital and its immediate suburbs; this includes 70% of all Chileans between the ages of 15 and 24. No other city has more than about 300,000 residents. The last formal census was in 1992.

Most Chileans are mestizos, although many can still claim purely European descent. In much of the country, social class is still a greater issue than race – working-class people and others resentfully call the country's elite *momios* (mummies) because, to paraphrase the words of film director Miguel Littín, they are so resistant to change that they might as well be embalmed. The capital does, however, have a substantial population of urbanized Mapuche Indians from the southern region of La Araucanía.

Chile did not experience the massive 19th- and 20th-century European immigration that neighboring Argentina did – at the end of the 19th century, only a small percentage of Chileans were foreign-born. After the European upheavals of 1848, many Germans settled in southern mainland Chile, where use of the German language is still vigorous, if not widespread. Other immigrant groups included the French, Italians, European Jews and Palestinians.

European immigration did not alter the structure of Chilean society, but added non-Spanish elements to the middle and upper classes. The established aristocracy (the original landed gentry), of mostly Spanish Basque origin, welcomed wealthy immigrants with British, French or German surnames like Edwards, Subercaseaux and Gildemeister. Despite their small numbers, European immigrants became economically powerful, controlling rural estates and commercial, financial and industrial institutions.

EDUCATION

Chile's 95% literacy rate is one of Latin America's highest. For children ages five to 12, education is free and compulsory, although school attendance is low in some rural areas.

Universities were traditionally free and open, but after the 1973 coup the military dictatorship installed its own rectors throughout the country; its sweeping university reform of the 1980s reduced state funding, raised student fees, and either downgraded or eliminated ostensibly 'subversive' careers such as sociology and psychology. The Universidad de Chile was a particular target because of its reputation for aggressive dissent, and suffered further downsizing in the 1990s during the administration of Christian Democrat Eduardo Frei Ruiz-Tagle. The more conservative Universidad Católica came through in better shape, partly because its church funding gave it greater autonomy.

Both the Universidad Católica and the Universidad de Chile have several campuses around town, but their main buildings are along the Alameda in downtown Santiago; the other major campus is the Universidad de Santiago, across from the main railroad station. The military reform of higher education made it easy to open private universities, but most of these are glorified trade schools with part-time faculty, limited curriculum and dubious standards. Some, however, are rapidly improving.

Like other Latin American countries, Chile suffers from a glut of lawyers and similar professionals and a shortage of people trained in engineering and other more practical fields. This is also changing, however, because of Chile's entrepreneurial advances over the past decade-plus.

SCIENCE & PHILOSOPHY

Major foreign scientists, most notably Charles Darwin, documented their observations on Chile – Darwin chronicled his ascent of Cerro La Campana, near present-day Viña del Mar, in *The Voyage of the Beagle*. Other important figures included French scientist Claudio Gay (1800–1873), who produced an impressive illustrated atlas of Chilean flora and fauna and was the

Chaz D

first director of Santiago's Museo de Historia Natural. There was also Polish immigrant Ignacio Domeyko (1802–1899), who surveyed much of present-day Chile and eventually became rector of the Universidad de Chile; and Swiss botanist Rodolfo Philippi (1808–1904).

Chile is not widely explored in the modern sciences, but the crystal clarity of its northern desert skies has led many international observatories to locate major facilities there, and all of these have encouraged participation by the country's relatively small community of 30 or so astronomers. The Universidad de Santiago has a good planetarium, and the Universidad de Chile has an observatory on Cerro Calán in Las Condes, but smog and light pollution limit their potential in the Región Metropolitana.

Contemporary Chilean archaeologists, most of whom have taken advantage of ideal conditions in the arid north, have earned international reputations. Ricardo E Latcham (1869–1943) was probably the father of Chilean archaeology, but the Belgian Jesuit Gustavo Le Paige (1903–1980) left an impressive legacy in the northern desert village of San Pedro de Atacama.

Probably the greatest historical figure in Chilean philosophy was a Venezuelan. A contemporary and associate of Simón Bolívar, Andrés Bello (1781–1865) lived 19 years in London before returning to South America, settling in Santiago rather than his native Caracas. Among other achievements, the multitalented Bello drafted Chile's civil legal code, founded the Universidad de Chile and wrote an important Spanish language grammar. Former Venezuelan president Rafael Caldera summarized his countryman's life in *Andrés Bello* (London, Allen & Unwin, 1977).

ARTS

Santiago is the center of Chilean cultural life, and Chilean art, literature and music have been influential beyond the country's borders. Many Chilean intellectuals, however, have been educated in European capitals, notably Paris, and in the 19th and early 20th

centuries, Santiago self-consciously emulated European – especially French – cultural trends in art, music and architecture. There are many significant museums, galleries and cultural centers in the capital.

Poetry

Decades after their deaths, Nobel Prize-winning poets Gabriela Mistral and Pablo Neruda remain major figures in Chilean, Latin American and world literature. Much of their work is available in English translation, such as Neruda's *The Heights of Macchu Picchu*, *Canto General*, *Passions and Impressions* and his rambling, selective, but still readable *Memoirs* (1977). For an interestingly conceived view of Neruda and his work, see Luis Poirot's *Pablo Neruda, Absence and Presence* (1990), a collection of outstanding black-and-white photos with accompanying text from Neruda and friends and admirers (both Chilean and foreign). Especially poignant are the photos of Neruda's houses in Santiago, Valparaíso and Isla Negra after their vandalization by the military.

US poet Langston Hughes translated some of Gabriela Mistral's work in *Selected Poems of Gabriela Mistral* (Indiana University Press, 1957), while a different book with the same title was published by the Library of Congress and Johns Hopkins Press in 1971. For an interpretation of her work, try Margot Arce de Vásquez's *Gabriela Mistral, the Poet and Her Work* (1964).

Important contemporary poets include Nicanor Parra, who has drawn Nobel Prize attention, and Jorge Teillier, whose work has been translated and analyzed by Carolyne Wright in *In Order to Talk with the Dead* (1993).

Fiction

With novels in the 'magical realism' tradition of Latin American fiction, California-based Isabel Allende (niece of the late president Salvador Allende) has become a popular writer overseas as well as in Chile. Among her works are *House of the Spirits* (1986), *Of Love and Shadows* (1988), *Eva Luna* (1989) and *Daughter of Fortune* (1999).

The Paths of Mistral & Neruda

Gabriela Mistral and Pablo Neruda have opened a window on Chile and Latin America through their poetry, but their biographies are no less revealing. In some ways, no two individuals could be more different than these two Nobel Prize winners, but the parallels and divergences in their lives disclose both unifying and contrasting aspects of Chilean life and culture.

They were contemporaries, but of different generations; Mistral was born in 1889, Neruda in 1904. Both belonged to the provinces: Mistral to the remote Elquí Valley of the Norte Chico, Neruda to the southern city of Temuco, though his birthplace was Parral, in the heartland province of Maule, and he lived in Santiago, Valparaíso and in a small beach community at Isla Negra. Both poets used pseudonyms: Gabriela Mistral's given name was Lucila Godoy Alcayaga, while Pablo Neruda's was Neftalí Ricardo Reyes Basoalto. Both adopted their aliases out of timidity: the young rural schoolmistress Lucila Godoy sat in the audience at Santiago's Teatro Municipal while a surrogate received a prize for her 'Sonnets on Death,' in memory of a young suitor who had committed suicide; Neftalí Reyes feared the ridicule of his working-class family.

Both enjoyed literary success at a young age. The government rewarded both with diplomatic posts that subsidized their creative writing; in consequence, both traveled extensively and became celebrities outside their own country and the South American continent, which hadn't produced a Nobel Prize winner in literature until Mistral's award in 1945. In 1971, Neruda became the third Latin American writer to receive the Swedish Academy's prize (Guatemalan novelist Miguel Angel Asturias was the second, in 1967).

Their lifestyles, however, diverged in many ways. After the death of her beloved, Mistral never married and devoted her life to children and their education at schools from La Serena to Punta Arenas – when she taught in Temuco, the young Neruda and his friends worshiped her. She even traveled abroad to reform the Mexican system of public instruction. She lived austerely, but her stern features masked the sensitivity of a woman whose poetry was compassionate and mystical. Though friendly with political figures, most notably President Pedro Aguirre Cerda, her politics were not a matter of public controversy.

Neruda, by contrast, became a flamboyant figure whose private life was public knowledge, who built eccentric houses and filled them with outlandish objects, and whose politics more than once landed him in trouble. Unlike the somber Mistral, his face was usually smiling, often pensive, but never grim. While consul in Java in the 1930s, he married a Dutch woman, but left her for Delia del Carril (a decade older than himself) a few years later, and after nearly 20 years left Delia for the much younger Matilde Urrutia. It was Matilde for whom he built and named La Chascona, his Santiago house at the foot of Cerro San Cristóbal.

Neruda's houses, including his beachfront favorite at Isla Negra and La Sebastiana in Valparaíso, were material expressions of his personality,

The Paths of Mistral & Neruda

improvised with eclectic assemblies of objects amassed on his travels and at his diplomatic posts. Entire rooms are filled with shells, bowsprit figureheads, ships in bottles and of course books, all of which delighted him and his guests and now draw thousands of visitors. The houses themselves break all the rules of standard architecture and, for that reason, intrigue the visitor as much as they pleased the owner. In his autobiography, he wrote that 'I have ... built my house like a toy house and I play in it from morning till night.'

After Francisco Franco's rebels defeated the Spanish Republic, the Chilean diplomat devoted his energies to helping refugees escape the dictator's revenge. In Spain he had made a personal commitment to the Communist Party, although he did not enroll officially until his return to Chile, where he was elected senator for Tarapacá and Antofagasta, the mining provinces of the Norte Grande. After managing Gabriel González Videla's successful presidential campaign of 1946, he fell afoul of the president's caprice and went into hiding and then exile in Argentina, escaping by foot and horseback across the southern Andes.

After González Videla left office, Neruda returned to Chile and continued his political activities without reducing his prolific output of poetry. In 1969 he was the Communist candidate for the presidency, but resigned in support of Salvador Allende's candidacy and later became Allende's ambassador to France. He received the Nobel Prize during his tenure in France, but died less than a fortnight after the military coup of 1973.

For all his wealth, Neruda never forgot his modest origins nor abandoned his political convictions, and did not consider his privileged lifestyle incompatible with his leftist beliefs – lacking heirs, he left everything to the Chilean people through a foundation.

Neruda's poetry could be committed and combative, and although no government could suppress literature that could be found in almost every household that could spare a penny to buy it, General Pinochet's dictatorship did its best to erase his memory. After Neruda's death, his houses were vandalized with police and military complicity, but his widow Matilde and dedicated volunteers persisted to establish the Fundación Neruda in spite of legal and extralegal obstacles. It administers the estate and has successfully restored all three houses, now open to the public. Both Chileans and foreigners flock to them and, with a very few truly extreme exceptions, even those who disagreed with his politics enjoy and respect his work.

Gabriela Mistral, meanwhile, remains a modest but reassuring presence in Chilean life and literature. Every day, thousands of santiaguinos pass the mural of Gabriela and her 'children' on the Alameda, at the base of Cerro Santa Lucía, while many more pay her homage at the museum bearing her name in the village of Vicuña, in her native Elqui Valley. Though she died in New York, she is buried in her natal hamlet of Montegrande.

Chile's greatest contemporary novelist, José Donoso, died in late 1996. His *Curfew* (1988) offers a portrait of life under the dictatorship through the eyes of a returned exile. Antonio Skármeta's *I Dreamt the Snow was Burning* (1985) is a novel of the early postcoup years, but Skármeta has become famous for his novel *Burning Patience* (1987), a fictional exploration of Pablo Neruda's counsel to a shy but lovestruck mail carrier, which was adapted into the award-winning Italian-language film *Il Postino* (The Postman) by British director Michael Radford.

Marco Antonio de la Parra's *The Secret Holy War of Santiago de Chile* (1994) is a surrealistic novel of contemporary Chile, with numerous geographical and cultural references that anyone who has visited the capital will find fascinating and challenging.

Roberto Ampuero writes mystery novels whose main protagonist, Cayetano Brulé, is a Valparaíso-based Cuban expatriate. While none of Ampuero's work has yet appeared in English, his straightforward writing style makes stories like *El Alemán de Atacama* (The German of Atacama, 1996) accessible to nonnative speakers. Ampuero's contemporary geographical references – including thinly veiled restaurant recommendations – can be fun for visitors.

Music

Music, in a variety of styles, has also been one of Chile's greatest exports.

Folk Probably the best-known manifestation of Chilean popular culture is *La Nueva Canción Chilena* (New Chilean Song Movement), which wedded the country's folkloric heritage to the political passions of the late 1960s and early 1970s. Its most legendary figure is Violeta Parra, who collected folk songs during numerous research trips and brought them to urban audiences. Best known for her enduring theme *Gracias a la Vida* (Thanks to Life), she imparted her enthusiasms to her children Isabel and Angel, also performers, who established the first of many *peñas* (musical and cultural centers) in Santiago in the mid-1960s. Individual performers such as Patricio Manns and Victor Jara (brutally executed during the 1973 coup) and groups like Illapu, Quilapayún and Inti-Illimani acquired international reputations for both their music and their political commitment.

Many Chilean folk musicians, exiled during the Pinochet dictatorship, performed regularly in Europe, North America and Australia, and their recordings are still available both in Chile and overseas.

Rock & Pop Chilean rock music is not widely known throughout the continent and the world, but several groups are worth hearing, most notably the Paris-based Los Jaivas, who frequently perform in Europe and also tour Chile every summer. Also interesting are Los Tres (who, despite their name, are a four-piece band), La Ley (presently based in Mexico) and Los Dioses (a reincarnated version of Los Prisioneros, probably the country's most popular rock band ever). The politically conscious rap group Tiro de Gracia takes its ironic name from a Spanish-language phrase meaning 'bullet to the head.'

Classical The Orquesta Filarmónica de Santiago is resident at downtown's Teatro Municipal (see the Entertainment chapter).

Chile's most famous classical musician is the late pianist Claudio Arrau (1903–1991), a child prodigy who studied with Martin Krause (one of Franz Liszt's last pupils) and spent most of his career in Europe. Many recordings of his work are available, and streets in several comunas bear his name.

Before his death, poet Pablo Neruda collaborated with the then-young composer Sergio Ortega to create an opera version of Neruda's *Muerte y Fulgor de Joaquín Murieta* (Death and Brilliance of Joaquín Murieta), a work that did not see the stage until 1996 (in France). Its 1998 debut at the Teatro Municipal, with an almost entirely Chilean cast, drew critical acclaim but a tepid response from the largely conservative operagoers, because of its perceived political content (Ortega also composed the hymn for Salvador Allende's leftist Unidad Popular government).

Dance

One of Chile's cultural touchstones is the *cueca*, a folkloric dance in which both partners hold and maneuver a handkerchief, in a symbolic imitation of the courtship of cock and hen. Originating in Peru but differentiating itself since the end of colonial rule, it's a common sight around mid-September's patriotic holidays, even in downtown Santiago, and at virtually any rural festival.

Classical dance takes place at major performing arts venues. Like the Orquesta Filarmónica, the Ballet de Santiago is a resident company at the Teatro Municipal.

Painting & Sculpture

Chile has many art museums but, with a handful of exceptions, their focus is historical rather than contemporary, and the work is unexceptional. Venues like Santiago's Palacio de Bellas Artes tend to focus on traveling international exhibitions, but places like Providencia's Parque de las Esculturas (an open-air sculpture museum along the Río Mapocho; see the Things to See & Do chapter) focus on Chilean artists.

Valparaíso's Museo de Bellas Artes, presently undergoing renovation, stresses 19th-century Chilean landscapes like English painter Thomas Somerscales' 'Crepúsculo sobre Aconcagua' (Dusk over Aconcagua), which uses Andean light superbly. Manuel González, the father of Chilean impressionism, painted 'El Pago de Chile' (The Payment of Chile), depicting a mutilated soldier from the War of the Pacific; glory-conscious agents of the Pinochet dictatorship changed its title to 'Capitán Dinamita' (Captain Dynamite).

Chile's best-known living painter is Paris-based Roberto Matta (born 1911), the Latin American artist most closely identified with surrealism. Jesuit-educated in Chile, he went to France in 1934 to study architecture with Le Corbusier. He has also lived in New York and Mexico City, and though influenced by Mexican landscapes, his painting is more abstract than that would suggest. His work also includes forays into media such as sculpture and engraving.

Among Chile's notable contemporary artists are Máximo Pincheira, whose grim works deal with the anxieties of life under the dictatorship, and Mario Irarrázaval (born 1940) whose 'El Juicio' (The Judgment), shows a bound prisoner at the mercy of three judges – perhaps symbolizing Chile under military rule. Carmen Aldunate's paintings deal with more personal issues, as do the self-described 'frivolous' oils of her daughter María José Romero.

Santiago's metro system has contributed to the capital's arts scene by sponsoring a series of murals decorating various stations along the main east-west line.

Film

Chile began to produce feature films in the 1920s, but this initial boom proved unsustainable. There was a renaissance in the late 1960s, thanks to directors like Raúl Ruiz and Miguel Littín, with some truly experimental efforts – Alejandro Jodorowsky's surrealistic *El Topo* (The Mole), an underground success overseas, included a performance by the San Francisco–area band Country Joe and the Fish. Under the Socialist government of Salvador Allende, the state-run Chile Films floundered because of factionalism.

The then-exiled Littín's *Alsino & the Condor* (1983) was nominated for an Academy Award as Best Foreign Film and is readily available on video. Littín has recently gone over budget in the historical epic *Tierra del Fuego*, but his best work is the much earlier film *El Chacal de Nahualtoro* (The Jackal of Nahualtoro), a rural crime drama that was a tremendous success nationally.

Another exile's work, Patricio Guzmán's *La Batalla de Chile* (The Battle of Chile), is a powerful three-part documentary on the Allende years and the Pinochet coup that only recently made its way onto Chilean pay TV. The Paris-based Ruiz has been prolific in his adopted country but only recently released his first English-language film, the psychological thriller *Shattered Image* (1998). Starring William Baldwin and Anne Parillaud (the latter best known as *La Femme*

Nikita), it drew mostly tepid and critical reviews for its portrayal of a woman unable to distinguish between dream and reality.

Director Gustavo Graef-Marino's *Johnny 100 Pesos*, based on a true story about a gang of robbers who become trapped in a Santiago high-rise, made a favorable impression at 1994's Sundance Film Festival. This led to a Hollywood contract for *Diplomatic Siege*, a thriller shot in Romania in 1998–99 with Tom Berenger and Daryl Hannah in starring roles.

Theater

While traditional venues like Santiago's Teatro Municipal operated more or less normally during Pinochet's dictatorship, the return to democracy has seen a major burst of growth in Bohemian neighborhoods like Bellavista and even suburban comunas like Ñuñoa. Look for small experimental companies like La Tropa, a three-person outfit that plays public parks like Plaza Ñuñoa.

One of Chile's best-known playwrights is Ariel Dorfman, whose *Death and the Maiden* (1994) explored issues of brutality and reconciliation in the post-military years; the effortlessly bilingual Dorfman adapted it into an English-language film directed by Roman Polanski. The versatile playwright was also once notorious for his deconstruction of Disney in *How to Read Donald Duck* (1971), an indignantly clever critique of cultural imperialism coauthored with Belgian sociologist Armand Mattelart. Also a poet and novelist who spent his New York youth admittedly enamored with US culture (he now lives in North Carolina), Dorfman has mellowed in his memoir *Heading South, Looking North* (1998).

Of a younger generation, Marco Antonio de la Parra remained in Santiago during the Pinochet years, despite censorship of such works as *Lo Crudo, lo Cocido y lo Podrido* (The Raw, the Cooked and the Rotten) and *Carta Abierta a Pinochet* (Open Letter to Pinochet). Many of his plays have been performed in Europe and North America; he is also a novelist.

SOCIETY & CONDUCT

English-speaking visitors may find Santiago fairly accessible because of its superficial resemblance to their own societies. Foreign travelers are less conspicuous than in Latin American countries that have large indigenous populations, and can more easily integrate themselves into everyday life here. Chileans are hospitable and often invite foreigners to visit their homes and participate in daily activities, but may also be very reserved at times. In general, however, they are more physically demonstrative than most North Americans or Europeans, and regularly exchange kisses (on the cheek) in greeting. In formal situations, however, it's better to go with a handshake unless you are certain of the appropriate gesture.

Sport is extremely important here, and soccer is the national obsession, thanks to high visibility internationals like Iván Zamorano, Marcelo Salas and Sebastián Rozental. Tennis star Marcelo Ríos, briefly ranked No 1 in the world in 1998 before nagging injury problems, may be Chile's best-known athlete.

Dos & Don'ts

Being polite goes a long way in any encounter with Chilean officialdom – or with any other citizen for that matter. Do not forget to preface any request with the appropriate salutation – *buenos días* (good morning), *buenas tardes* (good afternoon) or *buenas noches* (good evening) – and use *usted* (the formal mode of address) unless you are certain that informality is appropriate.

Chilean dress is more casual than it used to be, especially for recreational activities, but as in other cities, informal clothing is normally inappropriate for business, some restaurants, casinos and events like the symphony or opera. Note that some places that are informal by day may become formal by night.

Talking Politics

Pinochet's 1998 London arrest brought human rights issues out into the open for the first time in recent memory – even after the return to democracy in 1989 under Pinochet's custom-designed constitution, many Chileans preferred to avoid public discussions of such matters. Though the lid is off now, visitors of any political persuasion should still be circumspect – many people's opinions are still polarized, and it's best to refrain from offering yours unless you know the person you're speaking with well, or that person has solicited your candid opinion.

RELIGION

Traditionally about 90% of Chileans are Roman Catholic, but evangelical Protestantism is rapidly gaining converts. There are also Lutherans, Jews, Presbyterians, Mormons and Pentecostals. The proselytizing Mormons have caused great controversy, and their churches have been the target of bombings by leftist groups, though this has diminished of late.

Catholicism has provided Chile some of its most compelling cultural monuments, such as Santiago's Catedral Metropolitana and colonial Iglesia San Francisco. Countless roadside shrines, some of them extraordinary manifestations of folk art, also testify to the pervasiveness of religion in Chilean society.

Like Chilean political parties, the Church has serious factions, but its Vicaria de la Solidaridad compiled such an outstanding human rights record during the dictatorship that it became the major object of General Pinochet's vitriolic scorn in his four-volume autobiography. At great risk to themselves, Chilean priests frequently worked in the shantytowns of Santiago and other large cities. Such activism has continued in today's more lenient political climate.

On the other hand, the Church's attitude toward other social issues is starkly reactionary. Its obstinacy has contributed to Chile's status as the world's only democracy without a divorce law, though annulments are not unusual for those who can pay for the legal maneuvering (a new but still restrictive divorce law is under consideration by Congress). The government has found it difficult to institute critically important sex education programs over ecclesiastical opposition, and the Church's absolutist position on abortion has driven the practice underground, with predictable results.

LANGUAGE

Spanish is Chile's official language and is almost universally understood, but there are also a handful of native languages spoken by a very few individuals. English has long superseded French as the foreign language of choice among the elite, and many santiaguinos speak at least a smattering of English, especially in the tourist sector. This is less common in the regions.

See the Language chapter toward the end of this book for pronunciation details and useful phrases.

Facts for the Visitor

WHEN TO GO

Chile offers the prospect of two summers in the same year, but the country's geographical variety can make a visit rewarding in any season. Santiago and its surroundings are best in the verdant spring (September through November) or during the fall harvest (late February into April). Conversely, Chilean ski resorts draw many visitors during the Northern Hemisphere's summer (June through August).

It's worth mentioning that the month of September, which includes the anniversaries of contentious dates like the election of Salvador Allende in 1970 (September 4), Pinochet's military coup of 1973 (September 11) and Armed Forces Day (September 19), often sees civil disturbances in the capital. Foreign visitors will rarely find these events more than an inconvenience, but should be aware of them and preferably not wander into the middle.

ORIENTATION

Santiago is immense, but Santiago Centro is a relatively small, roughly triangular area bounded by the Río Mapocho and woodsy Parque Forestal to the north, the Vía Norte Sur to the west, and the Avenida del Libertador General Bernardo O'Higgins (more commonly and manageably known as the Alameda, short for the earlier 'Alameda de las Delicias') to the south. The triangle's apex is Plaza Baquedano, more commonly known as Plaza Italia, where the Alameda intersects two other main thoroughfares, Avenida Providencia and Avenida Vicuña Mackenna. Should you get disoriented, the Andean front range is visible to the east – smog permitting.

Within this triangle, centered on the Plaza de Armas, downtown Santiago's street plan largely conforms to the standard grid pattern that the Spaniards imposed on all their American possessions. Surrounding the plaza are many of the most notable public buildings, including the Municipalidad (City Hall), the Catedral Metropolitana and the Correo Central (main post office). Paseo Ahumada, a pedestrian mall, leads south to the Alameda, and a block south of the Plaza de Armas it intersects with Paseo Huérfanos, another pedestrian mall. Other public buildings, including the presidential palace, domi-

Law of the Indies

Perceptive visitors to Santiago and other Latin American cities will immediately notice their structural similarity. Except in the great indigenous empires of Mexico and the Andes, where the Spaniards adapted pre-Hispanic cities to their own ends, the colonial *Leyes de Indias* (Law of the Indies) decreed the imposition of a regular grid pattern traceable to Roman times.

The Spaniards were largely an urban people and drew on their European experience to build the new colonial settlements. In Spain, the slow-growing medieval city had resulted in dispersal of major urban institutions like the *cabildo* (town council), the church and the market, but in the colonies all of these clustered around the central plaza. Because of the plaza's defensive functions on the frontier, settlers often called it the Plaza de Armas. As the leading Spanish citizens settled near the institutions of power, the plaza became the city's economic and social center.

There were exceptions to the rule, of course. Officials were directed to choose town sites in open, level areas, but the spontaneous development and irregular topography of many ports (colorfully disorderly Valparaíso is the best example) and mining towns discouraged uniform application of the system. Nevertheless, the rectangular grid became the template for urban development throughout the region, and this legacy greatly simplifies the task of orientation for visitors.

26

nate the Barrio Cívico around Plaza de la Constitución, west of Paseo Ahumada and just north of the Alameda.

West of the Via Norte Sur, Barrio Brasil is an intriguing enclave of early-20th-century architecture that is presently experiencing an urban renaissance. Farther west and south are the agreeable open spaces of Parque Quinta Normal and Parque O'Higgins, both popular weekend refuges for santiaguinos and their families.

One of Santiago's most attractive parks, Cerro Santa Lucía, overlooks the Alameda about halfway between the Plaza de Armas and Plaza Italia. Across the Mapocho from Plaza Italia, on either side of Pío Nono, Barrio Bellavista is Santiago's lively 'Paris quarter.' Overlooking Bellavista is the enormous Cerro San Cristóbal, which rises dramatically from the plain to the north of Avenida Providencia, which leads eastward toward the comunas of Providencia, Las Condes and Vitacura. Avenida Vicuña Mackenna leads southeast toward increasingly fashionable Ñuñoa.

Spanish-speaking travelers planning an extended stay in Santiago might want to acquire Carlos Ossandón Guzmán's *Guía de Santiago*, which is especially strong on architectural history. It contains a valuable summary in English.

MAPS

JLM Cartografía (☎ 225 1365, 236 4808, jmatassi@interactiva.cl), General del Canto 105, Oficina 1506, Providencia, publishes *Santiago*, the best map of the city; its scale is unspecified. Perhaps not totally up to date, but still useful, Atlas de Chile's *Plano de Santiago y Mini Atlas Caminero de Chile 1995* combines an indexed plan of the capital (1:25,000) with a respectable highway map (1:2,000,000). Inupal's *Gran Mapa Caminero de Chile* provides comparable highway coverage but lacks city maps.

The Instituto Geográfico Militar (IGM) produces the *Guía Caminera* (1992). It could use updating but it's still a reasonably good highway map in a convenient ring-binder format, with scales ranging from 1:500,000 to 1:1,500,000; it also includes several city maps at varying scales. Telefonica's *Plano de Santiago* (1999) has maps, at a scale of 1:20,000, and a street index in book form; the binding is flimsy, but it's one of the most up-to-date maps available.

The IGM's 1:50,000 topographic series is useful for hikers, although maps of some sensitive border areas (where most national parks are) may not be available. Individual maps cost about US$15 each in Santiago, where the IGM (☎ 696 8221) is at Dieciocho 369, just south of the Alameda. It's open 9 am to 5:30 pm Monday, 9 am to 5:50 pm Tuesday through Friday.

The following maps will be helpful if you plan to take any of the many day trips detailed in the Excursions chapter. Lonely Planet's *Chile & Easter Island Travel Atlas* maps the entire country in full color at a scale of 1:1,000,000. For members of the American Automobile Association (AAA) and its affiliates, there is a general South American road map that is adequate for initial planning. International Travel Maps of Vancouver's (ITMB's) widely available *Southern South America*, at a scale of 1:4,000,000, covers most of Chile, as does their *Argentina*, at an identical scale. The popular Turistel guidebook series (see Guidebooks, later in this chapter) contains detailed highway maps and excellent plans of Chilean cities and towns, but lacks scales.

Some of these maps may be available at specialist bookshops like Stanford's in London, or in the map rooms of major university libraries. In most major Chilean cities, the Automóvil Club de Chile (Acchi) has an office that sells maps, although not all of them are equally well stocked. If you belong to an auto club at home, ask for a discount.

TOURIST OFFICES
Local Tourist Offices

Sernatur (☎ 236 1420, 236 1416; Map 8), Chile's national tourist service, occupies most of the old market building at Avenida Providencia 1550, midway between the Manuel Montt and Pedro de Valdivia metro stations. The friendly and capable staff, which always includes an English speaker, offers maps and other information, including lists of accommodations, restaurants and bars, museums and art galleries, transport options out of Santiago and leaflets on other parts of the country. It's open 9 am to 5 pm weekdays, 9 am to 1 pm Saturday.

Sernatur also operates an information booth (☎ 601 9320) on the ground floor of the international terminal at Aeropuerto Arturo Merino Benítez at Pudahuel, and another at the San Borja bus terminal, alongside the train station on the Alameda. Both are open 9 am to 9 pm weekdays, 9 am to 5:30 pm weekends.

The Municipalidad maintains a tourist kiosk (no ☎), helpful but less well stocked, near the intersection of the Ahumada and Huérfanos pedestrian malls, a block from the Plaza de Armas, open 9 am to 9 pm daily (Map 5). Open 10 am to 6 pm weekdays only, the main municipal Oficina de Turismo (☎ 632 7785) occupies part of the colonial Casa Colorada, Merced 860, near the Plaza de Armas (Map 5). There's also a branch (☎ 664 4206, tur-ims@entelchile.net) on Cerro Santa Lucía (Map 5), open 9 am to 6 pm Monday through Thursday, 9 am to 5 pm Friday.

All these offices distribute free maps detailing downtown, Providencia and other inner comunas of the capital, with the main metro stations included. More detailed maps are available from the Municipalidad for about US$2.

Most hotels distribute *What's On*, a thorough bilingual guide to events around town, also known as *Que Hacer, Que Ver* in Spanish. It has maps of key tourist-oriented areas. Another useful source on what's happening in the capital is the bilingual, bimonthly magazine *Traveling Chile*, which gives a thorough rundown on theater and arts events.

Tourist Offices Abroad

Chilean embassies and consulates in major cities usually have a tourist representative in their delegation (see the embassies and consulates listings). Also try representatives of LanChile, Chile's only intercontinental airline, for tourist information.

DOCUMENTS
Passports

Passports are obligatory, except for nationals of Argentina, Brazil, Uruguay and Paraguay, who need only their national identity cards. Citizens of Canada, the UK, the USA, Australia, New Zealand and most Western European countries need passports only. Nationalities needing advance visas include Koreans, Poles, Indians, Thais, Jamaicans and Russians.

Note that the Chilean government now collects a US$45 processing fee from arriving US citizens in response to the US government's imposition of a similar fee on Chilean citizens applying for US visas; this onetime payment is valid for the life of the passport. Canadians pay US$55, Australians US$30.

It is advisable to carry your passport – though the military are keeping a low public profile under the present civilian government, the carabineros (national police) can still demand identification at any moment. In general, Chileans are document-oriented, and a passport is essential for cashing traveler's checks, checking into a hotel and many other routine activities.

Visas

Relatively few nationalities now need an advance visa, but those who do should not arrive at the border without one, or they may be sent straight to the city with the nearest Chilean consulate. On arrival, visitors receive a tourist card and entry stamp, which allow a stay of up to 90 days but are renewable for an additional 90.

Visa Extensions To renew an expiring tourist card, visit the Departamento de Extranjería (☎ 672 5320; Map 5), Moneda 1342, between 8:30 am and 3:30 pm weekdays, or one of their offices in other cities. However, since this now costs about US$100, requires two color photographs and takes two to three days, many visitors prefer a quick dash across the Argentine border. Even the quickest trip to Mendoza (see the Excursions chapter) and back won't cost much less than that, but it's probably more interesting than spending several days standing in lines.

Do not lose your tourist card, which border authorities take seriously; for a replacement, visit the Policía Internacional (☎ 737 1292; Map 7) at General Borgoño 1052, Independencia, just across the river from the old Mapocho station, from 8:30 am to 12:30 pm or 3 to 7 pm weekdays. One LP reader reports that, with the help of airline staff, a card can be replaced more quickly at the international airport.

Re-Entry Visas If you're staying longer than six months, it's simplest to make a brief visit to Argentina, Peru or Bolivia, then return and start your six months all over again. There is no formal obstacle to doing so, but some border officials monitor entry and exit stamps closely enough to question returnees from Mendoza as to whether they are working illegally in Chile.

Work & Resident Visas Chile's array of work visas is complex. Visitors on tourist cards may apply for a Tarjeta Especial de Trabajo (Special Work Card) that allows them to work month-to-month while arranging a longer work visa, but this temporary card costs US$200 to US$500 per month, depending on the applicant's nationality. Moreover, the applicant's minimum monthly salary must be at least US$1000.

Usually, this is a temporary expedient while the applicant seeks a Visa Residente Sujeto al Contrato (Resident Visa Subject to Contract), often assisted by a Chilean employer. Those wishing to work as consultants or start businesses should apply for a Visa de Residencia Temporaria, which requires evidence of substantial financial solvency, usually at least US$8000 deposited in a Chilean bank. After two years on a contract visa, or a year's temporary residence, a foreigner may apply for Visa de Residencia Permanente, a permanent residence visa. Students who have spent two years in Chile on a student visa may also apply for permanent residence.

After obtaining residence, foreigners must register with the Policía Internacional and obtain a Cédula de Identidad (Identity Card) from the Registro Civil (Civil Register).

Onward Tickets

Theoretically, Chile requires a return or onward ticket for arriving travelers, and some airlines may ask for evidence of an onward ticket if the date of your return ticket is beyond the initial 90-day tourist-card limit. However, the author has crossed numerous Chilean border posts, including international airports, dozens of times over many years without ever having been asked for an onward ticket.

Travel Insurance

A travel insurance policy to cover theft, loss (including plane tickets) and medical problems is a good idea. Some policies offer lower and higher medical-expense options; the higher ones are chiefly for countries that have extremely high medical costs, such as the USA. There is a wide variety of policies available, so check the small print.

Some policies specifically exclude 'dangerous activities,' which can include scuba diving, motorcycling or even trekking. A locally acquired motorcycle license is not valid under some policies.

You may prefer a policy that pays doctors or hospitals directly rather than making you pay on the spot and claim later. If you do have to claim later, make sure that you keep all documentation. Some policies ask you to call back collect (reverse charges) to a center in your home country, where an immediate assessment of your problem is made.

Check that the policy covers ambulances or an emergency flight home.

Driver's License & Permits

Foreigners resident in Chile may obtain a Chilean driver's license through the municipality in which they live.

International Driving Permit Visiting motorists need an International Driving Permit to complement their national or state license. Carabineros at highway check-points or on the road are generally firm but courteous and fair, with a much higher reputation for personal integrity than most Latin American police. *Never* attempt to bribe them.

Vehicle Documents For hints on purchasing and registering a car in Chile, see the Getting Around chapter. Permits for temporarily imported tourist vehicles may now be extended beyond the initial 90-day period, but not all customs officials are aware of this; it may be easier to cross the border into Argentina and return with new paperwork.

Hostel Cards

Chile has a small but growing network of official hostels and affiliates throughout the country. For information, contact the Asociación Chilena de Albergues Turísticos Juveniles (☎/fax 233 3220, achatj@entelchile.net), the local affiliate of Hostelling International, Avenida Hernando de Aguirre 201, Oficina 602, Providencia (Ⓜ Tobalaba). Hostel cards can also be purchased at the Hostelling International hostel (☎ 671 8532, 688 6434, fax 672 8880, histgoch@entelchile.net), Cienfuegos 151 (Ⓜ Los Héroes; Map 6).

Student & Youth Cards

The Instituto Nacional de la Juventud (INJ or Injuv, ☎ 688 1072), Agustinas 1564 (Ⓜ Los Héroes or Moneda; Map 5) issues an inexpensive *Tarjeta Joven* (youth card) that entitles the holder to discounts on many travel services, including some airline fares, and admission to national parks. It may, however, only be available to Chilean nationals and permanent residents.

Seniors' Cards

Travelers over the age of 60 can sometimes obtain *tercera edad* discounts on museum admissions and the like. Usually a passport with date of birth will be sufficient evidence of age.

International Health Card

Chile does not require an International Health Certificate, but it might be a good idea to obtain one if you plan to visit other South American countries, especially in the Tropics. It's advisable to have a medical checkup before your trip.

Copies

Make photocopies of the data pages of your passport and other documents, especially airline tickets, travel insurance documents with emergency numbers, credit cards (and phone numbers to contact in case of loss), driver's license and vehicle documentation. Keep all of this, and a list of traveler's checks, separate from the originals, and leave a copy with someone reliable at home. If your passport is lost or stolen, notify the carabineros, get a statement and then notify your consulate as soon as possible.

It's also a good idea to store details of your vital travel documents in Lonely Planet's free online Travel Vault in case you lose the photocopies or can't be bothered with them. Your password-protected Travel Vault is accessible online anywhere in the world – create it at www.ekno.lonelyplanet.com.

EMBASSIES & CONSULATES
Chilean Embassies Abroad

Chile has diplomatic representation in most parts of the world; those listed are the ones most likely to be useful to intending visitors. In some places there is a tourist information section with a separate address.

Argentina
(☎ 4394 6582)
San Martín 439, 9th floor, Buenos Aires

Australia
(☎ 6286 2430)
10 Culgoa Circuit, O'Malley ACT 2606

Bolivia
(☎ 785 275)
Avenida H Siles 5843, Barrio Obrajes, La Paz

Brazil
(☎ 552 5349)
Praia do Flamengo 344, 7th floor, Flamengo Rio de Janeiro
(☎ 284 2044)
Avenida Paulista 1009, 10th floor, São Paulo

Canada
(☎ 613-235-4402)
50 O'Connor St, Suite 1413,
Ottawa, Ontario K1P 6L2

Tourist Information:
(☎ 613-235-4402)
56 Sparks St, Suite 801 Ottawa, Ontario K1P 5I4
Consulates:
(☎ 416-924-0106)
2 Bloor St W, Suite 1801, Toronto, Ontario M4W 3E2
(☎ 514-499-0405)
1010 Sherbrooke St W, Suite 710, Montréal, Québec H3A 2R7

France
(☎ 470 54661)
64 Blvd de la Tour Maubourg, Paris

Germany
(☎ 204 4990)
Leipzigerstrasse 63, Berlin

New Zealand
(☎ 471 6270)
7th floor, Willis CorroonHouse, 1-3 Welleston St, Wellington

Paraguay
(☎ 600 671)
Guido Spano 1687, Asunción

Peru
(☎ 221 2817)
Javier Prado Oeste 790 San Isidro, Lima

UK
(☎ 020 7580 1032)
12 Devonshire St, London W1N 2DS

Uruguay
(☎ 908 2223)
Andes 1365, 1st floor, Montevideo

USA
(☎ 202-785-3159)
1736 Massachusetts Ave NW
Washington, DC 20036
Tourist Information:
(☎ 202-785-1746)
1732 Massachusetts Ave NW
Washington, DC 20036
Consulates:
(☎ 212-980-3706)
866 United Nations Plaza, Suite 302, New York, NY 10017
(☎ 617-426-1678)
79 Milk St, Suite 600, Boston, MA 02109
(☎ 215-829-9520)
Public Ledger Building, Suite 1030, 6th & Chestnut Sts, Philadelphia, PA 19142
(☎ 305-373-8623)
800 Brickell Ave, Suite 1230, Miami, FL 33131
(☎ 809-725-6365)
American Airlines Building, Suite 800, 1509 López Landrón, Santurce, San Juan PR 00911
(☎ 312-654-8780)
875 N Michigan Ave, Suite 3352

Chicago, IL 60611
(☎ 713-621-5853)
1360 Post Oak Blvd, Suite 2330
Houston, TX 77056
(☎ 415-982-7662)
870 Market St, Suite 1062
San Francisco, CA 94105
(☎ 310-785-0047)
1900 Avenue of the Stars, Suite 2450
Los Angeles, CA 90067
(☎ 619-232-6361)
550 West C St, Suite 1820, San Diego, CA 92101
(☎ 808-949-2850)
1860 Ala Moana Blvd, No 1900
Honolulu, HI 96815

Embassies & Consulates in Santiago

All major European and South American countries, and many others as well, have embassies in Santiago. It's important to realize what your own embassy can and can't do to help you if you get into trouble. Generally speaking, it won't be much help in emergencies if the trouble you're in is remotely your own fault. Remember that you are bound by the laws of the country you are in. Your embassy will not be sympathetic if you end up in jail after committing a crime locally, even if such actions are legal in your own country.

In genuine emergencies, you might get some assistance, but only if other channels have been exhausted. If you need to get home urgently, a free ticket home is exceedingly unlikely – the embassy would expect you to have insurance. If all your money and documents are stolen, it might assist you with getting a new passport, but a loan for onward travel is out of the question.

Argentina (☎ 222 8977) Vicuña Mackenna 41

Australia (☎ 228 5065) Gertrudis Echeñique 420, Las Condes

Austria (☎ 223 4774) Barros Errázuriz 1968, 3rd floor, Providencia

Belgium (☎ 232 1071) Avenida Providencia 2653 Oficina 1104, Providencia

Bolivia (☎ 232 8180) Avenida Santa María 2796, Providencia

Brazil (☎ 639 8867) MacIver 225, 15th floor

Canada (☎ 362 9660) Nueva Tajamar 481, 12th floor, Las Condes

Denmark (☎ 218 5949) Jacques Cazotte 5531, Vitacura

France (☎ 225 1030) Avenida Condell 65, Providencia

Germany (☎ 633 5031) Agustinas 785, 7th floor

Israel (☎ 246 1570) San Sebastián 2812, 5th floor, Las Condes

Italy (☎ 225 9020) Román Díaz 1270, Providencia

Japan (☎ 232 1809) Avenida Ricardo Lyon 520, Providencia

Mexico (☎ 206 6132) Félix de Amesti 128, Las Condes

Netherlands (☎ 223 6825) Las Violetas 2368, Providencia

New Zealand (☎ 231 4204) Isidora Goyenechea 3516, Las Condes

Norway (☎ 234 2888) San Sebastián 2839, Oficina 509, Las Condes

Paraguay (☎ 639 4640) Huérfanos 886, Oficina 514

Peru (☎ 235 4600) Padre Mariano 10, Oficina 309, Providencia

Spain (☎ 233 4070) Avenida 11 de Septiembre 2353, 9th floor, Providencia

Sweden (☎ 231 2733) Avenida 11 de Septiembre 2353, 4th floor, Providencia

Switzerland (☎ 263 4211) Avenida Américo Vespucio Sur 100, 14th floor, Las Condes

UK (☎ 231 3737) Avenida El Bosque Norte 0125, 3rd floor, Las Condes

Uruguay (☎ 223 8398) Avenida Pedro de Valdivia 711, Providencia

USA (☎ 232 2600) Avenida Andrés Bello 2800, Las Condes

CUSTOMS

There are no restrictions on import and export of local and foreign currency. Duty-free allowances include 400 cigarettes or 50 cigars or 500 grams of tobacco, 2½ liters of alcoholic beverages, and perfume for personal use. Though Chilean officials generally defer to foreign visitors, travelers crossing the border frequently and carrying electronic equipment like camcorders or laptop computers might consider carrying a typed list of these items, with serial numbers, stamped by authorities for ease and convenience.

Inspections are usually routine, although some travelers have had to put up with more rigorous examinations because of the occurance of drug smuggling from Peru and Bolivia.

At international borders, officials of the SAG (Servicio Agrícola-Ganadero, Agriculture and Livestock Service) check luggage for fruit, the entry of which is strictly controlled to prevent the spread of diseases and pests that might threaten Chile's booming fruit exports.

Photographers should note that at major international border crossings like Los Libertadores (the crossing from Mendoza, Argentina), Chilean customs officials put baggage through X-ray machines; do not leave film in your luggage.

MONEY

A combination of cash, traveler's checks and credit or ATM cards is the best way to take your money.

Currency

The unit of currency is the peso (Ch$). Bank notes come in denominations of Ch$500, Ch$1000, Ch$5000 and Ch$10,000, with a new Ch$2000 bill entering circulation. Coin values are Ch$1, Ch$5, Ch$10, Ch$50 and Ch$100, although one-peso coins are rare. Copper-colored coins have replaced lightweight aluminum coins, which are no longer legal tender. In small villages, it can be difficult to change bills larger than Ch$1000.

Demand for pesos is minimal outside Chile, except in a few border towns and capitals, so it's best to change all your money at the border unless you're returning to Chile in the near future.

Exchange Rates

Santiago generally has the best exchange rates in the country. The following rates, current as of mid-2000, provide an idea of relative values:

country	unit		Chilean$
Argentina	Arg$1	=	Ch$521
Australia	A$1	=	Ch$298
Bolivia	Bol1	=	Ch$86
Canada	Can$1	=	Ch$351

'Loop-de-loop' sculpture, World Trade Center

KRZYSZTOF DYDYNSKI

Busy Paseo Ahumada

KRZYSZTOF DYDYNSKI

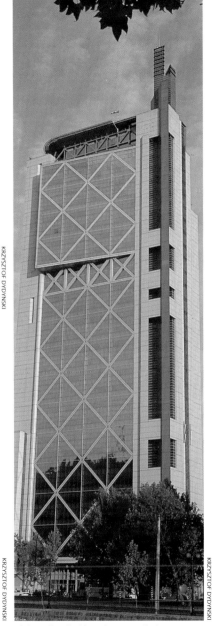

Chile's tallest building, biggest cell phone

KRZYSZTOF DYDYNSKI

Club Colo Colo gargoyles

Tick tock goes the Bolsa de Comercio

Gardener on holiday, Calle Lastarría

Wrought iron gate, Palacio Irarrázaval

European Union	€1	=	Ch$473
France	1FFr	=	Ch$72
Germany	DM1	=	Ch$242
Italy	It£1000	=	Ch$244
Japan	¥100	=	Ch$477
New Zealand	NZ$1	=	Ch$246
Peru	Sol1	=	Ch$153
Spain	Pta100	=	Ch$284
Switzerland	SwFr1	=	Ch$304
UK	UK£1	=	Ch$782
USA	US$1	=	Ch$521

For the most up-to-date information, see *Estrategia* (Chile's equivalent of the *Wall Street Journal* or *Financial Times*), the financial pages of *El Mercurio* or the online *Santiago Times* (www.santiagotimes.cl/news/).

Exchanging Money

US dollars are by far the preferred foreign currency, and the dollar has gradually been gaining strength against the Chilean peso, ranging from about Ch$450 to just upwards of Ch$530 during the period of research, with some fluctuations. Santiago is the only ready market for European currencies.

Argentine pesos can be readily exchanged in Santiago, at border crossings and in tourist centers like Viña del Mar. If arriving from Argentina, it's better to exchange surplus Argentine currency directly into Chilean pesos – though the rate is a little lower than for dollars, the double exchange is more costly. Commissions are insignificant except on traveler's checks in some areas.

Chile has no black market at present, though some businesses may give an especially favorable exchange rate for purchases in cash dollars. There is nothing illegal about this.

Cash Cash dollars can be exchanged at banks, *casas de cambio* (exchange houses), hotels and some travel agencies, and often in shops or on the street. Cash dollars earn a slightly better exchange rate and avoid commissions sometimes levied on traveler's checks. If you are confident of your ability to carry cash safely, it's the best alternative.

Traveler's Checks Traveler's checks are unquestionably safer than cash, but in smaller towns and out-of-the-way locations it can be difficult to find a bank that will change them, so carrying some cash dollars is a good idea. Some travelers have reported that lost Thomas Cook checks will not be replaced unless you notify the Santiago office of the loss within 24 hours; contact the Cook representative Turismo Tajamar (☎ 231 5112), Orrego Luco 023, Providencia, or phone the US office (☎ 609-987-7300) collect.

If you have US dollar traveler's checks, it may be better to convert them to cash and then change the cash for pesos. This is more problematic than it once was, but some cambios along Agustinas will still do it.

ATMs Automated teller machines affiliated with the Plus and Cirrus systems make it easy to get withdrawals or cash advances in most Chilean cities, but Banco del Estado's ATMs in smaller towns are incompatible with foreign ATM and credit cards.

Credit Cards Credit cards, particularly those that allow cash advances or traveler's check purchases (American Express, Visa and MasterCard), can be useful. Revaluation of local currency can make your bill higher than anticipated (though devaluations can make it cheaper), so be aware of fluctuations in the rate. Credit cards are also useful if you must show 'sufficient funds' before entering another South American country or in an emergency. Note that some banks and credit card companies are beginning to collect higher service charges on overseas transactions – check these out before you go.

International Transfers To receive money from abroad, have your home bank send a draft. Money transferred by cable should arrive in a few days; Chilean banks will give you your money in US dollars on request.

Security

Santiago is not a high-crime city, but pickpocketing is not unknown, and travelers should avoid carrying large amounts of money in vulnerable spots like the back pocket. Both money belts and leg pouches are secure means of carrying cash and other important monetary documents, like traveler's checks.

Costs

While Chile's inflation has been slightly higher than that of neighboring Argentina, gradual devaluation has meant stabilization, at least in US dollar terms. It's still relatively expensive compared with the Andean republics of Peru and Bolivia, but modest lodging, food and transport are still more economical than in Europe, North America or even Argentina.

Budget travelers should allot a minimum of US$25 per day for food and lodging, but if you purchase food at markets or eat at modest restaurants you may be able to get by on less. It's even possible to lunch economically at some very fine restaurants that offer fixed menus.

Mid-range travelers can do very well on about US$50 per day, though some of the best family-style accommodations are better values than mid-range hotels. Visitors for whom budget concerns are not primary will find some outstanding values, both in accommodations and food.

Tipping & Bargaining

In restaurants, it's customary to tip about 10% of the bill, except in exclusively family-run places. In general, waitstaff are poorly paid, so if you can afford to eat out you can afford to tip, and even a small *propina* will be appreciated. Taxi drivers do not require tips, although you may round off the fare for convenience.

Usually only purchases from handicrafts markets will be subject to bargaining. Hotel prices are generally fixed and prominently displayed, but in the off-season or a slow summer, haggling may be possible; for long-term stays it is definitely possible. It's worth asking if the first price quoted is their best.

On occasion, long-distance bus or *taxi colectivo* (shared taxi) fares are open to negotiation, especially those between Santiago and Mendoza, Argentina.

Taxes & Refunds

At many mid-range and top-end hotels, payment in US dollars (either cash or credit) legally sidesteps the crippling 18% IVA *(impuesto de valor agregado)*, the value-added tax. If there is any question as to whether IVA is included in the rates, clarify before paying. A few places that get only a handful of foreign visitors can't be bothered with the extra paperwork, but most find it advantageous to be able to offer the discount (for which it's imperative to show your tourist card).

POST & COMMUNICATIONS

Correos de Chile's postal services are reasonably dependable but sometimes rather slow. Over the past decade-plus, telephone infrastructure has gone from Paleolithic to postmodern and is probably the best on the continent. Telegraph, telex and fax services are of equally high quality.

Postal Rates

Within Chile, sending an ordinary domestic letter costs about US$0.25. An airmail letter costs about US$0.85 to North America and US$1 to overseas destinations, while aerograms cost US$0.75 anywhere. Postcards are slightly cheaper.

Addresses

In Chilean cities and towns, names of streets, plazas and other features are often long and elaborate, such as Calle Cardenal José Maria Caro or Avenida Libertador General Bernardo O'Higgins. Long names are often shortened on maps, in writing or in speech, so the former might appear on a map as JM Caro, or just Caro, while the latter might appear as Avenida Gral O'Higgins, Avenida B O'Higgins, just O'Higgins or even by a colloquial alternative (Alameda). The word *calle* (street) is usually omitted on maps.

Some addresses include the expression *local* (locale) followed by a number, for example Cochrane 56, Local 5. 'Local' means it's one of several offices at the same street address.

Some street numbers begin with a zero, for example, Avenida El Bosque Norte 084.

This confusing practice usually happens when an older street is extended in the opposite direction, beyond the original number 1. If, for instance, street numbers increase heading from north to south, El Bosque Norte 084 will be north of El Bosque 84, which will in turn be north of El Bosque 184.

The abbreviation 's/n' following a street address stands for *sin número* (without number) and indicates that the address has no specific street number. Particularly perplexing to foreign visitors, this is far more common in small towns than in the capital itself.

Sending Mail

Most Chilean post offices are open 9 am to 6 pm weekdays and 9 am to noon Saturday. Send essential overseas mail *certificado* (registered) to ensure its arrival. Mail that appears to contain money is unlikely to arrive at its final destination.

Santiago's Correo Central (main post office), on the north side of the Plaza de Armas (Map 5), handles poste restante services and also has a philatelic desk. It's open 8 am to 10 pm weekdays, 8 am to 6 pm Saturday; closed Sunday. Kiosks at the entrance sell envelopes and postcards and will also wrap parcels for a small fee. Correos de Chile has another large downtown post office at Moneda 1155 and a convenient Providencia branch at Avenida Providencia 1466.

Sending parcels is straightforward, although a customs official may have to inspect your package before a postal clerk will accept it. There are vendors in or near the post office who will wrap parcels upon request.

Courier Services International courier services are readily available in Santiago, less so outside the capital. Try Federal Express (☎ 231 5250), Avenida Providencia 1951 (Ⓜ Pedro de Valdivia; Map 8); DHL Express at Santa Rosa 135 (☎ 639 4342; Map 5), Huérfanos 1109 (☎ 697 2817; Map 5); or General Holley 70 (☎ 335 4388, Ⓜ Los Leones; Map 8).

Receiving Mail

You can receive mail via *lista de correos* or poste restante (equivalent to general delivery) at any Chilean post office. Santiago's American Express office offers client mail services, while some consulates will also hold correspondence for their citizens. To collect mail from a post office (or from American Express or an embassy), you need your passport as proof of identity. Instruct correspondents to address letters clearly and to indicate a date until which the post office should hold them; otherwise, they may be returned or destroyed. There is usually a small charge, about US$0.25 per item.

Chilean post offices maintain separate lists of correspondence for men and women, so check both if your correspondent has not addressed the letter 'Señor,' 'Señora' or 'Señorita.' If expected correspondence does not arrive, ask the clerk to check under every possible combination of your initials, even 'M' (for Mr, Ms etc). There may be particular confusion if correspondents use your middle name, since Chileans use both paternal and maternal surnames for identification, with the former listed first. Thus a letter to the Chilean 'Augusto Pinochet Ugarte' will be found under the listing for 'P' (the paternal surname) rather than 'U,' (the maternal) while a letter to North American 'Ronald Wilson Reagan' may be found under 'W' even though 'Reagan' is the proper surname.

Telephone

Santiago's area code is ☎ 02; Chile's country code is ☎ 56. All telephone numbers in Santiago and the Metropolitan Region have seven digits; most other telephone numbers in Chile have six digits. Exceptions include certain toll-free and emergency numbers, and cellular telephones throughout the country, which have seven digits prefixed by 09.

Despite occasional glitches due to rapid technological change, Chilean telephone services are among the best and cheapest in the world. The former state telephone monopoly Entel, as well as Telefónica (until recently the Compañía de Teléfonos de Chile,

Carrier Codes

Both Entel and Telefónica (formerly CTC) have access codes to overseas operators, though it is often cheaper to pay for the calls in Chile (the opposite is true in neighboring Argentina and most other Latin American countries). The following are local carrier codes, but rates change on a weekly or even daily basis – for the latest, consult the English-language *News Review* or any Santiago daily. If you are calling from a Telefónica or Entel public phone, you don't need to dial the respective carrier codes.

Carrier	Code
BellSouth	☎ 181
Chilesat	☎ 171
Entel	☎ 123
Firstcom Chile	☎ 155
Manquehue	☎ 122
Telefónica	☎ 188
Telefónica del Sur	☎ 121
Transam	☎ 113
VTR	☎ 120

CTC) and several other carriers offer domestic and international long-distance services throughout most of the country.

When calling or answering the telephone, the proper salutation is *aló* or *hola* (hello). Exchange pleasantries before getting to the point of your conversation.

Pay Phones Local calls from public phones cost Ch$100 (about US$0.20) for five minutes, but outside peak hours (8 am to 8 pm weekdays, 8 am to 2 pm Saturday) they cost only Ch$50. On most modern phones, a liquid crystal readout indicates the remaining credit on your call; when it reaches zero and you hear a beeping sound, insert another coin unless you plan to finish within a few seconds. Public phones do not make change, but if there is at least Ch$50 credit remaining you may make another call by pressing a button rather than inserting another coin.

Some Telefónica CTC Chile phones accept only coins, others only magnetic phone cards, and still others accept both. *Cobro revertido* (reverse-charge or collect) calls overseas are simple, as are credit card calls. Only a handful of phones have direct fiber-optic connections to operators in North America and Europe.

Telefónica CTC Chile magnetic phone cards are available in values of Ch$2000 to Ch$5000, valid in most but not all Telefónica phones. Entel's 'Entel Ticket' has a similar appearance but has an individual number instead of a magnetic strip. The user dials ☎ 800-800 123, then 2, then the ticket number; at this point, a computer voice states the remaining peso amount and, after you dial the number, tells you the time that amount will permit you to speak.

Because of the so-called multicarrier system, whereby a number of companies compete for long-distance services, charges for both foreign and domestic calls can be astonishingly cheap, but the system is complicated. Most Entel and Telefónica CTC Chile offices close by 10 pm, after which you'll need to use a pay phone elsewhere.

Collect Calls To make a collect call, dial the number of the carrier, then 182 for an operator.

Entel international codes appear below; for countries not on this list, dial ☎ 800-123-123.

Australia	☎ 800-360 150
Belgium	☎ 800-360 121
Canada	☎ 800-360 280
France	☎ 800-360 110
Germany	☎ 123-003 491
Italy	☎ 800-360 099
Netherlands	☎ 123-003 311
Spain	☎ 800-360 055
UK (BT)	☎ 800-360 066
USA (AT&T)	☎ 800-800 311
USA (MCI)	☎ 800-360 180
USA (Sprint)	☎ 800-360 777

Telefónica CTC Chile codes appear below; for other countries, contact Telefónica at ☎ 800-200 300.

Australia	☎ 800-800 287
Canada	☎ 800-800 226
France	☎ 800-800 372
Germany	☎ 800-800 049
Italy	☎ 800-800 039
Spain	☎ 800-207 334
UK (BT)	☎ 800-800 044
USA (AT&T)	☎ 800-800 288
USA (MCI)	☎ 800-207 300
USA (Sprint)	☎ 800-800 777

International Calling Cards There's a wide range of international calling cards. Lonely Planet's eKno Communication Card provides budget international calls, a range of messaging services, free email and travel information. You can join online at www.ekno.lonelyplanet.com or by phone from Chile by dialing the eKno access number (☎ 800 360 193).

Cellular Communications Cellular telephones have become very common in Chile, thanks to companies like BellSouth, which rent them for about US$50 per month plus additional charges beyond a certain amount of usage. Services often include voicemail, call waiting and three-way calling. In early 1999, all cellular service switched to a 'caller-pays' format, which eats up magnetic phone cards very quickly for anyone calling *to* a cell phone.

Cell phones throughout the country have seven digits, even in areas where conventional telephones have six; when calling a cell phone, dial the prefix 09 first.

Entel has a nationwide toll-free information number (☎ 800 367 700). Rates are as low as US$24 per month for 100 minutes, US$30 for 200 minutes, not counting the phone itself.

Fax & Telegraph

Entel, Telefónica CTC Chile, Telex-Chile and VTR offer telex, telegraph and fax services at their long-distance telephone offices; there are also many small private offices with fax service. Like other telecommunications services in Chile, prices are very reasonable.

Email & Internet Access

It's becoming more routine for Chilean businesses and individuals to have email and Internet access. The increasing number of cybercafés and other public outlets is making this more convenient. Getting access to your own phone line is usually possible only at top-end hotels that place surcharges on local calls (which are, in any event, on a metered rather than flat fee basis).

Some Internet service providers (ISPs), such as AOL and Compuserve, have local dial-in numbers in Chile. For other suggestions contact the following local providers:

Telefónica CTC Chile	☎ 800 200 300
Entel	info@entelchile.net
Chilesat	info@chilepac.net

Cybercafés Public access Internet sites include the Café Virtual (☎ 638 6846), Alameda 145 (Map 5); Dity Office (☎ 269 2610), Fidel Oteíza 1930, Providencia (Ⓜ Pedro de Valdivia); and CyberCenter (☎ 231 4207), General Holley 170, Providencia (Ⓜ Los Leones), open 11 am to 10 pm daily except Sunday. The South Central American Information Club (☎ 673 3166), in the Hotel Indiana at Rosas 1339 (Map 5), also has Internet access, as does the Bivouac Café (☎ 777 6173), Calle del Arzobispo 0635 on the Providencia side of Barrio Bellavista (Ⓜ Salvador; Map 7).

The best deal in town, though, is the public access at the Torre Telefónica CTC Chile at Avenida Providencia and General Bustamante (Map 8). Open 10 am to 8 pm Tuesday through Saturday, it does require reservations for one free hour per person per day – the downside, of course, is that demand is high, and there's no guarantee you'll get the slot you want.

INTERNET RESOURCES

The World Wide Web is an excellent resource for travelers. You can research your trip, hunt down bargain airfares, book hotels, check on weather conditions and chat with locals and other travelers about the best places to visit (or avoid).

Lonely Planet's site (www.lonelyplanet .com) is a great place to start your Web explorations. You'll find summaries on travel experiences, postcards from other travelers and the Thorn Tree bulletin board, where you can ask questions before you go or dispense advice when you get back. Also handy is the subWWWay section, which links you to the most useful travel resources elsewhere on the Web.

BOOKS

Most books are published in different editions by different publishers in different countries. As a result, a book might be a hardcover rarity in one country but readily available in paperback in another. Fortunately, bookstores and libraries can search by title or author, so your local bookstore or library is best placed to advise you on the availability of the following recommendations.

See Arts in the Facts about Santiago de Chile chapter for Chilean literature.

Lonely Planet

Other books can supplement or complement this one. The pocket-size *Latin American Spanish Phrasebook* is helpful for those just starting in the language. Geared toward the first-time traveler, *Read This First: Central & South America* is from a new series, providing practical information for budgeting and planning your trip. *Healthy Travel Central & South America* has answers to travelers' commonly asked health questions.

If you plan to travel more widely in Chile, the *Chile & Easter Island* guide has everything you'll need. For travel even farther afield, LP's guidebook series includes the following titles: *Argentina, Uruguay & Paraguay*; *Ecuador & the Galápagos Islands*; *Bolivia*; *Peru*; *Colombia*; and *Brazil*. Budget travelers covering a large part of the continent should look for *South America on a Shoestring*. There are also several other city guides, including *Buenos Aires*.

Guidebooks

One of the most useful sources of information is the Turistel guide series, published by the Telefónica CTC Chile (the former Compañía de Teléfonos de Chile), which is updated annually and reasonably priced, but the single-volume English translation *Chile: a Remote Corner of the Earth* is badly out of date. The Spanish version contains a separate Centro volume that includes Santiago and environs; there's also a pocket-size Telefónica guide to camping and campgrounds with more detailed maps of some important areas.

Oriented toward motorists, Turistel guides provide excellent highway and city maps (the latter beautifully drawn, despite frequent minor errors and the absence of scales) and thorough background information, but they rarely cover budget accommodations. Their biggest drawback, though, is the flimsy paper binding, which makes them unusable after one season – handle with care.

Travel

Sara Wheeler's *Travels in a Thin Country* (1996) is humorous and sometimes insightful, but suffers from an irritating 'product placement' approach to a certain international car rental agency. Ariel Dorfman's *Heading South, Looking North* (1998) is the personal and political memoir of a bicultural activist, also one of contemporary Chile's major literary figures, that fits partly into the travel literature category. John Hickman's *News from the End of the Earth: a Portrait of Chile* (1998) uses the author's five years (1982–87) as British ambassador to Santiago as a takeoff point for an inter-pretation of the country.

Don't overlook works of greater antiquity. Charles Darwin's *Voyage of the Beagle*, available in many editions, is as fresh as yesterday. His accounts of the Chilean landscape are truly memorable, and a lightweight paperback copy is a perfect companion for any trip to Chile. Besides insights on the early Chilean polity, María Graham's *Journal of a Residence in Chile* (1824) conveys the beauty of the landscape in both words and illustrations.

History

Studies of Santiago proper are hard to find in English, but several books contain information on the capital and its hinterland. One widely available source on Chile from the Spanish conquest to the late 1970s is Brian Loveman's rather glib *Chile: The Legacy of Hispanic Capitalism* (1979), which, despite its polemical and conde-scending tone, presents a common point of view. A better choice, though more re-stricted in its coverage, is the collection *Chile Since Independence* (1993), edited by Leslie Bethell.

With a narrower focus, based on painstak-ing archival research, Arnold Bauer's *Chilean Rural Society from the Spanish Con-quest to 1930* (1975) traces the evolution of the Chilean countryside on which the capital depended. Though dated in many ways, George McCutcheon McBride's *Chile: Land and Society* (1936) is a vivid portrait of life on the *latifundio* (large landholding), which changed little until the late 1960s.

Two recent illustrated books, with Spanish language text, are worth looking for in Santiago. José Moreno and Miguel Laborde's *Santiago 1850–1930* (Dolmen Ediciones, 1997) is a selection of historic black-and-white photographs from the archives of the Universidad de Chile. Raúl Rojas (text) and Pedro Carrasco Pávez (photos) collaborated on *Santiago de Chile … Ciudad para Recordar* (Editorial Renacimiento), a color album celebrating the capital's historic legacy and contempo-rary developments.

Allende & the Pinochet Dictatorship

Publishing on the Allende years is a minor industry in its own right, and, as in the 1970s, it's still hard to find a middle ground. Events in Ñuñoa's Estadio Nacional (National Stadium) following the military coup are part of the scenario in *Victor: An Unfinished Song* (1983), a personal account of life during the 1960s and 1970s by Joan Jara, the English wife of murdered folksinger Victor Jara. The death of a politically involved US citizen at the Estadio Nacional was the subject of Thomas Hauser's book *The Execution of Charles Horman: An American Sacrifice* (1978), which implicated US officials and was the basis of the film *Missing*. A riveting account of an exile's secret return is the famous Colombian writer Gabriel García Márquez's *Clandestine in Chile* (1987), which tells the story of filmmaker Miguel Littín's secret working visit to Santiago in 1985.

Contemporary Chilean Politics

An outstanding, nonpolemical explanation of the complexities of 20th-century Chilean politics is César Caviedes' *The Politics of Chile: a Sociogeographical Assessment* (1979), which has detailed information on the capital. For an account of the Pinochet years and their aftermath that eschews par-tisan rhetoric and focuses on the complexi-ties of political events over two decades, see Pamela Constable and Arturo Valenzuela's *A Nation of Enemies* (1991).

Geography & Natural History

Several readable texts integrate Latin American history with geography. Try Arthur Morris' *South America* (1979), which has several worthwhile pages on Santiago; the detailed chapter on Chile in Harold Blakemore and Clifford Smith's collection *Latin America* (1983); and *The Cambridge Encyclopedia of Latin America* (1985), which is rather broader in conception.

NEWSPAPERS & MAGAZINES

Still recovering from the repression of the Pinochet years, Chilean journalism is rapidly improving, but conditions are far from perfect. State security laws favor the powerful, even when allegations may be true – in 1999, when journalist Alejandra Matús published *El Negro Libro de la Justicia Chilena* (The Black Book of Chilean Justice) exposing corruption in the Supreme Court, the Chief Justice ordered it confiscated and briefly jailed the publishers. Matús fled to Miami, where the US government's grant of political asylum embarrassed the Chilean government, which seemed incapable of altering the Pinochet dictatorship's draconian state security laws.

El Mercurio de Valparaíso (founded 1827) is Chile's most venerable daily, but Santiago is the country's media center. *El Mercurio* (estimated readership 336,000 daily, 643,000 Sunday; www.elmercurio.cl/), the capital's oldest and most prestigious daily, follows a conservative editorial policy but has a diverse letters section, excellent cultural coverage and an outstanding Sunday travel magazine; its *Wikén* supplement, which comes out Friday, is a guide to entertainment in the capital. *Mercurio*'s parent corporation also owns the sleazy tabloids *La Segunda* (estimated readership 112,000) and *Ultimas Noticias*, which sensationalize crime and radical political dissent (which they seem to consider synonymous). *La Cuarta*, however, makes these two look like the *New York Times*, and if you wrapped fish in it, you wouldn't know which was the source of the odor.

La Tercera (estimated readership 634,000 daily, 467,000 Sunday), another tabloid, has improved coverage and broadened its editorial stance, but is still pretty conservative. *La Nación* (estimated readership 41,000) is the official government daily, but the editorial dominance of its conservative competition makes it sound like an opposition paper. The new kid on the block is *El Metropolitano*, a tabloid descended from the failed but serious Christian Democratic daily *La Epoca*; while it's not sensationalist, *El Metropolitano*'s news coverage is a bit thin compared with its sports and entertainment pages. *Estrategia* (estimated readership 94,000; www.estrategia.cl) is the weekday voice of Chile's financial community and the best source on trends in the exchange rate.

The radical press has not fared well because of trouble attracting advertising. *El Siglo*, voice of the Communist party, has become a monthly rather than a weekly because of financial difficulties; the other major leftist paper is the uncompromising fortnightly *Punto Final*. A recent entry, inspired by General Pinochet's detention in London, is the truculently satirical biweekly *The Clinic*; some of its articles border on the juvenile, but others are right on target, most notably the facetious medical report on the general, using the body of a plucked chicken to point out the physical ailments he and his supporters allege. Despite the English-language name, all the articles are in Spanish.

Since its beginning in late 1991, Santiago's English-language *News Review* has improved substantially, but it's had to cut back from twice weekly to once weekly. It's still hard to find outside the capital, but try upscale hotels in the regions. The *News Review*'s German-language counterpart is *El Cóndor*, now in its 59th year.

The weekday English-language digest of the Chilean press, *Santiago Times* (☎ 777 5376, fax 735 2267, www.chipnews.cl), PO Box 53331, Correo Central, is available by fax or email subscription.

One of the more useful papers for anyone buying or selling anything is the twice-weekly tabloid *El Rastro*, which consists exclusively of classified ads for rental apartments, automobiles and virtually any other merchandise.

Chilean magazines include the general-interest newsweeklies *Ercilla*, *Qué Pasa*, and *Hoy* (oriented toward Christian Democrat politics). Monthlies include *Rocinante*, which stresses the arts, culture and society, and *América Economía*, edited in Santiago but distributed throughout Latin America, which specializes in international business.

RADIO & TV

In recent years, the end of government monopoly in the electronic media has opened the airwaves to a greater variety of programming than in the past. Broadcasting is less regulated than before, and there are many radio stations on both AM and FM bands.

TV stations include the government-owned Televisión Nacional (TVN) and the Universidad Católica's Channel 13, plus several private stations. International cable service is widely available and is common even in many *hospedajes* (budget accommodations, usually a large family home with extra bedrooms) and *residenciales* (also budget accommodations, generally buildings designed for short-stay lodging). There is a weekly English-language newsmagazine *Chile Today*, shown three times daily on cable channel 64. Networks such as CNN (in both English and Spanish), HBO, Discovery, ESPN and MTV are present in many Chilean homes and nearly all hotels mid-range and above.

Chile's most famous television personality is Mario Kreuzberger, popularly known as 'Don Francisco,' host of the weekly variety program *Sábado Gigante*, also seen on Spanish-language TV stations in the USA. The portly, multilingual Francisco, whose smiling visage endorses products on billboards throughout the country, also hosts the annual *Teletón* to raise money for disabled children.

There are 24 AM and 33 FM radio stations in the Región Metropolitana. Many stations use lowest-common-denominator syndicated formats like Futuro (88.9 FM) and Rock & Pop (94.1 FM), but there are also classical stations like El Conquistador (91.3 FM) and Beethoven (96.5 FM). Radio Universidad de Santiago (94.5 FM) offers noncommercial programming.

PHOTOGRAPHY & VIDEO

There are many shops that sell and process color print film fairly cheaply. Color slide film, exclusively for E6 processing, is not difficult to find but is more expensive than overseas – it's better to bring your own and have it processed at home.

For prompt and efficient, but not cheap, camera repair service, contact Harry Müller Thierfelder (☎ 698 3596), Ahumada 312, Oficina 312 (Map 5). Other possibilities are

Tec-Fo (☎ 695 2969), Nueva York 52, Oficina 204 (Map 5); Photo von Stowasser (☎ 232 1138), Santa Magdalena 16, Providencia (Ⓜ Los Leones); and Photo Service (☎ 335 4460), Avenida Suecia 84, 8th floor, Oficina 81, Providencia (Ⓜ Los Leones).

Santiago's usually hazy atmospheric conditions make a UV filter indispensable and a polarizing filter desirable. Even these can't assure perfection, but they improve the odds.

Santiago's airport security is generally responsive to requests to inspect film and cameras visually, rather than forcing you to send them through X-ray machines. Incoming customs inspections, however, sometimes require arriving passengers to put their luggage through X-rays, and this also happens to bus passengers at some land borders, most notably the crossing from Mendoza, Argentina. It's better not to leave film in your luggage or, if you must do so, place it in a lead-lined protective container.

TIME

For most of the year, Chile is four hours behind GMT/UTC, but from mid-December to late March, because of daylight saving time (summer time), the difference is three hours. The exact date of the changeover varies from year to year, especially in drought years when there may be hydro-electricity shortages.

ELECTRICITY

Electric current operates on 220 volts, 50 cycles. In Santiago, numerous electrical supply stores on San Pablo, west of the Puente pedestrian mall, sell transformers for appliances.

WEIGHTS & MEASURES

The metric system is official, but for weight the traditional *quintal* of 46kg is still common. For motorists, it's common to find tire pressure measured in pounds per square inch, and the Chilean military often uses feet as a standard measure, for instance for airport elevations. There's a conversion chart inside the back cover of this book.

LAUNDRY

In recent years, *lavanderías autoservicio* (self-service laundromats) have become more common. At most of these, 'self-service' means dropping off your clothes and picking them up later. Most inexpensive hotels will have a place where you can wash your own clothes and hang them to dry. In some places, maid service will be reasonable, but agree on charges in advance. Dry cleaners are abundant.

Try Lavandería Autoservicio (☎ 632 1772) at Monjitas 507 (Map 5), or Lavandería Lolos (☎ 699 5376) at Moneda 2296 in Barrio Brasil (Ⓜ República). There's also Laverap at Avenida Providencia 1645 (Ⓜ Pedro de Valdivia; Map 8).

RECYCLING

Santiago, unfortunately, has embraced disposable plastics. It's still possible, however, to buy soft drinks, beer and the like in returnable bottles. Usually, equally unfortunately, it's necessary to return the bottle to the original seller to obtain the deposit. An increasing number of neighborhoods, most notably Bellavista with its active nightlife, have large sidewalk containers to deposit used glass bottles.

On the other hand, scavengers are adept at salvaging almost anything of value, and many items thought useless by their original owners end up at flea markets around the city.

TOILETS

Ordinary toilet paper does not readily disintegrate in Chilean sewers, so most bathrooms have a basket where you discard what you have used. Cheaper accommodations and public toilets rarely provide toilet paper, so carry your own wherever you go. For the truly squeamish, the better restaurants and cafés are good alternatives.

LUGGAGE STORAGE

All of Santiago's bus stations have left-luggage facilities that are reliable and reasonably priced. Hotels in almost all categories will hold luggage after checkout time for travelers catching a late flight or bus, or even for those on an extended excursion. There is rarely any charge for this.

HEALTH

For medical emergencies, try the Posta Central (☎ 634 1650) at Avenida Portugal 125, which has English-speaking personnel (Ⓜ Universidad Católica; Map 5). Private clinics include the Clínica Universidad Católica (☎ 633 4122) at Lira 40 (Map 5) and the Clínica Dávila (☎ 735 4030) at Avenida Recoleta 464 in Recoleta (Ⓜ Puente Cal y Canto; Map 7). Less central, but highly regarded, are Clínica Las Condes (☎ 211 1002), Lo Fontecilla 411, Las Condes; and Clínica Alemana (☎ 212 9700), Avenida Vitacura 5951, Vitacura.

If you need an injection or a blood test (obligatory if you are a driver involved in an auto accident), purchase a new syringe from a pharmacy and ask the doctor or nurse to use it.

HIV/AIDS Organizations

As of December 1998, Chile had 2736 registered cases of AIDS and another 3601 carriers of HIV (human immunodeficiency virus). About 90% are male, mostly between the ages of 20 and 49. The port city of Valparaíso has the highest rate of infection.

For information contact the Corporación Chilena de Prevención del Sida (☎ 222 5255), General Jofré 179, Providencia, or Información sobre Sida y Enfermedades de Transmisión Sexual (☎ 736 5542), Melipilla 3432, Conchalí (just northwest of the Hipódromo Chile), which also provides medical and legal advice.

WOMEN TRAVELERS
Attitudes Toward Women

Many Chilean men are *machista* (chauvinist) but rarely violent in public behavior toward women. The main nuisances are unwelcome attention and vulgar language, which usually emphasizes feminine physical attributes, and is generally used in the presence of other men. If you respond aggressively ('Are you talking to me?'), you will probably put the aggressor to shame, but this requires considerable confidence on your part. Otherwise, it's best to ignore it and walk on.

Single women checking in at budget hotels, both in Santiago and elsewhere, may find themselves objects of curiosity or suspicion since prostitutes often frequent such places. If you otherwise like the place, ignore this and it should disappear. Chilean women generally do not travel alone, thus, outside the larger cities, women traveling alone are often objects of curiosity. You should interpret questions as to whether you are running away from parents or husband as expressions of concern.

Some foreign women living in Chile have complained that they find it difficult to make female friends, since some Chilean women view them as competitors for Chilean men. This may contribute to a sense of social isolation.

Scandinavian women (or women who look Scandinavian) may find that some Chilean men associate them with liberal attitudes toward sex and pornography.

Safety Precautions

For women traveling alone, Chile is probably safer than most other Latin American countries, but you should not be complacent. Unwelcome physical contact, particularly on crowded buses or trains, is not unusual. If you're physically confident, a slap or a well-aimed elbow should discourage any further incident. If not, try a scream – another very effective measure.

Should you hitchhike, exercise caution and especially avoid getting into a vehicle with more than one man. Though hitching is never totally safe, it is much safer in pairs.

GAY & LESBIAN TRAVELERS

While Chile is a strongly Catholic country, and homosexuality or even talk of it is taboo to many, there are enclaves of tolerance, most notably in parts of the capital. Since Chilean males are often more physically demonstrative than their counterparts in Europe or North America, behaviors like a vigorous embrace may seem innocuous even to some who dislike homosexuals.

Likewise, lesbians walking hand-in-hand may attract little attention, since Chilean women frequently do so, but this would be very indiscreet behavior for males.

After unwarranted raids on gay bars in Santiago in early 1996, homosexual rights advocates managed to get the Policía de Investigaciones to destroy videotapes of the raids, which had resulted in arrests but no charges, and to pledge not to repeat the incidents. In June 1999, about 250 gay activists marched through downtown Santiago in a gay pride celebration.

Chile's main homosexual rights organization is Movimiento Unificado de Minorías Sexuales (MUMS, ☎ 634 7557; Map 5), Viollier 87, which also has a Web site (www.minorias.in.cl) in both Spanish and imperfect but readable English.

For information on AIDS/HIV organizations, see Health, earlier in this chapter.

DISABLED TRAVELERS

Travelers with disabilities may find Santiago difficult; the wheelchair-bound in particular will find the narrow sidewalks, which are frequently in disrepair, hard to negotiate. Crossing streets can also be a problem, though most Chilean drivers are courteous toward individuals with obvious handicaps.

According to Chile's last census (1992), 288,000 Chileans claimed some sort of disability, while a recent government study suggests a figure of around 616,000. The Fondo Nacional del Descapacitado (Fonadis, National Fund for the Handicapped) believes the World Health Organization (WHO) figure of 1.4 million is closer to the truth. The law now requires new public buildings to provide disabled access, but public transport remains poor in this regard – though the metro's new Línea 5 has been retrofitted.

Santiago's Tixi Service (☎ 800 223 097) caters specifically to disabled individuals, with hydraulic elevators to accommodate wheelchairs. Trips within the capital generally cost around US$12.

SENIOR TRAVELERS

Senior travelers should not encounter any particular difficulties in Santiago, where older citizens typically enjoy a great deal of respect. On crowded buses, for instance, most santiaguinos will readily offer their seat to an older person who needs it. See Documents, earlier in this chapter, for information of discounts for seniors.

SANTIAGO FOR CHILDREN

Santiago is child-friendly on all levels, including people's attitudes, safety, health and family-oriented activities. For small children, a folding stroller is a good idea, especially where there is a chance of getting lost in crowds. People are also very helpful on public transport; often someone will give up a seat for parent and child, but if that does not happen, an older person may offer to put the child on his or her lap.

In terms of food and health, there are no special concerns, but bottled water may be a good idea for delicate stomachs. Most restaurants offer a wide variety of dishes suitable for children (vegetables, pasta, meat, chicken, fish), and Chilean cuisine is generally bland despite the occasional spicy sauce. Portions are abundant enough that smaller children probably won't need separate meals, and there is usually no problem in securing additional cutlery.

In general, public toilets are poorly maintained; always carry toilet paper, which is almost nonexistent in them. While a woman may take a young boy into the women's room, it would be socially unacceptable for a man to take a girl into the men's room.

Santiago and most other cities have large public parks with playgrounds, so it's easy for children to make international friendships. There are also many activities specifically for children; consult newspapers like *El Mercurio* for listings.

For general information on the subject, look for Maureen Wheeler's *Travel with Children* (Lonely Planet, 1995).

USEFUL ORGANIZATIONS

Travelers interested in environmental conservation may wish to contact Comité Pro Defensa de la Fauna y Flora (Codeff, ☎ 251 0287, fax 251 8433, info@codeff.mic.cl), Avenida Francisco Bilbao 691, Providencia;

Greenpeace Pacífico Sur (☎ 777 9570, fax 735 8990, greenpeacechile@dialb.greenpeace.org), the Chilean branch of the international conservation organization, at Montecarmelo 37 (Map 7); or Defensores del Bosque Chileno (☎ 204 1914), Diagonal Oriente 1413, Ñuñoa. Ancient Forests International (☎/fax 707-923-3015), PO Box 1850, Redway, CA 95560, USA, has close links to Chilean forest conservation organizations.

German visitors, businesspeople or intending residents may wish to contact the Deutsch-Chilenischer Bund (☎ 212 6474), Avenida Vitacura 5875, Vitacura, which publishes the useful guide *Chile: Ein Land zum Leben, Arbeiten und Investieren* (1997).

LIBRARIES

Santiago's (and the country's) major library is the massive Biblioteca Nacional (☎ 360 5200), Alameda 651, also a national monument (Map 5). For visiting scholars, the same building also contains the Archivo Nacional Histórico (National History Archive, ☎/fax 632 5735), entered from Miraflores 50. The library also offers occasional museum-style exhibitions on Chilean topics in its Salón Fundadores and Sala Ercilla, and hosts events such as book releases and film series in its Sala América.

Most of the binational cultural centers mentioned below also have libraries with books, magazines and newspapers in their respective languages.

UNIVERSITIES

Santiago is the educational center of the country. The oldest institutions are the Universidad de Chile and the Universidad Católica, both with primary campuses in historic buildings on the Alameda (see the Things to See & Do chapter for details) and have metro stops named for them. Both have additional campuses in Ñuñoa and Macul, among other locations. The Universidad de Santiago (ex-Universidad Técnica) is opposite the Estación Central, the main railway terminal, and reached via the eponymous metro station.

Santiago's many private universities, most of them created since the military coup of 1973, are scattered throughout the city, mostly in recycled buildings in areas like Barrio Brasil.

CULTURAL CENTERS

Where passenger trains to Viña del Mar and Valparaíso once arrived and departed, the Centro Cultural Estación Mapocho (☎ 361 1761) has become Santiago's premier cultural center, offering live theater, concerts, art exhibits, a café and special events like the annual book fair. It's on the south bank of the Río Mapocho at the north end of Bandera (Ⓜ Puente Cal y Canto; Map 5).

The Centro de Extensión de la Universidad Católica (☎ 222 0275), Alameda 390, also regularly presents artistic and photographic exhibits (Ⓜ Universidad Católica). The Centro Cultural Carmen (☎ 665 2695), Carmen 340, shows films, presents live folkloric music, has occasional art exhibits and also has a selection of crafts for sale (Map 5).

Several suburban comunas have their own cultural centers, all of which change programs frequently. The Instituto Cultural de Providencia (☎ 209 4341), Avenida 11 de Septiembre 1995, offers free lectures, film cycles and art exhibits. On the north bank of the Mapocho, on the Providencia side of Bellavista, the Centro Cultural Monte-carmelo (☎ 777 0882, 735 6251, 735 7016), at Bellavista 0594, offers art, theater programs and film cycles on the grounds of a former Carmelite monastery. It also has a cafeteria and restaurant (Map 7).

Other centers include the Casa de la Cultura de la Municipalidad de Ñuñoa (☎ 225 3919), Avenida Irarrázaval 4055, open 10 am to 8 pm daily, and the Instituto Cultural de Las Condes (☎ 336 9393), Avenida Apoquindo 6570, open 10:30 am to 1:30 pm and 3:30 to 7 pm daily except Monday, which has art and archaeology exhibits.

The Centro Cultural de España (☎ 235 1105), Avenida Providencia 927, is one of Santiago's most active foreign cultural representatives, hosting book parties, contemporary art exhibits, film cycles and many other events (Ⓜ Salvador; Map 8). Other comparable cultural centers include the Instituto Chileno-Británico (☎ 638 2156), Santa Lucía 124, with current British newspapers and periodicals; the Instituto Goethe (☎ 638 3815), Esmeralda 650; and the Instituto Chileno-Francés (☎ 633 5465), Merced 298 (all Map 5).

The Instituto Chileno-Norteamericano de Cultura (☎ 696 3215), Moneda 1467, offers frequent photographic and artistic exhibits on various topics in various media. It also has a decent English-language library, which carries North American newspapers and magazines, and free films, usually in video format (Map 5).

In the shape of a cell phone, the kitschy skyscraper at Avenida Providencia 111 houses the Sala de Arte Telefónica, which provides an outlet for the capital's figurative artists (Map 8).

DANGERS & ANNOYANCES

Santiago is far less hazardous than most other Latin American cities, as well as those in many other parts of the world, but certain precautions will reduce risks and make your trip more enjoyable.

Theft

Truly violent crime is still unusual in Santiago; both men and women can travel in most parts of the city at any time of day or night without excessive apprehension. The crowded metro and buses, however, can be havens for pickpockets.

Valparaíso has an unfortunate reputation for robberies in some of its southern neighborhoods. Summer is the crime season in beach resorts like Viña del Mar and Reñaca. Though these are by no means violent places, be alert for pickpockets and avoid leaving valuables on the beach while you go for a swim.

Take precautions against petty theft, such as purse snatching. Be especially wary of calculated distractions, such as someone tapping you on the shoulder or spilling something on you, since these 'accidents' are often part of a team effort to relieve you of your backpack or other valuables. Grip your bag or purse firmly, carry your wallet in a front pocket and avoid conspicuous displays of expensive jewelry. Valuables like passports and air tickets can be conveniently carried in a light jacket or vest with one or two zip-up or button-up pockets. Money belts and neck pouches are common alternatives, though some travelers find them uncomfortable; an elastic leg pouch is less cumbersome, but can get very sweaty in hot weather.

Baggage insurance is a good idea. Since many budget hotels have only token locks or none at all (you may want to bring one), do not leave valuables like cash or cameras in your hotel room. Lower to mid-range accommodations usually have secure left-luggage areas, while upscale hotels often have secure strongboxes in each room.

Demonstrations

Unauthorized political demonstrations still take place and can be very raucous; the police will sometimes use tear gas or truck-mounted water cannons – known as *guanacos* after the spitting wild New World camels – to break them up. The single most contentious site in Santiago may be Providencia's Avenida 11 de Septiembre, named by the dictatorship after the date of the coup that overthrew the Allende government; on every anniversary of the coup, truculent demonstrators demand that the street be renamed.

Ever since General Pinochet's arrest in London in 1998, the British and Spanish embassies and consulates have regularly been the targets of noisy, disorderly demonstrations by Pinochet supporters. A newly contentious date is October 16, the anniversary of the arrest (celebrated by Pinochet's opponents).

Police & Military

Chile's carabineros, less known for corruption than other South American police, behave professionally and politely in ordinary circumstances, but there have been credible reports of mistreatment of foreign travelers, especially in Santiago. In one 1999 case, police apparently attempted to frame a French citizen on weapons charges during a pro-Mapuche demonstration in the southern city of Traiguén, though a judge later dismissed the complaint.

Carabineros can demand identification at any time, so you should carry your passport.

Chileans often refer to carabineros as *pacos*, a disrespectful (though not obscene) term that should *never* be used to a policeman's face. Speed bumps are sometimes known as *pacos acostados* (sleeping policemen).

The military still take themselves seriously, even under civilian government, so avoid photographing military installations. In the event of a national emergency, the military-dominated Consejo de Seguridad Nacional (National Security Council) can impose martial law, suspending all civil rights, so make sure someone knows your whereabouts and contact your embassy or consulate for advice.

Terrorism

For several years after the return of civilian rule in 1990, leftist guerrilla groups like the Frente Patriótico Manuel Rodríguez (FPMR) continued to operate at a subdued level, with occasional attacks on police stations and the like, but this has virtually disappeared. Mormon churches, viewed as instruments of North American cultural imperialism, have been bombing targets, but this has also diminished.

More recently, however, right-wing forces like the shadowy Patria y Libertad (Fatherland and Freedom) organization have reorganized in the aftermath of Pinochet's detention in England, and the honorary British consul in Valparaíso resigned in October 1999 after anonymous death threats. Visitors should not overestimate the importance of these groups, but should be aware of their existence.

Earthquakes

South America's Pacific Coast is part of the 'ring of fire' that stretches from Asia to Alaska to Tierra del Fuego. There are no active volcanoes in the immediate vicinity of Santiago, but earthquakes are common and occur without warning. Local construction often does not meet seismic safety standards – adobe buildings are especially vulnerable. Travelers staying in budget accommodations should make contingency plans for safety, including evacuation, before falling asleep at night.

Recreational Hazards

Many of Chile's finest beach areas have dangerous offshore rip currents – strong currents that often pull swimmers out to sea. Swimming against the current can be exhausting and futile – it's better to stay with the current, which weakens in deeper water, and then return to shore by a different route. Ask about these before entering the water and be sure someone on shore knows your whereabouts.

The Pacific is also colder than many bathers expect, so hypothermia can be a serious matter. Hypothermia occurs when the body loses heat faster than it can produce it, causing the core temperature of the body to fall so rapidly that death is a possibility. Disorientation, dizziness, slurred speech, stumbling, shivering, numb skin and physical exhaustion are all symptoms of hypothermia and are indications that you should seek warmth, shelter and food.

In the wild high country east of Santiago, which is popular with hikers and skiers, changeable weather can also be a hazard. On steep, slippery terrain, especially with loose volcanic rock, it takes constant attention to avoid accidents.

EMERGENCIES

Throughout the country the toll-free emergency telephone number for carabineros is ☎ 133. Because all calls to this number have caller ID, they should be able to pinpoint your location if necessary, but it still helps to give directions if at all possible.

LEGAL MATTERS

Traditionally, Chile's Napoleonic legal code establishes judges as both prosecutors and jury – but a recent reform has created the *ministerio público*, a public prosecutor's office intended to eliminate such conflicts of interest. Since this approach is still a novelty in Chile, there are likely to be inconsistencies in its implementation. There is still no jury trial, though there has been talk of it.

Foreign embassies and consulates generally maintain referral lists of lawyers for their nationals in need of legal assistance. The police generally permit foreign nationals to contact their diplomatic representatives.

Criminal Procedures

Until current reforms take hold, should you be so unfortunate as to be arrested in Chile, you must appear before a judge within five days. The judge will decide whether to dismiss charges and release you, confirm the charges (and continue detention) or grant a temporary stay (meaning the case could be reopened). In the *plenario* – the stage the accused can respond to the charges, usually in writing – open court trials are unusual. In the sentencing phase, the judge can release the accused or sentence him or her to jail or impose a fine.

Traffic Accidents

If you are involved in *any* traffic accident involving other drivers, public property or insurance claims, your license will be confiscated until the case is resolved. Local officials, however, will usually issue a temporary driver's permit within a few days. A blood alcohol test is obligatory; purchase a sterile syringe at the hospital or clinic pharmacy when the carabineros take you there. After this you will be taken to the police station to make a statement and then, under most circumstances, released. Ordinarily you cannot leave Chile until the matter is resolved; consult your consulate, insurance carrier and a lawyer.

Carabineros do not harass drivers for minor equipment violations (unlike the police in neighboring Argentina). You should *never* attempt to bribe the carabineros, whose reputation for institutional integrity is very high.

Drugs

Amazingly, possession of drugs like cannabis and cocaine for personal use is not illegal in

Chile – but production and possession for sale are; since most drugs have illegal origins, the police will likely presume the possessor is involved in such activities unless he or she can prove otherwise. It's easier to avoid the drug scene altogether than to have to talk your way out of such a situation or have to hire a lawyer to do so for you.

BUSINESS HOURS

Traditionally, business hours in Chile commence by 9 am, but shops close around 1 pm for three or even four hours, when people often return home for lunch and a brief siesta. After the siesta, shops reopen until 8 or 9 pm. In Santiago, government offices and many businesses have adopted a more conventional 9 am to 6 pm schedule. Government offices are often open to the public only in the morning. Banking hours are generally 9 am to 2 pm, but exchange houses are open much later.

PUBLIC HOLIDAYS

Throughout the year, but especially in summer, santiaguinos celebrate a variety of local, national and international cultural, political and religious dates. Aside from the activities surrounding holidays like Easter and Christmas, the most significant are mid-September's Fiestas Patrias, but many localities have their own favorites.

There are numerous national holidays, on which government offices and businesses are closed. There has been pressure to reduce these or to eliminate so-called sandwich holidays, which are taken by (officially or unofficially) moving the actual holiday to the nearest Monday, sandwiching it between the weekend and the holiday. The following are notable holidays, with such changes indicated:

January 1
Año Nuevo (New Year)
March/April
Semana Santa (Easter Week)
May 1
Día del Trabajo (Labor Day)
May 21
Glorias Navales (commemorating the naval Battle of Iquique)

2nd Monday of June
Corpus Christi (moved from 2nd Thursday of June)
Nearest Monday to June 29
Día de San Pedro y San Pablo (St Peter & St Paul's Day, officially moved)
August 15
Asunción de la Virgen (Assumption)
First Monday of September
Día de la Unidad Nacional (Day of National Unity, replacing the controversial *Pronunciamiento Militar de 1973*, the military coup of 1973. The future of this holiday is still in doubt since General Pinochet's detention in London.)
September 18
Día de la Independencia Nacional (National Independence Day)
September 19
Día del Ejército (Armed Forces Day)
Nearest Monday to October 12
Día de la Raza (Columbus Day, officially moved)
November 1
Todo los Santos (All Saints' Day)
December 8
Inmaculada Concepción (Immaculate Conception)
December 25
Navidad (Christmas Day)

SPECIAL EVENTS

Santiago is the site of several special events throughout the year, such as early November's **Feria de Libro** (Book Festival), which fills the Mapocho station for about 10 days and sometimes attracts authors the caliber of Peru's Mario Vargas Llosa. Almost immediately after the Feria del Libro, the **Expo Nuevo Mundo Rural** is a new, but to this point highly successful, exhibition of Chilean agricultural products from the llama herds of the north to the fruits of Middle Chile and the woolens of Tierra del Fuego. It also has live folkloric entertainment and a wide selection of crafts for sale by the artisans.

Santiago's biggest and longest-running event, the **Feria Internacional de Santiago** (Santiago International Fair or FISA) usually takes place in December but suffered its first cancellation in 130 years in 1999 because of a financial crisis. The venue is the FISA fairgrounds (☎ 530 7000) at Camino a Melipilla 10339, Maipú (Map 1).

DOING BUSINESS

At about 15 million people, Chile's internal market is relatively small, but it's also very concentrated – about 40% of the population lives within 160km of Santiago, most companies have their offices in the capital, and most economic activity takes place there. Chile actively courts foreign investors, but on the condition that capital remain in the country for a minimum term of one year to discourage rapid disinvestment. Profits, however, may be repatriated immediately.

There are many promising sectors for foreign investment in Chile. They include medical equipment, travel and tourism, telecommunications equipment, port facilities (especially with impending privatization), pollution control equipment, building materials, mining equipment, electrical power equipment, plastics production machinery, security equipment, computers, construction machinery, refrigeration and air-conditioning, and food processing equipment.

The US, Canadian and Mexican governments have responded positively to Chile's wish to join NAFTA, the North American Free Trade Agreement, but the US Congress has obstructed approval of Chilean admission. Mexico and Canada have since reached separate bilateral free trade agreements with the Chileans, who are associate members of South America's Mercosur free trade group (comprising Argentina, Brazil, Paraguay and Uruguay).

For information on work visas and other documents, see Documents, earlier in this chapter.

Tax Documentation

Anyone establishing a business in Chile must register with the Servicio de Impuestos Internos (SII, International Revenue Service), requesting a Rol Unico Tributario (RUT, or tax ID number) and making a Declaración de Inicio de Actividades (Declaration of Intent to Start a Business). The RUT requires filling out only a few lines of Formulario 4415 (Form 4415) at SII offices, but the Declaración requires far more detail,

and it's best to consult an attorney before completing it.

The most convenient SII offices are at Santa Rosa 108, Santiago Centro, and San Pascual 1, Las Condes. Generally, if your mailing address is west of Avenida Vicuña Mackenna, you must apply at the former office, while if it's east of Avenida Vicuña Mackenna, you may apply at the latter office. Obtaining a RUT, which is also necessary for activities like purchasing a car and opening a bank account, takes only a few minutes. It is not necessary to be a Chilean citizen or legal resident, but obtaining it does not imply permission to work in the country.

El Pituto

Anyone undertaking business or many other activities in Santiago needs to be aware of the informal institution of the *pituto*, whose rough English-language equivalent would be the 'old boy network.' Though the pituto is not necessarily male, it is often a long-term or even lifetime contact who greases the wheels for bureaucratic chores like obtaining an essential tax document. Neither does it necessarily imply corruption, but it can cover some very gray areas. For foreigners, it can take some time to develop these relationships, which can greatly simplify the practicalities of living and doing business in the city.

Foreign suppliers will need a partner to help crack the Chilean market, and should contact their local embassy or consulate for suggestions and procure a reliable local attorney to help draw up and review contracts. Franchises and joint ventures are increasingly common. Bribery and corruption are unusual (according to Transparency International's 1999 survey, Chile is Latin America's least corrupt country), but not unheard of.

While Chileans are casual about time in social occasions, they are almost invariably punctual for business meetings. Many Chileans in the export sector speak English, but business visitors with fluent Spanish will have a distinct advantage.

References

For anyone doing business in Chile, one of the essential resources is the *Directorio de Instituciones de Chile*, popularly known as the *Guía Silber* after its publisher Silber Editores. Updated twice annually, it includes contact names, addresses, telephones and other critical information for institutions of government, labor, business, politics, culture and even nonprofits and nongovernmental organizations (NGOs). While expensive at about US$80, it's an indispensable item, available from Silber Editores (☎ 232 2400), Avenida Providencia 2019, Oficina A-31 (Map 8); the US contact is Silber Publishers (☎ 305-759-5998), 7711 Center Bay Drive, North Bay Village, FL 33141.

The US State Department's Web-published Country Commercial Guides include a detailed, annually updated, report on Chile. For more information, visit their Web site (www.state.gov).

Chambers of Commerce

Santiago has several binational chambers of commerce that can offer advice on doing business in the country.

Cámara Chileno Alemana de Comercio e Industria
(☎ 203 5320, fax 203 5325, ahkchile@reuna.cl) Avenida El Bosque Norte 0440, Oficina 601, Las Condes

Cámara Chileno Australiana de Comercio
(☎/fax 335 9980) Don Carlos 2986, Oficina 8, Las Condes

Cámara Chileno-Británica de Comercio
(☎ 231 4366, fax 335 1906, cambrit@entelchile .net) Avenida Suecia 155-C, Providencia

Cámara Chileno Canadiense de Comercio
(☎/fax 201 1571) Los Estanques 9482, Vitacura

Cámara Chileno-Neozelandesa de Comercio
(☎ 231 8785, fax 232 0374) San Sebastián 2839, Oficina 310, Las Condes

Cámara Chileno-Norteamericana de Comercio
(AmCham)
(☎ 290 9700, fax 206 0911, amcham@entelchile .net) Avenida Américo Vespucio Sur 80,9th floor, Las Condes

Cámara de Comercio e Industria Franco-Chilena
(☎ 225 5547, fax 225 5545, cfcci@netline.cl) Marchant Pereira 201, Oficina 701, Providencia

Cámara de Comercio Italiana de Chile
(☎ 232 2618, fax 233 0973, camit@ia.cl) Avenida Luis Thayer Ojeda 073, 12th floor, Providencia

Cámara Oficial Española de Comercio de Chile
(☎ 231 7160, fax 233 5280, camacoes@ctcreuna .cl) Carmen Sylva 2306, Providencia

WORK

It's increasingly difficult to obtain residence and work permits. Consequently, many foreigners do not bother to do so, but the most reputable employers will insist on the proper visa. If you need one, visit the Departamento de Extranjería (☎ 672 5320; Map 5), Moneda 1342. Business hours are 8:30 am to 3:30 pm weekdays. For more information, see Documents, earlier in this chapter.

A good orientation to working and living in Santiago, including suggestions on obtaining residence and starting a business, is *The International Settler*, an informational booklet published by the *News Review*, Santiago's weekly English-language newspaper. If you're unable to find it around town, contact the *News Review* (☎ 236 1423, newsrevi@mcl.cl), Almirante Pastene 222, Providencia. The *News Review* also sponsors a monthly 'Advice for New Arrivals' night at Flannery's Irish Geo Pub, Encomenderos 83, Las Condes; for information, contact ☎ 235 1212 or check the paper for the date and time.

Teaching English

It is not unusual for visiting travelers to work as English-language instructors in Santiago. Wages are fairly good on a per-hour basis, but full-time employment is hard to come by without a commitment to stay for some time.

Volunteer Work

Options for volunteer work are worth exploring, especially with social and environmental organizations. Two good sources to consult are the comprehensive biannual *Directorio de Instituciones de Chile* (popularly known as the *Guía Silber*; see References in the Doing Business section, earlier in this chapter), a directory of political, labor, church, cultural and other institutions both official and nongovernmental. Also helpful is the annual *Directorio de Organizaciones Miembros* published by Renace (Red Nacional de Acción Ecológica), a loosely affiliated network of environmental organizations throughout the country. Renace (☎ 223 4483, fax 225 8909, renace@rdc.cl) is at Seminario 774, Ñuñoa.

Bar Work

The best options for bar work are the numerous pubs along Avenida Suecia and General Holley ( Los Leones), and in Barrio Bellavista. Wages, however, are substantially lower than they would be in Europe or North America, and tips are not as good either.

Getting There & Away

Santiago's main long-distance transport options are air and bus, though there is limited train service to some cities to the south.

AIR

There are often significant seasonal discounts, so try to avoid peak travel times such as Christmas/New Year or Holy Week (Semana Santa). Advance purchase of a ticket for a given period of time, usually less than six months, generally provides the best, most flexible deal.

Fares for day-of-purchase flights within Chile are expensive, but paying as little as 24 hours in advance can reduce the bite substantially, even for one-way flights. Roundtrip fares with seven-day advance purchase offer the best bargains.

Airports

Nearly all international flights to Chile arrive at Santiago, landing at Aeropuerto Interna-

---

Warning

The information in this chapter is particularly vulnerable to change: Prices for international travel are volatile, routes are introduced and canceled, schedules change, special deals come and go, and rules and visa requirements are amended. Airlines and governments seem to take perverse pleasure in making price structures and regulations as complex as possible. You should check directly with the airline or a travel agent to make sure you understand how a fare (and ticket you may buy) works. In addition, the travel industry is highly competitive, and there are many lurks and perks.

The upshot of this is that you should get opinions, quotes and advice from as many airlines and travel agents as possible before you part with your hard-earned cash. The details given in this chapter should be regarded as pointers, and are not a substitute for your own careful, up-to-date research.

---

cional Arturo Merino Benítez in the suburb of Pudahuel. There are also flights from neighboring countries to regional airports like Arica, Iquique, Temuco, Puerto Montt and Punta Arenas, with connections to Santiago.

LanChile is the national carrier, with the most extensive system of connecting internal routes, but many other reputable airlines also serve Santiago – see Airline Offices, later in this section.

Departure Tax

Chilean departure tax for international flights is US$18 or its equivalent in local currency. For domestic flights, departure tax is about US$8.

Note that *arriving* US air passengers pay a onetime fee of US$45, valid for the life of their passport. Chilean authorities imposed this fee after US officials increased a onetime US$20 visa application fee for Chilean nationals and have since applied it to Australians, who pay US$30, and Canadians, who pay US$55.

Other Parts of Chile

Santiago lies roughly midway between the cities of Arica, near the Peruvian border, and Punta Arenas, on the Strait of Magellan – a latitudinal extent roughly equivalent to the distance from Havana to Hudson Bay. The only significant east-west routes are to the Juan Fernández Archipelago, served only by air taxis, and Easter Island (Rapa Nui), a Chilean possession five hours across the Pacific Ocean.

LanChile and its close affiliate Ladeco serve all major domestic airports north and south of Santiago. Avant is another major airline, while a recent start-up called Aeromet expects to provide some competition for the established carriers. In the thinly populated far south there are also air taxi services.

Peru, Bolivia & Argentina

LanChile has three daily flights from Lima to Santiago for US$357 one-way, but there are many discount roundtrip fares. Lacsa, Copa and Saeta all fly daily, while Aeroflot flies twice weekly.

Peruvian domestic airline Aerocontinente flies from Lima to the southern city of Tacna, only 50km from the Chilean border city of Arica, for US$90 one-way. Crossing overland from Tacna and flying from Arica to Santiago is a substantial saving on the nonstop airfare from Lima to Santiago.

LanChile flies daily from Santiago to La Paz, Bolivia, via Iquique and Arica.

Many airlines fly between Santiago and Buenos Aires from about US$190 one-way, but European airlines that pick up and discharge most of their passengers in Buenos Aires try to fill empty seats by selling roundtrip tickets between the Argentine and Chilean capitals for around US$160 – not much more than the bus fare. Even throwing away the return portion, one-way passengers still come out ahead.

There are also LanChile (twice daily) and Avant (twice weekly) flights from Santiago to Mendoza (around US$98 one-way, but with discount roundtrip tickets for as little as US$90), and LanChile flights to Córdoba (twice daily, US$175 one-way, but with discount roundtrips for as little as US$139).

LanChile's weekly flight from Santiago to the Falkland Islands stops in Río Gallegos, Argentina, on the third Saturday of each month; the return flight from the Falklands stops in Río Gallegos on the fourth Saturday.

Other South American Countries

LanChile flies from Santiago to Guayaquil, Ecuador; Bogotá, Colombia; Caracas, Venezuela; Asunción, Paraguay, in conjunction with TAM; and São Paulo and Rio de Janeiro, Brazil, and from Iquique to Asunción three times weekly in conjunction with TAM.

Avianca links Santiago with Bogotá daily, either nonstop or via Buenos Aires. Ecuatoriana flies five times weekly to and from Quito and Guayaquil, while Saeta flies to Guayaquil and Quito daily except Sunday. TAME flies three times weekly to Guayaquil and Quito.

Pluna flies five times weekly to Montevideo, the only nonstop service to the Uruguayan capital. TransBrasil and Varig fly to Brazilian destinations.

Mexico & Central America

Aeroméxico and LanChile combine for eight flights weekly to Mexico City. LanChile also flies twice weekly to Cancún. Copa flies daily to Panama via Lima, while Lacsa flies daily to Costa Rica and Guatemala City via Lima.

The USA

From the USA, the principal gateways to South America are Miami, New York and Los Angeles. Airlines that serve Santiago from the USA include LanChile, Aerolíneas Argentinas (via Buenos Aires), American, Avianca (via Bogotá and Buenos Aires), Continental, Copa (via Panama), Ecuatoriana, Líneas Aéreas de Costa Rica (Lacsa), Lloyd Aéreo Boliviano (LAB), Saeta, TransBrasil, United and Varig (via Brazil).

CIEE (or Council Travel, ☎ 800-226-8624 in the USA, cts@ciee.org) has agencies in the following cities and in many college towns:

Austin, TX
  (☎ 512-472-4931) 2000 Guadalupe St
Berkeley, CA
  (☎ 510-848-8604) 2486 Channing Way
Boston, MA
  (☎ 617-266-1926) 273 Newbury St
Denver, CO
  (☎ 303-571-0630) 900 Auraria Parkway, Tivoli Bldg
La Jolla, CA
  (☎ 619-452-0630) UCSD Price Center B-023
Los Angeles, CA
  (☎ 213-208-3551) 10904 Lindbrook Drive
Miami, FL
  (☎ 305-670-9261) 9100 S Dadeland Blvd, Suite 220
New York, NY
  (☎ 212-822-2700) 205 E 42nd St, ground floor
Pacific Beach, CA
  (☎ 619-270-6401) 953 Garnett Ave
San Francisco, CA
  (☎ 415-421-3473) 530 Bush St
Seattle, WA
  (☎ 206-632-2448) 1314 NE 43rd St, Suite 210

Washington, DC
(☎ 202-337-6464) 3300 M Street NW, 2nd floor

Like Council Travel, the Student Travel Network (STA, ☎ 800-777-0112) has offices in the following cities plus many college towns:

Berkeley, CA
(☎ 510-642-3000) ASUC Travel Center, University of California

Boston, MA
(☎ 617-266-6014) 297 Newbury St

Chicago, IL
(☎ 312-786-9050) 429 S Dearborn St

Los Angeles, CA
(☎ 213-934-8722) 7202 Melrose Ave
(☎ 310-824-1574) 920 Westwood Blvd

Coral Gables, FL
(☎ 305-284-1044) University of Miami, 1306 Stanford Dr

New York, NY
(☎ 212-627-3111) 10 Downing St

Philadelphia, PA
(☎ 215-382-2928) 3730 Walnut St

San Francisco, CA
(☎ 415-391-8407) 51 Grant Ave

Seattle, WA
(☎ 206-633-5000) 4341 University Way NE

Washington, DC
(☎ 202-887-0912) 2401 Pennsylvania Ave, Suite G

In the USA, New York and Miami are the only choices for courier flights to South America. For the widest selection of destinations, try Now Voyager (☎ 212-431-1616, fax 212-334-5253), 74 Varick St, Suite 307, New York, NY 10013; or Air Facility (☎ 718-712-1769), 153 Rockaway Blvd, Jamaica, NY 11434.

For up-to-date information on courier and other budget fares, send US$5 for the latest newsletter or US$25 for a year's subscription to Travel Unlimited, PO Box 1058, Allston, MA 02134. Another source of information is the International Association of Air Travel Couriers (☎ 407-582-8320, fax 407-582-1581, iaatc@courier.org, www.courier.org), PO Box 1349, Lake Worth, FL 33460; its US$45 annual membership fee includes the monthly newsletter *Shoestring Traveler* (not related to Lonely Planet).

Canada

LanChile no longer has direct service to Canada, but there are good connections to Toronto via Miami and to Vancouver via Los Angeles with Canadian Airlines.

Travel Cuts (☎ 416-977-2185, 888-838-2887, fax 416-977-4796), the Canadian counterpart of Council Travel and STA, is at 243 College St, 5th floor, Toronto, Ontario M5T 2Y1.

Australia & New Zealand

Fares from Australia and New Zealand to South America have fallen – it's no longer cheaper to get a roundtrip flight to Los Angeles or Miami and buy a roundtrip ticket to South America from there, though that's still an option for those who plan to visit the US anyway. Qantas flies direct to Buenos Aires and, in combination with LanChile, to Tahiti (stopovers permitted) and Santiago. It's also possible to make the Tahiti connection with Air New Zealand.

From Australia, fares to Santiago, permitting a stopover on Easter Island, start at A$1659 low season, A$1925 high season, and also allow a side trip to another South America city, say Lima or Buenos Aires. Qantas' direct flights to Buenos Aires also permit a side trip to another South American city, say Santiago, with Aerolíneas Argentinas; fares start at A$1689 low season, A$1909 high season. Aerolíneas' transpolar flight from Sydney to Buenos Aires also stops in Río Gallegos for easy connections to Chilean Patagonia and Tierra del Fuego.

STA Travel (☎ 800-637-444), with the following Australian locations, is a good place to inquire for bargain airfares; student status is not necessary to use their services.

Adelaide
(☎ 08-223-6620/6244) Level 4, Union House, Adelaide University

Brisbane
(☎ 07-3221-3722) Shop 25 & 26, 111-117 Adelaide St

Air Travel Glossary

Cancellation Penalties If you have to cancel or change a discounted ticket, there are often heavy penalties involved; insurance can sometimes be taken out against these penalties. Some airlines impose penalties on regular tickets as well, particularly against 'no-show' passengers.

Courier Fares Businesses often need to send urgent documents or freight securely and quickly. Courier companies hire people to accompany the package through customs and, in return, offer a discount ticket which is sometimes a phenomenal bargain. However, you may have to surrender all your baggage allowance and take only carry-on luggage.

Full Fares Airlines traditionally offer 1st class (coded F), business class (coded J) and economy class (coded Y) tickets. These days there are so many promotional and discounted fares available that few passengers pay full economy fare.

Lost Tickets If you lose your airline ticket an airline will usually treat it like a travellers cheque and, after inquiries, issue you with another one. Legally, however, an airline is entitled to treat it like cash and if you lose it then it's gone forever. Take good care of your tickets.

Onward Tickets An entry requirement for many countries is that you have a ticket out of the country. If you're unsure of your next move, the easiest solution is to buy the cheapest onward ticket to a neighbouring country or a ticket from a reliable airline which can later be refunded if you do not use it.

Open-Jaw Tickets These are return tickets where you fly out to one place but return from another. If available, this can save you backtracking to your arrival point.

Overbooking Since every flight has some passengers who fail to show up, airlines often book more passengers than they have seats. Usually excess passengers make up for the no-shows, but occasionally somebody gets 'bumped' onto the next available flight. Guess who it is most likely to be? The passengers who check in late.

Promotional Fares These are officially discounted fares, available from travel agencies or direct from the airline.

Reconfirmation If you don't reconfirm your flight at least 72 hours prior to departure, the airline may delete your name from the passenger list. Ring to find out if your airline requires reconfirmation.

Restrictions Discounted tickets often have various restrictions on them – such as needing to be paid for in advance and incurring a penalty to be altered. Others are restrictions on the minimum and maximum period you must be away.

Round-the-World Tickets RTW tickets give you a limited period (usually a year) in which to circumnavigate the globe. You can go anywhere the carrying airlines go, as long as you don't backtrack. The number of stopovers or total number of separate flights is decided before you set off and they usually cost a bit more than a basic return flight.

Transferred Tickets Airline tickets cannot be transferred from one person to another. Travelers sometimes try to sell the return half of their ticket, but officials can ask you to prove that you are the person named on the ticket. On an international flight tickets are compared with passports.

Travel Periods Ticket prices vary with the time of year. There is a low (off-peak) season and a high (peak) season, and often a low-shoulder season and a high-shoulder season as well. Usually the fare depends on your outward flight – if you depart in the high season and return in the low season, you pay the high-season fare.

Canberra
(☎ 06-247-0800) Arts Centre, ANU
Hobart
(☎ 02-243-496) Union Bldg, ground floor, Univ of Tasmania
Melbourne
(☎ 03-9349-2411) 220 Faraday St, Carlton
Perth
(☎ 09-380-2302) 1st floor, New Guild Bldg, Univ of W Australia, Crawley
Sydney
(☎ 02-360-1822) 9 Oxford St, Paddington

STA also has offices at the following New Zealand locations:

Auckland
(☎ 09-307-0555) 2nd Floor, Union Bldg, Auckland University
Christchurch
(☎ 03-379-909) 90 Cashel St
Wellington
(☎ 04-385-0561) 233 Cuba St

The UK & Continental Europe

It is no longer necessarily cheaper to fly through New York or Miami than it is to go directly to South America from Europe. There are no nonstops, but many airlines have direct flights to Santiago via Buenos Aires, Rio de Janeiro or São Paulo from major European cities like Paris, Rome, Zurich, London, Moscow, Frankfurt and Amsterdam.

London's so-called bucket shops can provide the best deals; check out newspapers or magazines such as the *Evening Standard* or *Time Out* for suggestions. Advertised fares from London to Santiago have fallen recently and now start as low as £380 roundtrip.

Since bucket shops come and go, it's worth inquiring about their affiliation with the Association of British Travel Agents (ABTA), which will guarantee a refund or alternative if the agent goes out of business. The following are reputable London bucket shops:

Bridge the World
(☎ 020 7922 0900, www.b-t-w.co.uk) 47 Chalk Farm Rd, London NW1 8AN

Campus Travel
(☎ 020 7730 3402) 52 Grosvenor Gardens, London SW1W 0AG
Journey Latin America
(☎ 020 8747 3108) 16 Devonshire Rd, Chiswick, London W4 2HD
Passage to South America
(☎ 020 8767 8989) Fovant Mews, 12 Noyna Rd, London SW17 7PH
South American Experience
(☎ 020 7976 5511) 47 Causton St, London SW1
STA Travel
(☎ 020 7361 9962, www.statravel.co.uk) 86 Old Brompton Rd, London SW7 3LQ 117 Euston Rd, London NW12SX
Trailfinders
(☎ 020 7938 3939, www.trailfinders.com) 194 Kensington High St, London W8
(☎ 020 7938 3366) 42-50 Earls Court Rd, London W8

In Berlin, check out the magazine *Zitty* for bargain-fare ads. The following agencies in Europe are good possibilities for bargain fares:

France
Council Travel
(☎ 0144-41-89 80) 1 Place de l'Odeon, 75006 Paris
Germany
STA Travel
(☎ 030-283 3903) Marienstraße 25, Berlin
(☎ 069 -430 191) Bergerstraße 118, Frankfurt
Travel Overland
(☎ 089-2727 6300) Barerstraße 73, München
Ireland
(☎ 01-602 1600) USIT Travel Office, 19 Aston Quay, Dublin
Italy
(☎ 06-462 0431) CTS, Via Genova 16, Rome
Netherlands
(☎ 020-642 0989) NBBS, Rokin 38, Amsterdam
(☎ 020-623 6814) Malibu Travel, Damrak 30, Amsterdam
Spain
(☎ 91-347 7778) TIVE, José Ortega y Gasset 71, Madrid
Switzerland
(☎ 01-297 1111) SSR, Leonhardstrasse 10, Zürich

The only apparent Europe-South America courier flights are with British Airways (☎ 0870-606 1133), which has roundtrips to

Ticket Options

There are several types of discount tickets to South America. Generally, discounted fares are either officially (promotional fares) or unofficially discounted. The lowest prices often impose limitations such as flying with unpopular airlines, inconvenient schedules or unpleasant routes and connections. A discounted ticket can save you things other than money – you may be able to pay Apex prices (see below) without the associated Apex advance booking and other requirements. Discounted tickets only exist where there is fierce competition.

Some excellent bargains are possible on 'Round-the-World' tickets (see the Air Travel Glossary). A British Airways/Qantas Global Explorer (the only fare that takes in Easter Island, as a LanChile codeshare with Qantas and BA) costs A$2375 low season, A$2775 high season; and the BA/Qantas European Explorer, which can take in Bangkok, London and Santiago, costs A$2019 low season, A$2550 high season. Similar 'Circle Pacific' fares allow excursions between Australasia and South America.

Highlighted below and in the Air Travel Glossary are some options you may not have been familiar with:

Apex Advance purchase excursion tickets must be bought well before departure, but they can be a good deal if you know exactly where you will be going and how long you will be staying. Usually only available on a roundtrip basis, with a 14- or 21-day advance purchase requirement, these have minimum- and maximum-stay requirements (usually 14 and 180 days respectively), allow no stopovers and stipulate cancellation charges.

Economy Class Airlines traditionally offer first-class (coded F), business-class (coded J) and economy-class (coded Y) tickets. These days there are so many promotional and discounted fares available from the regular economy class that few passengers pay full economy fare. Valid for 12 months, economy-class (Y) tickets have the greatest flexibility within their time period. However, if you try to extend beyond a year, you'll have to pay the difference of any interim price increase.

Excursion Fares Priced midway between Apex and full economy fare, these have no advance booking requirements but may require a minimum stay. Their advantage over advance purchase is that you can change bookings and/or stopovers without surcharge.

MCO 'Miscellaneous charges orders' (MCOs) are open vouchers for a fixed US dollar amount, which can be exchanged for a ticket on any IATA (International Air Transport Association) airline. In countries that require an onward ticket as a condition for entry, such as Panama or Colombia, this will usually satisfy immigration authorities. In a pinch, you can turn it into cash at the local offices of the airline from which you purchased it.

Point-to-Point This discount ticket is available on some routes in roundtrip for waiving stopover rights, but some airlines have entirely eliminated stopovers.

Buenos Aires for £400, taxes included; given falling bucket shop prices, the incentive to be a courier is also falling. More information is available by sending a self-addressed, stamped envelope to British Airways Travel Shop, Room E328, E Block, BA Crane Bank S551, Off Jubilee Way, PO Box 10, Heathrow Airport, Hounslow TW6 2JA.

Asia & Africa

Carriers serving Santiago from Asia, usually via North America, include All Nippon Airways (with LanChile) via Los Angeles and Varig (via Brazil). Varig also flies to São Paulo via Johannesburg.

Malaysia Airlines (with LanChile) connects Santiago with Kuala Lumpur via Buenos Aires, Johannesburg and Capetown, while South African Airways (with British Airways) flies from Santiago to Johannesburg via Buenos Aires, São Paulo and Rio de Janeiro.

Airline Offices

LanChile (see International, below) and Ladeco share offices around Santiago, but the latter has a few offices of its own. Avant also has a number of offices around the city.

Avant
 (☎ 290 5000) Alameda 107
 (☎ 639 8969) Huérfanos 885
 (☎ 252 0300) Avenida Pedro de Valdivia 041, Providencia

Ladeco
 (☎ 639 5053, fax 633 8343) Huérfanos 1157
 (☎ 334 7629) Avenida Providencia 2286, Providencia

International Many major international airlines have offices or representatives in Santiago. The following list includes the most important ones:

Aeroflot
 (☎ 331 0244) Guardia Vieja 255, Oficina 1010, Providencia
Aerolíneas Argentinas
 (☎ 639 3922) Moneda 756
Aeroméxico
 (☎ 234 0001) Ebro 2738, Las Condes
Air France
 (☎ 290 9330) Alcántara 44, 6th floor, Las Condes
Air New Zealand
 (☎ 231 8626) Andrés de Fuenzalida 17, Oficina 62, Providencia
Alitalia
 (☎ 698 3336) Alameda 949, Oficina 1003
American Airlines
 (☎ 679 0000) Huérfanos 1199
 (☎ 231 0299) Las Urbinas 043, Providencia
 (☎ 334 4746) Avenida El Bosque Norte 0107, Local 11, Las Condes

Avianca
 (☎ 231 6646) Santa Magdalena 116, Local 106, Providencia
British Airways
 (☎ 330 8600) Isidora Goyenechea 2934, Oficina 302, Las Condes
Canadian Airlines International
 (☎ 679 0100) Huérfanos 1199
Continental
 (☎ 204 4000) Nueva Tajamar 481, Oficina 905, Vitacura
Copa
 (☎ 209 4838) Fidel Oteíza 1921, Oficina 703, Providencia
Cubana de Aviación
 (☎ 274 1819) Fidel Oteíza 1971, Oficina 201, Providencia
Ecuatoriana
 (☎ 671 2334) Moneda 1170
Iberia
 (☎ 698 1716) Bandera 206, 8th floor
Japan Airlines
 (☎ 232 5961) Isidora Goyenechea 2934, Oficina 301, Las Condes
LanChile
 (☎ 632 3442) Agustinas 640
Líneas Aéreas de Costa Rica (Lacsa)
 (☎ 235 5500) Barros Borgoño 105, 2nd floor, Providencia
Lloyd Aéreo Boliviano (LAB)
 (☎ 672 6163) Moneda 1170
Lufthansa
 (☎ 630 1655) Moneda 970, 16th floor
Northwest
 (☎ 233 4343) Avenida 11 de Septiembre 2155, Torre B, Oficina 1204, Providencia
Pluna
 (☎ 707 8008) Avenida El Bosque Norte 0177, 9th floor, Las Condes
Qantas
 (☎ 232 9562) Isidora Goyenechea 2934, Oficina 301, Las Condes
SAS
 (☎ 233 5283) Mardoqueo Fernández 128, Oficina 502, Providencia
Saeta
 (☎ 334 4427) Santa Magdalena 75, Oficina 410, Providencia
Swissair
 (☎ 244 2888) Barros Errázuriz 1954, Oficina 810, Providencia
Transportes Aéreos Mercosur (TAM)
 (☎ 381 1333) Santa Magdalena 94, Providencia

TAME (Ecuador)
(☎ 334 1758) Ebro 2747, Las Condes

United Airlines
(☎ 632 0279) Tenderini 171
(☎ 337 0000) El Bosque Norte 0177, 19th floor, Las Condes

Varig
(☎ 707 8000) Avenida El Bosque Norte 0177, Oficina 903, Las Condes

BUS
Buses are so numerous and frequent that schedules are rarely an issue except during holidays, when services can fill up fast. For an array of destinations within Chile and how much they cost see 'Sample Bus Fares from Santiago.'

Other Parts of South America
Santiago has four main bus terminals, but most international services leave from the Terminal de Buses Santiago (also known as Terminal de Buses Sur, ☎ 779 1385), Alameda 3850 between Ruiz Tagle and Nicasio Retamales (Map 6). A few also leave from, or stop by, the Terminal Los Héroes (☎ 696 9798), on Tucapel Jiménez near the Alameda (Map 5).

There are direct buses to every country on the continent except the Guianas and Bolivia, but only masochists are likely to attempt the 4½- to 10-day marathons to destinations like Quito, Ecuador (US$110), Bogotá, Colombia (US$160) and Caracas, Venezuela (US$200). Tepsa (☎ 779 5263) and Ormeño (☎ 779 3443) cover these northern routes, with stops in Lima, Peru (48 hours, US$70), about the single longest stretch any traveler is likely to undertake.

Argentina is the most frequent destination; the trans-Andean city of Mendoza has a much wider selection of buses and destinations within Argentina than is available from Santiago. Carriers crossing the Andes to Mendoza (seven hours, US$25) and Buenos Aires (18 hours, US$65) include Ahumada (☎ 778 2703, also at Terminal Los Héroes), Covalle Bus (☎ 778 7576), Fénix (☎ 776 3253), Nueva O'Higgins San Martín (☎ 779 5727), TAC (☎ 779 6920), Tur-Bus (☎ 776 3690) and Cata (☎ 779 3660).

Sample Bus Fares from Santiago

Travelers should remember that bus fares are subject to substantial variations among companies and can also rise dramatically on and near holidays. Note that Pullman seats recline, while salón seats recline farther, making it easier to sleep.

destination	hours	Pullman	salón cama
Antofagasta	18	US$31	US$42
Arica	28	US$38	US$56
Castro	19	US$27	US$45
Chillán	6	US$9	
Concepción	8	US$14	
Copiapó	11	US$20	US$30
Iquique	26	US$37	US$46
La Serena	7	US$15	US$22
Osorno	14	US$19	US$32
Puerto Montt	16	US$20	US$35
Punta Arenas	60	US$100	
Temuco	11	US$14	US$29
Valdivia	13	US$17	US$32
Valparaíso	2	US$4	
Villarrica	13	US$15	US$29
Viña del Mar	2	US$4	

Chile Bus (☎ 776 5557) goes to Mendoza, São Paulo, Brazil (72 hours, US$112), Rio de Janeiro (US$107) and intermediates and to Bolivia via northern Chile. Pluma (☎ 779 6054) goes to Mendoza, Montevideo, Uruguay (25 hours, US$80) and Brazilian destinations. Tas Choapa (☎ 779 4925) serves Mendoza, Córdoba (15 hours, US$57), Buenos Aires (US$64), Montevideo (US$70) and Bariloche (21 hours, US$36). EGAS (☎ 779 3536) also goes to Montevideo and Brazilian destinations, while El Rápido Internacional (☎ 779 0316) goes to Argentina and Uruguay. Pullman Bus (☎ 779 5243) goes to Asunción, Paraguay, (30 hours, US$70) at 1 pm Tuesday and Friday.

Igi Llaima (☎ 779 1751) and Buses Jac (☎ 776 1582) go to Junín de los Andes, San Martín de Los Andes and Neuquén via Temuco, as does Cruz del Sur (☎ 779 0607).

From Terminal Santiago, Coitram (☎ 776 1891) and Nevada (☎ 776 4116) run shared taxi colectivos to Mendoza that are only slightly more expensive (about US$28) and far quicker than buses – and drivers sometimes stop on request for photo opportunities on the spectacular Andean crossing. Prices may be open to haggling outside the peak summer season.

TRAIN

Since the late 1970s, there has been no international rail passenger service to or from Santiago, though there has been talk about restoring the former Santiago-Mendoza line, which parallels the international highway over the Libertadores pass and would be a massive undertaking. Otherwise, the 8870km rail network, only a small portion of which offers passenger service, desperately needs upgrading.

For the foreseeable future, having unsuccessfully attempted to encourage privatization of passenger services, the Empresa de Ferrocarriles del Estado (EFE) will continue to run southbound trains to Chillán, Concepción, Temuco and intermediates from the Estación Central (☎ 689 5199, 698 5401), Alameda 3322 (Ⓜ Estación Central; Map 6). Trains to Chillán leave at 8:30 am and 2:15

and 6:30 pm. Temuco-bound service leaves at 8 pm only, while the overnighter to Concepción leaves at 10:30 pm. Station hours are 7 am to 11 pm daily.

If the Estación Central is inconvenient, book passage at the Venta de Pasajes (☎ 639 8247; Map 5) in the Galería Libertador, Alameda 853, Local 21. It's open 8:30 am to 1 pm weekdays, 9 am to 1 pm Saturday. There is another office (☎ 228 2983) at the Galería Comercial Sur, Local 25, at the Escuela Militar metro station, open 9 am to 1 pm weekdays.

EFE also runs frequent commuter service between Santiago and Rancagua, capital of Region VI, for about US$2 (one hour).

Classes & Fares

Trains have three classes: economía, salón and cama. Cama refers to 'sleeper' class, which has upper and lower bunks; the latter are more expensive. On long overnight journeys, the charming between-the-wars sleepers may be worth consideration, but travelers have observed that decades of heavy use have left the bunks less comfortable than they once were.

Typical one-way fares for economía and salón classes are listed below; a roundtrip fare is slightly cheaper than two singles. The approximate time of the journey from Santiago appears after the destination.

destination	hours	economía	salón
Talca	5	US$5	US$9
Chillán	7	US$8	US$14
Concepción	9	US$11	US$19
Temuco	13	US$14	US$24

Cama fares to Concepción are around US$21/27 upper/lower, while to Temuco they are around US$27/35.

CAR & MOTORCYCLE

Even though Chile's public transport system is extensive, many interesting areas are more easily accessible by motor vehicle. Off the main highways, where buses may be few or nonexistent, it's not easy to stop where you want and then continue by public transport. Note, however, that because of smog problems there may be weekday restrictions on private vehicle use in Santiago and the Región Metropolitana; usually these are organized according to the last digit of the car's license plate. Since foreign-licensed vehicles will not carry the obligatory decal, they may be stopped by police (who are generally reasonable, however).

BICYCLE
Bicycling is an interesting and inexpensive alternative for traveling around Chile. Because even the best paved roads usually have dirt or gravel shoulders, a *todo terreno* (mountain bike) is a better choice than a racing bike.

Cycling is an increasingly popular recreational activity, and there are many good routes, especially along the coast and in the mountains east of Santiago. Chilean motorists are usually courteous, but on narrow, two-lane roads without shoulders, they can be a real hazard.

LP reader Paul Arundale, who has cycled extensively through the Southern Cone countries, offers the following suggestions on bicycle travel in Chile:

Chile offers ideal cycling conditions on rough unsurfaced roads in the north and south of the country, but in the middle it is difficult to avoid using the Panamericana; while this is not dangerous, having a wide hard shoulder for much of the central part, it is certainly no fun with the mountains far away and the diesel fumes all too close. January and February are months best avoided as all of Santiago seems to be on the road in pickup trucks and vans heading north or south and the unsurfaced roads are usually little more than one vehicle wide, making continual traffic in either direction a frazzling experience. For those on a longer tour, Chile has the best-stocked bike shops

in South America and even the smallest town has at least one bike shop offering all the latest Japanese parts. If flying between New Zealand and Chile, LanChile carries bikes wrapped in cardboard free between Chile, Easter Island and Tahiti.

Another reader claims that spare parts are hard to come by, though easier for mountain bikes than for racing bikes; 27-inch tires are particularly hard to find. There's a cluster of shops along Calle San Diego in Santiago.

Readers interested in detailed information on cycling in South America can find more material in Walter Sienko's *Cycling in Latin America* (1993).

HITCHHIKING
Along with Argentina, Chile is probably the best country for hitchhiking in all of South America. The major drawback is that Chilean vehicles are often packed with families with children. Truck drivers will often help backpackers, however. *Servicentros* on the outskirts of Chilean cities on the Panamericana, where truckers gas up their vehicles, are often a good place to solicit a ride. From Arica to Puerto Montt along the Panamericana, hitching is fairly reliable, but competition may be great in the summer months, when Chilean students hit the highway with their backpacks.

Women can and do hitchhike alone in Chile, but should exercise caution and especially avoid getting into a car with more than one man. Because hitching is never entirely secure, Lonely Planet does not recommend the practice. Travelers who decide to hitchhike should understand that they are taking a small but potentially serious risk. People who do choose to hitch will be safer if they travel in pairs and let someone know where they are planning to go.

Getting Around

TO/FROM THE AIRPORT

Aeropuerto Internacional Arturo Merino Benítez (☎ 601 9001, 601 9709), which also serves as the airport for most domestic flights, is in Pudahuel, 26km west of downtown Santiago. Note that, although Línea 1 of the metro ends at Pudahuel, the metro does *not* reach the airport.

The cheapest transportation to the airport, Centropuerto (☎ 601 9883; Map 6) buses charge only US$1.30 from Plazoleta Los Héroes, outside the Los Héroes metro station; between 5:55 am and 10:30 pm, there are 40 departures daily. Return times from the airport are 6:40 am to 11:30 pm. Slightly more expensive, Tour Express (☎ 671 7380; Map 5), Moneda 1529, charges US$2 one-way, US$3.50 roundtrip.

Buses from the airport leave from the front of the international terminal, and will drop you at the city terminal or just about anywhere along the route.

Minibuses belonging to Delfos (☎ 226 6020) or Transfer (☎ 777 7707) carry passengers door-to-door between the airport and any part of Santiago for US$5 to US$7.50 depending on distance. Departing passengers should call the day before their flight if possible, but these minibuses will sometimes pick up on short notice.

Taxi fares are negotiable; a cab to or from downtown can cost anywhere from about US$10 (if your Spanish is good) to US$25.

BUS

Santiago's buses go everywhere cheaply, but it takes a while to learn the system – check the destination signs in their windows or ask other passengers waiting at the bus stop. Many buses now have signed, fixed stops, especially in the downtown area, but that doesn't necessarily mean they won't stop at other points. Fares vary slightly depending on the bus, but all are within a few cents of US$0.40 per trip; hang on to your ticket, since inspectors may ask for it.

For convenience and security reasons, municipal authorities are promoting automatic fare machines, but the expense and difficulty of getting the myriad private companies to adopt the new technology have been daunting.

TAXI COLECTIVO

Taxi colectivos are, in effect, five-passenger buses on fixed routes. They are quicker and more comfortable than most buses and not much more expensive – about US$0.75 within most of Gran Santiago, although some to outlying suburbs like Puente Alto are a bit costlier. Taxi colectivos resemble ordinary taxis, but have an illuminated roof sign indicating their destination and a placard in the window stating the fixed fare.

METRO

Carrying nearly a million passengers daily, Santiago's metro system has three separate lines that interlink, and further extensions under construction. For destinations along these lines, it's far quicker than city buses, which must contend with the capital's narrow, congested streets. The metro operates 6:30 am to 10:30 pm Monday to Saturday, 8 am to 10:30 pm Sunday and holidays. Trains are clean, quiet and frequent, but at most hours it's difficult to get a seat.

Signs on station platforms indicate the direction in which the trains are heading. On east-west Línea 1, 'Dirección Las Condes' heads toward Escuela Militar station in the wealthy eastern suburbs, while 'Dirección Pudahuel' goes to San Pablo (it does *not* reach the international airport). On the north-south Línea 2, 'Dirección Centro' reaches Puente Cal y Canto station a few blocks north of the Plaza de Armas, while 'Dirección La Cisterna' heads toward the southern comuna of Lo Ovalle. Los Héroes, beneath the Alameda, is the only transfer station between these two lines.

Línea 5 (planners have apparently decided to skip Líneas 3 and 4) uses Baquedano (on

Línea 1) as a transfer station, passing through Ñuñoa and Macul en route to the southeastern comuna of La Florida; a western extension of Línea 5 to the Santa Ana station on Línea 2 opened in early 2000, including new stations at Bellas Artes and Plaza de Armas.

Fares vary slightly depending on the time of day and the line, but range from about US$0.30 to US$0.50. Tickets can be pur-chased from agents at each station; a convenient *boleto inteligente* or *boleto valor* (multitrip ticket) is also available at a slight discount. Charges are according to the following schedule; note that weekends and holidays are always charged as middle hours.

hora alta	hora media	hora baja
(peak)	(middle)	(low)
7:15–9 am	9 am–6 pm	6:30 am–7:15 am
6–7:30 pm	7:30–9 pm	9–10:30 pm

Tickets have a magnetic strip on the back. After slipping your ticket into a slot, pass through the turnstile and continue to the platform; your ticket is not returned unless it's a boleto inteligente with remaining value (several individuals may use the same boleto inteligente by simply passing it back across the turnstile). No ticket is necessary to exit the system.

Metrobús
Supplementing the metro is a feeder system known as metrobús, which connects outlying destinations with direct service to and from each metro station. The bright blue metrobús costs about US$0.65 per ride, about 50% more than regular city buses. Metro stations distribute a small map of the metro with a simplified diagram of metrobús routes, of which there are about 30.

CAR & MOTORCYCLE
If you're spending several months in Santiago and plan to travel to outlying areas, purchasing a car merits consideration, but it has both advantages and disadvantages. On the one hand, it's more flexible than public transport and likely to be cheaper than multiple rentals; reselling it at the end of your stay can make it even more economical. On the other hand, any used car can be a risk, especially on rugged back roads. Fortunately, even the smallest hamlet seems to have a competent and resourceful mechanic.

Chile's domestic automobile industry is insignificant – nearly 90% of vehicles are

---

Underground Art

Through its MetroArte program, Santiago's subway system has sponsored murals and other artworks by prominent Chilean artists on several of the city's more central underground stations, all except one of them on the central Línea 1. There are four at the Baquedano transfer station: Hernán Miranda's *Ojo en Azul* (Blue Eye), Francisco Smythe's *Vía Láctea* (Milky Way), Matías Pinto de Aguiar's *La Bajada* (The Descent) and Samy Benmayor's *Declaración de Amor* (Declaration of Love).

The Los Héroes transfer station has two, Ramón Vergara Grez's *Geometría Andina* (Andean Geometry), an abstract representation of the shapes and colors of the Andes, and Pablo McClure's *Constelación II* (Constellation II). Estación Universidad de Chile also has two murals: Mario Toral's 1200-sq-meter *Memoria Visual de una Nación* (Visual Memory of a Nation) deals with violence in Chilean history, while another of Miranda's, *Interior Urbano* (Urban Interior), is a commentary on the vastness of the urban landscape.

Estación Santa Lucía contains Rogerio Ribeiro's *Azulejos para Santiago* (Tiles for Santiago), consisting of 44,000 tiles, donated by the city of Lisbon, that form four thematic panels on the sea, the land, the voyage and discovery. The collective Niños de Integra created *La República de los Niños* (The Children's Republic) at Estación República. The only work on Línea 5 is Pablo Rivera's sculpture *El Sitio de las Cosas* (The Place of Things), at Estación Parque Bustamante.

imported. Good imported vehicles are more expensive here than in Europe or the USA, but more reasonable than in Argentina. Japanese and Korean vehicles like Toyota and Hyundai are especially popular, but Argentine Peugeots are also common. Parts are readily available, except for some older models. Do not expect to find a serviceable used car for less than about US$3000; much more for recent models.

Documents & Insurance

If you purchase a car you must change the title within 30 days; failure to do so can result in a fine of several hundred dollars. In order to buy a vehicle, you must have a RUT (Rol Unico Tributario) tax identification number, available through Servicio de Impuestos Internos, the Chilean tax office. Issuance of a temporary RUT takes only a few minutes at any SII office, though the permanent card arrives later by mail (for details on obtaining a RUT, see Doing Business in the Facts for the Visitor chapter).

The actual title transfer is done at any notary through a *compraventa* (contract of sale) for about US$10. It's worth mentioning that short-term visitors often avoid this paperwork by leaving the title in the hands of the original owner and obtaining notarial authorization to use the vehicle, but this has its own risks if it's someone you don't know or trust.

All vehicles must carry *seguro obligatorio* (minimum insurance), which covers personal injuries up to a maximum of about US$3000 at a cost of about US$20 per year. All insurance companies issue these policies, which run from April 1 to March 31 of the following year. Additional liability insurance is highly desirable.

Since Chilean policies are not valid in Argentina, but Argentine policies are valid in Chile and other neighboring countries, it's worth buying a reasonably priced Argentine policy across the border if you plan to visit several countries.

Note that while many inexpensive vehicles are for sale in the free zones of Regions I and XII (Tarapacá and Magallanes), only legal permanent residents of those regions

may take a vehicle beyond their borders, for a maximum of 90 days per calendar year.

Motorists with their own imported vehicles should be aware that, while customs regulations once stipulated that the 90-day import permit for foreign vehicles could not be extended (unlike tourist cards), this is no longer the case, and some border officials routinely issue 180-day permits. Not all customs officials are aware of this, however, and it may be easier to leave the country and return.

Road Rules & Hazards

While Chileans sometimes drive carelessly or a bit too fast (especially in the cities), if you have come from neighboring Argentina you will think them saints. Most Chilean drivers are courteous to pedestrians and rarely do anything willfully dangerous. Driving after dark is not advisable in some rural areas, where pedestrians, domestic animals and wooden carts are difficult to see on or near the highways. If you are involved in an automobile accident, consult the Legal Matters section in the Facts for the Visitor chapter for guidance.

Unless otherwise posted, speed limits are 50km/h in town and 100km/h in rural areas. In contrast to police in Argentina, Chile's carabineros strictly enforce speed limits with US$75 fines; bribing them is *not* an option.

Road Assistance

The Automóvil Club Chileno (Acchi), with offices in most major Chilean cities, provides useful information, sells maps and rents cars. It also offers member services and grants discounts to members of its foreign counterparts, such as the American Automobile Association (AAA) in the USA or the Automobile Association (AA) in the UK. Acchi's main office (☎ 212 5702) is at Avenida Vitacura 8620, Vitacura, while its tourism and member services office (☎ 225 3790) is at Fidel Oteíza 1960, Providencia. Membership includes free towing and other roadside services within 25km of an Automóvil Club office.

Shipping a Vehicle

Given its openness toward foreign trade and tourism, Chile is probably the best country on the continent for shipping a vehicle from overseas. After the author shipped his pickup truck from California to the port of San Antonio, southwest of Santiago, it took less than two hours of routine paperwork to get the vehicle out of customs. If the car is more than a few days in customs, however, storage charges can accumulate quickly.

To find a reliable shipper, check under Automobile Transporters in your local phone directory. Most transporters are accustomed to arranging shipments between North America and Europe, rather than from North America or Europe to South America, so it may take some of them time to work out details. One reliable US shipper is McClary, Swift & Co (☎ 650-872-2121), 360 Swift Avenue, South San Francisco, CA 94080.

When shipping a vehicle into Chile, do not leave anything whatsoever of value in the vehicle if at all possible. Theft of tools in particular is very common.

For shipping a car from Chile back to your home country, try the consolidator Ultramar (☎ 630 1817, fax 698 6552, italia@ultramar.cl), Moneda 970, 18th floor (Map 5). For the paperwork, it helps to have assistance from a reliable, conscientious customs agent, such as Juan Alarcón Rojas (☎ 225 2780, fax 204 5302, alrcon@entelchile.net), Fidel Oteíza 1921, 12th floor, Providencia.

Rental

Santiago has dozens of car rental agencies, from internationally known franchises to lesser-known local companies that tend to be cheaper. Even at smaller agencies, basic rental charges are now very high, the cheapest and smallest vehicles going for about US$50 to US$65 per day with 150km to 200km included, or sometimes with unlimited mileage. Adding the cost of insurance, petrol and IVA (*impuesta de valor agregado*, the value-added tax or VAT), it becomes very pricey to operate a rental vehicle without several others to share expenses. Weekend or weekly rates, with unlimited mileage, are better bargains. Small vehicles with unlimited mileage cost about US$350 to US$450 per week, while 4WD vehicles cost in excess of US$100 per day. Some companies will give discounts for extended rentals, say a month or more.

A number of companies have airport offices at Pudahuel in addition to the city offices listed below, many of which are in the eastern suburbs:

Alameda Rent a Car
(☎ 269 0553) Avenida 11 de Septiembre 1945, Oficina 702, Providencia

Alamo
(☎ 233 4343, fax 233 4766) Avenida 11 de Septiembre 2155, Oficina 1204, Providencia

Ansa Rent a Car
(☎ 251 0256) Avenida Eliodoro Yáñez 1198, Providencia

Atal Rent a Car
(☎ 235 9222, fax 236 0636) Avenida Andrés Bello 1051, Providencia

Automóvil Club Chileno (Acchi)
(☎ 225 3790) Fidel Oteíza 1960, Providencia

Vehicle Restrictions

Motorists must be aware of weekday vehicle restrictions because of air pollution, especially during the smoggy autumn months. Applicable to vehicles without catalytic converters, restrictions are based on the last digit of the license plate and are regularly published in newspapers and publicized in electronic media as well. Usually only two digits per day are affected, but in emergency situations it may be four or even six digits.

When smog levels are particularly high, the new government has instituted controls on vehicles with catalytic converters as well.

Before renting a vehicle, verify whether it has a catalytic converter, which is indicated by a decal that allows the police to determine whether it may operate or not on a given day.

Avis
(☎ 601 9966, fax 601 9757) Avenida Santa María 1742, Providencia

Budget Rent a Car
(☎ 220 8292, fax 224 1175) Manquehue Sur 600, Las Condes

Chilean Rent a Car
(☎/fax 737 9650) Bellavista 0183, Providencia/ Barrio Bellavista

Costanera Rent a Car
(☎ 235 7835, fax 236 1391) Avenida Andrés Bello 1255, Providencia

Dollar Rent a Car
(☎ 245 6175, fax 228 0995) Málaga 115, Local 101, Las Condes

First Rent a Car
(☎ 225 6328) Rancagua 0514, Providencia

Hertz
(☎ 235 9666, fax 236 0252) Avenida Andrés Bello 1469, Providencia

Just
(☎ 232 0900) Helvecia 228, Las Condes

Lacroce Rent a Car
(☎ 665 1325) Avenida Seminario 298, Providencia

Lys
(☎ 633 7600) Miraflores 541

Mann Seel Rent a Car
(☎ 239 8849) Las Encinas 3057, Ñuñoa

New Rent a Car
(☎ 277 6726) Avenida Ossa 2127, La Reina

Toluka Rent a Car
(☎ 207 3837) Isabel La Católica 5019, Las Condes

United Rent a Car
(☎ 236 1483) Padre Mariano 420, Providencia

The South Central American Information Club (SCAI Club, ☎ 673 3166, fax 673 3165), in the Hotel Indiana at Rosas 1339 (Map 5), deals largely but not exclusively with Israeli travelers. Daily rates range from US$55 per day for passenger cars to US$89 for 4WD pickups; monthly rates range from US$1300 to US$2200.

TAXI
Santiago has abundant metered taxis – black with yellow roofs. Fares vary, but it costs about US$0.60 to *bajar la bandera* ('drop the flag,' ie, start the meter) and about US$0.15 per 200m. Most Santiago taxi drivers are honest, courteous and helpful, but a few will take roundabout routes, and a handful have 'funny' meters.

There is also a system of radio taxis, which can be slightly cheaper – hotels and restaurants are usually happy to make calls for clients. One reliable, moderately priced company is Radio Taxi Andes Pacífico (☎ 225 3064, 204 0104, 225 2888). Other choices include Abadia (☎ 224 5931, 201 1230), Flash (☎ 689 4112, 689 8516), Radio Móvil Santiago (☎ 634 1147, 635 2777), Providencia (☎ 209 0445, 209 0371), Alto Las Condes (☎ 213 1369, 213 1379) and Limousine (☎ 228 1858, 207 5518).

BICYCLE
Santiago's mostly level and gradually sloping terrain is conducive to cycling, but its heavy traffic and narrow downtown streets are not. Some of the less densely settled outer comunas and suburbs are good for mountain biking.

WALKING
Again, the capital's mostly level and gradually sloping terrain is conducive to walking for practical reasons, but some of the busiest streets can be hazardous to cross. Hilly areas like Cerro Santa Lucía and Parque Metropolitano's Cerro San Cristóbal provide opportunities for recreational hiking.

ORGANIZED TOURS
If time is limited, consider a tour of Santiago and its surroundings. The municipal tourist kiosk on Ahumada offers free thematic walking tours of the downtown area at 10:30 am Tuesday mornings and at 3 pm Wednesday afternoons, but verify these times. Tours include free admission to selected museums, and sometimes accommodate English speakers. You can also arrange tours at the tourist office on Cerro Santa Lucía, taking in Cerro Santa Lucía, the Barrio Cívico Fundacional, Parque Forestal, museums and the Ruta Herencia Señorial, including Palacio Cousiño and other elite buildings.

Several agencies organize day and night tours of the capital (around US$20 each), excursions to Viña del Mar and Valparaíso (around US$40), visits to some combination of the Cousiño Macul, Errázuriz and Concha y Toro wineries (around US$35) and ski trips to the Farellones area (see Ski Resorts in the Excursions chapter*x-ref). Among them are Turismo Cocha (☎ 230 1000) at Avenida El Bosque Norte 0430 in Las Condes (Ⓜ Tobalaba), Sportstour Chile (☎ 549 5200), Moneda 970, 14th floor (Map 5) and Turistour (☎ 551 9370 for reservations).

Turismo Frontera (☎ 687 4390 for reservations) does a city tour of Santiago that takes you to La Chascona, the Palacio Cousiño and Parque Metropolitano for US$22, not including admission charges, and a full-day excursion to Isla Negra (US$35), not including lunch. There are also tours to vineyards, Pomaire and the Cajón del Maipo.

Note that most of the above agencies avoid subjects like recent political events – in fact, their guides are often instructed to do so. One doesn't, however. Chip Day Tours (☎ 777 5376), Avenida Santa María 227, Oficina 12, on the Recoleta side of Barrio Bellavista, offers a human-rights-oriented 'Historical Memory' tour that includes, among other features, visits to Parque por la Paz (see the Things to See & Do chapter) and, for a different point of view, the Fundación Pinochet. A half-day tour costs US$35, while a full-day tour, including lunch, costs US$50 to US$75 depending on the number of passengers. Chip also offers tours in the vicinity of Santiago, including Neruda's Isla Negra and regional vineyards.

Other tours and activities farther afield are highlighted in various sections of the Excursions chapter.

Things to See & Do

Santiago's various comunas and barrios have a wealth of interesting places, though the pace of change is obscuring the remaining historical sites. The greatest density of things to see is within Santiago Centro's historic core, a triangular area bounded by the Río Mapocho, the Alameda and the Via Norte Sur. West of the Via Norte Sur, rapidly evolving Barrio Brasil rewards the adventurous urban explorer. North of the Mapocho, overlapping the comunas of Recoleta and Providencia, Barrio Bellavista is one of the capital's prime nightlife areas, but with its assemblage of distinctive houses and active street life it's also a delightful area for walking.

The eastern suburbs of Providencia, Las Condes and Vitacura are more oriented toward upscale shopping, dining and accommodations, but there are a handful of worthwhile sights. Middle-class Ñuñoa has a remarkably active cultural life and is becoming a popular restaurant zone. La Reina and working-class Peñalolén have scattered points of interest.

SANTIAGO CENTRO (MAP 5)
Walking Tour

An apropos starting point for an orientation walk through downtown Santiago is the **Estación Mapocho**, at the corner of Bandera and Balmaceda on the south bank of the Río Mapocho, where rail passengers from Valparaíso, Viña del Mar and the Argentine city of Mendoza used to arrive from 1912 until the mid-1980s. It is now the city's foremost cultural center. Across Balmaceda, between 21 de Mayo and Puente, the wrought-iron **Mercado Central**, designed by architect Fermín Vivaceta in 1872, is one of Santiago's most colorful attractions; any of its numerous seafood locales is a fine choice for lunch or an early dinner.

Two blocks southeast, at Esmeralda 749, no colonial magistrate ever inhabited the misnamed **Posada del Corregidor** (1765), a whitewashed, two-story adobe structure

with an attractive wooden balcony; its art gallery (☎ 633 5573) is open to the public 10 am to 5 pm weekdays, 10 am to noon Saturday. Continue down MacIver to the corner of Santo Domingo, where the **Casa Manso de Velasco** (1730) resembles the Posada del Corregidor, then head west to the **Templo de Santo Domingo** (1747, but not completed until 1808), a massive stone church at Santo Domingo 961.

A block west and then south on Paseo Puente stands the distinctive **Cuerpo de Bomberos** (fire station, 1863-1893), a French-style building with a mansard roof. Its bell tower sounds only to commemorate a fireman's death in action. One block south is the remodeled **Plaza de Armas**, the city's historical center, flanked by the **Correo Central** (main post office, 1882), the Museo Histórico Nacional in the **Palacio de la Real Audiencia** (1804), the **Municipalidad de Santiago** (1785) and the **Catedral Metropolitana** (1745).

Two blocks west of the plaza, at Morandé 441, the former **Congreso Nacional** (1876) has become the Ministerio de Relaciones Exteriores (Foreign Ministry) since the military coup of 1973 (the present congress occupies new quarters in Valparaíso). The Ministry's Academia Diplomática (Diplomatic Academy) occupies the nearby **Palacio Edwards**, Catedral 1183, once the mansion of an elite Anglo-Chilean family. Immediately south of the ex-Congreso, fronting on Compañía, are the neoclassical **Tribunales de Justicia** (Law Courts, 1912-1930), one of the country's first reinforced concrete buildings.

Across the street, at Bandera and Compañía, the late colonial **Real Casa de Aduana** (Royal Customshouse) contains the outstanding Museo Chileno de Arte Precolombino. Two blocks west, at Compañía 1340, Chañarcillo silver magnate Francisco Ignacio Ossa Mercado lived in the Moorish-style **Palacio La Alhambra** (1862), inspired by its Spanish namesake at Granada. It's now an art gallery and cultural center

(☎ 689 0875), open 11 am to 1 pm and 5 to 7:30 pm weekdays.

The modern headquarters of **Codelco**, Huérfanos 1276, Chile's powerful state-run copper company, are on pedestrian street **Paseo Huérfanos**. If you continue east on Huérfanos you'll hit **Paseo Ahumada**, Santiago's main pedestrian thoroughfare, which runs south from the Plaza de Armas to the Alameda. Municipal pressure has reduced the number of street vendors, but buskers of diverse style and quality still congregate in the evening (though shrill Evangelicals sometimes drown out the others). Paralleling Ahumada a block farther east, **Paseo Estado** was recently transformed into a similar pedestrian mall by the municipal government. Half a block east of the plaza and Paseo Estado, the colonial **Casa Colorada** (1769) houses the city museum and tourist office.

A couple blocks southeast, at Agustinas 794, the elegant **Teatro Municipal** (1857), Santiago's prime performing arts venue, occupies the original site of the Universidad de San Felipe. Nearby, at Tenderini 187, the **Sociedad Nacional de Agricultura** (1936) is the seat of Chile's influential

Highlights

Many of Santiago's highlights are more subtle than conspicuous, but there's plenty to satisfy the curious visitor.

Palacio de La Moneda The masterpiece of Italian architect Joaquín Toesca, Chile's neoclassical presidential palace looks much as it did in late colonial times – thanks largely to a solid restoration job after air force bombs and bullets damaged it in the military coup of 1973. Parts of the building are open to the public, on organized tours only.

Museo Chileno de Arte Precolombino Superb archaeological collections in an equally superb late-colonial building make for one of Santiago's finest museums.

Iglesia de San Francisco One of Santiago's oldest buildings (1618) has withstood the earthquakes and wrecking balls that have transformed much of the rest of the city.

Palacio Cousiño Portuguese merchants built one of Santiago's landmark 19th-century mansions, open to the public, south of the Alameda.

Cerro Santa Lucía In the 19th century, the visionary city mayor Benjamín Vicuña Mackenna transformed an arid, rocky outcrop into a verdant garden retreat, only minutes from the crowded downtown streets.

Barrio Bellavista North of the Mapocho, the tree-shaded streets on both sides of Avenida Pío Nono are Santiago's principal dining and nightlife area. Within Bellavista, one of the high points is poet Pablo Neruda's Santiago residence **La Chascona**, open to the public.

Parque Metropolitano High above the city, north of Bellavista, this spacious park offers the best possible views – on a rare clear day, at least.

Parque por la Paz The best way to confront the meaning of 17 years of military dictatorship is to visit the former site of Villa Grimaldi, a torture center now transformed into a memorial park for the victims, in Peñalolén.

landowners' organization, founded in 1838. A block south sits the monolithic **Biblioteca Nacional**.

East of Cerro Santa Lucía near the Providencia border (a slight stretch away from the rest of these sites), the main campus of the **Universidad Católica** (1913), at the corner of Alameda and Portugal, is one of the city's main cultural centers. Its spacious interior patio, with ample natural light, attractive colonnades and a café, rates a detour. This is also the home of the Universidad's notoriously conservative Canal 13 TV.

Back toward the center, on the south side of the Alameda, the striking **Iglesia de San Francisco** (1618, with subsequent modifications), at Alameda 834, is one of Santiago's oldest buildings, housing the **Museo de Arte Colonial**, a notable collection of colonial art.

Some landmarks south of the Alameda are more scattered, though the cluster of 1920s buildings known as **Barrio París Londres** deserves a stroll along its namesake streets (París and Londres). Southwest, a stretch away from these other sites, in what was once an aristocratic neighborhood, architect Ricardo Larraín Bravo modeled the Byzantine-domed **Iglesia Santísimo Sacramento** (1931), Arturo Prat 471, on Paris' Eglise de Sacre Coeur. Since the 1985 earthquake, the exterior needs repairs, but the interior features a marble altar and mosaics.

Back north to the Alameda is the imposing **Universidad de Chile** (1874), Alameda 1058, which superseded the colonial-era Universidad de San Felipe; this is the main site, but the university has several other campuses. West of the university, at Alameda and Zenteno, much of Chile's political power still resides in the brutally utilitarian **Edificio de las Fuerzas Armadas**, the armed forces headquarters. A touch west stands the **Altar de la Patria**, which crowns the crypt of Chilean liberator General Bernardo O'Higgins.

Farther west and back across the Alameda, at the corner Amunátegui, the 128m **Torre Entel** (1976) resembles London's Post Office Tower; Santiago's New Year's fireworks take place here.

Heading east again, past the small **Plaza de la Libertad**, are a few other buildings of note, including the **Club de La Unión** (1925) at Alameda 1091, where Santiago's stockbrokers hold their power lunches; the **Bolsa de Comercio** (Stock Exchange, 1917) at La Bolsa 64; the depression-era **Ministerio de Hacienda** (Treasury Department, 1933) with its ornate doors at Teatinos 120; and the **Intendencia de Santiago** (1914), at Moneda and Morandé, a regional government site that began life as a newspaper office. Occupying an entire block in the middle of them all is the late-colonial **Palacio de La Moneda**. Formerly the presidential residence, La Moneda was badly damaged by air force attacks during the 1973 coup but restored before the return to democracy. And north, offering unobstructed views of La Moneda, is the **Plaza de la Constitución**, between Teatinos and Morandé.

Catedral Metropolitana

Begun in 1745, the present cathedral is the fifth church to occupy the site at the northwest corner of the Plaza de Armas, but was the first to actually face the plaza. Italianborn architect Joaquín Toesca, also responsible for the Palacio de La Moneda, added classical and baroque features to the façade in the late 18th century. The towers date from the late 19th century, when Italian architect Ignacio Cremonesi's otherwise ill-advised remodeling eliminated the elaborately carved cedar beams and covered the intentionally austere stone walls with ornamental stucco. The earthquake of March 1985 loosened the stucco, which was removed shortly thereafter.

Palacio de La Moneda

Under Toesca's direction, construction of a royal mint started in 1788 near the current Mercado Central on the Río Mapocho. When the flood-prone site proved inadequate, the project soon moved to its present location, a onetime Jesuit farm, where it was finally completed in 1805. In the mid-19th century, La Moneda became the residence of Chilean presidents, but the last to actually live there was Carlos Ibáñez del Campo, during his second term (1952–58).

After air attacks during his military coup of 1973 left the building unusable, General Pinochet governed from the Edificio Diego Portales, on the Alameda near Cerro Santa Lucía, but since La Moneda's 1981 restoration, Pinochet and elected presidents Patricio Aylwin and Eduardo Frei have kept their offices here. The rooms open to the public (see below) are impeccable, but the aging orange trees in the **Patio de los Naranjos** could use replacement.

The building itself occupies the entire block bounded by Morandé and Teatinos, between Plaza de la Libertad and Plaza de la Constitución; the main entrance on Moneda faces the latter. On even-numbered days at 10 am, the tallest of the carabineros hold a 30-minute changing-of-the-guard ceremony here.

With 20 days' advance notice, it's possible to take a guided tour of the interior by contacting the Dirección Administrativa del Palacio de La Moneda (☎ 671 4103). This can often be done more quickly, however, by making an in-person appearance at the subterranean office on Plaza de la Constitución, entered from Morandé. Present your passport to make a reservation by filling out a brief *Solicitud de Visita Palacio de La Moneda*.

Mercado Central

Occupying an entire block bounded by San Pablo, Paseo Puente, 21 de Mayo and Avenida Balmaceda, just across from the Río Mapocho, is Santiago's distinctive central market. It's at the site of the former Plaza de Abasto, an open-air market established by orders from independence hero Bernardo O'Higgins to remove the disorderly commerce around the Plaza de Armas in 1817. The current wrought-iron edifice dates from 1872; note the repeating Chilean star in its superstructure. In addition to an appealing selection of fresh fruit, vegetables and fish, the market contains a number of eateries ranging from modest to fine dining.

Centro Museums

For a complete listing of downtown Santiago museums, ask for Sernatur's leaflet *Galerías de Arte y Museos*, which also gives opening hours and transport details. Most museums are free Sunday and closed Monday. A few are just beyond the central triangle.

Museo de Santiago Part of the colonial Casa Colorada, this museum (☎ 633 0723), at Merced 860, documents the capital's growth from its modest nucleus to the current sprawl. Permanent exhibits include maps, paintings, dioramas and colonial dress. Particularly informative are the diorama of the 1647 earthquake (when 10% of the population died), a model of the Iglesia de La Compañía after the fire of 1863 and the diorama of the departure of troops for the north in the War of the Pacific, in which Chile fought against Peru and Bolivia. There is also a life-size recreation of a *sarao*, a parlor gathering of Santiago's late-colonial elite.

The museum is open 10 am to 6 pm Tuesday to Friday, 10 am to 5 pm Saturday, and 11 am to 2 pm Sunday and holidays (US$1). There is also a well-stocked combination bookstore-giftshop.

Museo Chileno de Arte Precolombino In the late-colonial Real Casa de Aduana (Royal Customshouse; 1805), this beautifully arranged museum (☎ 695 3851), Bandera 361, chronicles 4500 years of pre-Columbian civilization. There are separate halls for Mesoamerica (Mexico and Central America), the central Andes (Peru and Bolivia), the northern Andes (Colombia and Ecuador), and the southern Andes (modern Chile and Argentina plus, anomalously, parts of Brazil). Most of the well-preserved items come from the personal collections of the Larraín family, but there are also occasional special exhibits.

The museum is open 10 am to 6 pm Tuesday to Saturday, 10 am to 2 pm Sunday and holidays (about US$3); it's closed for Semana Santa (Holy Week), May 1, September 18, Christmas and New Year's Eve. It also has a good bookstore and an excellent, attractive café.

Museo de Arte Colonial Exhibits at the Museo de Arte Colonial, in Santiago's landmark Iglesia de San Francisco, include a wall-size painting, attributed to an 18th-century artist, detailing the genealogy of the Franciscan order and its patrons. The several rooms depicting the life of St Francis of Assisi will test the stamina of all but the most earnestly devout.

At Londres 4, just off the Alameda, the museum (☎ 639 8737) is open 10 am to 1:30 pm and 3 to 6 pm Tuesday to Saturday, 10 am to 2 pm Sunday and holidays (US$1 for adults, US$0.50 for children).

Palacio de Bellas Artes Modeled on Paris' Petit Palais, with a Belgian-built glass-and-metal cupola, Santiago's neoclassical, late-19th-century fine arts museum (☎ 633 0655) fronts an entire block in the Parque Forestal, on José M de La Barra near Avenida José María Caro. It has permanent collections of

French, Italian, Dutch and Chilean paintings, plus occasional, sometimes spectacular, special exhibits from overseas.

It's open 11 am to 7 pm Tuesday to Saturday, 11 am to 2 pm Sunday and holidays (US$1 adults, US$0.50 children).

Palacio Cousiño Probably the most elaborate of Santiago's 19th-century mansions open to the public, the Palacio Cousiño (☎ 698 5063) is south of the Alameda at Dieciocho 438, near Parque Almagro. The prominent Chilean wine family (originally of Portuguese descent) had additional successes in coal and silver mining, which enabled them to build what was probably Santiago's foremost mansion. Dating from 1871, it's embellished with Francophile artwork and features one of the country's first elevators. Some years back, fire destroyed the 3rd-floor interior, but the remaining floors are well-preserved reminders of elite life in the late 19th century. Interior

KRZYSZTOF DYDYNSKI

Façade detail of Museo de Arte Colonial

photography is prohibited, but the building's exterior and the surrounding gardens, designed by Spanish landscaper Miguel Arana Bórica, may be photographed.

It's open 9:30 am to 1:30 pm daily except Monday and 2:30 to 5 pm weekdays only. Admission is US$2 for adults, US$1 for children, including excellent guided tours in Spanish or sometimes in English (M Toesca).

Cerro Santa Lucía

Honeycombed with 65 hectares of gardens, footpaths and fountains, Cerro Santa Lucía (known to the Mapuche as Welen) has been

a handy hilltop sanctuary from the bustle of downtown Santiago for over a century. At its base, on the Alameda, sits a large stone engraved with the text of a letter in which Pedro de Valdivia extolled the beauty of the newly conquered territories to Spain's King Carlos V. A short distance north is a striking tiled mural of Nobel Prize–winning poet Gabriela Mistral.

Also fronting the Alameda is the refurbished, attractive **Plaza Neptuno**, where staircases encircle French-built fountains and eventually lead to the summit, where the parapet reveals a perfect view of the

Vicuña Mackenna & His Legacy

Even despite the last two decades of fast-food franchises, probably no single individual since Pedro de Valdivia has left a greater imprint on the cityscape of Santiago than Benjamín Vicuña Mackenna. During his relatively short life (1831-1886), Vicuña Mackenna was a lawyer, editor, journalist, historian, politician and diplomat.

Vicuña Mackenna began his public life as a member of the anticlerical Sociedad de Igualdad (Society for Equality) and barely avoided a death sentence as a member of the losing side in the civil war of 1851. Fleeing to California, he wrote extensively about Chilean history before returning to become the editor of *El Mercurio de Valparaíso*, and by the time of his death, he had authored over a hundred books. Elected to congress, he also served as a diplomat in North America and Europe, where Parisian urbanism left a lasting impression.

Between 1872 and 1875, as Intendente (Mayor) of Santiago, Vicuña Mackenna was able to impose his vision of *afrancesamiento* (Frenchification) on the city. Symbolically inaugurating the Mercado Central (which antedated his taking office), he worked from offices in the colonial Palacio de la Real Audiencia (today's Museo de Historia Nacional, to which he added a tower). He cobbled Calle Ahumada, turning it into a chic commercial area, conceived the Camino de Cintura, a ring road known today as Avenida Vicuña Mackenna (the eastern border of Santiago proper), and promoted cultural events such as art exhibitions.

His masterwork, though, was the visionary transformation of Cerro Santa Lucía from a stony wasteland into a verdant park that would do any city proud. Many of its constructions, such as the fountains of Plaza Neptuno, the winding paths that honeycomb the hillside and the chapel of La Ermita, date from this time, though the Castillo Hidalgo, recently recycled as an events center, dates from 1820. By the early 1890s, tree plantings had obscured damages to a hillside that had been used as a quarry.

Vicuña Mackenna's improvements set an example for surrounding areas like Barrio Lastarria, a stylish area east of the park, and much of the rest of the capital. Mourned widely on his death, the mayor himself rests appropriately in the modest chapel of La Ermita, near the summit of the hill.

There was a dark side to this progress, though, that continues today. The mayor's administration confiscated and demolished substandard housing on the lower slopes, attracting wealthier santiaguinos to the area and displacing those with fewer resources. Even today, after perceived security problems, the city now requires all visitors to sign a register – and while anyone can presumably enter, there's clearly a profile of undesirables that may have as much to do with class as real danger.

city, Cerro San Cristóbal and the Andes – smog permitting. The north side of the park, along Avenida Subercaseaux, features a pleasant **Jardín Japonés** (Japanese Garden).

Santa Lucía's transformation is a modern development – when Santiago mayor Benjamín Vicuña Mackenna opened the park in 1872 it was mostly barren rock. In 1914 British diplomat James Bryce remarked, 'The buildings which had defaced it having been nearly all removed, it is now laid out as a pleasure ground, and planted with trees.' Vicuña Mackenna's tomb lies in the **Capilla La Ermita**, a small chapel near the summit.

The municipal tourist office branch on Cerro Santa Lucía offers exceptional 1½-hour guided tours, in Spanish and English, at 11 am Thursday. These include a visit to Vicuña Mackenna's tomb and a chance to view the traditional midday cannon shot (ear protection provided, but the recoil is still powerful, and the explosion is loud enough to set off car alarms in the street below).

Hovering at an altitude of 629m, Cerro Santa Lucía is an easy walk from downtown. At the east end of Huérfanos, there is a glass *ascensor* (elevator) that carries passengers up the steep hillside. It has acquired an unfortunate reputation for nighttime muggings but is generally safe during the day, although visitors should not be complacent. The city has made serious efforts to improve security, and visitors must now sign in. The park is open 9 am to 8 pm daily (Ⓜ Estación Santa Lucía).

Museo Arqueológico de Santiago

Featuring outstanding exhibits on Chile's indigenous peoples from colonial times to the present, this misleadingly named museum (☎ 638 3502), Lastarria 321, is more accurately ethnohistorical than archaeological. Its major defect is outdated rhetoric that makes its subjects sound more like Chilean possessions than people in their own right.

At the Plaza del Mulato Gil de Castro, on the east side of Cerro Santa Lucía, the museum is part of an interesting neighborhood that includes many art galleries, excellent bookshops and varied restaurants.

It's open 10 am to 2 pm and 3:30 to 6:30 pm weekdays, 10 am to 2 pm Saturday (free).

BARRIO BRASIL & AROUND (MAP 6)

Undergoing a renaissance in recent years, the area immediately west of the Vía Norte Sur, reached via the new Paseo Huérfanos pedestrian suspension bridge and several surface streets, features good but affordable accommodations and restaurants, plus universities and cultural centers, in what remains one of Santiago's best-preserved traditional neighborhoods. The quarterly publication *Barrio Brasil* is a good guide to what's happening in the neighborhood, especially during mid-November's Semana de Barrio Brasil festival (which, despite its name, takes place on a weekend).

The main site of the festival, and the barrio's centerpiece, is relandscaped **Plaza Brasil**, which includes a small memorial to samba musician Antonio Carlos Jobim, dedicated by President Fernando Enrique Cardoso of Brazil. Other landmarks include the quake-damaged, neo-Gothic **Basílica del Salvador** (1892) and the gargoyle-festooned **Club Colo Colo** (1926) at Cienfuegos 41. Headquarters of the famous soccer club, but originally built by architects Guillermo Edwards Matte and Federico Bieregel for the Ismael Edwards family, the latter building is one of the city's most outlandish.

The private Universidad La República is one of the barrio's major benefactors, thanks to restoration of classic buildings like its **Escuela de Arquitectura** at the corner of Cienfuegos and Huérfanos.

South of Parque Quinta Normal, the comuna de Estación Central takes its name from the imposing French-built prefab **railway station**, dating from 1900, at the corner of the Alameda and Avenida Exposición. While Chilean rail service has declined, daily trains still reach the southern cities of Temuco and Concepción, and frequent commuter trains go as far as the city of Rancagua.

The comuna of Estación Central is mostly an industrial and residential area, but across the street, on the campus of the Universidad de Santiago, is a modern **planetario** (planetarium). It presents the latest on Chilean astronomy, which is probably the most advanced in South America, as there are several major international observatories near the northern desert cities of La Serena and Antofagasta. The planetarium (☎ 681 2171), Alameda 3349 at Matucana, offers summer audiovisual presentations at 5:15 pm weekdays except Monday, at 7 pm Wednesday, Friday, Saturday and Sunday, also at 5 pm Saturday and Sunday, and at noon Sunday only. Winter schedules are 7 pm Wednesday, Friday, Saturday and Sunday, 5 pm Saturday and Sunday, and also at noon Sunday. Admission is US$5 for adults, US$2.50 for children age 10 and under.

Basílica del Salvador

Archbishop Rafael Valdivieso ordered the construction of this neo-Gothic national monument (89m long, 37m wide and 30m high) in 1864. The country's only basilica, its founding stone was set in 1870, and work began in 1873, but persistent delays postponed its inauguration until 1892, and completion of the interior lagged until 1920. Still, German architect Teodoro Burchard and his local assistant Ignacio Zuazagoitía could have used even more time to design a building less vulnerable to the seismic activity that closed it for many years after the March 3, 1985, earthquake, a 7.8 on the Richter scale.

Several artists contributed to the final product, including Aristódemo Lattanza Borghini (murals and other paintings), Virginio Arias (design, candelabras and bronzes) and Onofre Jarpa (sketches, altars and altarpieces). The exterior statuary deserves a look.

Now supported by exterior buttresses, along with 20 interior columns – two of them utilitarian concrete replacing elaborately painted originals – that sustain the roof, the basilica is once again open to the public. Parts of the building, however, are still unsafe and cordoned off, and any major restoration may be decades away at the estimated cost of US$2.5 million.

The basilica is at Huérfanos 1781, just beyond the pedestrian suspension bridge over the Via Norte Sur.

Museo de la Solidaridad Salvador Allende

Begun in 1971 with donations from artists around the world in sympathy with Chile's socialist experiment, this museum (☎ 681 4954) literally went underground after the military coup of 1973. The entire collection spent 17 years in the warehouses of the Museo de Arte Contemporáneo, awaiting the return of civilian rule.

Supplemented by works from Chilean artists in exile, a part of the collection is now on display in this unpretentious museum. While the paintings and sculptures themselves are less overtly political than one might expect, the museum also includes a video salon presenting the history of Allende and the Unidad Popular. The museum recently moved from its location on Virginia Opazo to Herrera 360 between Huérfanos and Agustinas. It's open 9 am to 7 pm Tuesday to Sunday.

Salvador Allende

Parque Quinta Normal

Once an area of prestigious mansions, the comuna of Quinta Normal is now much less exclusive but of great historical interest. West of downtown, the cool, woodsy 40-hectare Parque Quinta Normal attracts strolling santiaguinos, picnicking families, impromptu soccer games and (on Sunday) increasing numbers of parading Evangelicals. On the western margins of Barrio Brasil, the park itself is actually a panhandle of the comuna of Santiago.

The most notable of several museums is the **Museo Nacional de Historia Natural** (☎ 681 4095), whose exhibits include a credible replica of the mummified body of a 12-year-old child. Sacrificed at least 500 years ago, the body was discovered in 1954 on the icy summit of El Plomo, a 5000m peak near Santiago, by a team from the Universidad de Chile. Also on display are bone fragments of the giant Pleistocene ground sloth known as the 'milodon,' from the famous cave near Puerto Natales in Chilean Patagonia. Open 10 am to 5:30 pm Tuesday through Saturday all year, it has varying Sunday hours: 11 am to 6:30 pm September to March, noon to 5:30 pm the rest of the year (US$1 for adults, US$0.50 for kids).

In the center of the park, there's an artificial lagoon where you can rent rowboats and, for kids, the floating equivalent of bumper cars. Beyond the lagoon, visit the **Museo de Ciencia y Tecnología** (☎ 681 6022), open 10 am to 5:30 pm Tuesday to Friday all year; weekend hours are 11 am to 7 pm October to mid-March, 11 am to 6 pm the rest of the year (US$1.50 for adults, US$1 for kids).

Specifically for children, about 50m north of the lagoon, is the **Museo Infantil** (☎ 681 6022). It's open 9:30 am to 5 pm weekdays (US$1).

Near the southern entrance, the 14 lovingly maintained steam locomotives at the open-air **Parque Museo Ferroviario** (☎ 681 4627) are a tribute to pioneers of the Chilean railroads, including the one that crossed the Andes to Argentina. There is also audiovisual material. From mid-October to mid-March, it's open 10 am to 6 pm Tuesday to Friday, 11 am to 7 pm weekends; the rest of the year, it's open 10 am to 5:30 pm Tuesday to Friday, 11 am to 5:45 pm weekends (US$1 for adults, US$0.60 for children).

Across from the southern entrance, housed in an offbeat structure designed for the Paris Exhibition of 1889 then dismantled and installed here after the start of the 20th century, is the **Museo Artequín** (☎ 681 8687), Avenida Portales 3530, an interactive museum of replica art, mostly European masters. December to February, it's open 10:30 am to 6:30 pm Tuesday to Friday, 11 am to 7:30 pm weekends; the rest of the year, hours are 9 am to 5 pm Tuesday to Friday, 11 am to 6 pm weekends. Admission is by voluntary contribution.

To get to Parque Quinta Normal, take the metro to Estación Central and then walk or catch a northbound bus up Matucana. There are park entrances on Avenida Portales, Matucana, Santo Domingo and Avenida General Velásquez. Public hours are 8 am to 8:30 pm daily except Monday.

Parque O'Higgins

South of the Alameda, 80-hectare Parque O'Higgins was the preserve of Santiago's elite in a previous incarnation as Parque Cousiño, but is now a more egalitarian place. Bordering the Via Norte Sur, parts of the park are dilapidated, making it less appealing than Parque Quinta Normal, but it still provides an entertaining glimpse of what many working-class Chileans do on weekends.

The sector known as **El Pueblito** features full-size replicas of rural buildings and a gaggle of inexpensive restaurants with raucous salsa bands on Sunday afternoon. Its **Museo del Huaso** (☎ 555 0054), honoring Chile's counterpart to the Argentine gaucho, often features good folkloric music; open 10 am to 5 pm weekdays, 10 am to 2 pm weekends. El Pueblito also contains the small **Museo Acuario** (Municipal Aquarium, ☎ 556 5680), the **Museo de Insectas y Caracoles** (Museum of Insects and Snails) and the **Museo de Fauna Menor**, a mini-zoo – all open 10 am to 7 pm daily.

Fantasilandia (☎ 689 3035) is a children's amusement park, open 2 to 8 pm weekdays except Monday and 11 am to 8 pm weekends in summer; 11 am to 8 pm weekends only the rest of the year. Admission, which includes unlimited rides, is free for children shorter than 90cm, while those between 91cm and 140cm pay US$9, and all others US$10 (**Ⓜ** Parque O'Higgins).

Club Hípico de Santiago

Just west of Parque O'Higgins, Club Hípico (☎ 693 9600), Avenida Blanco Encalada 2540, Santiago's premiere racetrack, dates from 1870. Set on 78 hectares of French baroque gardens, it also has tennis courts, a swimming pool and an artificial lake. Architect Josué Smith modeled the main building (1918) and grandstands, fronted by fountains, upon the Longchamps track in the Bois de Boulogne, west of Paris. Races take place on Sunday and alternate Wednesdays (**Ⓜ** Unión Latinoamericana or República).

BARRIO BELLAVISTA (MAP 7)

Across the Río Mapocho beneath Cerro San Cristóbal, on both sides of shady Avenida Pío Nono and many side streets, Bellavista is one of Santiago's liveliest neighborhoods on weekends, but relatively placid the rest of the time. Overlapping the comunas of Providencia and Recoleta, its houses painted in lively pastels like those of Valparaíso's hill areas, Bellavista has countless ethnic restaurants and an active Friday-Saturday evening crafts fair, starting at Parque Gómez Rojas across from the **Facultad de Derecho de la Universidad de Chile** (law school) and continuing up Avenida Pío Nono.

The barrio is the main entry point to Cerro San Cristóbal and the sprawling Parque Metropolitano. On the Providencia side, the **Plazuela Camilo Mori** is a popular meeting place.

La Chascona (Museo Neruda)

Nicknamed for the poet's widow Matilde Urrutia's unruly hair, Pablo Neruda's eclectic Bellavista house sits on a shady cul-de-sac at the foot of Cerro San Cristóbal, a short distance off Pío Nono.

The Fundación Neruda (☎ 737 8712), Márquez de La Plata 0192, conducts tours of La Chascona on a first-come, first-served basis 10 am to 1 pm and 3 to 6 pm daily except Monday. Admission costs US$2.50 for adults, half that for children; very thorough visits last about an hour. The Fundación also arranges one-day bus tours (lunch included) taking in the poet's three houses: here, at Isla Negra and in Valparaíso (see the Excursions chapter for descriptions of the latter two).

Cementerio General

Both Chile's distant and recent past are on display at this cemetery at the north end of Avenida La Paz, north of the Río Mapocho via the Cal y Canto Bridge. The tombs of public figures like José Manuel Balmaceda and Salvador Allende (both presidents who died violently in office) and diplomat Orlando Letelier (assassinated in Washington, DC by agents of the Pinochet dictatorship) are reminders of political turmoil from the 19th century to the present. A recent addition, erected in 1994, is a memorial to the 'disappeared' victims of the Pinochet era, but many ordinary Chilean citizens have been interred here as well since Bernardo O'Higgins ordered the Cementerio General's creation in 1819. It's open every day during daylight hours.

Centro Cultural Montecarmelo

Carmelite nuns once strolled the cobbled patio of what originally served as Molino El Rosario (a colonial grain mill) and then the Escuela San José, a Catholic school. Dating from 1897, the former La Capilla (chapel) is now a 200-seat theater, while the 300-seat Sala Cordillera also serves as an exhibition hall for Chilean artists in various media. Acquired by Providencia's municipal government in 1986, Montecarmelo became a cultural center in 1991. It's at Bellavista 0594, on the Providencia side of Bellavista; for details of offerings, see the Cultural Centers entry in the Facts for the Visitor chapter.

PARQUE METROPOLITANO (MAP 7)

Crowned by a chalky 36m statue of the Virgin Mary, 869m **Cerro San Cristóbal** towers above downtown Santiago from the north side of the Mapocho. Reached by funicular railway, *teleférico* (aerial tramway or cable car), bus or on foot, it dominates Parque Metropolitano, central Santiago's largest open space and a major recreational resource for capital residents. There are several restaurants, snack bars and coffee shops at the summit and throughout the park.

The most direct route to San Cristóbal's summit is the funicular (built in 1925) that climbs 485m from Plaza Caupolicán, at the north end of Pío Nono. It makes an intermediate stop at the **Jardín Zoológico** (zoo, ☎ 777 0387), which has a modest collection of scandalously neglected exotic animals (a tiger actually escaped and roamed the area for several hours in early 1996); improvements are supposedly underway (US$3 for adults, US$1.25 for children).

The climb continues to the **Terraza Bellavista** where, on a rare clear day, there are extraordinary views of the city and its surroundings. At the summit proper, Pope John Paul II said mass at the **Santuario Inmaculada Concepción** during his 1984 Santiago visit.

A short walk from the Terraza is the **Estación Cumbre**, from which the teleférico begins its 2000m-long trek from Cerro San Cristóbal, via Tupahue, to a station near the north end of Avenida Pedro de Valdivia Norte (about 1200m from the Pedro de Valdivia metro station).

At the Tupahue teleférico station is the **Piscina Tupahue**, a large swimming pool. A short walk east from Tupahue are the **Casa de la Cultura** (an art museum, open 9 am to 5 pm daily), the **Enoteca**, (a restaurant and wine museum) and the **Jardín Botánico Mapulemu** (a so-so botanical garden). Farther east, there's another large pool, the **Piscina Antilén**, reachable only by bus or on foot.

The funicular operates 10 am to 7 pm weekdays, 10 am to 8 pm weekends and holidays. The teleférico keeps slightly different hours, 10:30 am to 6:30 pm weekdays, extended to 7:30 pm weekends and holidays. From either direction, the funicular-teleférico combination (about US$3.50 for adults, US$1.75 for children), plus the metro, is a good means of orienting yourself to Santiago's complex geography. The funicular alone costs US$1.25 to Estación Cumbre, US$2 for a roundtrip. From Plaza Caupolicán, Buses Tortuga Tour also reaches Avenida Pedro de Valdivia Norte via Tupahue, on a winding, roundabout road.

PROVIDENCIA (MAP 8)

Providencia's points of interest are more spread out, but since Línea 1 of the metro and many bus lines run the entire length of Avenida Providencia, it's convenient to use public transportation to get to most of them. Perhaps emblematic of modern Santiago, just west of Plaza Italia on Avenida Providencia, the **Torre Telefónica CTC Chile** houses Chile's dominant telecommunications enterprise in a building that, embracing the kitsch aesthetic, looks like a 50-story cell phone. The main floor has a first-rate art gallery, the Sala de Arte Telefónica, open 10 am to 8 pm Tuesday to Saturday, with frequently changing exhibitions that are free of charge.

At Avenida Vicuña Mackenna 44 is the **Museo del Deporte** (Museum of Sport), also home to Chile's Olympic Committee. At Avenida Providencia 1550, the redbrick offices of Sernatur, the national tourist service, once housed the **Mercado Providencia**, the main local market; an attenuated market still exists directly behind the main building. Across from Sernatur, built by Italian-born architect Eduardo Provasoli Pozzoli, the **Parroquia Nuestra Señora de la Divina Providencia** dates from 1880.

Museo Nacional y Biblioteca Histórica Benjamín Vicuña Mackenna

On the western edge of Providencia, in the former residence of the Vicuña Mackenna-Subercaseaux family, this museum (☎ 222 9642), Avenida Vicuña Mackenna 94, honors the individual who, at least prior to the military coup of 1973, exercised the greatest influence on the city of Santiago (thanks largely to his transforming vision of Cerro Santa Lucía).

In addition to the family's personal possessions, the building deals with Vicuña Mackenna's career as historian, journalist, traveler, diplomat, politician and mayor of Santiago. A 23-minute video entitled *Benjamín Vicuña Mackenna y la transformación de Santiago, 1872-1875* shows at 11 am and 4 pm. The museum is open 9:30 am to 1 pm and 2 to 6 pm Tuesday to Saturday (US$1.20).

Parque de las Esculturas

On the north banks of the Mapocho, between the Pedro de Valdivia and Padre Letelier Bridges, this open-air abstract sculpture garden is a pleasant hangout on sunny days – especially for affectionate couples. There is also a semi-subterranean exhibition hall (☎ 340 7303), Avenida Santa María 2201, with changing exhibits from Chilean artists; open 10 am to 7 pm daily (free). It's a short walk across the river from the Pedro de Valdivia or Los Leones metro stations.

LAS CONDES & VITACURA (MAP 9)

Most of Las Condes' attractions are gastronomical and commercial, with a handful of scattered landmarks among the high-rise, high-rent apartment blocks.

Museo Histórico de la Escuela Militar

At the end of Línea 1 of the metro, at the corner of Avenida Apoquindo and Avenida Américo Vespucio, the Escuela Militar has indoctrinated generations of army officers in the doctrine that they know what's best for the country. Its museum (☎ 208 3701), entered at Los Militares 4500, celebrates the army's accomplishments since independence. Among those accomplishments are the 'pacification' of the southern Mapuche frontier (which took Spain and Chile more than three centuries) and the defeat of Peru

and Bolivia in the War of the Pacific (which took Chile only a few years, 1879-1883).

The museum's most revealing exhibit, though, is the separate room known as the **Sala Presidente Augusto Pinochet**, which, on a modest Chilean scale, exposes a personality cult that seems straight out of Stalin's Russia. On top of this, the general has displayed his own tendencies by donating his enormous collection of Napoleon memorabilia, including several busts and a huge library in Spanish, French and English. The museum is open 3 to 6 pm weekdays, but by appointment only (free; Ⓜ Escuela Militar).

Museo Ralli

More approachable, and accessible, than the Escuela Militar, is the Ralli Museum (☎ 206 4224), Alonso de Sotomayor 4110, part of a chain of international art museums with other branches in Spain, Israel and Uruguay. In a largely residential area, this remarkable, spacious facility has 16 rooms of modern paintings and sculptures by mostly Latin American artists, including Chile's own Roberto Matta and Carmen Aldunate among others, but also well-known European figures like Salvador Dalí and Henry Moore. About a fourth of the exhibits turn over in any given year. It's open 10:30 am to 4 pm daily except Monday and Thursday (free). To get there, take any bus out Avenida Vitacura to Candelaria Goyenechea and walk one block north.

Museo de Artes Decorativas Casas de lo Matta

More significant for its past than its contents, this museum (☎ 212 4633), Avenida Presidente Kennedy 9350, set among well-kept rose gardens, occupies a restored 18th-century home – one of few of its kind within the city – whose balconies run both sides of the length of the house. The museum holds a derivative collection of contemporary landscapes that, for all their scant imagination, might have been painted a century ago. The Corporación Cultural de Vitacura does, however, arrange special exhibits and events like outdoor jazz concerts, so it's worth dropping by if you're in the area or phoning to ask what's on. Museum hours are 9 am to 6 pm weekdays, 9 am to 2 pm Saturday (free).

ÑUÑOA (MAP 10)
As upscale high-rise development dissolves the community feeling of once-suburban areas like Providencia and Las Condes, santiaguinos have gained a new appreciation of areas like middle-class Ñuñoa, where attractive single-family houses and tree-lined streets recall what other parts of the capital have lost. It's close enough to the Andean front range that the mountains are usually visible despite the city's frequent smog.

Middle-class does not mean dull, however – Ñuñoa has an active cultural life centered around Plaza Ñuñoa, where the Universidad Católica has one of Santiago's most important theater venues, and a progressive municipal administration has promoted live concerts and a crafts and flea market. Restaurants and dance clubs pull visitors from downtown, especially on weekends, and the Estadio Nacional hosts soccer matches and rock concerts. Foreign students from the Universidad de Chile's nearby Macul campus add a cosmopolitan element, and there's even an outpost of Chile's Middle Eastern community symbolized by the **Mesquita As-Salam**, a mosque on Avenida Chile-España at Campoamor.

To get to Plaza Ñuñoa from elsewhere in the city, take bus Nos 212, 338 or 382 from Plaza Italia (the area around Plaza Baquedano), No 433 from Alameda and Vicuña Mackenna, No 606 from the Terminal de Buses Santiago, No 600 from Estación Central, or No 243 from Compañía. Metrobús directly connects Estación Salvador with Plaza Ñuñoa.

Estadio Nacional
Built for the 1960 World Cup, this stadium, on Avenida Grecia at Campos de Deportes, retains an aura of infamy for its role in the incarceration and death of many Chilean activists, including folksinger Víctor Jara, in the aftermath of the military coup of 1973. Most Chileans, though, would prefer to remember it for classic soccer matches with teams like Colo Colo, Universidad de Chile and Universidad Católica.

PEÑALOLÉN
The mostly working-class comuna of Peñalolén, in Santiago's eastern foothills, is far off most tourist circuits, but its recent history, although grim, and community dynamics make it one of the city's most interesting areas. At the east end of Avenida Grecia, its population is a sometimes volatile mix of squatters with ties to the left-wing Movimiento Izquierdista Revolucionario (MIR, among the most fervent supporters of Salvador Allende and most implacable opponents of the Pinochet dictatorship), counterculture Bohemians and upwardly mobile professionals who value its relative seclusion. In some of the modern subdivisions, the houses look like suburban New England transplants, but on the day General Pinochet assumed his lifetime Senate seat, enraged activists from the squatter settlements burned a supermarket to the ground (it was quickly rebuilt).

Parque por la Paz
The onetime estate of Villa Grimaldi was the main detention and torture center for now-imprisoned General Manuel Contreras' notorious DINA. Razed by the military to cover up evidence in the last days of the Pinochet dictatorship, it was converted into a memorial park. It's a powerful testament that assumes the visitor need only read the descriptions and see the names of the dead and disappeared to imagine what happened here.

Little remains of the original structures, most notably the former DINA photo lab (containing a model of Villa Grimaldi, ask attendant for key) and the swimming pool, where DINA used to frighten people by feigning executions. There are 224 names on the list of those who died here, but only a handful of these appear in military records as executed. The main gates by which prisoners entered are now closed – 'never to be opened again.'

Parque por la Paz, in the 8300 block of José Arrieta near La Capilla, is open 11 am to 8:30 pm daily except Monday (free; Map 4). Take bus No 242 from Avenida Providencia, No 433 from Plaza Italia, or No 337 from Estación Central, on the Alameda.

Barrio Ecológico

Also in Peñalolén, where the foothills steepen toward the Andean front range, the so-called Barrio Ecológico began as an agrarian-reform subdivision of a *fundo* (rural estate) in the late 1960s under the late President Eduardo Frei Montalva. As wheat crops failed because of poor soils in what was then a remote location, counter-culture hippies began to move in, acquiring land from campesinos (peasants) and creating an innovative architecture – thanks largely to a lack of municipal oversight – but the area had no electricity or running water until relatively recently. Residents have planted extensively to stem erosion on the hillsides.

Some peasants remain, providing a social mix, but there is an agreement with Peñalolén officials that the Barrio Ecológico should remain an area of low-density housing as a barrier against Santiago's sprawl. None of the streets are paved – by preference of the residents, to preserve the natural drainage – but some houses have become elaborate. Some assert that it has become an elitist enclave, but it's clearly more a community than nearby cookie-cutter suburban housing developments that have clashed with the MIR-oriented *callampas* (squatter settlements).

At the entrance to the barrio, which is precisely at the end of the No 318 bus line from Mapocho, Santa Lucía or Diagonal Paraguay, there's a small but worthwhile crafts market and a picada serving good, moderately priced lunches. Weekends are the best time to visit. If driving, the best way is probably to go to the east end of Avenida Grecia and ask for directions.

CERRILLOS & MAIPÚ

Southwest of Estación Central, in the comuna of Cerrillos on the highway toward San Antonio, the **Museo Nacional de Aeronáutica y del Espacio** (National Air & Space Museum, ☎ 557 0344), Avenida Pedro Aguirre Cerda 5100, occupies part of the grounds of Aeropuerto Los Cerrillos (Map 1), which used be Santiago's main domestic airport but now has only a handful of air taxi charter services. Focusing on local aviation history, it also includes the Chilean flag that was carried to the moon by Apollo 14 in 1971. The museum is open 10 am to 6 pm daily except Sunday.

Just beyond Cerrillos, in the southwestern suburban comuna of Maipú, the **Templo Votivo de Maipú** is a monstrous manifestation of patriotic and ecclesiastical hubris, a 10-story concrete bunker that probably only a truly devout structural engineer can appreciate, as it struggles vainly to redeem itself through the filtered light of its stained-glass windows (Map 1). The attached **Museo del Carmen** (☎ 247 9669) contains exhibits on religious history and customs, while the Templo's grounds contain late-colonial ruins that are fenced off because of earthquake damage.

The Templo is open to the public 8:30 am to 7:30 pm, while the museum is open 3:30 to 6 pm Saturday, 11 am to 2 pm and 3:30 to 6:30 pm Sunday and holidays. From the Alameda, take any bus that says Templo. Taxi colectivos leave from the Alameda and Amunátegui.

ACTIVITIES
Wine Classes

Wine aficionados who plan to spend some time in Santiago might contact the Club de Amantes del Vino (☎ 365 0724, fax 365 0723), Avenida Américo Vespucio Norte 2920-B, Vitacura (Map 9), which offers regular classes on wine and, to put things in perspective, arranges appropriate dinners at some of Santiago's better restaurants.

Similarly, the Escuela de Vino (☎ 207 3520, fax 207 0581), Avenida Vitacura 3446 in Vitacura (Map 9), offers introductory, middle and advanced wine courses, consisting of four to seven two-hour sessions with instruction by Chilean vintners, enologists and university faculty. Classes take place

Monday to Thursday, monthly between March and December, in Spanish only, but the students are international. The cost is about US$100, and there are about 20 students per class.

Affiliated with the Miguel Torres wineries, the Centro Cultural del Vino (☎ 245 1101, ccv@miguel-torres.cl), Roger de Flor 2900, Las Condes (Map 9), offers a series of six-hour courses (three hours each on consecutive nights), dealing with topics like viticulture and gastronomy, for about US$60.

For visits to wineries in and around Santiago, see the Excursions chapter. For suggested wine outlets, see the Shopping chapter.

Cycling
Downtown Santiago's heavy traffic makes cycling unpleasant, but the suburbs and surrounding areas like the Cajón del Maipo have plenty of open space. Lys Rent A Car (☎ 633 7600), Miraflores 537, rents bikes from US$18 per day and also does tours of the cordillera (Map 5).

Swimming
Santiago has several public pools, though per person charges are pretty steep. The most reasonable is at Parque O'Higgins (☎ 556 1927), where adult fees are US$3.50 weekdays, US$4 weekends, but US$2 for children at any time (Map 6). There are two pools in Parque Metropolitano (☎ 777 6666) on Cerro San Cristóbal (Map 7): Piscina Tupahue charges US$9 for adults, US$6 for children weekdays and slightly more on weekends; Piscina Antilén costs US$10 for adults, US$6 for children weekdays, and also slightly more on weekends. The Asociación Cristiana de Jóvenes (YMCA, ☎ 696 5106), Compañía 1360, has a pool along with gym facilities (Map 5).

Tennis
The International Sporting Club, on Bellavista at Loreto, rents courts on a first-come, first-served basis for US$8 per hour for

singles matches, US$12 per hour for doubles. Hours are 8 am to 8 pm weekdays, 8 am to 6 pm Saturday, and 8 am to 3 pm Sunday (Map 7). There are also courts at the Club de Ténis Estadio Nacional (☎ 238 8943), Avenida Marathon s/n, Ñuñoa.

Polo
The Club de Polo San Cristóbal (☎ 206 0294) is at Avenida Monseñor Escrivá de Balaguer 5501, Vitacura, just beyond the Américo Vespucio ring road.

Cricket
In the eastern comuna of La Reina, the Prince of Wales Country Club (☎ 226 8374), Avenida Francisco Bilbao 6445, has regular Saturday matches open to any willing participant (Map 9).

Rugby
The capital's Anglophone community has organized the Santiago Touch Rugby Club (☎ 233 6966, 242 4586), a coed organization that plays a noncontact version of the sport at the Colegio St George (☎ 228 7611; Map 1), Avenida Américo Vespucio Norte 540, Quilicura.

Running
Santiago's spacious parks and eastern suburbs are good areas for runners. The English-language weekly *News Review* (☎ 235 1512), Almirante Pastene 222, sponsors the Hash House Harriers jogging club.

Climbing
The Bivouac Café (☎ 777 6173), Calle del Arzobispo 0635 in Barrio Bellavista, has a climbing wall and sells outdoor equipment (Ⓜ Salvador; Map 7). Cascada Expediciones (☎ 234 2274), Orrego Luco 040 in Providencia (Map 8), organizes summit climbs, mostly walkups, to Farellones-area peaks like 2750m Cerro Provincia (US$16) and 4300m Cerro Pintor (US$40).

Climbers in search of advice should contact the Federación de Andinismo (☎ 222 0888), Almirante Simpson 77, Providencia; for emergency help, contact the Cuerpo de

Socorro Andino (☎ 699 4764). Anyone climbing near the Argentine border needs permission from the Dirección de Fronteras y Límites del Estado (☎ 698 3502, fax 697 1090, difrol3@minrel.cl), Bandera 52, 5th floor.

Hiking

Cascada Expediciones (see Climbing, above) offers free guided hikes to Cerro Pochoco (4km, two to three hours), in Lo Barnechea, Wednesday at 7 am – phone for details. Take any bus out Avenida Las Condes to Plaza San Enrique, then catch a cab to the end of Camino del Alto, about 4km to the northeast, where the Universidad de Chile has a small astronomical observatory. In spring, California poppies cover the hillsides along the badly eroded trail, which climbs steeply to the 1804m summit for views of 5424m Cerro del Plomo and other glacier-covered Andean peaks. If doing this hike independently, start early to benefit from the shade, carry water and use good hiking boots, not sneakers – the descent can be treacherous without sufficient grip.

In the nearby Cajón de Farellones, Cascada offers another hike to Vallecitos (three to five hours, US$6), Saturday at 8 am. Again, call to confirm.

Tobogganing

One of Santiago's uncommon entertainments is the Rodelbahn, a toboggan on rails in the heights of the eastern suburb of La Reina. Popular with both adults and children, it also offers one of the best views of the sunset over Santiago (if not for the persistent smog, it would have one of the best views of the city, period). In summer, the Rodelbahn (☎ 273 4819), Avenida Larraín 11095, is open noon to midnight Tuesday to Friday, 11 am to midnight Saturday, and 11 am to 10 pm Sunday; the ride costs US$4, and two can fit, albeit precariously, on a single toboggan. The rest of the year, it's open weekends only, and hours are reduced (Map 4).

Nearby is *Gran Vista (☎ 275 0010)*, an outstanding Chilean-Patagonian restaurant

on the grounds of the Club de Equitación La Reina, a riding club at Talinay 11040, which will pick up diners at their hotel free of charge. It's fairly expensive; open for dinner Tuesday to Saturday, and for lunch only Sunday.

Golf

None of the courses in Santiago proper are open to the public, though visitors may sometimes play as guests of members. For information on courses around the country, contact the Federación de Golf (☎ 204 8956), California 1946, 3rd floor, Oficina F, Providencia.

Southwest of the city, near the town of Lonquén, the Club de Golf Las Palmas (☎ 855 9275) offers a full day on the links, including transfers, clubs, caddy, shoes and greens fees, for US$180. Lonquén is near Talagante, on the toll highway to San Antonio.

LANGUAGE COURSES

For intensive three-week Spanish courses, with five hours of instruction per day, try the Centro de Idiomas Bellavista (☎ 735 7651, fdo@cib.cl), Crucero Exeter 0325, Bellavista (Map 7). Rates are US$345 per person for groups no larger than six persons; individual classes are offered at higher rates. It also has its own guesthouse, charging US$14 per day for lodging, and arranges lodging with Chilean families.

Also in Bellavista, at Ernesto Pinto Lagarrigue 362-A, the Escuela Violeta Parra (☎ 735 8240, fax 229 8246, vioparra@chilesat.net) has drawn praise for emphasizing the social context of language instruction, by arranging field trips to community and environmental organizations, vineyards and the like, as well as tours to nearby national parks (Map 7).

The Instituto Goethe (☎ 638 3185), Esmeralda 650, offers intensive Spanish language courses, consisting of four weeks of 25 class-hours per week for US$390; classes are available for beginning, intermediate and advanced students. The Instituto also offers twice-weekly conversation classes for

US$120 for four weeks. Classes are no larger than 10 to 12 students (Map 5).

Another alternative is the Natalis Language Center (☎/fax 222 6470, natalis@intermedia.cl), Vicuña Mackenna 6, Departamento 3, where monthlong courses (20 to 25 hours per week) cost US$340, with a maximum of five students per class. Individual tuition and conversation classes are also possible (Map 8).

The Instituto Chileno de la Lengua (☎ 664 3114), Miraflores 590, also offers language instruction (Map 5), as does the Linguatec Language Center (☎ 233 4356, Interno 23), Avenida Los Leones 439, Providencia (Map 8).

Places to Stay

Santiago has a wide range of accommodation options, from youth hostels and *hospedajes* (family-run budget accommodations) to simple but fine *residenciales* (inexpensive hotels, usually with shared bath) to five-star luxury lodgings of jet-set stature. Budget accommodations tend to be past their prime, though not necessarily bad, while many mid-range hotels are either showing their age or have undergone shoddy remodeling (this is even true of some top-end accommodations). There are, however, some good values in all categories; remember that mid-range and upscale lodgings usually discount the 18% IVA to foreign visitors.

The main areas for budget accommodations are Santiago Centro and Barrio Brasil, but these areas have both very good and very bad places. Some budget hotels double as *hoteles parejeros*, short-term accommodations utilized by young couples in search of privacy.

In areas like Providencia and Las Condes, top-end accommodations are the rule rather than the exception; budget travelers will find few alternatives, though some mid-range places exist. Accommodations are relatively scarce in other parts of town.

Travelers should note that tourist offices are usually reluctant to recommend places in the budget range or even to admit that they exist. This is partly because some of the cheapest places can be pretty squalid, but also because the staff have the idea that foreign visitors should stay in *hoteles de categoria*, the best available (and usually very expensive) lodging. Often, with gentle persistence, travelers can extract information on more economical alternatives.

Checkout times vary, but may be as early as 10 am and are rarely later than noon. While most places are flexible within reason, some will add the cost of an extra day for those who overstay their limit; travelers should verify each hotel's policy and give advance notice if they need extra time. Most places are happy to provide temporary luggage storage for travelers with late afternoon or evening flights or bus trips, or even for several days for those who take brief excursions outside the capital.

PLACES TO STAY – BUDGET

Travelers should be selective – lodgings in this category differ much more in quality than in price.

Santiago Centro (Map 5)

Santiago's main budget zone is a seedy but not really dangerous neighborhood near the former Terminal de Buses Norte, around General Mackenna, Amunátegui, San Pablo and San Martín (**M** Puente Cal y Canto), where accommodations range from squalid to basically acceptable. Single women may feel uncomfortable here late at night, especially on General Mackenna, where many prostitutes hang out.

Hotel Indiana (☎ 671 4251, Rosas 1343), a dilapidated mansion with dependable hot water, is Santiago's Israeli hangout; beds cost around US$6. In an architecturally appealing, European-style building with large and bright rooms, the odd but friendly *Hotel Pudahuel* (☎ 698 4169, San Pablo 1419) nevertheless has a distinct odor of cat, and it can be noisy – not least from by-the-hour clients. Rates with shared bath are US$6.50 per person, while doubles with private bath go for US$15.

The area's best is labyrinthine *Hotel Caribe* (☎ 696 6681, San Martín 851), whose spartan rooms, some of them spacious, are still good values at US$7 per person with shared bath and hot showers. It's popular with travelers, but there's usually space, though singles may be at a premium. Ask for a room at the back or upstairs, since foot traffic on the squeaky-clean floors makes the lobby and passageway a bit noisy. The doors have flimsy hasps and padlocks, but you can leave valuables in the safe; the manager will happily and securely store your personal belongings at no charge if you go trekking or take some other excursion. Meals, snacks and drinks are available at reasonable prices.

Rivaling the Caribe is the more central, slightly cheaper **Nuevo Hotel Valparaíso** (☎ 671 5698, San Pablo 1182/Morandé 791), but the rooms are insecure – store your valuables safely. Even more central, on a cul-de-sac near the corner of Moneda and Amunátegui, **Residencial Tabita** (☎ 671 5700, fax 696 9492, Príncipe de Gales 81) charges US$13 per person with shared bath, US$15 with private bath, but has had its share of negative comments. At the slowly declining **Hotel España** (☎ 698 5245, Morandé 510) rates for singles/doubles start around US$11/16 with shared bath, US$16/20 with private bath for clean but stark rooms, some of them dark and with balky plumbing. Watch the surcharge on credit cards.

In stylish Barrio París Londres, south of the Alameda near Iglesia San Francisco (Ⓜ Universidad de Chile), popular **Residencial Londres** (☎/fax 638 2215, Londres 54) is an outstanding value at US$11 per person with hot water, clean and secure rooms with shared bath and a pleasant and helpful staff. Rates with private bath are only slightly higher. Make reservations or arrive early, since it fills up quickly – singles are almost impossible to get. If nothing's available, try around the corner at **Hotel París** (☎ 639 4037, París 813), where small but clean and comfy rooms with private bath start at US$16/24; some of these lack windows, but better, more spacious rooms with cable TV and other luxuries go for US$24/32 and up.

Barrio Brasil & Vicinity (Map 6)

Hostels On the Santiago Centro side of the boundary, about 10 minutes south of the Estación Central by *micro* (small bus), American-run **SCS Habitat** (☎ 683 3732, San Vicente 1798) is a cramped but still cheap and popular lodging in a quiet but fairly inconvenient neighborhood. Rates are US$7 to US$10 per person with an abundant breakfast.

Santiago's custom-built **Hostelling International** facility (☎ 671 8532, 688 6434, fax 672 8880, histgoch@entelchile.net, Cienfuegos 151) has a convenient Barrio Brasil location (Ⓜ Los Héroes). Rates for the 120 beds, in four- and six-bed rooms with locking closets, are US$10 per night for members, US$12.50 for nonmembers, but guests automatically become members after six nights. There are ample common areas, including a much-improved cafeteria, TV lounge and patio, and quick, inexpensive laundry service. If the hostel is not crowded, it's possible to have a single or double room for just a small additional charge.

Residenciales Highly recommended **Residencial del Norte** (☎ 695 1876, fax 696 9251, Catedral 2207) charges US$10 per person, with shared bath and breakfast, in a family atmosphere (Ⓜ Santa Ana or República); rooms are plain, clean and spacious, with ample furniture and balconies, but some beds are soft, and the numerous micros passing nearby make some noise – as do occasional evangelical gatherings across the street, which, mercifully, end early.

On the main metro line, the aging but still recommended **Residencial Alemana** (☎ 671 2388, Avenida República 220) charges US$14 per person with shared bath, US$19/31 for singles/doubles with private bath (Ⓜ República). Nearby, in a big old house that's been partitioned into some small but nevertheless sunny rooms, **Residencial Mery** (☎ 696 8883, Pasaje República 36) enjoys a surprisingly quiet location in a small alleyway just off the Alameda. Rates are US$14/26, but breakfast is extra.

Providencia (Map 8)

The only budget accommodations in the entire comuna, **Residencial Salvador** (☎ 223 9221, fax 204 6256, Avenida Salvador 297) is well worn and past its prime, but try finding anything else here for US$18 (single) with breakfast. It's passable, but there are better values in Barrio Brasil. Las Condes and Vitacura have no budget accommodations whatsoever.

PLACES TO STAY – MID-RANGE

Santiago's mid-range accommodations are sometimes better value than its budget selection. Many of these hotels have small but agreeable rooms with private bath; for a few bucks more there is often telephone, TV and refrigerator.

Santiago Centro (Map 5)

Tacky but friendly **Hotel di Maurier** (☎ 695 7750, fax 696 6193, Moneda 1510) is convenient to the airport bus; rates for singles/doubles are US$25/33 with private bath but without breakfast. **Hotel Europa** (☎ 695 2448, fax 697 1378, Amunátegui 449) has small, simple but tidy rooms in excellent shape for US$30/35 with breakfast; discounts are possible for extended stays.

In an interesting neighborhood near Cerro Santa Lucía, well-maintained **Hotel Foresta** (☎/fax 639 6262, fax 632 2996, Subercaseaux 353) is a first-rate choice for US$33/46. Judgments differ on **Hotel Cervantes** (☎ 696 5318, Morandé 631), where some rooms are cramped, with lumpy beds, and others are bright and spacious. Rates are US$26/36 with private bath and breakfast; it also has a decent restaurant.

Friendly, well-located **Hotel Gran Palace** (☎ 671 2551, fax 695 1095, Huérfanos 1178) is quiet and tidy, starting around US$37/45 with breakfast and cable TV. Other respectable downtown choices include ragged **Hotel Panamericano** (☎ 672 3060, fax 696 4992, Teatinos 320), which is a bit noisy, for US$38/46, and **Hotel El Libertador** (☎ 639 4212, fax 633 7128, Alameda 853) with rooms at US$46/55.

On a cul-de-sac off Catedral between Teatinos and Morandé, the recommended **Hotel Metrópoli** (☎ 672 3987, Sótero del Río 465) has worn but clean and comfortable rooms with private bath for US$41/49, though opinions are mixed. Try also the professionally run **City Hotel** (☎/fax 695 4526, Compañía 1063) for US$41/50, or the pleasant, better-located **Hotel Riviera** (☎ 633 1176, Miraflores 106), where smallish rooms cost US$43/50.

One of the best mid-range choices is **Hotel Montecarlo** (☎ 639 2945, fax 633 5577, Subercaseaux 209), opposite Cerro Santa Lucía. Rooms are small but cheery, all have private (if tiny) baths, and the staff are friendly, but be prepared for noise from the busy street; rates are US$43/50. Despite a slightly cheesy remodeling job, cheerful **Hotel Las Vegas** (☎ 632 2498, fax 632 5084, Londres 49) remains one of Santiago's better mid-range bargains for clean, spacious rooms at US$43/51, but breakfast costs US$6 extra.

Hotel Santa Lucía (☎ 639 8201, fax 633 1844, Huérfanos 779, 4th floor) is also a good value for US$50/60; rooms are attractive, with TV, telephóne, strongbox, refrigerator and private bath. While the street below can be noisy, double-paned windows make the rooms nearly soundproof.

Barrio Brasil (Map 6)

With spacious gardens and an English-speaking owner who exchanges books, **Hotel Turismo Japón** (☎ 698 4500, Almirante Barroso 160) is an excellent value at US$35/45 with breakfast, though it can get a little cool in winter. Some rooms are small at **Hotel Ducado** (☎ 696 9384, fax 695 1271, Agustinas 1990), but it's a good and friendly place charging US$35/45.

Highly regarded **Hotel Conde Ansurez** (☎ 699 6368, 696 0807, fax 697 0126, ansurez@ cepri.cl, Avenida República 25) offers European atmosphere for US$50/60 with buffet breakfast. The rooms are relatively small but well kept; those away from the street are noticeably quieter (Ⓜ República).

Barrio Bellavista (Map 7)

Accommodations of any kind are scarce in Bellavista, but **Hotel Parlamento** (☎ 735 2401, fax 777 1784, Avenida Santa María 281) is a three-star choice charging US$50/60. The busy thoroughfare is noisy during the day, but it's just far enough from the bar-and-restaurant scene that evenings and nights are fairly placid.

Providencia (Map 8)

Hotel Flores (☎/fax 264 2248, Antonio Varas 423) is a friendly, well-located, family-run place that's a bargain by Providencia standards – US$43 single or double, after IVA discounts. There's one small single available for US$30 (**M** Manuel Montt).

Another good, family-run value is *Hotel Lyon* (☎ *225 7732, fax 225 8697, lyon@entelchile.net, Avenida Ricardo Lyon 1525)*, a 15-room facility in a pleasant neighborhood. English, German and Spanish are spoken; rates start at US$65/75 with breakfast, but it also has a small nearby residencial charging only US$36/43.

The wood-paneled rooms at the remarkably congenial *Hotel Posada del Salvador* (☎ *235 9450, 251 8697, posatel@interactiva.cl, Eliodoro Yáñez 893)* are a bit dark but also spacious and quiet (thanks to double-paned windows); rates are US$40/51 with breakfast. The staff can manage English, German, French and Italian. The modern but attractive *Hotel María Angola* (☎ *235 1280, fax 235 5914, Halmaro@entelchile.net, Miguel Claro 425)* is a medium-size hotel with an airy dining room for breakfast and other meals; rates are US$54/60, including breakfast.

Opposite the Parque de las Esculturas near the Pedro de Valdivia Bridge, the cozy *Hotel Santa María* (☎ *232 3376, fax 231 6287, hotelsantamaria@entelchile.net, Avenida Santa María 2050)* is an excellent value for US$60/70 with breakfast. Suites with a sofa bed that could accommodate another person are an even better value at US$80.

Tiny (only eight rooms) but modern and well-equipped, *Hostal Thayer* (☎ *233 9703, fax 233 7022, Luis Thayer Ojeda 746)* occupies a quiet residential site in Providencia. Rates are US$65/75 for cozy, comfortable rooms with breakfast (**M** Tobalaba).

Nice-looking *Hotel Holley* (☎ *231 6931, General Holley 2284)* has 20 smallish but spotlessly comfy rooms for US$70/83, including a continental breakfast on the 4th-floor terrace, cable TV and in-room strongbox, but if you expect peace and quiet in this barhoppers' neighborhood, choose an interior room, especially on weekends,. There's a 10% discount for cash.

Las Condes (Map 9)

Mid-range accommodations are scarce in Las Condes, but *Hotel Irazú* (☎ *220 5941,*

Noruega 6340) is a bargain for this part of town, charging US$55/60 with buffet breakfast; it discounts IVA only for those paying cash dollars. Rooms are plain but comfortable and quiet, and there's a cluster of decent-looking restaurants within walking distance – as well as Cine Las Condes for movies and Cosmocentro Apumanque for shopping.

PLACES TO STAY – TOP END

Santiago has many expensive, first-rate hotels, including well-known international chains. Most provide gourmet restaurants, cafés, bars and money exchange services for their clients. All of them have English-speaking staff, and most handle other languages as well, usually French, German or Portuguese.

Many of these are in the upscale eastern boroughs of Providencia, Las Condes and Vitacura, but several are downtown as well. The rates indicated below are rack rates, but hardly anybody ever pays these – with reservations, or sometimes just by asking, it's possible to do better, especially toward the upper end of the category.

Santiago Centro (Map 5)

Some of the better values are in the lower end of the range, such as *Hotel El Conquistador* (☎/*fax 696 5599, Miguel Cruchaga 920)*, on a passageway off Paseo Estado near the Alameda, starting at US$67 single or double. For US$75/86, *Majestic Hotel* (☎ *695 8366, fax 697 4051, Santo Domingo 1526)*, which has been recommended, has fine service, but it's close to the Vía Norte Sur freeway and lacks air-con for hot days.

Glittering *Hotel Galerías* (☎ *361 1911, fax 633 0821, San Antonio 65)*, a block from the Alameda, has rooms from US$80/90, breakfast included, and features a swimming pool. Near Plaza Mulato Gil de Castro, alongside the Instituto Chileno-Francés, the business-oriented *Hostal del Parque* (☎ *639 2694, fax 639 2754, Merced 294)* charges US$99/110 for rooms with kitchenettes, and includes airport transportation.

Hotel Tupahue (☎ *638 3810, fax 639 2899, San Antonio 477)* charges US$110/120, including continental breakfast, but the air-con is suspect and it's a lesser value than some other places in this range. The well-located **Hotel Fundador** (☎ 632 2566, hotelfundador@ hotelfundador.cl, Paseo Serrano 34), on a quiet pedestrian mall but still close to the Alameda in Barrio París Londres, charges US$150/170 with breakfast; this modern hotel has classic touches like the stylish woodwork in the lobby, but also boasts a business center, pool and gym. Rooms at the **Holiday Inn Crowne Plaza** (☎ 638 1042, fax 633 6015, Alameda 136) start at US$189/260; the hotel has offices, shops, a gym and pool, car rentals and a post office.

Charging US$240/260, the **Hotel Plaza San Francisco** (☎ 639 3832, fax 639 7826, fcohotel@entelchile.net, Alameda 816) is a tastefully luxurious five-star facility that takes pride in having hosted guests like Mikhail Gorbachev, Mia Farrow and the Dalai Lama – not to mention LP founder Tony Wheeler.

At the venerable **Hotel Carrera** (☎ 698 2011, fax 672 1083, hotel.carrera@chilnet.cl, Teatinos 180), overlooking Plaza de la Constitución, rates start at US$260 for a double. It was from here, in 1985, that deadly serious opponents of the Pinochet dictatorship aimed a time-delay bazooka at the general's office at La Moneda – the recoil, however, was too strong for the photo tripod on which it rested, and the explosion destroyed the hotel room's interior instead.

Providencia (Map 8)

On the western edge of the borough, enthusiastically recommended **Hotel Principado** (☎ 222 8142, fax 222 6065, Avenida Vicuña Mackenna 30) charges US$68/79 (Ⓜ Baquedano). The 50-room **Hotel Los Españoles** (☎ 232 1824, fax 233 1048, Los Españoles 2539) charges US$80 per double with breakfast; it has free email and 24-hour room service.

In a well-preserved older building, **Hotel Orly** (☎ 231 8947, fax 252 0051, Avenida Pedro de Valdivia 027) recalls the Providencia of less commercial times; for US$84/95, rooms are a little small, but the hospitable staff are a big plus (Ⓜ Pedro de Valdivia). **Hotel Neruda** (☎ 231 0010, fax 231 1007,

Avenida Pedro de Valdivia 164) has rooms for US$120/130 with breakfast.

A fine value is the newish **Hotel Diego de Velásquez** (☎/fax 234 4400, Diego de Velásquez 2141), at US$110/125, including a room-service US-style breakfast, cable TV and other services (Ⓜ Pedro de Valdivia or Los Leones). Charging US$131/152 with a buffet breakfast, the modern **Hotel Aloha** (☎ 233 2230, fax 233 2494, Francisco Noguera 146) has accommodating English-speaking personnel (Ⓜ Pedro de Valdivia).

Rates at the **Sheraton San Cristóbal** (☎ 233 5000, fax 234 1729, sheraton@ chilepac.net, Avenida Santa María 1742), north of the Mapocho, start at US$210 (double) for luxurious rooms furnished with antiques, complemented by spacious baths; it also has the best gardens of any luxury hotel in town. The **Santiago Park Plaza** (☎ 233 6363, fax 233 6668, pplaza@netline.cl, Avenida Ricardo Lyon 207) charges US$230/240 for elegant, European-style rooms; its lobby is outfitted with antiques, Persian rugs and other lavish elements (Ⓜ Los Leones).

On a quiet block, the French-run **Eurotel** (☎/fax 251 6111, eurotel@ctc-mundo.net, Guardia Vieja 285), has small but impeccable singles/doubles for US$89 with breakfast, but their more spacious junior suites are a better value at US$103.

For US$160/170 and up with a buffet breakfast, the well-furnished rooms at **Hotel Torremayor** (☎/fax 234 2000, restorre@ panamericanahoteles.cl, Avenida Ricardo Lyon 322) are a bit smaller than others in that price range (Ⓜ Los Leones).

Recently remodeled and expanded to give it a lighter, airier, Mediterranean feel, the four-star **Hotel Bonaparte** (☎ 274 0621, fax 204 8907, hotel.bonaparte@entelchile.net, Avenida Ricardo Lyon 1229) has spacious, comfortable rooms in a good neighborhood for US$94/104. There's a small pool at the back of this mostly business-oriented hotel.

Rates at the **Hotel Embassy Suites** (☎/fax 341 7575, embassy@entelchile.net, Avenida Condell 40) range from US$175 to US$220 singles/doubles, including buffet breakfast, for spacious, well-appointed rooms with spectacular panoramas of the cordillera from the upper floors. It also has a spa, a business center and a free cocktail hour from 6 to 8 pm.

Las Condes & Vitacura (Map 9)

The quality of upscale accommodations in these eastern comunas is generally excellent, and should satisfy nearly everybody. At small but sparkling *Hotel Montebianco* (☎ 233 0427, fax 233 0420, Isidora Goyenechea 2911), rates start at US$83/105 for air-conditioned rooms with TV, telephone, continental breakfast and attractive attached patios. Unlike most of the hotels in this area, it is *not* a high-rise, so it lacks views (but not comforts). It's also close to many fine restaurants.

At the east end of Avenida Vitacura, *Hotel Acacias de Vitacura* (☎ 211 8601, fax 212 7858, acacias@ctcreuna.cl, El Manantial 1781) is a one-of-a-kind, mid-size (37 rooms), family-run hotel set on a cul-de-sac among expansive wooded grounds, with a large pool, a gym and a collection of antique machinery including a steam-powered locomotive. The common areas are also furnished with museum pieces, while the rooms themselves are spacious and comfortable, each with a balcony or small patio; rates are around US$84/92, but there are a couple smaller rooms for US$74 and suites for US$184.

Charging US$90/108, *Hotel Río Bidasoa* (☎ 242 1525, fax 228 9798, bidasoa@entelchile .net, Avenida Vitacura 4873) has expansive gardens and a large pool, but some of the rooms are smaller than one might expect in a four-star hotel. Still, in this part of town, the price isn't out of line.

The business-oriented *Hotel Tarapacá* (☎ 233 2747, fax 245 1440, tarapacá@ chilnet.cl, Vecinal 40) is a modern 53-room hotel with cable TV, and laundry and room service, midway between the Tobalaba and El Golf metro stations. Rates are US$110/120. More geared toward tour groups, its sister *Hotel Parinacota* (☎ 246 2788, fax 220 5386, parinacota@chilnet.cl, Avenida Apoquindo 5142) charges the same rates.

Affiliated with the Best Western chain, the *Hotel Director* (☎ 207 1580, fax 228 7503, dire1000@netline.cl, Avenida Vitacura 3600) is an excellent value from US$115/125 including buffet breakfast; rooms are very spacious, including the baths and walk-in closets. Rates at the faux-Roman-style *Hotel Leonardo da Vinci* (☎/fax 206 0591, fax 208 6629, criin@ctc-mundo.net, Málaga 194) start at US$150/170, including a buffet breakfast, but substantial discounts are possible; some rooms have Internet access. Its restaurant is the Ponte Vecchia (three guesses what sort of food it serves and the first two don't count).

Resembling many of Las Condes' other upscale hotels in its services, the new and elegant *Hotel Regal Pacific* (☎ 229 4000, fax 229 4005, regalpac@entelchile.net, Avenida Apoquindo 5680) starts at US$215/225. It has a fitness club and two restaurants, one Italian and the other Caribbean.

Hotel Kennedy (☎ 290 8100, fax 219 3272, hkennedy@ctcreuna.cl, Avenida Presidente Kennedy 4570) is a modern high-rise offering spacious rooms (some with walk-in closets), air-con, cable TV, a gym, swimming pool and the like; the baths are also large. Rates are US$230 for a single or double, including a buffet breakfast.

Rates at the massive *Radisson Royal Santiago Hotel* (☎ 203 6000, fax 337 3111, radisson@iusanet.cl, Avenida Vitacura 2610) start at US$260/271 singles/doubles with the usual luxuries, including a spa; it also offers cell phones for call forwarding while you're out of the room. The congenial staff help compensate for the sterile lobby, which is a poor approach to what are pleasant rooms with spectacular Andean vistas on clear days, or at least near sunset.

From US$265 single or double, but with frequent promotional prices, the expanding *Hotel Intercontinental Santiago* (☎ 234 2200, fax 251 7814, santiago@interconti.com, Luz 2920) can boast spacious, comfortably furnished rooms and a friendly staff. It also has an award-winning restaurant, the Carrara.

The *Hyatt Regency Santiago* (☎ 218 1234, fax 218 2279, hyattscl@chilepac.net, Avenida Presidente Kennedy 4601) has 310 rooms starting at US$310 single or double. It has a business center, tennis courts, gym, pool and the highly regarded restaurant Anakena. Some of the rooms are smaller than you might expect for the price, but the building's soaring interior is worth a look even for those who have no intention of staying here.

Santiago's tallest building, the 40-story *Marriott Hotel (☎ 426 2000, Avenida Presidente Kennedy 5741)* opened in early 2000.

LONG-TERM RENTALS

Finding a place to stay in Santiago is not difficult, but finding a good inexpensive place is not so easy. The obvious places to look are the twice-weekly classifieds tabloid *El Rastro* and the want ads pages of the daily *El Mercurio*.

Should you find a place to rent, be aware that, because of the slowly devaluating Chilean peso, rental contracts are based on a changing value called the Unidad de Fomento (UF), which was Ch$15,373 as of May 10, 2000 and had risen only about Ch$330 is the previous calendar year. Rents are expressed in numbers of UF.

Apart Hotels

A good option for longer stays, apart hotels are accommodations with cooking facilities, which usually have daily maid service and other motel-style amenities.

Bellavista's *Apart Hotel Monteverde (☎ 777 3607, fax 737 0341, Pío Nono 193)* is moderately priced and reasonably good for US$39/49, with breakfast, for rooms with kitchenettes that have microwaves. The barrio's hyperactive street life, however, can make sleep impossible Friday and Saturday nights (Map 7).

Apart Hotel La Sebastiana (☎ 232 7225, San Sebastián 2711), in Las Condes, caters to business travelers, with 16 nicely decorated apartments scattered throughout a high-rise, though most are near the 11th-floor office. Bedrooms and living rooms are spacious, with balconies, cable TV, radios with CD players and strongboxes; there are also full (if small) kitchens. Rates start at US$86 for a single (Ⓜ Tobalaba; Map 9).

Providencia's *Tempo Rent Apart Hotel (☎ 231 1608, fax 334 0374, tempo.rent@chilnet.cl, Santa Magadalena 116)* has immaculate hotel-style rooms starting at US$98 for a single or double, but spacious one-bedroom apartments with kitchen, living room and balcony are only slightly more at US$116 (Ⓜ Los Leones; Map 8).

Affiliated with the Best Western chain, the 49-suite *Apart Hotel Director (☎ 246 0101, fax 231 1007, directap@tmm.cl, Carmencita 45)* charges from US$135/145 with buffet breakfast; amenities include a gym and sauna. All rooms have Internet connections (Ⓜ El Golf; Map 9).

Places To Eat

Downtown Santiago has an abundance of eateries ranging from the basic (especially around the bus terminals, the Huérfanos and Ahumada pedestrian malls, the Plaza de Armas and the Alameda) to the elegant. The best choices, though, are in and around Cerro Santa Lucía, Barrio Bellavista, and the eastern comunas of Providencia, Las Condes, Vitacura and Ñuñoa.

Besides Chilean *parrillada* and seafood, and lots of Peruvian choices, there are many French, Italian and Chinese restaurants. But the variety also includes, among others, Indian, Middle Eastern, Mexican (both Tex-Mex and regional cuisine), Brazilian, German, Spanish and Thai. Sernatur's free publications offer some idea of this formidable range, but the *Centro* volume of Telefónica's Turistel series also has comprehensive and systematic listings.

There are many budget eateries in the downtown area, but it's possible to find a good inexpensive meal in almost any part of the city. Note that even some expensive restaurants have moderately priced lunches on weekdays, so it's often possible to sample some very fine places at moderate cost. This practice is less common on weekends.

Mid-range restaurants can cost anywhere from US$5 to US$15 for main dishes but, again, there are often bargain lunches. Meals in top-end restaurants are usually US$15 or more.

FOOD

From the Tropics to the Pole, Chile's varied cuisine features seafood, beef, fresh fruit and vegetables. Upwelling of the waters from the Pacific Ocean's cool Humboldt Current sustains a cornucopia of fish and shellfish for Chilean kitchens, while Middle Chile's fields, orchards and pastures fill the table with superb produce.

Chilean restaurants range from hole-in-the-wall snack bars to sumptuous international venues. Most cities feature a central market with many small, cheap restaurants –

usually known as *cocinerías* or *comedores* – of surprisingly high quality. Nearly every sizable town also has a *casino de bomberos* (fire station restaurant) with excellent, inexpensive meals.

There are several categories of eating establishments. Bars serve snacks and both alcoholic and nonalcoholic drinks, while *fuentes de soda* are similar but do not serve alcohol. *Cafeterías* serve modest meals; *hosterías* are more elaborate and usually located outside the main cities – they're often popular for weekend outings. A *salón de té* is not quite literally a teahouse but is a bit more upscale than a cafetería. While full-fledged *restaurantes* are technically distinguished by quality and service, this distinction is less than exact, and the term is generally applied to every category of establishment. Almost all serve alcoholic and nonalcoholic drinks.

One category unique to Chile is the *picada*, a family establishment that often begins informally and, because of its quality, acquires a following that enables it to flourish and even expand. Many if not most picadas are in coastal resorts, but they're not uncommon in Santiago. Chileans often abbreviate the term to *picá*.

Except in strictly family establishments like picadas, it is customary – and expected – to leave a 10% tip (some of the more elaborate picadas do expect tipping). The menu is *la carta*; the bill is *la cuenta*.

Breakfast

Breakfast *(desayuno)* often consists of toast *(pan tostado)* with butter *(mantequilla)* or jam *(mermelada)* and tea *(té)*; eggs or sandwiches are also common. *Huevos fritos* are fried eggs, usually served in a *paila* (small frying pan). *Huevos revueltos* are scrambled eggs, *huevos pasados* are boiled eggs, and *huevos a la copa* are poached eggs. *Bien cocidos* means well cooked and *duros* means hard-boiled.

Lunch & Dinner

Many places offer a cheap set meal *(comida corrida* or *almuerzo del día)* for lunch *(almuerzo* or *colación)* and, less often, for dinner *(cena)*. Some of the most common dishes are listed in this chapter, but there are many other possibilities. Do not hesitate to ask waitstaff for an explanation of any dish.

Lunch can be the biggest meal of the day. Set menus tend to be almost identical at cheaper restaurants, generally consisting of *cazuela*, a stew of potato or maize with a piece of beef or chicken, a main course of rice with chicken or meat, and a simple dessert. Soup is *caldo* or *sopa*. *Porotos* (beans) are a common budget entrée, but there are more elaborate versions with a variety of vegetables and condiments. One of Chile's most delicious and filling traditional dishes is *pastel de choclo*, a maize casserole filled with vegetables and chicken and/or beef, but this may be available only during the summer maize harvest.

Snacks

Cheap and available almost everywhere, one of the world's finest snacks is the *empanada*, a tasty turnover with vegetables, hard-boiled egg, olive, beef, chicken, ham and cheese or other filling. The most common fillings you'll find, however, are *pino* (ground beef) and *queso* (cheese). Empanadas *al horno* (baked) are lighter than empanadas *fritas* (fried). Travelers arriving from Argentina will find the Chilean empanada larger and more filling than its Argentine counterpart, so don't order a dozen for lunch or your bus trip.

Humitas are like Mexican tamales – cornmeal wrapped in husks and steamed; when served in this manner they are *humitas en chala* – a popular and tasty snack. There are numerous breads, including *chapalele*, made with potatoes and flour and boiled; *milcao*, another type of potato bread; and *sopaipa*, recognizable by its dark brown exterior, which is made from wheat flour and fruit, but not baked.

Pebre is a tasty condiment of chopped tomatoes, onion, garlic, chili peppers, cilantro and parsley, usually spread on bread.

Sandwiches are popular snacks throughout the day. Among sandwich fillings, *churrasco* (steak), *jamón* (ham) and queso are the most widely available. Cold ham and cheese make an *aliado*, while a sandwich with ham and melted cheese constitutes a *Barros Jarpa*

It's What's for Dinner

Beef, in a variety of cuts and styles of preparation, is the most popular main course at *parrillas* – restaurants that grill everything from steak to sausages over charcoal. The *parrillada* proper is an assortment of steak and other cuts that will appall vegetarians and heart specialists. A traditional parrillada will include offal like *chunchules* (small intestines), *tripa gorda* (large intestine), *ubre* (udder), *riñones* (kidneys) and *morcilla* (blood sausage). A token green salad *(ensalada)* will usually accompany the meal.

The biggest standard meal in Chile is *lomo a lo pobre*, an enormous slab of beef topped with two fried eggs and buried in french fries (you may wish to monitor your cholesterol level before and after eating). *Ajiaco* is a spiced beef stew that, traditionally, uses a variety of leftovers. Many restaurants of all kinds offer *pollo con papas fritas* (chicken with fries) and *pollo con arroz* (chicken with rice).

(named after a Chilean painter known for consuming them in large quantities). A steak sandwich with melted cheese is a *Barros Luco*, the favorite of former President Ramón Barros Luco (1910–15). Beefsteak with tomato and other vegetables is a *chacarero*.

Seafood

What really distinguishes Chilean cuisine is its varied seafood, among the world's most diverse. Popular seafood dishes include the delicious *sopa de mariscos*, or *cazuela de mariscos*, which is actually more of a shellfish stew than a soup. *Paila marina* is a fish and shellfish chowder, while *sopa de pescado* is fish soup. Try *chupe de cóngrio* (conger eel stew) or, if available, *chupe de locos* (abalone stew), both cooked in a thick sauce of butter, breadcrumbs, cheese and spices. Locos, however, may be in *veda* (quarantine) because of overexploitation.

Do not overlook the simple market restaurants at venues like Santiago's Mercado Central. Some dishes, like *erizos* (sea urchins) are acquired tastes, but they will rarely upset your stomach. Do insist on all shellfish being thoroughly cooked, which is obligatory since the cholera scare of 1991–92; even the traditional *ceviche* (marinated raw fish or shellfish) must now be cooked, although it is still served cold.

The following are a few seafood terms worth knowing:

clams	*almejas*
crab	*cangrejo* or *jaiva*
fish	*pescado*
giant barnacle	*picoroco*
king crab	*centolla*
mussels	*cholgas*
octopus	*pulpo*
oysters	*ostras*
prawns	*camarones grandes*
razor clams	*machas*
scallops	*ostiones*
sea urchins	*erizos*
shellfish	*mariscos*
shrimp	*camarones*
squid	*calamares*

Many basic restaurants prepare their fish by frying in heavy oil, which besides its dietary shortcomings also destroys the flavor; on request, though, most will prepare fish *al vapor* (steamed) or *a la plancha* (grilled).

Vegetarian

While most Chileans are carnivores, vegetarianism is no longer the mark of an eccentric. Santiago has some excellent vegetarian fare, but, other than in strictly vegetarian restaurants, you may have to make a special request. If presented with meat that you don't want, it may help to claim allergy *(alergia)*.

Markets have a wide variety of fruit and vegetables – produce from the Chilean heartland reaches the limits of the republic and overseas. Remember that agricultural regulations forbid importing fruit from foreign countries, including neighboring Argentina.

Desserts

Dessert *(postre)* is commonly fresh fruit or *helado* (ice cream). The latter has improved greatly over the past several years, at least at those ice creameries featuring *elaboración artesanal* (small-scale rather than industrial production). Also try *arroz con leche* (rice pudding), *flan* (egg custard) and *tortas* (cakes). In the southern lakes region, Chileans of German descent bake exquisite *kuchen* (pastries) filled with local fruit, and these desserts make occasional appearances in the capital.

Fast Food

Fast-food restaurants are mostly inferior clones of Kentucky Fried Chicken or Mc-Donalds, although these foreign franchises are themselves increasingly common. Except at better Italian restaurants, pizzas are generally small, greasy and inferior. The nationwide Dino's and Bavaria chains offer passable standard fare.

Chile's cheapest fast food is the *completo*, a hot dog with absolutely everything (including a massive cholesterol infusion).

DRINKS
Non-Alcoholic Drinks
Soft Drinks & Water Chileans guzzle prodigious amounts of soft drinks, from the ubiquitous Coca-Cola to 7 Up, Sprite and sugary local brands such as Bilz. Mineral water, both carbonated *(con gas)* and plain *(sin gas)*, is widely available, but tap water is potable almost everywhere. The most popular mineral waters are Cachantún and Chusmiza, but others are equally good.

Fruit Juices & Licuados *Jugos* (juices) are varied and excellent. Besides the common *naranja* (orange), *toronja* (grapefruit) and *limón* (lemon), others available include *damasco* (apricot), *piña* (pineapple), *mora* (blackberry), *frambuesa* (raspberry), *maracuyá* (passion fruit) and *sandía* (watermelon). The distinctively Chilean *mote con huesillo* is a peach nectar with barley kernels, sold by countless street vendors but closely monitored for hygiene.

Licuados are milk-blended fruit drinks, but on request can be made with water. Common flavors are *banana*, *durazno* (peach) and *pera* (pear). Unless you like yours *very* sweet, ask them to hold the sugar *('sin azúcar, por favor')*.

Coffee & Tea While the situation is improving, Chilean coffee will dismay serious caffeine addicts. Except in upscale restaurants and specialized coffee bars like Café Haití and Café Caribe (which serve espresso), semisoluble Nescafé is the norm. *Café con leche* is literally milk with coffee – a teaspoon of coffee dissolved in hot milk. *Café solo* (coffee only) or *café negro* (black coffee) is coffee with hot water alone.

Likewise, *té con leche* is a teabag submerged in lukewarm milk. Tea is normally served black, with at least three packets of sugar. If you prefer just a touch of milk, a custom that most Chileans find bizarre, it's easier to ask for *un poquito de leche* later rather than try to explain your eccentric habits in advance.

Yerba mate ('Paraguayan tea') is consumed much more widely in the River Plate countries of Argentina, Uruguay and Paraguay than in Chile, but some Chilean supermarkets do carry it. Chileans do consume herbal teas *(aguas)* such as *manzanilla* (chamomile), *rosa mosqueta* and *boldo* in considerable quantities.

Alcoholic Drinks
Wines By consensus, Chilean wines are South America's best and rate among the finest in the world; reds *(tintos)* and whites *(blancos)* are both excellent. Middle Chile's *zona de regadío* produces the country's best-known wines, mostly Cabernet Sauvignon and other reds planted under French tutelage in the 19th century. Acreages planted to whites like Chardonnay and Riesling are increasing. Many major wineries in this zone lack sufficient acreage to produce the quantity they require and buy quality grapes on contract.

Major labels include Concha y Toro (and its subsidiary Santa Emiliana), Undurraga, Cousiño Macul, Errázuriz Panquehue, Ochagavía, Santa Rita, Santa Carolina, San Pedro Canepa, Manquehue, Tarapacá and Carmen. An increasing number of these wineries are open to the public, but wine tourism is still not an everyday activity as it is in, say, California or France. The Internet news digest *Santiago Times* is currently preparing a guide to 80 Chilean wineries open to the public, many of them in and around Santiago.

Other Alcoholic Drinks Chile's table wines should satisfy most visitors' alcoholic thirst, but don't refrain from trying the tasty but powerful pisco, often served in the form of a pisco sour, with lemon juice, egg white and powdered sugar. It may also be served with ginger ale *(chilcano)* or vermouth *(capitán)*.

Escudo is the best bottled beer *(cerveza)* and Cristal the most popular, but Becker has recently gained popularity and imported varieties are also available. Bars and restaurants commonly sell draft beer (known as *chopp* and pronounced 'shop'), which is cheaper than bottled beer and often better.

Guinda is a cherrylike fruit that is the basis of *guindado*, a fermented alcoholic drink with brandy, cinnamon and clove. A popular holiday drink is the powerful but deceptively sweet *cola de mono* ('tail of the monkey'), which consists of *aguardiente* (cane alcohol), coffee, clove and vanilla.

SANTIAGO CENTRO & VICINITY (MAP 5)
Budget
Avoid greasy McDonalds clones like Burger Inn or Max Beef (for that matter, avoid Mc-Donalds). For cheap snacks, pastries and drinks there's a string of stand-up places in the Portal Fernández Concha on the south side of the Plaza de Armas, serving items like completos, sandwiches and fried chicken with fries. For lunch, one of Santiago's best choices is the Mercado Central, a few blocks north of the Plaza de Armas, where various locales offer a wealth of tremendous seafood choices – be adventurous. Its lively atmosphere makes the historic building worth visiting in its own right, while the food is often a bargain. The most obviously appealing places are those like ***Donde Augusto*** (☎ 672 2829, *Mercado Central, Local 66 & 166*), picturesquely set among the central fruit and vegetable stands, but such restaurants are not dramatically better than the smaller, cheaper places on the periphery.

Serving Chilean specialties like pastel de choclo, ***Bar Nacional 1*** (☎ 695 3368, *Bandera 317*) is a lunchtime favorite with downtown office workers. ***Bar Nacional 2*** (☎ 696 5986, *Huérfanos 1151*) is a nearby branch. For Italian fast food, try ***Pizza Napoli*** (☎ 633 0845, *Paseo Estado 149*).

Downtown's ***El Puente de Bórquez*** (☎ 633 4021, *Miraflores 443*) has inexpensive Peruvian lunches and dinners. Japanese restaurants tend to be expensive, yet the unprepossessing ***Izakaya Yoko*** (☎ 632 1954, *Merced 456*) manages to provide excellent, filling meals for around US$5 to US$6 without drinks, which are also reasonably priced.

For *onces* (afternoon tea), juices and sandwiches, a good central place is ***100% Natural*** (☎ 697 1860, *Valentín Letelier 1319*), directly west of the Palacio de La Moneda. ***Au Bon Pain*** (☎ 632 1688, *Miraflores 235*),

the North American chain, has sandwiches and croissants. ***Bavaria*** (☎ 698 3723, *Paseo Bulnes 178*) is one of Chile's better nationwide chains, serving sandwiches, beef and chicken.

With an oddball automotive décor, ***El Mesón de Fanor*** (☎ 695 6826, *Fanor Velasco 40*) is an informal pub-style spot with buffet lunches around US$4, not to mention a Friday happy hour from 6 to 9 pm (Ⓜ Los Héroes).

For inexpensive espresso and cocoa, go to any of the several stand-up bars, such as ***Café Haití*** (*Ahumada 140*), ***Café Caribe*** (*Ahumada 120*), almost next door, or ***Café Cousiño*** (*Matías Cousiño 107*), all of which have many other branches around town. Some women feel uncomfortable at these coffee bars, colloquially referred to as *café con piernas* (coffee with legs), since most of them attract male clientele by dressing their young female staff in tight, revealing minidresses.

Mid-Range
In the arcade on the south side of the Plaza de Armas, the very traditional ***Chez Henry*** (☎ 696 6612, *Portal Fernández Concha 962*) is not inexpensive, but neither is it outrageous – for about US$6 their famous pastel de choclo is the only meal you'll need all day (portions are huge). Other dishes are more expensive, but selective diners can still eat well at moderate prices, and ready-made items from the take-away deli are cheaper and no less appealing.

Carnivores can try ***El Novillero*** (☎ 699 1544, *Moneda 1145*). Popular with santiaguinos, ***Bar Central*** (*San Pablo 1063*) serves generous portions of excellent seafood. For Chinese food, try enthusiastically recommended ***Kam-Thu*** (☎ 639 9511, *Santo Domingo 769*).

Just south of the Mapocho, at the foot of Cerro Santa Lucía, several good restaurants are clustered in and around Plaza del Mulato Gil de Castro, on Lastarria near Merced; at ***Pérgola de la Plaza*** (☎ 639 3604, *Lastarria 321*), the tasty lunch specials (about US$6) are great bargains. Renovated and used as artists' studios, the surrounding

Mary looks skyward from Cerro Santa Lucía

Palacio de la Real Audiencia, Plaza de Armas

Artistry and color ceilings the Palacio La Alhambra – now an art gallery and cultural center

Ornate façade of Palacio Iñíguez – one of Santiago's many early 20th-century palaces – on the Alameda

Cementerio General, a treasure trove of art

More funerary art, Cementerio General

KRYSZTOF DYDYNSKI

KRYSZTOF DYDYNSKI

KRYSZTOF DYDYNSKI

buildings house a cluster of galleries and bookshops.

Alongside its namesake cinema, *Café del Biógrafo* (☎ 639 9532, *Villavicencio 398*) is a neighborhood hangout. Its US$5 lunches are excellent, as are the baguettes and the casual atmosphere, but service can be slow. *Don Victorino* (☎ 639 5263, *Lastarria 138*) is one of several venues that offer fine lunches at moderate prices, with an extensive but costlier dinner menu. Service is first-rate, and the atmosphere relaxed. In the same category are nearby *Gatopardo* (☎ 633 6420, *Lastarria 192*), which serves Bolivian food, and *Rincón Español* (☎ 633 9466, *Rosal 346*), with Mediterranean cuisine.

French cuisine is the rule at *Les Assassins* (☎ 638 4280, *Merced 297-B*), where outstanding fixed-price lunches cost only about US$7. It's better to go early or late for lunch, because it has fewer than 20 tables; the downstairs is tobacco-free. Don't miss the sushi at *Kintaro* (☎ 638 2448, *Monjitas 460*), a bargain compared with almost anywhere else in the world – taking advantage of Chile's varied finfish and shellfish, a portion large enough for two has recently gone up in price, but still only costs US$9.

Top End

Italian restaurants are good and numerous but surprisingly expensive, like *Da Carla* (☎ 633 3739, *MacIver 577*), *San Marcos* (☎ 633 6880, *Huérfanos 618*) and the classic *Le Due Torri* (☎ 633 3799, *San Antonio 258*). On the east side of Cerro Santa Lucía, *Squadritto* (☎ 632 2121, *Rosal 332*) is one of the city's top Italian venues, with prices to match.

Santiago has a growing number of outstanding Peruvian restaurants, the best of which is probably *Cocoa* (☎ 632 1272, *Lastarria 297*). It's fairly expensive but worth the splurge, with large and exquisite pisco sours and some of Santiago's best desserts as a bonus.

South of the Alameda, *Los Adobes de Argomedo* (☎ 222 2104, *Argomedo 411*) is a gaudy pseudo-folkloric restaurant-nightclub with stereotypical floor show entertainment, but the Chilean food is good and varied

(Ⓜ Santa Isabél; Map 5). Expect to pay around US$25 per person for the show and dinner with wine. Although it's huge, reservations are a good idea, at least on weekends.

BARRIO BRASIL (MAP 6)

West of the Via Norte Sur, Barrio Brasil's dining scene is a combination of older, traditional restaurants and newer, more innovative eateries that, at their best, rival Barrio Bellavista's in quality but are substantially cheaper. The nearest metro stations are Los Héroes and República.

Budget

Convenient to Santiago's youth hostel, *Pizzería Gigino* (☎ 698 2200, *Agustinas 2015*) keeps long hours, with standard pizza and pasta dishes for about US$5, but is also notable for a grossly mismatched collection of paintings covering virtually every open spot on the walls, imparting an undisciplined, informal atmosphere.

The new *Las Vacas Gordas* (☎ 697 1066, *Cienfuegos 280*) serves quality parrillada and pasta at below average prices, and drinks are cheap. *Tú y Yo* (☎ 696 4543, *Avenida Brasil 249*) is a neighborhood pub-restaurant with simple but good Chilean dishes.

Mid-Range

Ocean Pacific's (☎ 697 2413, *Avenida Ricardo Cumming 221*) is a reasonably priced, family-style seafood restaurant with friendly service and particularly good homemade bread, but the menu is misleading – many items listed are often not available. Nearby, slightly more expensive *Ostras Squella* (☎ 699 4883, *Ricardo Cumming 94*) also specializes in seafood, and usually has most of what appears on the menu.

Nearby are two branches of the popular seafood locale *Tongoy* (☎ 697 1144, *Bulnes 91*; ☎ 681 4329, *Bulnes 72*); despite inconsistencies, at their best they're very good, the former location more so than the latter.

Plaza Garibaldi (☎ 699 4278, *Moneda 2319*) has outstanding Mexican dishes, beers and margaritas, and an increasingly varied menu as santiaguinos gradually adapt to spicier food.

Though the quality's not so high as its counterparts at Cerro Santa Lucía and Bellavista, Santiago's best Peruvian bargain is *Puente de Chabuca* (☎ 696 7962, *Avenida Brasil 75*). It has changed its name four times in three-plus years without, however, altering typical lunches that include an appetizer, main course, wine and dessert for just US$6.

El Chachachá (☎ 699 4360, *Avenida Ricardo Cumming 536*) is a new Cuban restaurant that bears watching.

Chilean TV personality Mario Kreutzberger, popularly known as 'Don Francisco,' is the force behind *Estudio Gigante* (☎ 697 1727, *Catedral 1850*), named after his enormously popular Chilean (and international) TV show *Sábado Gigante*. Buffet lunches cost around US$12, dinners around US$20, US$6 for kids 12 and under. There are also many entertainment alternatives here.

Top End

Ostras Azócar (☎ 681 6109, 682 2293, *Bulnes 37*) is a traditional seafood restaurant, with delicate sauces and a complementary oyster appetizer, but it also serves meat. Prices are relatively high, but the quality is superb and the service impeccable.

Puro Chile (☎ 681 9355, *Maipú 363*) combines wildly imaginative, hip décor with upscale versions of Chilean specialties and outstanding, friendly service. It's popular with the arts crowd. *Los Buenos Muchachos* (☎ 698 0112, *Avenida Ricardo Cumming 1031*) is a Chilean favorite that doubles as a nightclub with elaborate floor shows.

BARRIO BELLAVISTA & VICINITY (MAP 7)

Full of Pablo Neruda's old haunts, Barrio Bellavista, north of the Mapocho, a short walk from the Baquedano metro station, is a great dining area (especially lively on weekends). Many, though not the least, restaurants line both sides of Pío Nono between the bridge and Plaza Caupolicán. There's an array of stylish new and generally expensive restaurants on the Providencia side of the barrio, while the Recoleta side has more traditional venues (along with its hyperactive nightlife).

Budget

El Antojo de Gauguin (☎ 737 0398, *Pío Nono 69*) is a good Middle Eastern eatery that's one of few places in the area to offer fixed-price lunches on Saturday. Down the block, *Al Karim* (☎ 737 8129, *Pío Nono 127*) serves kebabs and other Middle Eastern specialties.

La Venezia (☎ 737 0900, *Pío Nono 200*) is a moderately priced Chilean picada, but standards seem to be falling. Down the block, *Cristóforo* (☎ 737 7752, *Pío Nono 281*) serves Greek-Mediterranean food and has comfortable outdoor seating. Its reasonably priced *vaina doble* (a concoction of sherry or sweet wine, egg, sugar and cinnamon) packs a punch.

Café de la Dulcería Las Palmas (☎ 777 4586, *Antonia López de Bello 0190*) is worth a visit for fresh fruit juices and desserts, but the fixed-price lunches are mediocre. Argentine-run *Pizzas Gloria* (☎ 735 9968, *Dardignac 0188*) has quality pizza and pasta at bargain prices, primarily at lunchtime.

In Recoleta's Patronato district, a bit to the west, *El Rinconcito* (*Manzano at Eusebio Lillo*) is an economical Middle Eastern picada run by a Lebanese immigrant by way of Chicago – excellent for hummus, falafel and the like.

Mid-Range

Di Simoncelli (*Dardignac 197*) serves good pizza and modestly priced Italian lunches. *Armandita* (☎ 737 3409, *Pío Nono 108*) is an Argentine-style parrilla whose lomo a lo pobre (a typical Chilean dish; see 'It's What's for Dinner') is a good value for US$8 including french fries and juice or soft drink. The service can be sluggish, though.

Galindo (☎ 771 0116, *Dardignac 098*) is a traditional hangout for Bohemians and musicians, with sidewalk seating and Chilean food and sandwiches. *El Caramaño* (☎ 737 7043, *Purísima 257*) is a self-styled 'anti-restaurant' so informal that there's no sign outside (ring the bell to get in) and visitors scribble on the interior walls. It has fine Chilean food and friendly service. Across the street, *El Tallarín Gordo* (☎ 737 8567, *Purísima 254*) lags behind Bellavista's more innovative Italian locales. *El Rinconcito Peruano* (☎ 732 0076, *Antonia López de Bello 68*) can't match the distinction of elite Peruvian restaurants on the same block, but it's significantly cheaper, the quality's not bad and the service is attentive and friendly; whether it can survive such tough nearby competition is uncertain.

There are two branches of the Catalán-style *Tasca Mediterránea* (☎ 735 3901, *Purísima 165;* ☎ 737 1542, *Domínica 35*). The former has excellent fixed-price lunches, outstanding tapas, good service, an attached café-bookstore with an identical menu, and Bohemian atmosphere, while the latter is more of a dinner venue, specializing in dishes like paella and offering live jazz on weekends.

The intimate *Le Coq au Vin* (☎ 735 0755, *Antonia López de Bello 0110*) is a highly regarded, relatively moderate, French restaurant.

Mid-range Middle Eastern fare is available at *Omar Khayyam* (☎ 777 4129, *Avenida Perú 570*), the *Club Palestino* (*Avenida Perú 659*) and *El Amir Issa* (☎ 777 3651, *Avenida Perú 663*).

El Viejo Verde (☎ 732 0590, *Antonia López de Bello 94*) is a vegetarian restaurant whose punning name (literally, 'the old green one') idiomatically means 'dirty old man.' It also serves as a pub with live theater on weekends.

Top End

The outstanding Peruvian restaurant *Cocoa* (☎ 735 0634, *Antonia López de Bello 60*) has a branch on the Recoleta side. By no means inferior, in equally spectacular quarters across the street, is the equally Peruvian *El Otro Sitio* (☎ 777 3059, *Antonia López de Bello 53*). Another good Peruvian choice, though probably not quite so good a value, is *La Flor de la Canela* (☎ 777 1007, *Antonia López de Bello 125*), down the block, whose service is so rapid and attentive as to almost seem an affront, but there's a good tobacco-free section.

Rodizio (☎ 777 9240, *Bombero Núñez 388*) is a great-looking Brazilian parrilla, but even though it's an all-you-can-eat, the US$23 price tag will deter budget-watchers as well as dieters. Also a parrilla, *Eladio* (☎ 777 3337, *Pío Nono 241*) is the Bellavista branch of a longtime Santiago favorite.

Eneldo (☎ 732 0428, *Ernesto Pinto Lagarrigue 195*) serves seafood, but the best seafood choice, on the Providencia side, is *Azul Profundo* (☎ 738 0288, *Constitución 111*), whose elaborate maritime embellishments can be a distraction from the fine meals at admittedly premium prices.

Zen (☎ 737 9520, *Dardignac 0175*) has appealingly minimalist Japanese décor, but even the midday lunch, around US$10, is a lesser value than its Cerro Santa Lucía counterparts offer. So popular it sometimes has to close its doors (literally, until there's a free table), *Etniko* (☎ 732 0119, *Constitución 172*) serves reasonably good Japanese and Vietnamese food, but the noisy atmosphere is more like a bar than a restaurant.

The elaborate cinematic décor at *Muñeca Brava* (☎ 732 1338, *Mallinkrodt 170*) can sometimes overshadow the varied, outstanding menu and excellent service; prices are on the high side but not outrageous. Designed by the same architect as Azul Profundo, *Como Agua para Chocolate* (☎ 777 8740, *Constitución 88*) is an imaginative Mexican place painted in primary colors, with superb use of natural light, an interesting bar, and a menu conceived with help from the founder of Barrio Brasil's Plaza Garibaldi. They do fish very well, grilled lightly with tasty sauces.

Il Siciliano (☎ 737 2265, *Dardignac 0102*), the Italian version of all these new or newish upscale choices, matches Bellavista's other ethnic eateries in its surroundings; the US$10 lunches are good values with a choice of entrée, plus wine or juice and dessert, but the service is a little overpowering. *Acapela* (☎ 737 9340, *Loreto 509*) is another Italian eatery.

Sommelier (☎ 732 0034, *Dardignac 0163*) is a *very* upscale but surprisingly unpretentious Franco-Chilean restaurant that sometimes features live chamber music. The food is tasty and diverse, and the desserts exquisite – the almond mousse with raspberry sauce is to die for – but the service can be surprisingly casual and even amateurish for a restaurant that clearly has high aspirations.

Measuring the distance from Paris, *Kilomètre 11,680* (☎ 777 0410, *Dardignac 0145*) is a more casual, slightly less expensive locale that's also a wine bar (and consequently noisier than its more genteel counterpart down the block). Try the *filete a la crème chez nous*, a succulent beef dish with a white sauce, flanked by scalloped potatoes and a tomato-eggplant mélange.

Las Mañanitas (☎ 735 3742, *Antonia López de Bello 131*) is a Mexican venue that provides live mariachi music on weekends. The inconsistent *Cava Dardignac* (☎ 777 6268, *Dardignac 0181*) serves Portuguese cuisine, leaning toward meat but also including seafood.

PROVIDENCIA (MAP 8)
Budget
Some of the cheapest fixed-price lunches in town are at *Peters* (☎ 204 0124, *Marchant Pereira 132*); before 1 pm or after 3 pm weekdays, four-course meals, including a salad bar, cost only US$2.50 (Ⓜ Pedro de Valdivia).

For sandwiches and onces, one of Santiago's best traditional venues is *Liguria* (☎ 235 7914, *Avenida Providencia 1373*), also a hangout for actors (Ⓜ Manuel Montt). *Au Bon Pain* (☎ 233 6912, *Avenida Providencia 1936*) is part of a North American sandwich and baked goods chain that has several branches around town (Ⓜ Pedro de Valdivia).

For Italian fast food, try *Pizza Napoli* (☎ 225 6468, *Avenida 11 de Septiembre 1935*), near the Pedro de Valdivia metro station. Nearby *La Pizza Nostra* (☎ 231 9853, *Avenida Providencia 1975*) is only so-so. *Sbarro* (*Avenida Suecia 055*) is part of an Italian-style chain that sells food by weight; the selection is ample and the quality's not bad (Ⓜ Los Leones).

For fine ice cream and other desserts, a few places to try include *Sebastián* (☎ 231 9968, *Andrés de Fuenzalida 26*), midway between the Pedro de Valdivia and Los Leones metro stations; *Bravíssimo* (☎ 235 2511, *Avenida Providencia 1406*) near Manuel Montt station; and *La Escarcha* (*Avenida Providencia 1762*) near the Pedro de Valdivia metro station. The hands-down best ice creamery, though, is the classy Buenos Aires import *Freddo* (☎ 363 9911, *Avenida Providencia 2304*), which also does deliveries by moped (Ⓜ Los Leones).

Mid-Range
A perennial vegetarian favorite is *Café del Patio* (☎ 236 1251, *Providencia 1670, Local 8-A*), near the Manuel Montt metro station, but even nonvegetarians flock to *El Huerto* (☎ 233 2690, *Orrego Luco 054*), internationally renowned for imaginative meatless meals (Ⓜ Pedro de Valdivia). It's become more expensive, but the smaller menu at its adjacent café *La Huerta* offers quality food at lower prices.

Affiliated with Mexico's diplomatic mission, the *Casa de la Cultura de México* (☎ 334 3848, *Bucarest 162*) features outstanding regional dishes rather than Tex-Mex borderlands food; it also has superb crafts and a bookshop (Ⓜ Los Leones). In the same area, German food is the fare at *Der Münchner Hof* (☎ 233 2452, *Diego de Velásquez 2105*).

Homesick Brits will find good pub-style lunches for about US$7 to $8 at the *Phone Box Pub* (☎ 235 9972, *Avenida Providencia 1670*), whose grape arbor patio is a pleasant sanctuary from the busy avenue outside (Ⓜ Manuel Montt).

La Vera Pizza (☎ 232 1786, *Avenida Providencia 2630*) has good variety but is a bit pricey (Ⓜ Tobalaba). In the midst of a popular nightlife district, *Pizzería Morena* (☎ 231 8218, *Avenida Suecia 0120*) also has live music and dancing.

At *Rincón Brasileiro* (☎ 236 3475, *Avenida Manuel Montt 116*), the stress is more on meat than on some of the more diverse Brazilian cuisine. *Dos Cuates* (☎ 264 7376, *Avenida Manuel Montt 235*), down the block, is a mid-range Mexican place where maize tortillas are the rule rather than the exception. There's live mariachi music Thursday and Friday evenings and Saturday afternoon.

A new gastronomic axis is forming on and around Avenida Condell, where *Puerto Perú (☎ 363 9886, Avenida Condell 1298)* started as an informal family-style Peruvian restaurant and quickly became such a phenomenon that reservations are almost essential. The diverse menu nearly matches Bellavista's elite Peruvian eateries at far lower prices; portions are substantial, service attentive and the pisco sours tangy. Other restaurants in this area are just across the line in Ñuñoa; see Ñuñoa, later, for details.

Top End

Le Flaubert (☎ 231 9424, Orrego Luco 125) sometimes offers a weeknight *Cena del Vino*, a dinner with unlimited wine sampling, for US$25; it also has a tobacco-free area. *Trattoria Rivoli (☎ 231 7969, Nueva de Lyon 77)* has a huge, diverse pasta menu, an almost equally diverse variety of desserts and excellent service.

Aquí Está Coco (☎ 235 8649, La Concepción 236) is a seafood venue with conspicuously maritime décor, featuring items like crab cakes and corvina at upscale prices. So is nearby *Mare Nostrum (☎ 251 5691, La Concepción 281)*. *Eladio (☎ 231 4224, Avenida 11 de Septiembre 2250, 2nd floor)* is a Santiago institution for grilled meats.

LAS CONDES & VITACURA (MAP 9)
Budget

Near the Tobalaba metro station, as are most Las Condes restaurants, the complex of fast-food outlets at the *Food Garden (Avenida El Bosque Norte at Roger de Flor)* contains a number of decent, inexpensive eateries, including a branch of the Italian chain *Sbarro*, the juice bar *Jugomanía* and a good frozen-yogurt venue.

There are two of the North American bread and sandwich chain *Au Bon Pain (☎ 366 9145, Avenida El Bosque Norte 0177;*

☎ 331 5048, Avenida Apoquindo 3575). Though it imports nearly all its ingredients frozen, it's an exception to the rule that foreign franchises are not worth patronizing.

There are better choices, however, like *Café Melba (☎ 232 4546, Don Carlos 2988)*, which serves North American-style breakfasts all day, but is also a popular lunchtime choice. Another possibility is the *New York Bagel Bakery (☎ 246 3060, Roger de Flor 2894)*, which has a variety of bagels, cream cheeses and muffins.

Although the pun is reprehensible, popular *PubLicity (☎ 246 6414, Avenida El Bosque Norte 0155)* has excellent meals ranging from simple sandwiches to more elaborate fare. Recently reinvented as a Celtic venue, with Guinness on tap, the informal *Flannery's Irish Geo Pub (☎ 233 6675, Encomenderos 83)* has excellent lunches from US$5 to US$7 and is also a popular weekend hangout.

Mid-Range

TGIFriday's (☎ 334 4468, Isidora Goyenechea 3275) is a US import that's as much a pub as a place to eat. *Ruby Tuesday (Isidora Goyenechea 2960)* is a similar franchise. For vegetarian specialties, there's *El Naturista (☎ 236 5147, Avenida Vitacura 2751)*.

Da Dino (☎ 208 1344, Avenida Apoquindo 4228) is expensive for pizza, but its variety is greater and quality is higher than most Santiago pizza places – try the scallops special (Ⓜ Escuela Militar).

Top End

A favorite with professionals on expense accounts, *München (☎ 233 2108, Avenida El Bosque Norte 0204)* serves German food. Beefeaters favor the *Hereford Grill (☎ 231 9117, Avenida El Bosque Norte 0355)*, or the *Asador del Golf (☎ 335 3947, Enrique Foster Norte 0141)* for its buffet parrillada.

There's a branch of downtown's *Le Due Torri (☎ 231 3427, Isidora Goyenechea 2908)* for Italian food. Stylish *Gioia (☎ 335 3610, Isidora Goyenechea 3456)* has a huge, diverse pasta menu, and good fish as well, but the vegetables sometimes look a bit withered; entrées start around US$10. Across the street, **Da Renato** (☎ 231 6196, *Isidora Goyenechea 3471)* is also Italian, but has a stronger seafood orientation.

Shoogun (☎ 231 1604, *Enrique Foster Norte 172)* is substantially more expensive than its Japanese counterparts near Cerro Santa Lucía, but its quality is not demonstrably superior. **Ginza Teppanyaki** (☎ 365 0801, *Avenida Vitacura 2905)* is an alternative. **Chang Cheng** (☎ 212 9718, *Avenida Las Condes 7471)* is an excellent upscale Chinese restaurant, serving both Mandarin and Cantonese dishes. The **Wok House** (☎ 207 4757, *Avenida Vitacura 4355)* prepares Asian international cuisine, including tofu dishes, which are uncommon in Chile.

The seafood restaurant **Cangrejo Loco** (☎ 335 3952, *Isidora Goyenechea 3455)* shares quarters with **La Cocina Peruana** (☎ 335 3947), which has an inexpensive lunch service. **Coco Loco** (☎ 233 8930, *Avenida El Bosque Norte 0215)* grills fish like corvina and congrio, and also serves king crab and lobster. **Puerto Marisko** (☎ 233 2096, *Isidora Goyenechea 2918)* is also a seafood venue.

Popular enough that reservations are advisable even on weeknights, Vitacura's Canadian-run **Santa Fe** (☎ 215 1091, *Avenida Las Condes 10690)* features well-prepared Tex-Mex specialties like fajitas, enchiladas and burritos. The salsas are milder than one would find in the North American borderlands, but given the large portions, the US$10 to US$15 entrées are still good values. More conveniently located is **El Mexicano** (☎ 231 6467, *Avenida Vitacura 2946)*, easy walking distance from the Tobalaba metro station.

Having recently changed hands, **Jaipur** (☎ 233 7246, *Isidora Goyenechea 3215)* remains one of few places in the city to eat Indian food. Thai dinners cost US$35 per person at **Benyarong** (☎ 208 7427, *Avenida Américo Vespucio Norte 2970)*; the city's other notable Thai restaurant is the Hyatt's **Anakena** (☎ 363 3177, *Avenida Presidente Kennedy 4601)*.

Pinpilinpausha (☎ 232 5800, *Isidora Goyenechea 2800)* is a traditional Spanish restaurant, though its Las Condes locale is relatively new. The **Taberna de Papagayo** (☎ 231 4965, *Avenida Vitacura 2880)* serves Spanish buffet lunches for US$8, dinners for US$18 with live entertainment. **La Cascade** (☎ 231 1887, *Isidora Goyenechea 2930)* prepares pricey French food.

When President Bill Clinton visited Santiago, the US embassy chose **El Madroñal** (☎ 233 6312, *Avenida Vitacura 2911)*, renowned for its Spanish cuisine emphasizing fresh Chilean produce, for the presidential dinner.

El Suizo (☎ 208 3603, *Avenida Vitacura 3285)* serves wild game like deer and boar. Nearby **Delmónico** (☎ 206 2704, *Vitacura 3379)* is a well-regarded French locale. **Sakura** (☎ 206 7600, *Vitacura 4111)* serves Japanese lunches from US$9 and a buffet dinner for US$17.

ÑUÑOA (MAP 10)
Budget
Decorated in a Cuban motif, **Café de la Isla** (☎ 341 5389, *Avenida Irarrázaval 3465)* prepares good sandwiches and excellent juices, to the accompaniment of recorded jazz. Serving sandwiches and other snacks at budget prices, the informal **Las Lanzas** *(Trucco 11)* is noteworthy as an actors' hangout.

Mid-Range
Increasingly chic Plaza Ñuñoa offers moderate choices like **República de Ñuñoa** *(Trucco 33)*, open until 5 am on weekends, and **El Amor Nunca Muere** *(Trucco 43)*, which is open for dinner only. Across Avenida Irarrázaval, **La Terraza** (☎ 223 3987, *Jorge Washington 58)* is more patrician in style. On the east side of the Plaza, **Taverna della Piazza** (☎ 341 5192, *Avenida Irarrázaval 3600)* serves good pizza and other Italian specialties at moderate prices.

Many restaurants are west of the Plaza, along Avenida Irarrázaval. For Chinese food, there's **Xiong Mao** *(Irarrázaval 3470)* and **Sam-Sing** (☎ 274 7978, *Irarrázaval 3168)*. **Rhenania** (☎ 341 8386, *Irarrázaval 1301)* is a traditional schopería, a German-style beer bar with sandwiches, in the same spot since 1935.

La Vaca Mecánica (☎ 223 8884, *Avenida Los Leones 3093*) specializes in meats and pasta, with lunches from US$5 to US$9 and more expensive dinners.

Vietnamese food is unusual in Chile, but *Jardín de Bambú* (☎ 225 1706, *Avenida Salvador 1827*) serves some spicy Southeast Asian dishes and has a standard Chinese menu for more conservative diners.

Other new locales worth checking out include two Argentine-run places, moderately priced *Mexicana* (*Avenida Condell 1576*) and *Da Noi* (☎ 274 2001, *Avenida Italia 1791*), which specializes in pasta.

Top End

Ñuñoa's upscale restaurant row is along José Domingo Cañas, north of the Estadio Nacional, with venues like *Solar de Sancho Panza* (☎ 225 1413, *JD Cañas 982*), specializing in Spanish cuisine. Another fine choice is *Walhalla* (☎ 209 8492, *Campo de Deportes 329*), corner of JD Cañas, with moderately priced Swiss food in attractive surroundings, with excellent service.

Il Bogavante (☎ 343 1137, *JD Cañas 2306*) specializes in meat and seafood, including lobster from the Juan Fernández Archipelago. Occupying a typical barrio-style house, *La Parrilla* (☎ 204 7434, *JD Cañas 1301*) also specializes in beef, as do *Todo Papa* (☎ 223 1693, *JD Cañas 1879*) and amiable *Casa Argentina* (☎ 225 6934, *JD Cañas 1620*), which has tango evenings on weekends.

Entertainment

Santiago's main nightlife districts are Barrio Bellavista (Ⓜ Baquedano), Providencia's Avenida Suecia (Ⓜ Los Leones) and Plaza Ñuñoa (most easily reached by bus or taxi), though other venues are scattered throughout the city. In any event, remember that the metro closes around the hour that many of these places open, so it's not really a viable transportation option, at least not to get home.

While the venues below are divided into categories, readers should not take these categories too literally – many places have different types of entertainment on different nights. The best source of information on what's happening in town is *El Mercurio*'s Friday magazine supplement *Wikén*. Another publication, distributed free of charge in many locales in and around the eastern suburbs, is *GET out!*, a glossy monthly whose listings cover current cultural events and nightlife, including theater, concerts, live music, films and sports.

PUBS & BARS

The numerous bars clustered around Avenida Suecia and General Holley (Ⓜ Los Leones) in Providencia have adopted the North American custom of happy hour (two drinks for the price of one), even until midnight in some cases, and serve decent if unexceptional food. Nearly all have live music – mostly but by no means exclusively cover versions of international hits. Among them are ***Brannigan's*** (☎ 232 5172, *Avenida Suecia 035*), the ***Old Boston Pub*** (☎ 231 5169, *General Holley 2291*), Australian-run ***Boomerang*** (☎ 334 5081, *General Holley 2285*), ***Mister Ed*** (☎ 231 2624, *Avenida Suecia 0152*) and ***Wall Street*** (☎ 232 5548, *General Holley 99*).

Across Avenida Providencia, waiters in bolo ties serve reasonably priced beer (including Guinness on tap) and palatable food at the ***Electric Cowboy*** (☎ 231 7225, *Guardia Vieja 35*), which features live rockabilly music on weekends. One of the newly fashionable Providencia spots is ***El Deseo*** (☎ 232 2052, *Nueva de Lyon 139*), a Bohemian-style place with reasonably priced drinks, plus good snacks like cheese platters and sushi, but it's a little disorganized as yet.

Near Cerro Santa Lucía, one of Santiago's liveliest, least formal bars is ***Bar Berri*** (☎ 638 4734, *Rosal 321*); it also has good, inexpensive lunches. The ***Bar Excéntrico*** (☎ 632 8953, *Esmeralda 636*) spins music from hip-hop to easy listening to film soundtracks, and has a 6 to 10 pm happy hour daily (Map 1).

Nichola's Pub (☎ 246 0277, *Avenida Apoquindo 3371*), a neighborhood spot in Las Condes, has the cheapest pisco sours in town. Not too far away, ***Los Andes*** (☎ 231 1911, *Avenida Apoquindo 3012*) is a brewpub that's made good first impressions.

DANCE CLUBS

Dance clubs open late, around 11 pm, and stay open almost all night, at least on weekends. Recorded music is the norm, but some clubs offer live bands.

One of Santiago's most fashionable discos is the techno ***Oz*** (☎ 737 7066, *Chucre Manzur 6*), in a converted warehouse on a cul-de-sac just off Antonia López de Bello in Bellavista, but it collects a hefty cover charge, around US$15 per person. On the same block, its rival ***Rase*** (☎ 735 6105, *Chucre Manzur 3*) has a lower cover charge (about US$7) and admits women free until 1 am; it's open Friday and Saturday only.

Bellavista's ***Tadeo's*** (*Ernesto Pinto Lagarrigue 282*) has a spacious dance floor, with a crowd in the mid-20s range. ***La Barra de Mamil*** (*Antonia López de Bello 043*) attracts a similar public, as does ***Discotheque Puerto Bellavista*** (☎ 737 2116, *Antonia López de Bello 20*).

Also in Bellavista, ***Zoom*** (☎ 735 1167, *Antonia López de Bello 56*) offers canned DJ music, with cover at around US$6. Across the street, the ***Jammin' Club*** (*Antonia López de Bello 49*) deals in reggae, with a quality sound system; the US$4 cover includes one drink, but women get in free until 12:30 am.

Kasbba (☎ 231 7419, Avenida Suecia 081) is one of Providencia's top dance clubs, but many other bars in and around Avenida Suecia (see Pubs & Bars, earlier in this chapter) double as dance and live music locales. On the border of Ñuñoa, but on the Santiago Centro side of the street, **Laberinto** (☎ 635 5368, Avenida Vicuña Mackenna 915) is a large, popular live music club that charges US$10 cover but admits women free until 11:30 pm; lines can be long even several hours later (Map 1).

Near Barrio Brasil, **Blondie** (Alameda 2879), one of Santiago's longest-running dance clubs, features three different floors, each with a distinct style. This place often gets closed by the police.

In Las Condes, the club of the moment is the elitist **Skuba** (☎ 243 3380, Avenida Las Condes 11271), where dress is semiformal (no sneakers, at least), the cover is US$12, and the doorman better like your looks. It's in the Paseo San Damián, a huge complex of restaurants and pubs that can accommodate up to a thousand partygoers; open Thursday to Sunday.

SALSA

There are a number of clubs in Bellavista. The décor at cavernous **Havana Salsa** (☎ 737 1737, Domínica 142) stylishly recreates the ambience of Old Havana, encouraging even neophytes onto the dance floor; they also serve good food. For live salsa music, though, it's necessary to visit **Salsoteca Maestra Vida** (☎ 735 7416, Pío Nono 380) Thursday evening; on other nights the music is recorded. Cover is about US$5. Other salsa venues include **El Rincón Habanero** (Santa Filomena 131) and **Club 4-40** (Santa Filomena 81). **Tomm** (☎ 777 9985, Bellavista 098) varies from live rock to Latin music, mostly salsa; cover charges are US$6 for men, US$4 for women.

NIGHTCLUBS

Dating from 1879, **Confitería Las Torres** (☎ 698 6220, Alameda 1570) reinforces its

Make sure you have the right *Skuba* gear.

turn-of-the-19th-century atmosphere – complete with spectacular woodwork – with live tango on weekends (Ⓜ Los Héroes; Map 5). The stage set features enormous blowups of Argentine tango legend Carlos Gardel, while the walls are lined with photographs of Chilean presidents – perhaps the only place in the world where portraits of Allende and Pinochet hang side by side. The food is good but expensive, the service excellent.

Another locale offering tango Friday and Saturday nights is Providencia's **Tango Bar Siglo XX** (☎ 233 4949, Guardia Vieja 188). Admission is free.

Barrio Brasil's **Los Buenos Muchachos** (☎ 698 0112, Avenida Ricardo Cumming 1031), a popular Chilean restaurant, doubles as a nightclub with elaborate floor shows.

GAY & LESBIAN VENUES

The Recoleta side of Barrio Bellavista is the hub of Santiago's gay life, thanks to venues like **Bunker** (☎ 777 3760, Bombero Núñez 159), a popular cousin of its Buenos Aires namesake that attracts an upper-class clientele (especially with its US$12 cover charge). It's open Thursday, Friday and Saturday with dancing, and there's a two-for-the-price-of-one admission special before

1 am on Friday. It's known as a gay venue, but anyone is welcome.

Open from 8:30 pm daily except Sunday, the nearby *Bar Dionisio* (☎ 737 6065, *Bombero Núñez 111)* is more casual, with no cover charge, reasonably priced drinks, drag shows and karaoke. Also in Bellavista, *Máscara's (Purísima 129)* is mainly a lesbian club, while *Vox Populi (Ernesto Pinto Lagarrigue 364)* is a new gay nightspot.

Capricho Español (☎ 777 7674, *Purísima 65)*, in Bellavista, has recently become a gay venue (each table has its own phone for making contact) with a more mature crowd, though all ages and orientations are welcome. Recent visitors, though, say the food is not what it once was.

Also in Bellavista, *Bokhara* (☎ 732 1050, *Pío Nono 430)* is primarily a gay venue; relatively small though strategically placed mirrors make it seem larger than it is, and even livelier. Its *lunes sin restricción* (Monday without limits) tests the boundaries of the permissible in Chile.

Just across the Mapocho, in an ill-lit alleyway, *Queen (Coronel Santiago Bueras 128)* attracts a less pretentious crowd than Bunker (Map 5). On the fringes of Bellavista, *Fausto* (☎ 777 1041, *Avenida Santa María 0832)* is a stylish, multilevel club with techno music.

ROCK

Just west of Plaza Ñuñoa, the *Bar Sin Nombre (Irrarázaval 3442)* features excellent live rock bands on their way up; befitting its name, there is no sign. Just north of the Plaza, *La Batuta* (☎ 274 7096, *Jorge Washington 52)* also features quality live rock bands. Admission varies depending on the act, but women sometimes get in free until 11 pm. Other Ñuñoa rock venues include *Long Play* (☎ 225 6659, *JD Cañas 2828)* and *Le Pub (Avenida Irarrázaval at Brown Norte)*.

Clan Destino (☎ 777 1346, *Antonia López de Bello 146)* is probably the best spot for live rock & roll and amplified jazz-rock – if you walk by the side entrance on Bombero Núñez you can usually catch a glimpse of who's playing (Map 7).

BLUES & JAZZ

Blues is not easy to come by in Santiago, but you will find it live at Bellavista's *Il Rittorno (Santa Filomena 132)* at 11 pm on Friday night.

The capital's main jazz venue is Ñuñoa's *Club de Jazz de Santiago* (☎ 274 1937, *Avenida José Pedro Alessandri 85)*. Cover usually runs around US$4 to US$6 for what are usually New Orleans-style acts, rather than avant-garde improvisation, in an intimate surrounding.

In a typical Ñuñoa house of the early 1930s, *Café Ñuñoa* (☎ 341 1971, *JD Cañas 1675)* has occasional live jazz and small-scale theater presentations.

FOLK &TRADITIONAL MUSIC

Offering theater, poetry readings and live music, *La Casa en el Aire* operates two branches, one in Providencia (☎ 222 8789, *Santa Isabel 0411)* and the other in Bellavista (☎ 735 6680, *Antonia López de Bello 0125)*. *Peña Nano Parra* (☎ 735 6093, *Ernesto Pinto Lagarrigue 80)* is an intimate locale that offers a tremendous rapport between performers and audience (Map 7).

Other Bellavista venues with live music include *Altazor* (☎ 777 9651, *Antonia López de Bello 0189)* and *Da Lua (Antonia López de Bello 0126)*, both of which favor folk-style performers. *Don Mario Gutiérrez (Antonia López de Bello 0199)* has live Latin-fusion music on weekends.

South of the Alameda (Map 5), *La Habana Vieja* (☎ 638 5284, *Tarapacá 755)* has live Latin American music, from Cuba and Mexico south to the island of Chiloé. In Providencia, *La Mitad del Mundo* (☎ 204 0541, *Rancagua 0398)* is a folkloric venue with Ecuadorean food and music from throughout Chile and Latin America; admission is about US$4 for most shows, which take place Friday and Saturday nights.

Many of the municipal, private and binational cultural centers listed in the Facts for the Visitor chapter also offer traditional-music shows.

CLASSICAL MUSIC

Santiago has numerous performing-arts venues for both music and drama. Most prestigious is the *Teatro Municipal* (☎ 369 0282, Agustinas 794), with offerings from classical to popular (Map 7). The box office is open 10 am to 7 pm weekdays, 10 am to 2 pm weekends, but since members have priority, seats can be hard to come by. The repertoire is generally conservative, befitting the theater's wealthy patrons and contributors.

Providencia's *Teatro Universidad de Chile* (☎ 634 5295, Baquedano 043) presents ballets, and orchestral and chamber music in its fall season, but also hosts occasional popular-music concerts; the acoustics are exceptional. Another notable Providencia venue is the *Teatro Oriente* (☎ 232 1360, Avenida Pedro de Valdivia 099), which doubles as a cinema; the theater ticket office is at Avenida 11 de Septiembre 2214, Oficina 66.

CINEMAS

The number of cinemas in Santiago has been increasing, but the advent of multiplexes showing pretty much the same fare means that the selection of films may be decreasing. These show mostly Hollywood blockbusters, subtitled in Spanish, but smaller art houses and university cinemas show a wider variety, also subtitled in Spanish when appropriate.

Commercial Cinemas

Downtown Santiago's commercial cinema district is along Paseo Huérfanos and nearby side streets, where many large former theaters now have two or three screens showing different films. There are also cinemas and multiplexes in suburban comunas like Las Condes, Vitacura and Providencia. Most of the following cinemas have half-price discounts on Wednesday:

Santiago Centro

Cine Central
(☎ 633 3555) Huérfanos 930

Cine Hoyts
(☎ 664 1861) Huérfanos 735

Cine Huelén
(☎ 633 1603) Huérfanos 779

Cine Huérfanos
(☎ 633 6707) Huérfanos 930

Cine Lido
(☎ 633 0797) Huérfanos 680

Cine Rex
(☎ 633 1144) Huérfanos 735

Gran Palace 1-4
(☎ 696 0082) Huérfanos 1176

Las Condes & Vitacura

Cine Las Condes
(☎ 220 8816) Apoquindo & Noruega

Cine Lo Castillo
(☎ 242 1342) Candelaria Goyenechea 3820, Vitacura

Showcase Cinemas Parque Arauco
(☎ 224 7707) Avenida Presidente Kennedy 5413, Local 250, Las Condes

Providencia

Teatro Oriente
(☎ 231 7151) Pedro de Valdivia 099

Art Cinemas

For film cycles and independent or unconventional movies, the following venues are the best bets. These also usually have half-price Wednesday discounts:

Centro de Extensíon de la Universidad Católica
(☎ 635 1994) Alameda 390

Cine Alameda
(☎ 639 2479) Alameda 139 (Map 5)

Cine Arte Aiep
(☎ 264 9698) Avenida Miguel Claro 177, Providencia

Cine Arte Vitacura
(☎ 219 2384) Embajador Doussinague 1767

Cine El Biógrafo
(☎ 633 4435) Lastarria 181 (Map 5)

Cine Normandie
(☎ 697 2979) Tarapacá 1181 (Map 5)

Cine Tobalaba
(☎ 231 6630) Avenida Providencia 2563, Providencia

THEATER

Near Cerro Santa Lucía, the well-established *Teatro La Comedia* (☎ 639 1523, Merced 349) offers contemporary drama Thursday to Sunday. Other downtown venues include the Universidad de Chile's **Sala Agustín Sire** (☎ 696 5142, *Morandé 750*); the **Teatro Casa Amarilla** (☎ 672 0347, *Balmaceda 1301*) and the **Teatro Estación Mapocho** (☎ 735 6046, *Balmaceda 1301*), both in the Centro Cultural Mapocho; and the **Teatro Nacional Chileno** (☎ 671 7850, *Morandé 25*).

More likely to have experimental theater than other areas, Barrio Bellavista is home to companies like **Teatro El Conventillo** (☎ 777 4164, *Bellavista 173*), **Teatro Taller** (☎ 235 1678, *Ernesto Pinto Lagarrigue 191*), **Teatro Bellavista** (☎ 735 6264, *Dardignac 0110*), **Teatro Galpón 7** (☎ 737 5786, *Chucre Manzur 9-B*) and **Teatro La Feria** (☎ 737 7371, *Crucero Exeter 0250*). Particularly hard to categorize is **Sala Shakespeare's** (☎ 737 1577, *Bombero Núñez 289*), which offers live theater but also live pop music and even techno at times.

In summer, there's an inexpensive open-air theater program at Parque General Bustamante (also known as Parque Manuel Rodríguez), south of Plaza Baquedano, in Providencia; check the newspapers for details. The **Teatro de la Universidad Católica** (☎ 205 5652, *Jorge Washington 24*) gets much of the credit for Plaza Nuñoa's renaissance. The **Centro Cultural Las Condes** (☎ 231 3560, *Avenida Apoquindo 3364*) also offers live theater.

An additional venue for live theater and music is the **Teatro Monumental** (☎ 692 2000, *San Diego 850*), which handles major rock acts (Map 4).

SPECTATOR SPORTS
Soccer

Santiago has several first-division soccer (*fútbol*) teams. Major matches usually take place at the Estadio Nacional, at the corner of Avenida Grecia and Marathon in Ñuñoa. For tickets, contact the following teams:

Club Colo Colo
  (☎ 695 2251, 695 1094) Cienfuegos 41
Universidad Católica
  (☎ 231 2777) Avenida Andrés Bello 2782,
  Las Condes
Universidad de Chile
  (☎ 239 2793) Campos de Deportes 565, Ñuñoa

Horse Racing

Santiago has two major racecourses, which are usually open weekends but sometimes on weekdays, too. The Hipódromo Chile (☎ 736 9053) is at Fermín Vivaceta 2753, north of the Mapocho along Avenida Independencia in the comuna de Independencia (Map 4), while the Club Hípico de Santiago (☎ 683 5998) is at Almirante Blanco Encalada 2540 (Ⓜ Unión Latinoamericana; Map 6). The latter is also an architectural landmark and has spectacular views from the grandstand across the infield to the distant Andes, at least on a clear day. Admission is about US$1.50.

Shopping

WHAT TO BUY
Wine & Food

For a superb selection of Chilean wines, visit The Wine House (☎ 207 3533, fax 207 0581, winehous@entelchile.net, www.thewinehouse.com), Avenida Vitacura 3446 (Map 9). Other possibilities include the Vinoteca (☎ 334 1987), Isidora Goyenechea 3520 (Map 9), and Vinópolis (☎ 232 3814), Avenida El Bosque Norte 038 (Map 9).

Santiago's numerous supermarkets are well stocked with most items that anyone might conceivably want, but if you're desperate for Kellogg's Corn Flakes, Pop-Tarts, Hershey's chocolate syrup, Campbell's soup and the like, the only place in town is A Touch of Home (☎ 09-818 1461, eurofrut@ ctcreuna.cl), Don Carlos 2990, Las Condes.

Clothing

Casimires Castrodonoso, with locations at Moneda 950 (☎ 695 4091) and Bucarest 25, Providencia (☎ 233 4789), is authorized to deal legally in prime vicuña cloth products, which are now being produced in Italy with wool exported from Chile, Peru, Bolivia and Argentina, where populations of this small wild relative of the llama and alpaca have rebounded spectacularly over the past two decades. Anyone intending to buy vicuña products, however, should note that the US Department of the Interior's Fish and Wildlife Service has only just proposed reclassifying the vicuña from endangered to threatened under the US Endangered Species Act; until this proposal becomes final, it remains illegal to import such products into the US.

For leather, go to Mará Inés Matte (☎ 207 0536), Nueva Costanera 3961, Vitacura. Women's silk, cotton and linen clothing is available at Colomba (☎ 206 5026), Renato Sánchez 4082, Las Condes.

Jewelry

Bellavista shops specializing in lapis lazuli jewelry include Lapiz Lazuli at Pío Nono 3, Lapiz Lazuli House (☎ 732 1419) at Bellavista 014 and Callfúcura (☎ 732 5004) at Bellavista 096. North of the Mapocho in Providencia, try Morita Gil (☎ 232 6853), at Los Misioneros 1991, or Bellavista's Blue Mountain (☎ 738 0275), Bellavista 0918.

The best selection in Vitacura is at Faba (☎ 208 9526), Avenida Alonso de Córdova 4227, which also has some of the most elaborate creations – such as a near life-size lapis lazuli horse head.

For reproductions of pre-Columbian jewelry, there's Joyas LA Cano (☎ 233 4788), Santa Magdalena 41, Providencia.

Antiques & Collectibles

The north side of Cerro Santa Lucía has a gaggle of antique shops worth a visit, including Antigüedades Haddad (☎ 639 2157), José Miguel de la Barra 496, and Antigüedades Mujala (☎ 638 2434), José Miguel de la Barra 492 (both Map 5). Well-traveled Sergio Zurita created Barrio Bellavista's Arte del Mundo (☎ 735 2507), Dardignac 67, a particularly eclectic shop that defies description.

There are also antique shops in the eastern suburbs. Los Pájaros is a cluster of 75 separate shops at Avenida Providencia 2348,

---

Pinochet Kitsch

If your tastes run to ceramic dolls and coffee mugs honoring General Pinochet, the place to go is Nautigift (☎ 235 7364; Map 8), whose maritime memorabilia are less topical than the former English patient's present plight.

Providencia. Others include Antigüedades Eliecer Miranda Sánchez (☎ 225 5490), Caupolicán 414, Providencia, and Anfiteatro Lo Castillo, Candelaria Goyenechea 3820, Vitacura.

A number of antiquarians and booksellers from throughout the city have recently begun a small but high-quality antiques market in Bellavista, on the Providencia side of Dardignac, between Constitución and Mallinkrodt. If it does continue, it's well worth a visit on Saturday or Sunday morning.

Regional Crafts

Los Graneros del Alba (☎ 246 4360), Avenida Apoquindo 9085, Las Condes, popularly known as 'Los Dominicos' after its nearby church and convent, boasts Santiago's largest crafts selection, imported from throughout the country. It also has good food for a variety of budgets and often features folkloric music and dancing on weekends. Among possible purchases are copperware, huaso horsegear, furniture, sculpture, jewelry and alpaca woolens. The church, designed by architect Joaquín Toesca in late colonial times, features twin domes. Los Dominicos is open 11 am to 7:30 pm daily all year. The quickest way to get there is to take the metro to the end of

Línea 1 at Escuela Militar and then catch a taxi (US$4) out Avenida Apoquindo, but it's also possible to catch bus No 327 from Avenida Providencia, No 344 from the Alameda or Avenida Providencia, No 229 from Catedral or Compañía, or No 326 from Alameda and Miraflores.

For another selection of crafts from throughout the country, the nonprofit Artesanías de Chile has two locales. One is at the Centro Cultural Estación Mapocho (Ⓜ Puente Cal y Canto; Map 5), the other at Antonio Varas 475, Providencia (☎ 235 5375, Ⓜ Manuel Montt); both are open 10 am to 8 pm weekdays, 10:30 am to 1:30 pm Saturday.

For the best selection of indigenous crafts made by the Mapuche, Aymara and Rapa Nui peoples, visit the Centro de Exposición de Arte Indígena (☎ 664 1352) in the Grutas del Cerro Welen at Alameda 499, at the southwest corner of Cerro Santa Lucía (Map 5). It's open 10 am to 7:30 pm daily in summer, 10 am to 6 pm daily except Sunday the rest of the year. Across the Alameda is the Centro Artesanal Santa Lucía, also bounded by Carmen and Diagonal Paraguay, which has numerous stalls with goods that tend to be of varying quality (Map 5).

Crafts from Around Chile

There are many crafts that are common throughout Chile. Ceramics with different variations can be found in many regions, as well as musical instruments like the *zampoña* (pan pipes), wood and stone carvings, basketry, weavings, lapis lazuli and copperware. Each of Chile's regions, however, also has distinctive crafts.

The desert and Andean north is known for llama and alpaca woolens with geometric designs, while some of Central Chile's best-known goods include *huaso* (horseman) gear resembling that of Argentine gauchos, the unusual horsehair weavings known as *crin* – and of course, wine. The Mapuche country of the southern lakes regions is famous for spectacular silverwork. Just to the south, the archipelago of Chiloé is renowned for model boats and stilted houses and dolls.

Chile's Pacific Ocean outlier of Easter Island (Rapa Nui) is especially known for wood and stone carvings of its celebrated *moai* (statues), brought to global attention by Norwegian explorer Thor Heyerdahl in the 1950s, but their shell jewelry also deserves notice.

Some of the best shopping possibilities occur outside the capital, in places covered in the Excursions chapter. The village of Pomaire, for instance, has a remarkable pottery tradition. For antiques, there's no beating the port city of Valparaíso.

Bellavista is also a popular area for crafts, both at Pío Nono's weekend street fair and at shops like Artesanía Nehuen (☎ 777 7367), Dardignac 59, which has a wide selection of materials from throughout the country and will pick up customers at their hotels. The nearby Cooperativa Almacén Campesina (☎ 737 2117), Purísima 303, specializes in peasant crafts.

Music
Santiago has many places to buy CDs and cassettes, such as Disquería Fusión, Avenida Providencia 2124, Locales G & H (Map 8). There are many locations of the Feria del Disco chain, among them Ahumada 286 (☎ 698 6934; Map 5) and Avenida Providencia 2301 (Map 8).

WHERE TO SHOP
There are several well-stocked general crafts shops downtown, including Chile Típico (☎ 696 5504) at Moneda 1025, Local 149, and Huimpalay (☎ 672 1395) at Huérfanos 1162. Chile Típico also has locales at Avenida Alonso de Córdova 4017, Vitacura (☎ 228 8819) and at the Parque Arauco shopping center, Avenida Presidente Kennedy 5413, Mall 3, Local 434 (☎ 218 3588; Map 9). Rincón Chileno (☎ 207 9206), Alonso de Córdova 2359, Vitacura, also has a diverse inventory.

Malls
For most items, santiaguinos themselves generally head for modern shopping centers such as downtown's Mall del Centro, Paseo Puente 689. Other malls include the Mall Panorámico (☎ 231 6509) at Avenida 11 de Septiembre and Ricardo Lyon in Providencia (Ⓜ Pedro de Valdivia or Los Leones), and Parque Arauco (☎ 299 0500) at Avenida Presidente Kennedy 5413, Las Condes (Ⓜ Escuela Militar), whose heavy-handed security recalls the Pinochet dictatorship (try taking a picture of the parking lot from the pedestrian overpass on Avenida Presidente Kennedy). Also in Las Condes are Cosmocentro Apumanque (☎ 246 2614), Manquehue Sur 31, and Alto Las Condes (☎ 229 1383), Avenida Presidente Kennedy 9001.

Most of these shopping centers have free shuttles from upscale hotels downtown and in the eastern suburbs.

Art Galleries
Galería del Cerro (☎ 737 3500), Antonia López de Bello 0135, Barrio Bellavista (Providencia side) sells original works by Chilean painters. Other galleries include the following:

Galería R
   (☎ 638 4011) in the Hotel Galerías, San Antonio 65 (Map 5)
Galería Enrico Bucci
   (☎ 639 5103) Huérfanos 526 (Map 5)
Galería Ziebold
   (☎ 737 1197) Dominica 54, Barrio Bellavista (Recoleta side)
Galería Praxis
   (☎ 233 6092) Avenida Suecia 0161, Providencia
Galería Tomás Andreu
   (☎ 228 9594) Avenida Nueva Costanera 3731, Vitacura
Galería Artespacio
   (☎ 206 2177) Avenida Alonso de Córdova 2600, 2nd floor, Vitacura
Galería Isabél Aninat
   (☎ 246 8070) Avenida Alonso de Córdova 3053, Vitacura

Bookstores & Newsstands
Santiago's largest and best-stocked bookstore is the Feria Chilena del Libro, Huérfanos 623, a fine place to browse an excellent selection of books in both Spanish and English (Map 5); there are several other branches scattered around town. Other good, serious stores include Librería Manantial (☎ 696 7463) at Plaza de Armas 444 (the entrance is a corridor on the south side of the catedral; Map 5) and Librería El Cid (☎ 632 1540) at Merced 343, with a good selection of used books (Map 5). Fondo de Cultura Económica (☎ 695 4843), Paseo Bulnes 152, is a Latin American institution specializing in literature, social sciences, history and economics, with branches throughout the region (Map 5).

Calle San Diego, south of the Alameda, contains Santiago's largest concentration of used-book stores, although quality varies. One of the best, Librería Rivano at San Diego 119, Local 7, has a fine collection on Chilean history, not all of which is displayed to the public (Map 5). In the Plaza del Mulato Gil de Castro complex at Lastarria 307, Local 100, Ricardo Bravo Murúa (☎ 639 7141) is another good antiquarian bookseller who also stocks maps and postcards (Map 5).

Behind the grape arbor at the Phone Box Pub, Librería Chile Ilustrado (☎ 235 8145, Avenida Providencia 1652; Map 8) has a superb selection of books on Chilean history, archaeology, anthropology and folklore. Specializing in rare materials, but with much general-interest stock, it's open 9:30 am to 1:30 pm and 4 to 7:30 pm weekdays, 10 am to 1:30 pm Saturday. Two other booksellers occupy the same complex: Books (☎ 235 1205), with a good selection of used but fairly expensive English-language paperbacks, and the feminist bookshop Lila.

For new books in English, try Librería Inglesa at Huérfanos 669, Local 11 (Map 5),

Ahumada kiosk

or at Avenida Pedro de Valdivia 47 in Providencia. For magazines and newspapers, Libro's has locations downtown (☎ 699 0319) at Huérfanos 1178 and in Providencia (☎ 232 8839) at Avenida Pedro de Valdivia 039. French speakers will find reading material at the Librería Francesa (☎ 639 2407) at Paseo Estado 337, Local 22 (Map 5).

For a nearly complete selection of LP titles, and many other books in both English and German, go to Librería Eduardo Albers (☎ 218 5371), Avenida Vitacura 5648, Vitacura.

Newspapers and magazines in English and many European languages, as well as from other Latin American countries, are available at two kiosks at the junction of the Ahumada and Huérfanos pedestrian malls. If a newspaper appears to have been around more than a few days, you can often haggle over the price. Before buying anything, check to see that no pages are missing, as vendors often salvage papers off incoming international flights.

N'aitún (☎ 671 8410), Avenida Ricardo Cumming 453 in Barrio Brasil, is a leftist bookstore/community center that doubles as a venue for live music and theater; drinks and snacks are available as well.

There's a good open-air book fair at Plaza Carlos Fezoa Véliz, at the corner of San Diego and Santa Isabél (Map 5).

Markets & Ferias

Santiago has numerous flea markets, locally known as *Ferias Persas* (Persian Fairs) or simply *Persas*. One of the city's longstanding institutions, the Mercado Franklin, has recently moved a few blocks to the new Plaza Techadas, on Placer between San Francisco and San Diego (Ⓜ Franklin; Map 4). There's a lot of postmodern junk and kitsch at this market, which has lasted 40 years in the area, but also the occasional treasure.

A convenient market, open daily in summer only, is the crafts market located on the north side of Avenida Providencia, at the exit from the Pedro de Valdivia metro station.

From October through December only, in the Southern Hemisphere spring, the suburban comuna of Lo Barnechea sponsors the Feria San Enrique, featuring antiques and bric-a-brac, artwork and outstanding crafts with a minimum of kitsch. It also offers folkloric and popular music presentations on themes like *La Nueva Ola*, the Chilean music of the '60s. For information, contact the Corporación Cultural de Lo Barnechea (☎ 243 4758). The crafts fair proper starts around 10:30 am and lasts until about 2:30 pm Sunday only. To get there, from San Pablo or Compañía in downtown Santiago, or from Avenida Providencia, take bus No 205, 206, 233, 248, 324, 419 or 614.

Excursions

Beyond the Metropolitan Region of Santiago, the most notable feature of Chile's heartland is the fertile central valley which is, at its widest, just 70km between the Andean foothills and the coastal range. Endowed with rich alluvial soils, a pleasant Mediterranean climate and Andean meltwater for irrigation, this is Chile's chief farming region, ideal for cereals, orchards and vineyards.

Since the arrival of Europeans, large estates have dominated Chile's regional economy and society, but landowners' failure to develop their properties efficiently provoked a contentious agrarian reform in the 1960s and early 1970s. After the 1973 coup, the Pinochet dictatorship returned many large farms to their former owners and dissolved co-operatives in favor of individual family farms.

'Middle Chile,' from the Río Aconcagua south to the Biobío, contains almost 75% of the country's population and most of its industry. Nearly a third live in the sprawling capital, but the region also includes the major port of Valparaíso and Chile's most famous resort, the 'garden city' of Viña del Mar. Copper mines dot the sierras of the Metropolitan, Valparaíso and O'Higgins regions, and throughout, the imposing Andean crest is never far out of sight.

Though it's a bit farther than most other excursions in this chapter, the Argentine city of Mendoza is the nearest place to cross the border to renew an expiring Chilean visa. The route over the Andes is spectacular, passing the Western Hemisphere's highest peak, 6962m Cerro Aconcagua, and descending the valley of the Río Mendoza, past some of Argentina's greatest vineyards.

Around Santiago

☎ 02

There are many worthwhile sights outside the capital proper but still within the Región Metropolitana, as well as others outside the region but near enough for reasonable day trips.

CALEU

From Santiago, northbound Ruta 5 (the Panamericana) passes Tiltil and Punta Peuco (site of the luxury prison holding General Manuel Contreras, convicted of the car-bomb assassination of former Chilean diplomat Orlando Letelier in Washington, DC in 1976) en route to the village of Rungue, a distance of 55 km. At Rungue, a westbound gravel road leads 4km to a junction where another gravel road climbs to the rustic coastal-range hamlet of Caleu. The main road continues west over the winding Cuesta La Dormida to the town of Olmué, the gateway to Parque Nacional La Campana (see Around Viña del Mar, later in this chapter).

Fast becoming a weekend retreat for santiaguinos, including Chile's new president, Ricardo Lagos, Caleu has some simple accommodations, but with a swimming pool, for about US$20 per person with breakfast. There's a small crafts market, including artisanal preserves and sweets, and typical Chilean food at November's Feria Artesanal y Gastronómico.

Public transportation is very limited, leaving once daily from outside the Mapocho Station in Santiago. Chip Travel (☎ 777 5376), Avenida Santa María 227, Oficina 12, does weekend day tours of Caleu and its surroundings for US$75 per person for a minimum of three persons; larger groups pay less per person. Tours include transportation, a morning snack, lunch and a hiking excursion; a horseback riding option costs an additional US$25 per person.

POMAIRE

In this small, dusty village near Melipilla, southwest of Santiago, skilled potters

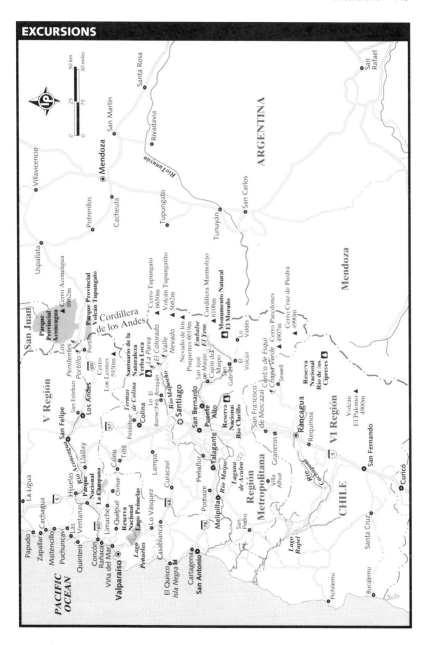

spend their days at their wheels to produce unique and remarkably inexpensive ceramics – a punchbowl with half a dozen cups, for instance, costs only about US$10. Unfortunately, most items are too large and fragile for most travelers to take home, but it's still worth a day trip from the capital for a tour and a small souvenir.

For lunch, try **Restaurant San Antonio** (☎ 831 2168), San Antonio at Arturo Prat. From Santiago, take Buses Melipilla (☎ 776 2060) from Terminal San Borja, Alameda 3250.

WINERIES

While Santiago's growth has displaced many of the wineries that once surrounded the capital, it has spared others, even within the city limits. Note that while Chile's wines can be world class, wineries have been slow to exploit or promote wine tourism, and it may take some effort and patience to arrange a suitable itinerary. Besides those mentioned here, see also the entry for Pirque, in the Cajón del Maipo, and the Ruta del Vino, southwest of Rancagua and San Fernando (see Reserva Nacional Río de Los Cipreses, later in this chapter.

Viña Santa Carolina
Santiago's most accessible winery is Viña Santa Carolina (☎ 450 3000,

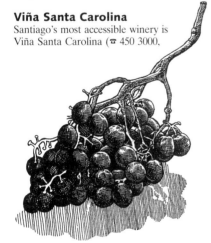

ask for Relaciones Públicas and try to avoid getting passed on to the voicemail system) at Rodrigo de Araya 1341 in the comuna of Macul, near the Estadio Nacional (Map 10). Although the sprawling capital has displaced the vineyards themselves, the historical *casco* (main house) of the Julio Pereira estate and the *bodegas* (cellars or storehouses) are still here, open to the public with 24 hours' advance notice. It's within walking distance of Rodrigo de Araya metro station.

Viña Cousiño Macul
Also within Santiago city limits, in the comuna of Peñalolén, Viña Cousiño Macul (☎ 284 1011), Anexo 45, has opened its bodegas but not its grounds to the public (the grounds are due for a major real estate development as the winery moves its growing activities out of the city). Tours take place at 11 am daily except Sunday, by reservation only, and are free of charge; the sales office is open 9 am to 1 pm and 2 to 6 pm weekdays, 9 am to 1 pm Saturday. Take bus No 39 or 391 from Santo Domingo out Américo Vespucio Sur to Avenida Quilín 7100, or No 210 from the Alameda.

Viña Santa Rita
In the village of Alto Jahuel, south of the capital and 5km east of Buin, is Viña Santa Rita (☎ 821 2707 for reservations, which are obligatory), Camino Padre Hurtado 0695. Tours including tasting (US$6) take place five times daily Tuesday to Friday. On Saturday and Sunday, 12:30 pm tours are free, but with a lunch that costs in the US$30 per person range with wine at their excellent restaurant **La Casa de Doña Paula** (☎ 821 4211); also open for lunch on weekdays. By public transportation, the simplest way to get here is to take Línea 2 of the metro to the end of the line at Lo Ovalle and then catch metrobús No 56, which passes the winery entrance.

Viña Undurraga
Thirty-four kilometers southwest of the capital on the old Melipilla highway between Peñaflor and Talagante, the grounds and

buildings of Viña Undurraga (☎ 817 2346) are open to the public weekdays 10 am to 4 pm (reservations obligatory). Buses Peñaflor (☎ 776 1025) covers this route from the Terminal San Borja, Alameda 3250; be sure to take the smaller Talagante micro rather than the larger Melipilla bus.

Cajón del Maipo

☎ 02

Southeast of the capital, easily accessible by public transportation, the Cajón del Maipo (canyon of the Río Maipo) is one of the main weekend recreation areas for santiaguinos. Camping, hiking, climbing, cycling, whitewater rafting, skiing and other activities are all possible. The area has experienced a recent environmental controversy over the location of a natural gas pipeline from Argentina through the Cascada de las Animas, a private nature reserve – see San Alfonso, later in this section.

Two main access routes climb the canyon: on the north side of the river, a good paved road passes from the suburban comuna of La Florida to San José de Maipo and above, while another narrower, less-traveled paved route follows the south side of the river from Puente Alto. The southern route crosses the river and joins with the other just beyond San José de Maipo.

Among the popular stops in the canyon are El Melocotón, San Alfonso, Cascada de las Animas, San Gabriel (where the pavement ends and beyond which the main gravel road follows the Río Volcán, a tributary of the Maipo), El Volcán, Lo Valdés, Monumento Natural El Morado and the rustic thermal baths at Baños Morales and Baños de Colina.

Buses Cajón del Maipo (☎ 850 5769) leave about every half hour from the Parque O'Higgins metro station.

The Cámara del Turismo del Cajón del Maipo intends to open an Oficina de Información Turística at Las Vizcachas, at the western entrance to the Cajón.

RAFTING THE RÍO MAIPO

From September to April, several adventure travel companies run descents of the Río Maipo in seven-passenger rafts, from

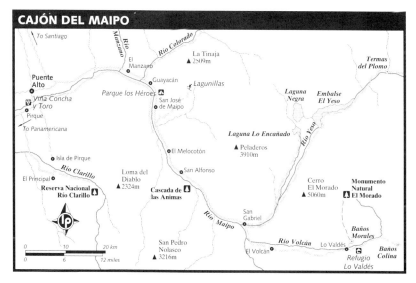

San Alfonso to Guayacán/Parque los Héroes. The hour-plus descent, passing through mostly Class III rapids with very few calm areas, is rugged enough that it's common for passengers to get tossed in the water. Still, it's perhaps less hazardous than it was in the 1970s, when the first kayakers descending found themselves facing automatic weapons as they passed the grounds of General Pinochet's estate at El Melocotón (the narrow bedrock chute here, containing one of the river's more entertaining rapids, is now known as 'El Pinocho').

Rafting excursions cost anywhere from US$30 to US$75, depending on whether they include lunch, transportation to and from Santiago, and other amenities; kayak descents and lessons are also possible. Operators provide helmets, wetsuits and buoyant lifejackets, as well as experienced guides and safety kayakers.

For operators, try Altué Active Travel (☎ 321 103, fax 336 799), Encomenderos 83, Las Condes; Cascada Expediciones (☎ 342 274, fax 339 768), Orrego Luco 040, Providencia; Grado Diez (☎ 344 130), Las Urbinas 56, Providencia; or Pared Sur (☎ 073 525), Juan Estéban Montero 5497, Las Condes.

PIRQUE

One of the gateways to the Cajón, Pirque is an easygoing village just beyond Puente Alto. On weekends there's a crafts fair featuring leather workers, goldsmiths and silversmiths. Cyclists will find the paved but narrow route up the south bank of the Maipo much less crowded and more pleasant than the north bank route.

The quickest way to Pirque is to take Línea 5 of the metro to the end of the line at La Florida, then catch metrobús No 73 or a taxi colectivo at Paradero 14, just outside the station.

Viña Concha y Toro

Chile's largest winery, Viña Concha y Toro (☎ 821 7000) has spacious grounds here. Guided tours in English take place at 9:30 and 11:30 am and 3 pm weekdays, 10 am, noon and 3:30 pm Saturday; call ahead to assure a spot, but if you're nearby it's worth stopping to see if there's space available.

Visits begin at the winery museum, with a brief video on Concha y Toro's history, followed by a tour of the vineyards, grounds and cellars and the massive brick catacombs held together by limestone mortar. At the end, you can taste three different wines for about US$1 each – guests favoring whites should try the sauvignon blanc and the fruity Late Harvest. Spanish-language tours take place at 10:30 am and 2 and 4 pm weekdays, 11 am and 2:30 pm Saturday.

About 3km east of Concha y Toro, on the road up the south side of the Cajón, the *Wailea Coffee Store* has good sandwiches, kuchen and coffee. There is also a string of restaurants, all very popular on weekends, most notably *La Vaquita Echá (☎ 854 6025, Ramón Subercaseaux 3355)*, famed for its *pastel de choclo*. There's great outdoor seating beneath massive shade trees.

RESERVA NACIONAL RÍO CLARILLO

One of the closest nature reserves to Santiago, 10,000-hectare Río Clarillo is a scenic tributary canyon of the Cajón del Maipo, 23km from Pirque. Its primary attractions are the river and the forest, with sclerophyllous (hard-leafed) tree species unique to the area (though similar to those in other Mediterranean climates, like California's). In addition to abundant bird life, the endangered Chilean iguana also inhabits the reserve; admission is US$5 weekdays, US$7 weekends.

From Pirque, Buses LAC has hourly departures to within 2km of the reserve. Bus No 32 ('El Principal') leaves every three hours or so from Gandarillas, half a block from Pirque's Plaza de Armas.

SAN JOSÉ DE MAIPO

One of the oldest towns in the Cajón, San José de Maipo dates from 1792; its national monument church, the **Iglesia Parroquial** on the Plaza de Armas, dates from 1798. About 48km southeast of Santiago, San José has several hosterías and restaurants and the last gas station for eastbound motorists.

In the cordillera northeast of San José, about 19km from town, the small ski resort of **Lagunillas** is a very modest counterpart to the region's other high-powered ski resorts, ranging from 2250m to 2580m above sea level. Accommodations are available through the Club Andino de Chile (☎ 269 0898), the Refugio Suizo (☎ 205 5423) or in any of several nearby towns, but it's also an easy day trip from the capital. Ask the Club Andino about transportation.

SAN ALFONSO

San Alfonso is home to **Cascada de las Animas**, a private nature reserve that, a few years back, successfully defied the Chilean government's plans to build a natural gas pipeline over the Andes and through it from Argentina. A former *fundo* (rural estate), it also operates a campground and cabañas, and arranges outings ranging from relaxing picnics, day trips and camping to more strenuous activities like hiking, horseback riding and rafting or kayaking. This is a very popular place on weekends and in summer, but much quieter during the week and off-season.

About 20m up the well-marked turnoff to Cascada de las Animas, one of the Cajón's oddest sights is the collection of antique railcars, and even an operating miniature railway, belonging to José Sagall, known as 'Pepe Tren' to his neighbors. About 100m farther down the road stands the old station for the military railroad that, until the 1960s, carried santiaguino weekenders up the Cajón.

From October to April, *Camping Cascada de las Animas* (☎ 861 1303) charges US$8 per person for shady campsites with good bathroom facilities; the rest of the year, rates are US$4 per person. Comfortable cabañas are also available from US$68 for a double.

Besides rafting, their Santiago office, Expediciones Las Cascadas (☎ 251 9223, 232 7214),

Chilean iguana

Orrego Luco 040 in Providencia (Map 8), does a full-day hiking excursion to Cascada de las Animas, including transportation to and from Santiago, lunch, and pool access at the end of the hike (US$73 per person). A similar program on horseback costs US$94.

REFUGIO LO VALDÉS

Overlooking the Cajón from a southside perch above the Río Volcán, across from Baños Morales and surrounded by poplars, the *Refugio Lo Valdés* (☎ 232 0476, terrainc@ entelchile.net), popularly known as the Refugio Alemán, is a popular weekend destination throughout the year.

Accommodations with full board cost US$51 per person; children to age seven pay half, while those two or younger stay free. Accommodations alone cost US$23; rates are US$35 with breakfast, US$45 with half board, but travelers with sleeping bags can crash in the attic for US$11.

The Refugio's restaurant also serves meals separately for non-guests: US$7 for breakfast, US$10 for an elaborate *onces* (afternoon tea) of sandwiches, kuchen, ice cream, cookies and coffee, and US$12 for lunch or dinner.

MONUMENTO NATURAL EL MORADO

Only 93km from Santiago, this relatively small (3000 hectares) but very scenic park rewards visitors with views of 5060m Cerro El Morado from **Laguna El Morado**, a two-hour hike from the humble hot springs of **Baños Morales**. While it's a stiff climb at the beginning, the trail soon levels off; motivated hikers can continue to the base of Glaciar El Morado, on the lower slopes of the Cerro.

Conaf maintains a small centro de información at the park entrance, where rangers collect an admission charge of US$1.25 for adults, US$0.50 for children. Horses are available for about US$5 per hour at Baños Morales, where there's also camping and simple accommodations.

Altué Active Travel (☎ 232 1103), Encomenderos 83, Las Condes (Map 9), arranges day trips, including lunch and transportation for a minimum of two persons, for US$155 per person. Larger parties pay substantially less per person.

T-Arrpue (☎ 211 7165) runs weekend buses from Santiago's Plaza Italia directly to Baños Morales. There are also buses from the Parque O'Higgins metro station at 7 am, returning at 6 pm.

Baños Colina

The road ends at ***Baños Colina*** (☎ 737 2844), a basic hot springs resort 12km beyond Lo Valdés. US$5 per person gets campers unlimited use of the thermal baths, but the campsites are bleak and exposed, and tents difficult to pitch because of the hard soil. There are also horse rentals; the border is about a six-hour ride, but only group trips planned far in advance may cross to Argentina here.

From September to April, Expediciones Manzur (☎ 643 5651, 777 4284) provides Saturday and Sunday transportation from Plaza Italia in Santiago for US$14 roundtrip, including access to the baths; in summer, there's an additional Wednesday departure. Miguel Acevedo (☎ 777 3881) does the same trip for US$10 roundtrip including access to the baths, leaving from the corner of Alameda and San Ysidro. Try also Buses Cordillera (☎ 777 3881) from Terminal San Borja.

Ski Resorts

Chile has acquired an international reputation among skiers, and Chile's best downhill skiing is to be found in Middle Chile's high cordillera, primarily up the valley of the Río Mapocho beyond Farellones, and along Ruta 60 to Mendoza, Argentina. Most ski areas are above 3300m, so they have long runs, a long season and generally deep, dry snow. Snowboarders are increasingly welcome.

The season generally runs June to early October. Most resorts adjust their rates from low season (mid-June to early July and mid-September to early October), to mid-season (mid-August to mid-September), to high season, the most expensive (early July to mid-August). For current conditions, check the English-language *Santiago Times* online at www.santiagotimes.cl/news/.

EL COLORADO

One of the closest ski areas, only 45km east of the capital and just beyond Farellones, El Colorado (☎ 211 0426, fax 220 7738) has 19 lifts climbing to 3333m above sea level, with 22 different runs and a vertical drop of 903m. Daily lift tickets cost US$33, with discounts for children and seniors; season passes are also available.

For information in Santiago, contact Centro de Ski El Colorado (☎ 246 3344, fax 206 4078, ski-colorado@ctcinternet.cl), Avenida Apoquindo 4900, Local 47/48, Las Condes, which is also the point of departure for direct transportation.

LA PARVA

Only 4km from Farellones, elevations on La Parva's 30 separate runs range from 2662m to 3630m (968m vertical drop). Daily lift tickets range from US$26 in low season to US$33 in high season; multi-day, weekly and seasonal passes are also available. It's also possible to buy an interconnected lift ticket with Valle Nevado (see below).

For accommodations, there's the *Hotel Condominio Nueva La Parva* for US$1950 to US$2250 per week, double occupancy, lift tickets included; for the most current information, contact Centro de Ski La Parva (☎ 264 1466, fax 264 1569), La Concepción 266, Oficina 301, Providencia (Map 8).

VALLE NEVADO

Another 14km beyond Farellones, Valle Nevado is a well-planned, high-altitude ski area, ranging from 2805m to 3670m, with 27 runs up to 3km in length. Full-day lift tickets run US$27 on weekdays to US$33 on weekends. Multi-day tickets are also available, but the savings are minimal. Rental equipment is available on site, and there's also a ski school.

At *Hotel Valle Nevado*, rates start at US$1344/2142 singles/doubles per week in low season and reach US$3234/4606 in high season, including half board and lift tickets. *Hotel Puerta del Sol* is about 30% cheaper, while *Hotel Tres Puntas* is another 15% to 20% cheaper.

Transportation to and from the international airport at Pudahuel costs US$60 roundtrip with Andina del Sud (☎ 697 1010); otherwise, more expensive taxi and helicopter service are available. For bookings, contact Valle Nevado (☎ 206 0027, ☎ 800-669-0554 in the USA, ☎ 888-301-3248 in Canada, fax 208 0695, info@vallenevado.com), Gertrudis Echeñique 441, Las Condes (Map 9).

PORTILLO

Known for its dry powder, Chile's most famous ski resort is the site of several downhill speed records. Altitudes range from 2590m to 3330m on its 11 runs, the longest of which is 1.4km. Just a short distance from the Chilean customs post, on the trans-Andean highway to Mendoza, Portillo is 152km from Santiago.

Hotel Portillo is not cheap, starting at US$825 per person for a week's stay in low season, rising as high as US$4615 to US$6550. Prices, however, include all meals and eight days of lift tickets, but not taxes, though foreign visitors are exempt from the 18% IVA. Lower-priced alternatives involve bunks and shared bath, but even those run US$640 per person in low season, US$770 in high season.

Ski facilities may or may not be open to non-guests, with lift tickets in the US$35 daily range. Additional services include a ski school, baby sitters, sauna and massage, and the like. Meals are available in the hotel restaurant, which has superb views of Laguna del Inca. Moderately priced accommodations are available in the city of Los Andes, below the snow line, 69km to the west.

In summer, the Hotel Portillo charges around US$66/99 to US$77/110 singles/doubles, with breakfast. For more information contact the Centro de Ski Portillo (☎ 263 0606, ☎ 800-829-5325 in the US, fax 263 0595, ptours@skiportillo.com), Renato Sánchez 4270, Las Condes (Ⓜ Escuela Militar; Map 9).

Central Coast

Northwest of Santiago, Valparaíso and its scenic coastline play a dual role in Chile. Valparaíso is a vital port and one of South America's most distinctive urban areas, while Viña del Mar, a resort of international stature, and other coastal towns to the north are choice summer playgrounds. The climate can be fickle, though – coastal towns are often fogbound into the early afternoon, and the average water temperature in summer is only around 15°C.

VALPARAÍSO

☎ 32

Growing spontaneously along the sea and up the surrounding coast range, Valparaíso – Valpo for short – more closely resembles a medieval European harbor than a modern commercial port. Often called La Perla del

Pacífico (Pearl of the Pacific), Chile's second-largest city occupies a narrow wave-cut terrace, overlooked by precipitous cliffs and hills covered by suburbs and shanty-towns linked to the city center by meander-ing roads, footpaths that more nearly resemble staircases, and nearly vertical as-censores (funicular railways).

Built partly on landfill between the wa-terfront and the hills, the commercial center is no less distinctive, with sinuous cobbled streets, irregular intersections and landmark architecture. Since many residents pay no garbage tax because their home values are low, parts of the city are not so clean, other parts, however, are improving rapidly. There is a prospect that some neglected older houses will be restored or remodeled as hotels or hostels.

History

Historians credit Juan de Saavedra, a lieu-tenant from Diego de Almagro's expedi-tion, as the founder of the city. Saavedra's troops met a supply ship from Peru in what is now the Bahía de Valparaíso in 1536. Despite Pedro de Valdivia's designation of the bay as the port of Santiago and the building of some churches, more than 2½ centuries passed before the Spanish crown established a *cabildo* (town council) in 1791. Not until 1802 did Valparaíso legally become a city.

Spanish mercantilism retarded colonial Valparaíso's growth, but after independence foreign merchants quickly established their presence. One visitor in 1822 remarked that Englishmen and North Americans so domi-nated the city that 'but for the mean and dirty appearance of the place, a stranger might almost fancy himself arrived at a British settlement.' Its commerce was disor-derly but vigorous:

The whole space between the beach and custom-house was filled with goods and merchandise of various kinds – timber, boxes, iron-bars, barrels, bales, etc – all exposed without any method or arrangement in the open street. Interspersed among them were a number of mules, some stand-ing with loaded, others with unloaded panniers; while the drivers, called peons, dressed in the char-

acteristic garb of the country, made the place ring with their noisy shouts. Here and there porters were busied in carrying away packages; boatmen stood ready to importune you with incessant demands....

Only a few months later, another visitor had similar impressions, noting that al-though 'even the governor's house and the custom-house are of poor appearance... all the symptoms of great increase of trade are visible in the many new erections for ware-houses.'

Valparaíso's population at independence was barely 5000, but demand for Chilean wheat brought on by the California Gold Rush prompted such a boom that, shortly after mid-century, the city's population was about 55,000. Completion of the railroad from Santiago was a further boost and, by 1880, the population exceeded 100,000. As the first major port-of-call for ships around Cape Horn, the city had become a major commercial center for the entire Pacific Coast and the hub of Chile's nascent banking industry.

A major earthquake in 1906 destroyed many downtown buildings, though some im-pressive 19th-century architecture remains. The opening of the Panama Canal soon after was an economic blow, as European shipping avoided the longer, more arduous Cape Horn route. Chilean exports of mineral nitrates declined as Europeans found synthetic substitutes, indirectly affect-ing Valparaíso by further reducing the region's maritime commerce. The Great Depression of the 1930s was a calamity, as demand for Chile's other mineral exports declined. Not until after WWII was there significant recovery, as the country began to industrialize.

Valparaíso remains less dependent on tourism than neighboring Viña del Mar, but many Chilean vacationers make brief ex-cursions from nearby beach resorts. As capital of Region V, the city is an adminis-trative center. Its major industries are food processing and exporting the products of the mining and fruit-growing sectors. Despite port expansion, the congested loca-tion of the city has diverted cargo south to

San Antonio, which handles nearly twice the volume of Valparaíso. The navy's conspicuous presence remains an important factor in the economy.

Orientation

The city of Valparaíso, 120km northwest of Santiago at the south end of the Bahía de Valparaíso, has an extraordinarily complicated layout that probably only a lifetime resident can completely fathom. In the congested commercial center, pinched between the port and the almost sheer hills, nearly all major streets parallel the shoreline, which curves north as it approaches Viña del Mar. Avenida Errázuriz runs the length of the waterfront, alongside the railway, before merging with Avenida España, the main route to Viña.

Downtown's focal point is remodeled Plaza Sotomayor, facing the port, but several other plazas encourage a lively street life. Families frequent Plaza Victoria, for instance, for its lively playground, while Plaza O'Higgins is the site of one of Chile's finest antique markets.

Behind the downtown area, Valparaíso's many hills are a rabbit's warren of steep footpaths, zigzag roads and blind alleys where even the best map sometimes fails the visitor. The city map in Turistel's *Centro* volume continues to show improvement, however, and the municipal Departamento de Turismo's cheaper *Valparaíso: Ciudad Puerto* is suitable for short-term visits.

Information

Valparaíso's improved, enthusiastic municipal Departamento de Turismo (☎ 221 001), Condell 1490, is open 8:30 am to 2 pm and 3:30 to 5:30 pm weekdays. Its new information office (☎ 236 322) at the Centro de Difusión on Muelle Prat (the pier), near Plaza Sotomayor, with friendly and well-informed personnel including English speakers, distributes free but adequate city maps and sells slightly better ones. It's open 10 am to 7 pm daily. There are also offices in the bus station (Terminal Rodoviario, ☎ 213 246), open the same hours in summer, but 10 am to 6 pm daily except Monday the rest of the

year. Another is on Plaza Victoria, open the same hours in summer but closed the rest of the year.

The Argentine Consulate (☎ 258 165) is at Blanco 890, 2nd floor. The British Consulate (☎ 256 117) is at Blanco 725, Oficina 26. The German Consulate (☎ 256 749) is at Blanco 1215, 11th floor, while the Peruvian Consulate (☎ 253 403) is two floors up at Oficina 1404.

Valparaíso's exchange houses include Inter Cambio on Plaza Sotomayor and Cambio Exprinter at Prat 895.

The main post office (Correos de Chile) is on Prat at its junction with Plaza Sotomayor. Telefónica has long-distance telephone services at Esmeralda 1054, Pedro Montt 2023 and at the Terminal Rodoviario. Entel is at Condell 1495 and at the corner of Avenida Pedro Montt and Cruz. Chilexpress, Avenida Brasil 1456, has fax, telephone and courier services.

DHL (☎ 881 299) has private courier service at Plaza Sotomayor 55.

The Centro Cultural Valparaíso is at Esmeralda 1083. A branch of the Instituto Chileno-Norteamericano de Cultura (☎ 256 897) is nearby at Esmeralda 1061.

Librería Crisis (☎ 218 504), Avenida Pedro Montt 2871, has a good selection of used books on Chilean history and literature.

Hospital Carlos van Buren (☎ 254 074) is at Avenida Colón 2454, at the corner of San Ignacio.

Dangers & Annoyances

Valparaíso's colorful hill neighborhoods have an unfortunate reputation for thieves and robbers – local people warn against any ostentatious display of wealth – but with the usual precautions these areas are safe enough, at least during daylight. Visitors to the area west of Plaza Sotomayor and even downtown have reported muggings, so be alert for suspicious characters and diversions. Exercise all reasonable caution, avoid poorly lit areas at night and if possible, walk with a companion.

Valparaíso has Chile's highest rate of AIDS, associated in part with the sex industry of one of the continent's major ports.

VALPARAÍSO

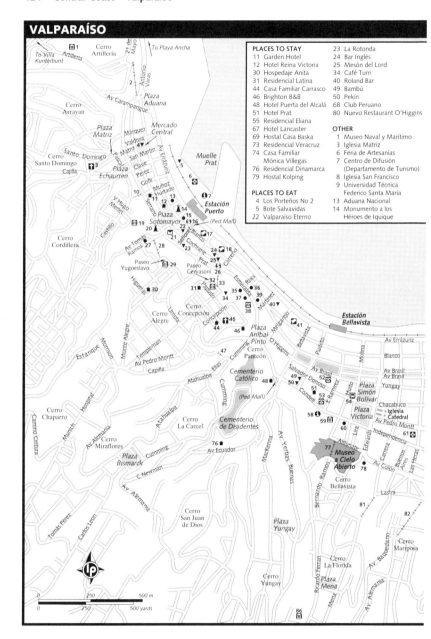

PLACES TO STAY
11 Garden Hotel
12 Hotel Reina Victoria
30 Hospedaje Anita
31 Residencial Latina
44 Casa Familiar Carrasco
46 Brighton B&B
48 Hotel Puerta del Alcalá
51 Hotel Prat
55 Residencial Eliana
67 Hotel Lancaster
69 Hostal Casa Baska
73 Residencial Veracruz
74 Casa Familiar
   Mónica Villegas
76 Residencial Dinamarca
79 Hostal Kolping

PLACES TO EAT
4 Los Porteños No 2
5 Bote Salvavidas
22 Valparaíso Eterno

23 La Rotonda
24 Bar Inglés
25 Mesón del Lord
34 Café Turri
40 Roland Bar
49 Bambú
50 Pekin
68 Club Peruano
80 Nuevo Restaurant O'Higgins

OTHER
1 Museo Naval y Maritimo
3 Iglesia Matriz
6 Feria de Artesanías
7 Centro de Difusión
   (Departamento de Turismo)
8 Iglesia San Francisco
9 Universidad Técnica
   Federico Santa María
13 Aduana Nacional
14 Monumento a los
   Héroes de Iquique

VALPARAÍSO

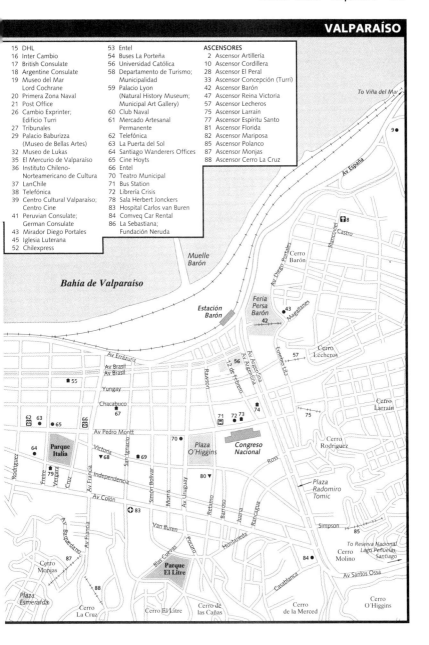

15 DHL
16 Inter Cambio
17 British Consulate
18 Argentine Consulate
19 Museo del Mar
   Lord Cochrane
20 Primera Zona Naval
21 Post Office
26 Cambio Exprinter;
   Edificio Turri
27 Tribunales
29 Palacio Baburizza
   (Museo de Bellas Artes)
32 Museo de Lukas
35 El Mercurio de Valparaíso
36 Instituto Chileno-
   Norteamericano de Cultura
37 LanChile
38 Telefónica
39 Centro Cultural Valparaíso;
   Centro Cine
41 Peruvian Consulate;
   German Consulate
43 Mirador Diego Portales
45 Iglesia Luterana
52 Chilexpress

53 Entel
54 Buses La Porteña
56 Universidad Católica
58 Departamento de Turismo;
   Municipalidad
59 Palacio Lyon
   (Natural History Museum;
   Municipal Art Gallery)
60 Club Naval
61 Mercado Artesanal
   Permanente
62 Telefónica
63 La Puerta del Sol
64 Santiago Wanderers Offices
65 Cine Hoyts
66 Entel
70 Teatro Municipal
71 Bus Station
72 Librería Crisis
78 Sala Herbert Jonckers
83 Hospital Carlos van Buren
84 Comveq Car Rental
86 La Sebastiana;
   Fundación Neruda

ASCENSORES
2 Ascensor Artillería
10 Ascensor Cordillera
28 Ascensor El Peral
33 Ascensor Concepción (Turri)
42 Ascensor Barón
47 Ascensor Reina Victoria
57 Ascensor Lecheros
75 Ascensor Larraín
77 Ascensor Espíritu Santo
81 Ascensor Florida
82 Ascensor Mariposa
85 Ascensor Polanco
87 Ascensor Monjas
88 Ascensor Cerro La Cruz

Highlights

Facing the historic **Primera Zona Naval** (ex-Intendencia de Valparaíso), an impressive structure with a mansard roof, **Plaza Sotomayor** is the official heart of Valparaíso, even more so as a new underground parking structure liberates for public use what had, until recently, looked like a used car dealership. Its dignified statuary crowns a simple, unadorned **Monumento a los Héroes de Iquique**, a subterranean mausoleum paying tribute to Chile's naval martyrs of the War of the Pacific. In addition to Arturo Prat, there are tombs of lesser known figures whose Anglo surnames – Reynolds, Wilson and Irving – hint at the role that northern European immigrants have played in Chilean history.

Other landmarks surrounding Plaza Sotomayor include the **Aduana Nacional** (customs, one of the port city's most important institutions), the **Estación Puerto** (terminal for Merval commuter trains but also noteworthy for its murals), and **Muelle Prat**, the redeveloped port area.

If Plaza Sotomayor is the city's official heart, the **Plaza Matriz** is its historic core, directly uphill from the Mercado Central, where the distinctive hills-architecture starts to take shape. Its major landmark is the **Iglesia Matriz**, a national monument dating from 1842. This is the fourth church on the site since construction of the original chapel in 1559.

Southeast of Plaza Sotomayor, where Prat and Cochrane converge to become Esmeralda, the **Edificio Turri** narrows to the width of its namesake clocktower. Topped by a mansard roof at Esmeralda and Ross, the neoclassical **El Mercurio de Valparaíso** (1903) is the home of Chile's oldest continuously published newspaper (since 1827, long antedating the building itself).

At Independencia and Huito, the neoclassical **Palacio Lyon** (1881) now houses the city's natural history museum and the municipal art gallery. One block east, at the southwest corner of Plaza Victoria, on Independencia between Huito and Molina, the French-style **Club Naval** dates from 1895. Overlooking Plaza Victoria, on Edwards

between Avenida Pedro Montt and Chacabuco, is the **Iglesia Catedral**, the site of ecclesiastical primacy.

At the east end of downtown, toward Viña del Mar, the most imposing landmark is the controversial **Congreso Nacional** (1990), which overlooks **Plaza O'Higgins**, site of the **Teatro Municipal** (municipal theater, 1931), and of the city's best antiques market on weekends. Two blocks north, the **Universidad Católica** is the city's most prestigious educational institution, but the most impressive edifice, dating from the 1930s, belongs to the **Universidad Técnica Federico Santa María**, which dominates Avenida España to the northeast.

Muelle Prat

This redeveloped pier, at the foot of Plaza Sotomayor, is a lively place on weekends, with a helpful tourist kiosk and a good handicrafts market, the Feria de Artesanías, open 10 am to 4 pm Thursday to Sunday. Several boats offer harbor tours for about US$1.50 – note that you should not photograph any of the numerous Chilean naval vessels at anchor. For US$2, some boats take passengers all the way to Viña del Mar – a nice change of pace from the bus.

Palacio Lyon

Once a private mansion, the neoclassical Palacio Lyon (1881) merits a visit in its own right, but also holds two of the city's key museums. Most of the large selection of natural history specimens in the **Museo de Historia Natural** (☎ 257 441), Condell 1546, are mediocre, but the upper exhibition halls compensate for this with outstanding accounts of Chile's pre-Hispanic cultures and their environments, including dioramas of subsistence activities. There is superb material on the oceans and their future, a subject of great importance to a maritime country like Chile. The museum is open 10 am to 1 pm and 2 to 6 pm Tuesday to Friday, 10 am to 6 pm Saturday, and 10 am to 2 pm Sunday and holidays. Admission is about US$1, half that for children, free Wednesday and Sunday.

In the basement of the building, but with a separate entrance, the **Galería Municipal de Arte** (Municipal Art Gallery, ☎ 220 062), Condell 1550, hosts fine arts exhibits throughout the year. It's open 10 am to 7 pm daily except Sunday (free).

Congreso Nacional

Mandated by Pinochet's 1980 constitution, which moved the legislature away from the Santiago-based executive branch, this last major public works project of the dictatorship cost US$100 million by its completion in 1990. With an area of 40,000 square meters, the imposing modern building, built on the site of Pinochet's boyhood homes, has proved to be a notable inconvenience since the return to constitutional government – rapid physical communication between the two cities is possible only by helicopter and there's been a rash of legislators busted for speeding on Ruta 68. Talk of returning congress to Santiago, hitherto opposed by conservative elements, has been gaining steam, but such action would leave Valparaíso with an unanticipated contemporary historical monument – or white elephant.

When congress is in session, the building is open to the public 3 to 5 pm Friday. It's at the junction of Avenida Pedro Montt and Avenida Argentina, opposite Plaza O'Higgins and the bus terminal.

Hills of Valparaíso

Valparaíso is undoubtedly the single most distinctive city in Chile and one of the most intriguing in all of South America. On a sunny afternoon, it's possible to spend hours riding the 15 ascensores, built between 1883 and 1916, and strolling back alleys. Some of the ascensores are remarkable feats of engineering – **Ascensor Polanco**, on the east side of Avenida Argentina, rises vertically through a tunnel, for example.

One of the best areas for urban explorers is Cerro Concepción, reached by **Ascensor Concepción** (the oldest in the city, it originally ran by steam power). Also known as Ascensor Turri, it climbs the slopes from the corner of Prat and Almirante Carreño, across from the landmark clocktower known as the **Reloj Turri**. At the top, the new **Museo de Lukas** (☎ 221 344), Paseo Gervasoni 448, exhibits historical sketches and cartoons by Italian-born porteño caricaturist Renzo Pecchenino. It's open 10:30 am to 2 pm and 3:30 to 6 pm daily except Monday (US$1).

Three blocks southeast, on Paseo Atkinson at Abtao, is the Gothic-style **Iglesia Luterana**.

Reached by **Ascensor El Peral**, near the **Tribunales** (law courts) just off Plaza Sotomayor, Cerro Alegre is home to the **Palacio Baburizza** (1916), housing the city's fine arts museum but presently undergoing an overdue renovation (see below). From here it's possible to loop over to Cerro Concepción, or vice versa. One block north of Plaza Sotomayor, **Ascensor Cordillera** climbs Cerro Cordillera to the **Museo del Mar Lord Cochrane** (see below).

Above the Feria Persa Barón, reached by **Ascensor Barón**, the **Mirador Diego Portales** offers a panorama of the city toward the west; nearby, the belltower of the historic

Ascensor Espíritu Santo

Iglesia San Francisco (1845) served as a landmark for approaching mariners, who gave the city its common nickname 'Pancho' (a diminutive of Francisco). Given Valpo's seismic susceptibility, it's astonishing that this lofty brick building is still standing.

For a quick, inexpensive tour of Valparaíso's hills, catch the Verde Mar 'O' micro on Serrano, near Plaza Sotomayor, all the way to Viña del Mar for about US$0.40. This bus also passes Pablo Neruda's Valparaíso home, now a museum (see La Sebastiana, later in this section).

Palacio Baburizza

Designed for an Italian nitrate baron but named for the Yugoslav who purchased it from him, this landmark art nouveau house (1916) is noteworthy for imaginative woodwork, forged-iron details and a steeply pitched central tower. Set among attractive gardens, it was a private residence until 1971, when the city acquired it as a fine arts museum. It's presently undergoing a much needed renovation with its collections in storage.

The museum (☎ 252 332), on Cerro Alegre's Paseo Yugoeslavo, is reached by Ascensor El Peral from near Plaza Sotomayor. It's normally open 9:30 am to 6 pm daily except Monday, but the building and its grounds alone justify a visit. Admission is free, but donations are accepted.

Museo del Mar Lord Cochrane

Overlooking the harbor, built in 1842 for Lord Thomas Cochrane but never occupied by him, this tile-roofed, colonial-style house above Plaza Sotomayor held Chile's first astronomical observatory – however unlikely that might seem, given Valparaíso's constant fogs. Its pleasant gardens offer excellent views, while the museum itself displays an excellent collection of model ships in glass cases, along with acrylic paintings.

To reach the museum (☎ 213 124), take Ascensor Cordillera from the west side of Plaza Sotomayor and walk east to Merlet 195. It's open 10 am to 6 pm daily except Monday (US$1 adults, US$0.50 children).

Museo Naval y Marítimo

One of few Chilean museums with sufficient resources for acquisitions and a truly professional presentation, Chile's naval and maritime museum focuses on the War of the Pacific (specifically honoring naval and national icon Arturo Prat). There are also major displays on Lord Cochrane (the navy's founder), Admiral Manuel Blanco Encalada and other lesser figures. The most interesting displays, though, deal with voyages around the Horn, giving credit to sailors of every European country.

Reached by Ascensor Artillería from the triangular Plaza Aduana (also known as Plaza Wheelwright), the immaculate museum building served as Chile's Escuela Naval (Naval Academy) from 1893 to 1967. At the top of the ascensor, Paseo 21 de Mayo offers souvenir stands, a small café with an attractive terrace and outstanding views of the port to the east. The museum (☎ 283 749) is open 10 am to 5:30 pm daily except Monday (US$1 adults, US$0.50 children).

Museo a Cielo Abierto

Between 1969 and 1973, students from the Universidad Católica's Instituto de Arte created the 20 brightly colored abstract murals that cover numerous hillside sites on Cerro Bellavista, reached by Ascensor Espíritu Santo. Concentrated on Aldunate and Paseos Guimera, Pasteur, Rudolph and Ferrari, Valparaíso's 'open sky museum' is not great art, but still adds a welcome spot of color to some otherwise rundown areas. The tourist kiosk on Muelle Prat distributes a locator map of the area.

La Sebastiana

Pablo Neruda probably spent less time at La Sebastiana, his least known and least visited house, than at La Chascona or Isla Negra, but he made it a point to watch Valparaíso's annual New Year's fireworks from his lookout on Cerro Bellavista. Restored and open to the public, La Sebastiana (Fundación Neruda) may be the best destination for Neruda pilgrims – it's the only one of his three houses that visitors can wander

Ornate façade of the Iglesia de la Merced, Rancagua

The neoclassical El Mercurio de Valparaíso

Monumento a los Héroes de Iquique, Valpo

AARON MCCOY

Andean skyscape: Monumento Natural El Morado in the Cajón del Maipo

AARON MCCOY

More El Morado mountains

WAYNE BERNHARDSON

Rafting the Río Maipo

around at will rather than subject themselves to regimented tours that seem out of character with the informal poet. In addition to the usual assemblage of oddball artifacts within the house, the Fundación Neruda has built a new Centro Cultural La Sebastiana alongside it, with rotating exhibitions, a café and a souvenir shop.

To reach La Sebastiana (☎ 256 606), Ferrari 692, take Verde Mar bus 'O' or 'D' on Serrano near Plaza Sotomayor and disembark in the 6900 block of Avenida Alemania, a short walk from the house. Alternatively, take Ascensor Espíritu Santo near Plaza Victoria and ask for directions. The house is open to the public 10:30 am to 2:30 pm and 3:30 to 6 pm daily except Monday. Admission is US$3, half that for students and retired people.

Neruda's most famous house, with an extensive collection of maritime memorabilia, is at Isla Negra (see Around Valparaíso, later in this chapter).

Special Events

Año Nuevo (New Year's) is one of Valparaíso's biggest events, thanks to the massive fireworks display that brings hundreds of thousands of spectators to the city to watch the spectacle.

April 17, marking the arrival of the authorization of the town council of Valparaíso in 1791, is the city's annual official day (imperial Spain's glacial bureaucracy and slow communications across the Atlantic delayed receipt of the authorization for more than three years).

Places to Stay

Viña del Mar has a broader choice of accommodations in all categories, but Valparaíso has a few alternatives, the most interesting of which are hospedajes in the scenic hills. Phone ahead before visiting any of these places, which can be difficult to find and may have a limited number of beds.

Budget Near the bus terminal, quiet, comfortable and amiable *Casa Familiar Mónica Villegas* (☎ 215 673, *Avenida Argentina 322)* charges US$9 (with some

space for negotiation, especially when it's not crowded) including a simple breakfast. Try also appealing, comparably priced *Residencial Veracruz (Avenida Pedro Montt 2881)*, opposite the Congreso Nacional, or *Residencial Eliana (☎ 250 945, Avenida Brasil 2164)* for US$12.

On Cerro Concepción, reached by Ascensor Concepción (Turri), family-oriented *Residencial Latina (☎ 237 733, Papudo 462)* comes highly recommended at a price of US$10 per person. Also on Cerro Concepción, the friendly *Casa Familiar Carrasco (☎ 210 737, Abtao 668)* is a phenomenal value at US$8 to US$10 for a single with shared bath, US$25 for doubles with fireplace and furnished with antiques; there are spectacular vistas from the rooftop deck (ideal for New Year's fireworks).

On Cerro Playa Ancha, at the west end of town near Ascensor Artillería, *Villa Kunterbunt (☎ 288 873, Avenida Quebrada Verde 192)* charges US$8 per person without breakfast; English and German are spoken. On Cerro Panteón, near the Cementerio de Disidentes, *Residencial Dinamarca (☎ 259 189, Dinamarca 535)* offers rooms with cable TV and private bath, as well as a bar and a cafeteria, for US$16 per person (there's one single with shared bath for US$12). On Cerro Alegre, recently renovated *Hospedaje Anita (☎ 239 327, Higueras 107)* may be worth a look for US$14 per person.

Conspicuous by its striking mansard roof but suffering from deferred maintenance and a noisy location, *Hotel Reina Victoria (☎ 212 203, Plaza Sotomayor 190)* starts around US$12 per person for 4th-floor singles with shared bath, rising to US$17/22 for 2nd-floor singles/doubles with private bath and breakfast. Around the corner, the similarly priced *Garden Hotel (Serrano 501)* has spacious rooms but is the subject of mixed reports, including surly staff.

Mid-Range & Top End One of downtown's best values is *Hostal Kolping (☎ 216 306, Francisco Valdés Vergara 622)* on the south side of Plaza Victoria, where singles/doubles cost US$18/24 with shared bath, US$25/33 with private bath, breakfast included. Not so good but more expensive are **Hotel Prat** (☎ *253 081, Condell 1443*) for US$25/29; or the rather better **Hotel Lancaster** (☎ *217 391, Chacabuco 2362*) for US$25/44. Highly recommended **Hostal Casa Baska** (☎ *234 036, Victoria 2449*) is a better choice for US$33/38.

On Cerro Concepción, the **Brighton B&B** (☎ */fax 223 513, Pasaje Atkinson 151*) is – despite its classic Valparaíso architecture – a new building, fitted with recycled materials. Also a pub-restaurant, its terrace offers great views of the city over Plaza Aníbal Pinto; rates are US$31/42, but rooms with sea views draw a 50% premium.

An exception to Valpo's shortage of upscale hotels is the new **Hotel Puerta del Alcalá** (☎ *227 478, fax 745 642, Pirámide 524*). Well-located and architecturally appealing, this business-oriented facility costs US$65 single or double.

Places to Eat

Traditionally, visitors dine in Viña del Mar, but Valparaíso can be an equally good place to eat. For the cheapest eats, try the area around the bus terminal.

Informal **Valparaíso Eterno** (☎ *255 605, Señoret 150, 2nd floor*) drips with bohemian atmosphere but is also an inexpensive lunch favorite for the city's downtown business crowd. **Los Porteños No 2** (☎ *252 511, Valdivia 169*) has large portions and excellent service but the menu is limited. Across the street, the 2nd-floor *marisquerías* (seafood stalls) at the **Mercado Central** charge less than US$3 for three-course meals, but the fish is usually fried.

Recommended **Bambú** (☎ *234 216, Pudeto 450*) has cheap vegetarian lunches, while nearby **Pekín** (☎ *254 387, Pudeto 422*) serves Chinese food.

In a classic building with high ceilings and chandeliers near Parque Italia, the elderly waitstaff at the **Club Peruano** (☎ *228 068, Victoria 2324*) serve moderately priced Peruvian specialties and it has tobacco-free areas. **Nuevo Restaurant O'Higgins** (*Retamo 506*) has a popular Sunday lunch for US$7.

The **Roland Bar** (☎ *235 123, Avenida Errázuriz 1152*) serves meat and seafood dishes, with a weekday lunch special for US$5. **Mesón del Lord** (☎ *231 096, Cochrane 859*) has good lunches (including vegetarian alternatives) in a traditional porteño atmosphere. Another traditional favorite is the **Bar Inglés** (☎ *214 625, Cochrane 851/Blanco 870*),

This churro cart provides a tasty snack option.

but prices have risen so that it's no longer a great bargain, even for lunch. At *La Rotonda* (☎ 217 746, *Prat 701*) the lunch menu includes a daily special for about US$10, but consider splitting à la carte dishes from the extensive menu – portions are huge. Both seafood and service are excellent.

Bote Salvavidas (☎ 251 477, *Muelle Prat s/n*) is a traditional but expensive seafood restaurant where open-air diners sometimes have to shoo away the pigeons; nevertheless, the quality is good and the service impeccable. *Café Turri* (☎ 252 091, *Templeman 147*), fronting on Paseo Gervasoni at the upper exit of Ascensor Concepción (Turri), has superb seafood in an agreeable setting, attentive but unobtrusive service, and panoramic harbor views from the 3rd-floor balcony. Although not really cheap, it's exceptional value.

Entertainment

Valparaíso has plenty of sleazy waterfront bars, but most visitors prefer the cluster of new pubs that has rejuvenated Avenida Ecuador, climbing the hill toward Cerro Panteón, just east of the cemetery.

The five-screen *Cine Hoyts* (☎ 594 709, *Pedro Montt 2111*) shows current films. The *Centro Cine* (☎ 216 953, *Esmeralda 1083*), part of the Centro Cultural Valparaíso, is more of an art house.

The *Teatro Municipal* (☎ 214 654, *Avenida Uruguay 410*) hosts live theater and concerts. The *Sala Herbert Jonckers* (☎ 221 680, *Colón 1712*) also offers live theater.

La Puerta del Sol (*Avenida Pedro Montt 2037*) has weekend tango shows.

Spectator Sports

The Santiago Wanderers (☎ 217 210), Independencia 2061, are Valparaíso's first-division soccer team; they play at the Estadio Municipal at Playa Ancha.

Shopping

For a fine selection of crafts, visit the Mercado Artesanal Permanente at the corner of Avenida Pedro Montt and Las Heras.

Valparaíso may be the best city in Chile for flea markets. One such is the Feria Persa Barón, on Avenida Argentina where it becomes Avenida España; it's open 9 am to 11 pm daily. Saturday, Sunday and holidays, there's a tremendous Feria de Antiguedades y Libros La Merced on Plaza O'Higgins, where the prices aren't cheap but the selection of books and antiques is outstanding. There's a more general interest flea market on Plaza Radomiro Tomic, the median strip between the lanes of Avenida Argentina, which includes some Mapuche crafts among the usual post-industrial dreck. There's also a modest Feria de Artesanías near Muelle Prat.

Getting There & Away

Air LanChile (☎ 251 441, fax 233 374) has a Valparaíso office at Esmeralda 1048, but there are no flights out of Viña del Mar's Aeropuerto Torquemada at present.

Bus Nearly all bus companies have offices at Valparaíso's bus station, the Terminal Rodoviario (☎ 213 246), Avenida Pedro Montt 2800, across from the Congreso Nacional. Because services from Valparaíso and Viña del Mar are almost identical, most information (including telephones) appears here and only information that differs appears under bus transportation for Viña. Note that some northbound long-distance buses, especially those at night, involve connections with buses from Santiago, which can mean waiting on the Panamericana – ask before buying your ticket.

The company with the most frequent service to Santiago (1¾ to two hours) is Tur-Bus (☎ 212 028 in Valpo, ☎ 882 621 in Viña). Buses leave every 10 to 15 minutes between 6 am and 10 pm. Some Viña buses go direct to Santiago, while others go via Valparaíso, but the fare is identical at about US$4 one-way.

Slightly cheaper, Cóndor Bus (☎ 212 927 in Valpo, ☎ 882 345 in Viña) leaves every 20 to 30 minutes. Sol del Pacífico (☎ 213 776 in Valpo, ☎ 883 156 in Viña) has hourly departures between 6:50 am and 9:30 pm, while Sol del Sur (☎ 252 211 in Valpo, ☎ 687 277 in Viña) has four daily. Pullman Lit (☎ 237 290) goes every two hours between 8:10 am and 7:10 pm.

Buses Farther Afield

There are many bus companies with service from Valparaíso and Viña del Mar to other towns in the region, as well as covering longer distances within Chile and international destinations. Most rates from Valpo and Viña are identical, with many trips making stops in one or the other and/or Santiago. Rates to, for example, La Ligua and Los Andes run from around US$2 to US$4, distances farther north and south run from around US$15 to US$40, while international trips range from US$25 to Mendoza, Argentina to US$112 to Rio de Janeiro, Brazil.

carrier	in Valpo	in Viña	*serves
Buses Ahumada	☎ 216 663		I
Buses Dhino's	☎ 221 298		R
Buses JM	☎ 256 581	☎ 883 184	R, L
Buses Géminis	☎ 258 322		I
Buses La Porteña	☎ 216 568		R
Buses Lit	☎ 237 200	☎ 690 783	L
Buses Norte	☎ 258 322		L
Buses Pluma	☎ 258 322		I
Buses TAC	☎ 258 922	☎ 685 767	I
Buses Zambrano	☎ 258 986	☎ 883 942	L
Chile Bus	☎ 256 325	☎ 881 187	L
Cóndor Bus	☎ 212 927		R
El Rápido	☎ 257 587	☎ 685 474	I
Fénix Pullman Norte	☎ 257 993		L, I
Flota Barrios	☎ 253 674	☎ 882 725	L
Intersur	☎ 212 297		L
Pullman Bus	☎ 253 125, 256 898	☎ 680 424	R, L
Pullman Bus Lago Peñuelas	☎ 224 025		R
Sol del Pacífico	☎ 288 577		R, L
Sol del Sur	☎ 252 211	☎ 687 277	L
Tas Choapa	☎ 252 921	☎ 882 258	L, I
Transportes Lasval	☎ 214 915	☎ 684 121	L
Tur-Bus	☎ 212 028	☎ 882 621	L, I

* R=service within the region   L=service longer distances within Chile   I=international service

Getting Around

Valparaíso and Viña del Mar are only a few kilometers apart, connected by countless local buses (about US$0.40) and slightly more expensive taxi colectivos.

Valparaíso's Estación Puerto (☎ 217 108) is at Plaza Sotomayor 711 at the corner of Errázuriz, with additional stations at Bellavista (on Errázuriz between Pudeto and Molina) and at Muelle Barón. Merval operates regular commuter trains between the Valparaíso/Viña area and the towns of Quilpué, Villa Alemana and Limache. The area's endemic traffic congestion makes the frequent, inexpensive service between Valparaíso and Viña a superior alternative to either bus or taxi, but there are fewer around midday or late evening, and they cease around 10 pm.

Driving in the congested Valparaíso/Viña area makes little sense, but cars can be useful for visiting beach resorts to the north or south. Most agencies have offices in Viña del Mar, but try Comveq (☎ 212 153) at Avenida Argentina 850.

AROUND VALPARAÍSO
Reserva Nacional Lago Peñuelas
Not really a lake, Lago Peñuelas is a reservoir built before the turn of the century to supply potable water to Valparaíso and Viña del Mar. Nevertheless, this 9260-hectare Conaf reserve along Ruta 68 is a popular site for weekend outings; fishing is possible, and it has a representative sample of coastal range vegetation and lesser fauna and birds. Lago Peñuelas is 30km southeast of Valparaíso. Any of the frequent buses linking Santiago with Valparaíso and Viña del Mar can drop passengers at the entrance.

Lo Vásquez
Every December 8, Chilean authorities close Ruta 68 and nearly half a million pilgrims converge on this small town's **Santuario de la Inmaculada Concepción**, 32km southeast of Valparaíso and 68km northwest of Santiago. Masses take place hourly from 6 pm the night before until 8 pm on the 8th.

Isla Negra (Museo Neruda)
Even more outlandish than La Chascona in Santiago, Pablo Neruda's favorite house sits on a rocky ocean headland between Valparaíso and Cartagena. Once vandalized by agents of the Pinochet dictatorship, it now houses the Museo Neruda, with the poet's collections of bowsprits, ships-in-bottles, nautical instruments, wood carvings and other memorabilia. His tomb is also here.

In summer, Isla Negra (☎ 035-461 284), which is *not*, by the way, an island, is open for visits from 10 am to 8 pm Tuesday to Sunday. Reservations are imperative, since there are up to 40 tours daily with guides whose interest and competence vary greatly. The rest of the year, when hours are 10 am to 2 pm and 3 to 6 pm Tuesday to Friday and 10 am to 8 pm weekends, tours are more relaxed. Admission and tour fees are US$2.50 for adults, US$1.25 for children, but tours are available in English or French for US$4 per person.

Tours last only half an hour, but visitors can hang around and photograph the grounds as long as they like. Pullman Bus

Lago Peñuelas (☎ 224 025 in Valpo) can drop pilgrims almost at the door (US$2.50). It's also possible to catch a bus from Santiago's Terminal Sur.

VIÑA DEL MAR
☎ 32
Viña del Mar (Viña for short) has long been Chile's premier beach resort, but it's also a bustling commercial center. Only a short bus ride north of Valparaíso, it is popularly known as the Ciudad Jardín (Garden City), for reasons obvious to any visitor: beginning with Avenida España's Reloj de Flores (Clock of Flowers), which greets visitors at the entrance to the town, Viña's manicured subtropical landscape of palms and bananas contrasts dramatically with the colorful disorder of its blue-collar neighbor. Many moneyed Chileans and other wealthy Latin Americans own houses here, but while Viña is not cheap, neither is it impossibly expensive.

Colonial Viña was the hacienda of the prominent Carrera family, who sold it to a Portuguese businessman named Alvarez in the mid-19th century. Alvarez's daughter and sole heir later married into the Vergara family, who have bestowed their name upon many city landmarks. Soon thereafter, Viña's history as the country's Pacific playground began as the railroad linked Valparaíso with Santiago – the porteños of Valparaíso, many of them foreigners, now had easy access to the beaches and broad green spaces to the north, and soon built grand houses and mansions away from the cramped harbor city.

With the construction of hotels and the subdivision of the sector north of the Estero Marga Marga, Viña became an increasingly attractive and popular weekend destination for santiaguinos. Viña, though, has recently lost popularity to competing resorts like La Serena.

Visitors anticipating balmy summer weather are often disappointed – like San Francisco, California, Viña and the entire central coast are subject to cool fogs that don't burn off until early afternoon, and ocean temperatures are downright chilly.

Sunseekers and surfers often wish they had brought woolens and wet suits.

Orientation

Viña is about 10km northeast of Valparaíso via the shoreline Avenida España. It consists of two distinct sectors: an established, prestigious area of traditional mansions south of the Estero Marga Marga, and a newer, more regular residential grid to its north. Several bridges, most notably Puente Libertad, connect the two sectors. North of the heavily polluted Marga Marga, most streets are identified by number and direction, either Norte (north), Oriente (east) or Poniente (west). Avenida Libertad separates Ponientes from Orientes. These streets are usually written as numbers, but are sometimes spelled out, so that 1 Norte may also appear as Uno Norte.

The commercial and activity centers of Viña are south of the Marga Marga, on Plaza Vergara and Avenida Arlegui and Avenida Valparaíso, which parallel the river. South of Alvarez is a zone of turn-of-the-19th-century mansions that belonged to the Santiago/Viña elite, whose centerpiece is the famous Quinta Vergara (see later in this section). Viña's main attraction, of course, is the white-sand beaches that stretch northward from Caleta Abarca to the suburbs of Reñaca and Concón. The city's limited industry is several kilometers inland.

Information

The municipal Central de Turismo e Informaciones (☎ 269 330) is near the junction of Libertad and Arlegui, just north of Plaza Vergara. Most of the year it's open 9 am to 2 pm and 3 to 7 pm weekdays, 10 am to 2 pm and 4 to 7 pm Saturday, but in the summer peak season it's open 9 am to 7 pm daily except Sunday. It distributes an adequate city map and an excellent monthly flyer entitled *Todo Viña del Mar Valparaíso*, including useful information and a calendar of events for both cities.

Sernatur's regional office (☎ 882 285, fax 684 117) is at Valparaíso 507, 3rd floor, but the entrance is a little difficult to find and the staff are oriented more toward

businesses than individuals. It's open 8:30 am to 5:30 pm weekdays. The Automóvil Club de Chile (Acchi, ☎ 689 505) is just north of the Marga Marga at 1 Norte 901.

For exchanging US cash or traveler's checks, try Cambios Guiñazú at Arlegui 686 or Inter-Cambio at 1 Norte 655-B.

The post office (Correos de Chile) is at the northwest side of Plaza Vergara, near Puente Libertad. DHL (☎ 683 913), Avenida Libertad 715, has international courier service.

Telefónica has long-distance offices at Valparaíso 628, as well as at Valparaíso and Villanelo, and at the corner of Avenida Libertad and 1 Norte. For cellular communications, contact Entel PCS at Avenida Libertad 1030; Startel at Avenida Libertad 1002; or BellSouth (☎ 975 891) at 9 Norte 870.

The Cyber Blues Café (☎ 690 529, cyber@café.cl), Avenida Valparaíso 196, offers Internet access, as does Planète Bleue, Avenida Valparaíso 279, Local 3.

Conaf (☎ 970 108), 3 Norte 541, has information on protected areas like Parque Nacional La Campana and other national parks.

For laundry there's Laverap, at Libertad 902, and Lavarápido (☎ 688 331) at Arlegui 440.

Hospital Gustavo Fricke (☎ 680 041) is east of downtown at Alvarez 1532, at the corner of Cancha.

Summer is the pickpocket season, so keep a close eye on your belongings, especially on the beach.

In-line skaters have become so ubiquitous in Viña that pedestrians must be alert to avoid collisions.

Cultural Centers

There are frequent exhibitions of art and sculpture at the Centro Cultural Viña del Mar (☎ 269 708), Avenida Libertad 250, which is open 10 am to 1 pm and 3 to 7:30 pm weekdays, 10:30 am to 1:30 pm and 4 to 8 pm weekends. Similar programs take place at the Sala Viña del Mar (☎ 680 633), Arlegui 683, which is open 10 am to 8 pm daily, except Sunday when hours are 10 am to 1 pm.

Viña's international cultural centers include the Instituto Chileno-Norteamericano

(☎ 686 191) at 2 Oriente 385 between 4 and 5 Norte, the Instituto Chileno-Británico (☎ 971 060) at 3 Norte 824, which has up-to-date British newspapers and magazines, as well as the Alianza Francesa (☎ 685 908) at Alvarez 314.

Museums

Specializing in Easter Island (Rapa Nui) archaeology and Chilean natural history, the **Museo de Arqueológico e Historia Francisco Fonck** (☎ 686 753), 4 Norte 784, features an original moai from Chile's remote Pacific possession at the approach to its entrance, but repeated vandalism may cause the moai to be moved. It has also been the site of the **Biblioteca William Mulloy**, probably the best concentration of books, maps and documents on the subject of Easter Island, but this facility is due to move to Hanga Roa's Museo Sebastián Englert in the year 2000. Duplicates of most of the material will remain in Viña. The museum is open 10 am to 6 pm Tuesday to Friday, 10 am to 2 pm weekends (US$1.50 for adults, US$0.20 for kids).

The **Museo Palacio Rioja** (☎ 689 665), at Quillota 214, is a turn-of-the-19th-century mansion that is now a municipal museum. Also hosting frequent musical and theater presentations, including films, it's open 10 am to 2 pm and 3 to 6 pm daily except Monday (US$0.60 adults, US$0.20 children).

On Avenida Marina near the outlet of the Estero Marga Marga, housed in the Castillo Wulff, the **Museo de la Cultura del Mar Salvador Reyes** (☎ 625 427) is open 10 am to 1 pm and 2:30 to 5:45 pm Tuesday to Friday, 10 am to 2 pm weekends and holidays. Admission is US$1 for adults, half that for children, free on weekends and holidays.

Among Viña's private art galleries are Galería de Arte Modigliani (☎ 684 991) at 5 Norte 168, and Arte Gallery at 2 Poniente 671.

Quinta Vergara

Once the residence of the prosperous Alvarez-Vergara family, now a public park, the magnificently landscaped Quinta Vergara contains the Venetian-style **Palacio Vergara**, which dates from 1908. The building houses the **Museo Municipal de Bellas Artes** (fine arts museum, ☎ 680 618), open 10 am to 2 pm and 3 to 6 pm daily except Monday. Admission is about US$0.60, US$0.20 for children.

Frequent summer concerts at the Quinta's **Anfiteatro** (amphitheater) complement the celebrated Festival Internacional de la Canción (see Special Events, later in this section). The grounds, whose only entrance is on Errázuriz at the south end of Quinta, are open 7 am to 7 pm daily.

Jardín Botánico Nacional

Chile's national botanical garden (☎ 672 566) comprises 61 hectares of native and exotic plants that, since 1983, have been systematically developed as a research facility with an expanded nursery, a library, educational programs and plaques for identification of individual specimens. Conaf has restricted cars and recreational activities like soccer and picnicking, making it a more interesting and relaxing place to spend an afternoon.

From Viana in downtown Viña, take bus No 20 east to the end of the line, then cross the bridge and walk about 10 minutes; the botanical garden is on your left. Grounds are open 9 am to 7 pm daily except Monday in summer; the rest of the year it's open 10 am to 6 pm daily. Admission is about US$0.75 for adults, US$0.20 for children.

Beaches

Many of Viña's beaches are either crowded or contaminated, but those in the northern suburbs are far better – from 2 Norte, take Pony Bus Nos 1, 10, 10-A (summer only) or 111 north to Reñaca and Concón, for example. For more details, see Around Viña del Mar, later in this chapter.

Organized Tours

A pleasant means of getting to know Viña is an hour's ride around town in a horse-drawn carriage, leaving from Plaza Vergara, which costs about US$15 for two people. More cheaply, at 3 and 5 pm daily, Sernatur-sponsored Trolley Tour conducts 1½-hour

VIÑA DEL MAR

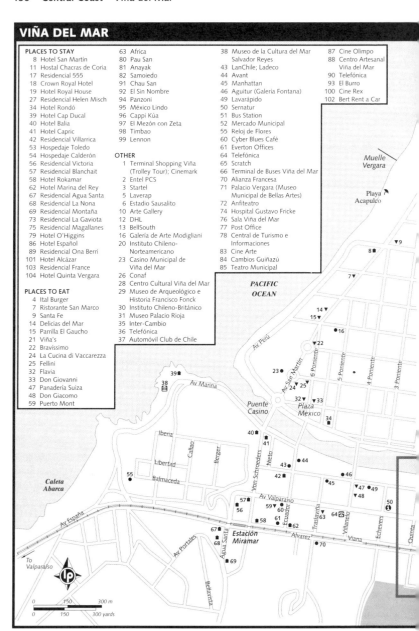

PLACES TO STAY
8 Hotel San Martín
11 Hostal Chacras de Coria
17 Residencial 555
18 Crown Royal Hotel
19 Hotel Royal House
27 Residencial Helen Misch
34 Hotel Rondó
39 Hotel Cap Ducal
40 Hotel Balia
41 Hotel Capric
42 Residencial Villarrica
53 Hospedaje Toledo
54 Hospedaje Calderón
56 Residencial Victoria
57 Residencial Blanchait
58 Hotel Rokamar
62 Hotel Marina del Rey
67 Residencial Agua Santa
68 Residencial La Nona
69 Residencial Montaña
73 Residencial La Gaviota
75 Residencial Magallanes
79 Hotel O'Higgins
86 Hotel Español
89 Residencial Ona Berri
101 Hotel Alcázar
103 Residencial France
104 Hotel Quinta Vergara

PLACES TO EAT
4 Ital Burger
7 Ristorante San Marco
9 Santa Fe
14 Delicias del Mar
15 Parrilla El Gaucho
21 Viña's
22 Bravíssimo
24 La Cucina di Vaccarezza
25 Fellini
32 Flavia
33 Don Giovanni
47 Panadería Suiza
48 Don Giacomo
59 Puerto Mont

63 Africa
80 Pau San
81 Anayak
82 Samoiedo
91 Chau San
92 El Sin Nombre
94 Panzoni
95 México Lindo
96 Cappi Kúa
97 El Mezón con Zeta
98 Timbao
99 Lennon

OTHER
1 Terminal Shopping Viña
   (Trolley Tour); Cinemark
2 Entel PCS
3 Startel
5 Laverap
6 Estadio Sausalito
10 Arte Gallery
12 DHL
13 BellSouth
16 Galería de Arte Modigliani
20 Instituto Chileno-
   Norteamericano
23 Casino Municipal de
   Viña del Mar
26 Conaf
28 Centro Cultural Viña del Mar
29 Museo de Arqueológico e
   Historia Francisco Fonck
30 Instituto Chileno-Británico
31 Museo Palacio Rioja
35 Inter-Cambio
36 Telefónica
37 Automóvil Club de Chile

38 Museo de la Cultura del Mar
   Salvador Reyes
43 LanChile; Ladeco
44 Avant
45 Manhattan
46 Aguitur (Galería Fontana)
49 Lavarápido
50 Sernatur
51 Bus Station
52 Mercado Municipal
55 Reloj de Flores
60 Cyber Blues Café
61 Everton Offices
64 Telefónica
65 Scratch
66 Terminal de Buses Viña del Mar
70 Alianza Francesa
71 Palacio Vergara (Museo
   Municipal de Bellas Artes)
72 Anfiteatro
74 Hospital Gustavo Fricke
76 Sala Viña del Mar
77 Post Office
78 Central de Turismo e
   Informaciones
83 Cine Arte
84 Cambios Guiñazú
85 Teatro Municipal

87 Cine Olimpo
88 Centro Artesanal
   Viña del Mar
90 Telefónica
93 El Burro
100 Cine Rex
102 Bert Rent a Car

PACIFIC
OCEAN

Muelle
Vergara

Playa
Acapulco

Av Perú
6 Poniente
5 Poniente
4 Poniente
3 Poniente
Av San Martín
Av Marina
Puente
Casino
Plaza
México
Iberia
Callao
Berger
Libertad
Balmaceda
Von Schroeders
Nieto
Ecuador
Av Valparaíso
Traslaviña
Villanelo
Echevers
Quinta
Caleta
Abarca
Av España
Av Santa
Av Portales
Estación
Miramar
Alvarez
Viana
Bellavista

To
Valparaíso

0   150   300 m
0   150   300 yards

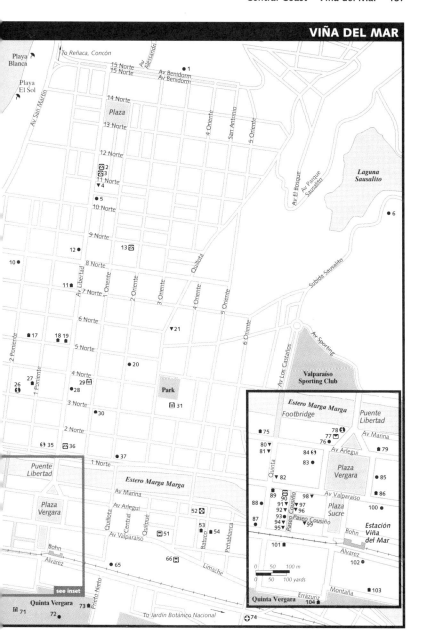

VIÑA DEL MAR

Playa Blanca

Playa El Sol

To Reñaca, Concón

Av San Martín

15 Norte
15 Norte

Av Benidorm
Av Benidorm

● 1

14 Norte

Plaza

13 Norte

12 Norte

Av Alessandri

4 Oriente

San Antonio

5 Oriente

Laguna Sausalito

● 6

🖼2
📷3
11 Norte
▼ 4

● 5

10 Norte

9 Norte

12 ●

13 📷

Av El Bosque

Av Parque Sausalito

8 Norte

Av Libertad

1 Oriente

2 Oriente

3 Oriente

4 Oriente

Quillota

Subida Sausalito

10 ●

11 🏛

7 Norte

6 Norte

▼ 21

5 Oriente

6 Oriente

Av Sporting

🏛 17

18 19

2 Poniente

5 Norte

● 20

Valparaíso Sporting Club

1 Poniente

26
🖂

27

4 Norte
29 🏛

● 28

Park

🏛 31

Av Los Castaños

● 30

3 Norte

2 Norte

🖂 35   📷 36

● 37

1 Norte

Puente Libertad

Plaza Vergara

Estero Marga Marga

Av Marina

Av Arlegui

Quillota

Central

Quilpué

52 🔲

Bohn

Álvarez

● 65

53 🏛   🏛 54

🔲 51

Batuco

Peñablanca

Av Valparaíso

see inset

66 🖂

Limache

🏛 71

Quinta Vergara

72 ●

73 🏛

Prieto Nieto

To Jardín Botánico Nacional

🖂 74

Inset

Estero Marga Marga
Footbridge

Puente Libertad

Av Marina

🏛 75

78 🖂
77 🖂
76 ●

79 🏛

80 ▼
81 ▼

84 🖂

83 ●

Plaza Vergara

● 85

Quinta

▼ 82

Av Arlegui

86 🏛

89 ●
90 📷
91 ▼
92 ▼

98 ▼

Paseo Cousiño

97 ▼
96 ▼

Av Valparaíso

Plaza Sucre

100 ●

88 ●

87 ●

93 ●
94 ▼
95 ▼

99 ▼

Paseo Cousiño

Bohn

Estación Viña del Mar

101 🏛

Álvarez

102 ●

0   50   100 m

0   50   100 yards

Quinta Vergara

Montaña

🏛 103

Errázuriz

104 🏛

Av Sporting

tours of Viña, leaving from Terminal Shopping Viña on 15 Norte between 2 and 3 Oriente. The cost is US$5 for adults, US$4 for children.

Aguitur, Viña's Asociación de Guías de Turismo (☎ 711 052) has moved out of the municipal tourist office and into the Galería Fontana at Arlegui 364, Oficina 223. It can arrange tours of Viña or Valparaíso (three hours, US$20), Viña *and* Valparaíso (four hours, US$25), Zapallar (eight hours, US$35), Isla Negra (eight hours, US$35) or Santiago (10 hours, US$40). There is also a three-hour night tour of Viña and Valparaíso for US$35.

Private guides are available from Aguitur for US$40 per half-day, US$80 per full day, in English, French, Italian and Greek; Spanish-language rates are about a third less.

Special Events

Viña del Mar's most wildly popular attraction is the annual Festival Internacional de la Canción (International Song Festival), held every February in the amphitheater of the Quinta Vergara. This pompous competition of the kitschiest artistes from the Spanish-speaking world (for balance, there's usually at least one really insipid Anglo performer) resembles the Eurovision Song Contest. Every evening for a week, everything stops as ticketless Chileans gaze transfixed at TV sets in their homes, cafés, restaurants and bars. Patient and discriminating listeners may hear some worthwhile folk music. The Latin American TV network Univisión has the overseas rights, and often broadcasts the better-known acts in the USA and elsewhere.

Places to Stay

Accommodations are so plentiful that it would be impossible to list everything, but the entries below are a representative sample. Prices rise in summer, but outside the peak months of January and February, supply exceeds demand and prices drop (except on major holidays like Easter and mid-September's Fiestas Patrias). March is an especially good month, when the weather is often ideal but most Chileans have finished their holidays.

Budget Budget travelers will find several alternatives on or near Agua Santa and Von Schroeders, as well as downtown near the bus terminal. Off-season prices run to about US$10 per person, in season twice that or more, but a weak Argentine economy can also mean negotiable prices even in summer and at mid-range hotels.

The *Hotel Royal House* (☎ 681 965, 5 Norte 683), is an outstanding, well-located facility charging US$12 in off-season, US$20 in summer.

The improving *Residencial Montaña* (☎ 622 230, Agua Santa 153) is one of Viña's cheapest options at about US$9 per person, slightly less off-season; breakfast is included. *Residencial Blanchait* (☎ 974 949, Valparaíso 82-A) charges US$10 per person, with shared bath.

In an attractive blue Victorian building, *Residencial Agua Santa* (☎ 901 531, Agua Santa 36) charges US$10 in peak season. Almost next door, *Residencial La Nona* (☎ 663 825, Agua Santa 48) costs US$15 per person, with breakfast.

Residencial Victoria (☎ 977 370, Valparaíso 40) costs US$12 per person with shared bath, US$16 with private bath. *Hotel Capric* (☎ 978 295, Von Schroeders 39) charges US$13 for singles with shared bath (there's only one of them) and a skimpy breakfast, but it's not bad; rooms with private bath cost US$22/33 singles/doubles. *Residencial Ona Berri* (☎ 688 187, Valparaíso 618) has rooms for US$15 per person with shared bath, US$25 with private bath.

Near the bus terminal, across the street from each other, are two friendly, comfortable family lodgings charging around US$20 to US$25 a double with private bath: *Hospedaje Calderón* (☎ 970 456, Batuco 147) and *Hospedaje Toledo* (☎ 881 496, Batuco 160).

On the 'wrong side of the tracks' (in Viña, at least), *Residencial France* (☎ 685 976, Montaña 743) is a bit ragged, but friendly for US$16 per person with shared bath. Some rooms are small and boxy, but it has pleasant common areas.

Mid-Range Near the grounds of the Quinta Vergara, family-run *Residencial La Gaviota*

(☎ 974 439, Alcalde Prieto Nieto 0332) is a bargain at US$15 per person with shared bath, US$20 per person with private bath, both with breakfast. Set back from the street, friendly, family-run **Residencial Magallanes** (☎ 685 101, Arlegui 555) is a rundown place that seems overpriced at US$20 per person with shared bath (US$30/45 with private bath), but it's possible to bargain. For US$18/26, **Residencial Villarrica** (☎ 942 807, Arlegui 172) is also a good choice.

In the quieter, more residential area north of the Marga Marga, rates at tranquil, comfortable and well-located **Residencial Helen Misch** (☎ 971 565, 1 Poniente 239) are US$25/30. Award-winning **Residencial 555** (☎/fax 972 240, 5 Norte 555) is a newish place charging US$25/33 with shared bath, US$32/44 with private bath. **Hotel Balia** (☎ 978 310, Von Schroeders 36) charges US$25/37, while **Hotel Rokamar** (☎ 690 019, Viana 107) costs US$30/35.

Hostal Chacras de Coria (☎ 901 419, 7 Norte 669) costs US$30/36 with breakfast. English is spoken at the recommended **Crown Royal Hotel** (☎ 682 450, 5 Norte 655), which costs US$45 a double with a substantial buffet breakfast. Also recommended, **Hotel Español** (☎ 685 145, Plaza Vergara s/n) is in the same range at US$37/50.

Service is good at **Hotel Rondó** (☎ 883 144, 1 Norte 157), which charges US$48/61. Enthusiastically endorsed **Hotel Quinta Vergara** (☎ 685 073, fax 691 978, Errázuriz 690) has an English-speaking owner whose rates are US$50/60 with breakfast. During the annual song festival, however, this can be a noisy location. The new **Hotel Marina del Rey** (☎ 883 505, Ecuador 299), a Best Western affiliate, charges US$65/78.

Top End Top-end accommodations start around US$80/109 at **Hotel San Martín** (☎ 689 191, San Martín 667), but people have criticized the size and quality of rooms, despite its views of Playa Acapulco. **Hotel Alcázar** (☎ 685 112, Alvarez 646) is a better value for US$82/110.

Visitors with a little more green, about US$105/130, can try the oddball **Hotel Cap**

Ducal (☎ 626 655, fax 665 478, Avenida Marina 51), a ship-shaped building set on a concrete foundation in the surf ('It's not next to the sea, it's on the sea'), whose restaurant is also worth a try.

At the venerable **Hotel O'Higgins** (☎ 882 016, Plaza Vergara s/n), rates start at US$102/122, but you can pay up to US$130/146 (including a buffet breakfast) and accumulate a huge room-service bill without even working up a sweat. It's worth mentioning, though, that this 1934 landmark is past its prime, and the service could stand improvement as well.

Places to Eat

Like many other seaside resorts, Viña is sinking under the weight of hotels and restaurants, but there are good values for diners. **Panadería Suiza** (Arlegui at Villanelo) has good, cheap pastries and kuchen. For sandwiches, coffee and desserts, try **Anayak** (☎ 680 093, Quinta 134) or, even better, **Samoiedo** (☎ 684 610, Valparaíso 637). **Pau San** (☎ 685 257, Quinta 122) has inexpensive Chinese lunches and dinners.

Several good, moderately priced eateries are clustered on Pasaje Cousiño, a small passageway off Valparaíso near Plaza Vergara. **Panzoni** (☎ 682 134, Pasaje Cousiño 12-B) features friendly service, excellent atmosphere and fine Italian and Middle Eastern specialties; it's especially popular for lunch. **Chau San** (☎ 884 943, Pasaje Cousiño 10) prepares cheap Cantonese lunches. The modest, inexpensive **México Lindo** (☎ 692 144, Pasaje Cousiño 136, 2nd floor) serves credible Tex-Mex specialties like enchiladas and burritos, but the sauces are bland and the drinks are expensive. Tobacco-free **El Sin Nombre** (Pasaje Cousiño s/n) has cheap lunches, as does friendly **Lennon** (Pasaje Cousiño 16), which doubles as a pub. Other possibilities are **Cappi Kúa** (☎ 977 331, Pasaje Cousiño 11, Local 4) and **El Mezón con Zeta** (☎ 690 494, Pasaje Cousiño 9), which also provides live entertainment at night.

Misleadingly named **Ital Burger** (Avenida Libertad 920) has reasonably priced pasta dinners, but most other Italian choices are upscale. ***Ristorante San Marco*** *(☎ 975 304, Avenida San Martín 597)*, ***Don Giacomo*** *(☎ 688 889, Villanelo 135, 2nd floor)*, ***Don Giovanni*** *(2 Norte and 6 Poniente)*, ***Flavia*** *(☎ 686 358, 6 Poniente 121)*, and ***La Cucina di Vaccarezza*** *(☎ 975 790, Avenida San Martín 180)* all serve Italian specialties. ***Fellini*** *(☎ 975 742, 3 Norte 88)* is more Franco-Italian, with excellent fish.

LP correspondents continue to praise ***Puerto Montt*** *(Valparaíso 158-A)*, reached by a narrow off-street passageway, for large portions of well-prepared and reasonably priced fish. ***Delicias del Mar*** *(☎ 901 837, Avenida San Martín 459)* is a good but expensive Basque seafood restaurant.

Viña's *(☎ 694 655, Quillota and 6 Norte)* serves full parrilladas, as does ***Parrilla El Gaucho***, Avenida San Martín and 5 Norte. Most notable for its outlandish façade and decor, ***Africa*** *(☎ 882 856, Valparaíso 324)* serves both meat and seafood. ***Santa Fe*** *(☎ 691 719, 8 Norte 303)* is the Viña branch of Santiago's fine and popular but expensive Tex-Mex restaurant.

Timbao *(Valparaíso 670)* and ***Bravíssimo***, Avenida San Martín and 4 Norte, both offer good ice cream.

Entertainment

First-run movies often hit Viña even before they get to Santiago. Try the two-screen ***Cine Olimpo*** *(☎ 711 607, Quinta 294)* or ***Cine Rex*** *(☎ 685 050, Valparaíso 758)*, or check out the eight-screen ***Cinemark*** *(☎ 993 391, 15 Norte 961, Local 224)*. The ***Cine Arte*** *(☎ 882 798, Plaza Vergara 142)* is an art house.

There's a place in Antofagasta called 'Disco Hell,' but Viña may run away with that title thanks to a plethora of night spots such as ***El Burro*** *(Pasaje Cousiño 12-D)*, ***Scratch*** *(☎ 978 219, Bohn 970)* and ***Manhattan*** *(Arlegui 302, 2nd floor)*.

It's not really a dance club per se, but ***Hotel Alcázar*** (see Places to Stay, earlier in this section) holds a *noche de tango* every Saturday from 9 pm. There's also dancing Friday and Saturday evenings at top-end ***Hotel O'Higgins***, and at ***Don Giacomo*** *(Villanelo 135)*.

Plays, films and concerts take place at the ***Teatro Municipal*** *(☎ 681 739, Plaza Vergara s/n)*.

The ***Casino Municipal de Viña del Mar*** *(☎ 689 200, Avenida San Martín 199)*, overlooking the beach on the north side of the Marga Marga, offers opportunities to squander your savings on slot machines, bingo and card games, in between dinner and cabaret entertainment. Open daily from 6 pm into the early morning, it collects a US$6 cover charge.

Spectator Sports

Everton, Viña's second-division soccer team, plays at Estadio Sausalito *(☎ 978 250)*. Team offices *(☎ 689 504)* are at Viana 161.

Horse racing takes place at the Valparaíso Sporting Club *(☎ 689 393)*, Los Castaños 404.

Shopping

The permanent crafts stalls along Pasaje Cousiño are a good place to search for jewelry, copperware and leather goods in particular. The Centro Artesanal Viña del Mar, on Quinta between Viana and Valparaíso, has a large selection.

Getting There & Away

LanChile *(☎ 690 365)* and Ladeco share offices at Ecuador 80, but all flights leave from Santiago. Avant *(☎ 975 532)* is at Ecuador 31. LanChile and Ladeco operate their own bus service directly to Santiago's international and domestic terminals.

Viña's Terminal Rodoviario at Valparaíso and Quilpué, two long blocks east of Plaza Vergara, is currently undergoing a major renovation; at present buses leave from the provisional Terminal de Buses Viña del Mar *(☎ 697 680)*, Limache 1001. Services are virtually identical to those from Valparaíso, and all northbound and international services from the port capital stop in Viña (see Getting There & Away in the Valparaíso section, earlier in this chapter, for details).

Getting Around

Running along Arlegui, frequent local buses marked 'Puerto' or 'Aduana' link Viña with Valparaíso.

For easier connections to Valparaíso, the Metro Regional Valparaíso (Merval) has two stations: Estación Miramar at Alvarez and Agua Santa, and Estación Viña del Mar at the southeast corner of Plaza Sucre.

Viña has taxis that are twice as expensive as those in Santiago.

For the cheapest car rental rates, try Bert (☎ 685 515) at Alvarez 762. There are several others, including Mach Viña (☎ 259 429) at Las Heras 428, and Euro (☎ 883 559) at Hotel O'Higgins.

AROUND VIÑA DEL MAR

North of Viña are several less celebrated but more attractive beach towns along a coastline with spectacular rock outcrops, crashing surf and blowholes, but Chile's moneyed elite are rapidly appropriating the best sites and cutting off public access in many places.

Reñaca & Concón

Among the nearby beach towns are over-built suburbs like Reñaca, which has its own tourist office (☎ 32-900 499) at Avenida Borgoño 14100, plus the area's most extensive beach (also one of the cleanest). Body-boarders frequent Concón's Playa Negra.

The wall-to-wall, multi-tiered apartment buildings at Reñaca and Concón exemplify urban claustrophobia and mean no budget accommodations, but Reñaca's *Hotel Montecarlo* (☎ 32-830 397, fax 32-835 739, Avenida Vicuña Mackenna 136) has earned recommendations for its US$45/70 singles/ doubles.

Reñaca's *Pacífico* (☎ 32-832 055, Avenida Borgoño 17120) has drawn effusive praise for quality seafood at moderate prices, with fine service. Another local dining treat is the seafood at Concón's *La Picá Horizonte* (☎ 32-903 665, San Pedro 120) at Caleta Higuerillas, a little hard to find but worth the effort. From the Muelle de Pescadores (Fisherman's Pier), climb the steps (behind Restaurant El Tiburón) and, at the top, walk one short block left along the dirt road to San Pedro. On Sunday afternoon it's hard to get a table, but other nearby restaurants like *Picá los Delfines* (☎ 32-814 919, San Pedro

130) are decent alternatives, though the latter's service leaves much to be desired.

The *Cine Plaza* (☎ 32-837 217, Mall Plaza Reñaca s/n) shows current films.

Dancing choices include Reñaca's *News* (☎ 32-831 158, Avenida Borgoño 13101); *Baby Oh* (Santa Luisa 501); and Concón's *César* at Playa Amarilla.

Quintero

Another 23km beyond Concón, Quintero is a peninsular beach community that was once part of Lord Cochrane's hacienda. **Las Ventanas**, just to the north, is a liquid petroleum gas port featuring a power plant, an old LPG tanker washed up on the beach, and, remarkably, the **Río Puchuncaví estuary**, a valuable wetland that's essentially an ecopreserve.

One could guess that the *Hotel Monaco* (☎ 32-930 939, 21 de Mayo 1500) must once have been a very fine place, but it's now rundown – and cheap for US$6 with shared bath, US$30 for a double with private bath. Rates are US$10 per person with shared bath at *Residencial Victoria* (☎ 32-930 208, Vicuña Mackenna 1460), which also has a good *picada*, but there are literally dozens of seafood locales along 21 de Mayo.

There are also reasonable accommodations at *Residencial María Alejandra* (☎ 32-930 266, Lord Cochrane 157), where singles with shared bath cost about US$10 and those with private bath are only slightly higher. *Residencial Brazilian* (☎ *32-930 590, 21 de Mayo 1336*), though architecturally drab, has decent rooms and attractive gardens. Singles/doubles are US$20/36 with breakfast.

Horcón

Across the bay to the north, the quaint working port of Horcón is also something of an artists' colony. Its short, narrow beach is nothing to speak of, but nearby Playa Cau Cau is the place for beach volleyball, body surfing and the like. Horcón's clutter of cheap seafood restaurants rank among the area's best – try *El Ancla*, which also offers accommodations. Sol del Pacífico buses from Viña come directly here (see Getting There & Away in the Valparaíso section, earlier in this chapter).

Maitencillo

Its long, sandy beaches, Playa Larga and Playa Aguas Blancas, attract many visitors, but no one can overlook the five-star *Marbella Resort Hotel* (☎ *32-772 020, fax 32-772 030, Km 35 Carretera Concón-Zapallar*). It has a conference center, three restaurants, two bars and an 18-hole golf course as well as a nine-hole par three, two swimming pools, tennis courts and horseback riding. While it's far from cheap – US$195 for a single or double with an elaborate buffet breakfast – there are more expensive places that offer much less.

Marbella's local mailing address is Casilla 17, Puchuncaví. In Santiago, contact Marbella Resort (fax 02-228 3198, resorts@chilesat.net), Cruz del Sur 133, Oficina 503, Las Condes.

Zapallar

At Zapallar, the Malibu of Chilean beach resorts about 80km north of Viña, multimillion-dollar houses cover the densely wooded hillsides from the beach nearly to the ridgetops, but public access is nevertheless excellent.

At the *Residencial La Terraza* (☎ *033-741 026, 033-711 409, Alcalde 142*), two short blocks west of the highway but a stiff climb from the beach, there are singles/doubles for US$40/50 in high season, US$24/30 in off-season, and a good restaurant. On the beach, *Restaurant César* (☎ *033-741 507, Rambla s/n*) is popular with upper-income Chileans but is really a lesser value than more modest places in Horcón – in Zapallar, the view commands premium prices.

Cachagua

Cachagua, about 3km south of Zapallar, lacks hotels but has plenty of summer houses and a couple of restaurants, most notably *Entre Olas*, directly on the beach at the south end of Avenida Los Eucaliptos. Just opposite the attractive crescent beach is Conaf-administered Isla Cachagua, one of the central coast's major seabird breeding sites – with an odor to match. Humboldt penguins are the most notable species.

On the triangular plaza, scrawny horses and burros are available for rent for the kids.

Papudo

Papudo, 10km north of Zapallar, is less exclusive than Zapallar and has a wider range of accommodations, but high-rise apartment buildings are starting to crowd the waterfront. Sheltered Playa Chica and the more open Playa Grande are the main attractions, linked together by Avenida Irarrázaval.

Buses up and down the coast connect Papudo with Valparaíso, Viña del Mar and intermediates, and with La Ligua.

Small, friendly, family-run *Residencial La Plaza* (*Chorrillos 119,* ☎ *033-791 391*) maintains prices of US$9 per person, with private bath and breakfast all year; it's even less with shared bath. *Hotel Restaurant La Abeja* (☎ *033-791 116, Chorrillos 36*) does good business even out of season; room rates are US$30/40 singles/doubles.

There are several beachfront restaurants along Irarrázaval, most notably the expensive *Banana*; the next-door pub/snack bar *Caleta Papudo* is more economical. At Caleta Zapallar, just beyond the yacht club, there's a shellfish market as well as the *Marisquería Chungunguito* for dining.

LA LIGUA

☎ 033

Inland from Papudo, motorists passing on the Panamericana will notice white-coated vendors hawking the famous 'dulces' (sweets) of La Ligua, a modest but tidy agricultural town. Banco de Chile has an ATM at Ortiz de Rosas 485, and there's a good artisans' market on the Plaza de Armas.

The **Museo de La Ligua** (☎ 712 143), Pedro Polanco 698, is a superb archaeological museum. Once the city slaughterhouse, this professionally organized and remodeled building re-creates a Diaguita/Inca burial site with materials uncovered in downtown La Ligua, and also displays a selection of materials from the 19th-century mining era, and historical photographs of the city's early days. It's open 9:30 am to 1:30 pm and 3 to 6:30 pm weekdays (US$0.50).

The bus terminal is on Papudo between Pedro Polanco and Uribe; frequent buses connect La Ligua with Santiago, and with the coastal towns of Papudo and Zapallar.

Places to Stay & Eat

Economical accommodations are available for about US$7 with shared bath at **Residencial Regine I** (☎ 711 192, Esmeralda 27), or about US$11 with private bath at **Residencial Regine II** (☎ 711 196, Condell 360). Modern, well-managed **Hotel Anchimallén** (☎ 711 685, Ortiz de Rosas 694) has rooms with private bath and breakfast for US$33/44. **Restaurant Lihuén** (☎ 711 143, Ortiz de Rosas 303) has good sandwiches and outstanding ice cream.

PARQUE NACIONAL LA CAMPANA

After scaling the 1828m summit of Cerro La Campana, which he called 'Bell Mountain,' Charles Darwin fondly recalled one of his finest experiences in South America:

The evening was fine, and the atmosphere so clear, that the masts of the vessels at anchor in the bay of Valparaíso, although no less than twenty-six geographical miles distant, could be distinguished clearly as little black streaks. A ship doubling the point under sail, appeared as a bright white speck ....

The setting of the sun was glorious; the valleys being black, whilst the snowy peaks of the Andes yet retained a ruby tint. When it was dark, we made a fire beneath a little arbor of bamboo, fried our charqui (dried strips of beef), took our mate, and were quite comfortable. There is an inexpressible charm in thus living in the open air ....

We spent the day on the summit, and I never enjoyed one more thoroughly. Chile, bounded by the Andes and the Pacific, was seen as in a map. The pleasure from the scenery, in itself beautiful, was heightened by the many reflections which arose from the mere view of the Campana range with its lesser parallel ones, and of the broad valley of Quillota directly intersecting them ....

Created in 1967 by private donation and managed by Conaf, La Campana occupies 8000 hectares in a nearly roadless segment of the coastal range that once belonged to the Jesuit hacienda of San Isidro. In geological structure and vegetation, its jagged scrubland resembles the mountains of southern California and protects remaining stands of the roble de Santiago (*Nothofagus obliqua*), the northernmost species of the common South American genus, and the Chilean palm (*Jubaea chilensis*).

The Chilean palm, also known as the Palma de Coquitos for its tasty fruits (one

Chilean writer called them miniature co-
conuts), grows up to 25m in height and
measures up to 1½m in diameter. In more
accessible areas, it declined greatly in the
19th century because it was exploited for its
sugary sap, obtained by toppling the tree
and stripping it of its foliage. According to
Darwin, each palm yielded up to 90 gallons
of sap, which cutters concentrated into
treacle by boiling it. In some parts of the
park you can see the ruins of ovens that
were used for this purpose; there are also
old-fashioned charcoal kilns.

Orientation & Information

In the province of Quillota in Region V
(Valparaíso), La Campana is about 40km
east of Viña del Mar and 110km northwest
of Santiago via the Panamericana. There
are Conaf stations at each entrance where
rangers collect the small entrance fee
(about US$2) and sometimes have maps.
The largest of these stations is the Administración at Granizo, on the south side of
the park near Olmué; open 8 am to 6 pm
weekdays.

Geography & Climate

Ranging in altitude from less than 400m
above sea level to 2222m on the summit of
Cerro Roble, the park has a Mediterranean
climate strongly influenced by the ocean.
Annual maximum temperatures average
19°C and minimum temperatures 9°C, but
these statistics obscure dramatic variation –
summer can be hot and dry, while snow
brushes higher elevations in winter. Mean
annual rainfall, about 800mm, falls almost
entirely between May and September.
Profuse wildflowers and a more reliable
water supply make spring the best time for
a visit, but the park is open all year.

Cerro La Campana

Thousands of Chileans and increasing
numbers of foreign visitors reach the
summit of La Campana every year from the
Administración at Granizo, most easily accessible from Viña del Mar. It's conceivable
to hitch to the campground at the abandoned mine site at the end of the old but

well-maintained road from the Administración, considerably shortening the hike to
the summit, but it's much more interesting
and rewarding to hike the trail from the
park entrance. Figure at least four hours to
the top, and three hours back down.

From the Administración, 373m above sea
level, the abruptly steep trail to the summit
climbs 1455m in only 7km – an average grade
of nearly 21%! Fortunately, most of the hike
is in shade, and there are three water sources
en route: at **Primera Aguada** at an elevation
of 580m; at **Segunda Aguada** (backcountry
camping is possible near a cold, clear spring,
about two hours from the Administración);
and the drive-in campground at the abandoned mine site, where the trail continues to
the summit.

At the point where the trail skirts a
granite wall, prior to the final vertiginous
ascent, is a plaque, placed by Sociedad Cien-
tífica de Valparaíso and the city's British
community, commemorating the 101st anniversary of Darwin's climb (which took
place August 17, 1834). At another point
slightly beyond this, the Club Montañés de
Valparaíso has placed another plaque, honoring climbers who died in 1968 when an
earthquake unleashed a landslide.

On a clear day, the view from La
Campana, from the Pacific to the Andes, is
no less spectacular than when Darwin saw it,
from the ships at anchor in the harbor to the
summit of Aconcagua. Unfortunately, some
people feel obliged to leave a visible record
of their climbing success and, consequently,
carry spray paint in their backpacks.

Good, sensible footwear is recommended. Chilean women in high heels have
made the summit, but good treaded hiking
boots are the best bet – parts of the trail are
slippery even when dry, so that even sneakers can be awkward.

Palmas de Ocoa

Reached by a sometimes-rough gravel road
from the village of Hijuelas on the
Panamericana, Palmas de Ocoa is the
northern entrance to La Campana.

At Casino, 2km beyond the park entrance, a good walking trail connects Palmas

de Ocoa (Sector Ocoa) with Granizo (see Orientation & Information, earlier in this section), 14km to the north. To reach the high saddle of the Portezuelo de Granizo takes about two hours of steady hiking through the palm-studded canyon of the Estero Rabuco. On clear days, which are becoming rarer, the Portezuelo offers some of the views that so impressed Darwin.

About halfway up the canyon is a good, flat campsite where wild blackberries are abundant and the fruit from abandoned grapevines ripens in late summer. Water is limited – farther up the canyon, just below the Portezuelo, is a conspicuous and dependable spring, but elsewhere livestock have fouled the water, so carry a water bottle. At the Portezuelo, the trail forks: the lower branch plunges into Cajón Grande, while the other follows the contour westward before dropping into Granizo.

The hike from Palmas de Ocoa to Granizo, or vice-versa, is an ideal weekend excursion across the coastal range, allowing the hiker to continue to either Santiago or Viña, depending on the starting point. It's probably better to start from Granizo, where public transportation is better; at Palmas de Ocoa, Conaf rangers will help you get a lift back to the Panamericana, where it's easy to flag a bus back to Santiago.

Also at Sector Ocoa, another foot trail leads 6km to Salto de la Cortadera, an attractive waterfall that's best during the spring runoff. Ask the rangers for directions to the trailhead.

Places to Stay & Eat

Camping is the only alternative in the park proper – Conaf has formal camping areas (US$15 for up to six persons) at Granizo, Cajón Grande and Ocoa. It's feasible to make day trips from Viña del Mar and even from Santiago, though a trip from Santiago would be time-consuming since there is no regular public transportation between Hijuelas and Sector Ocoa.

Conaf permits backcountry camping, but inform rangers before attempting the routes between Palmas de Ocoa and Granizo or Cajón Grande. This is steep, rugged country,

and fire is a serious hazard, especially in summer and autumn.

In nearby towns like Olmué, which is popular on weekends, there are good accommodations at *Hostería Copihue* (☎ 33-441 944, Diego Portales 2203), a luxury complex with pool, tennis courts and other facilities, charging US$94/145 with full board. For dining, there's also *Hostería Aire Puro* (☎ 33-441 381, Avenida Granizo 7672).

Getting There & Away

La Campana enjoys good access from both Santiago and Viña del Mar. From Valparaíso/Viña (1¾ hours, US$1), Ciferal Express (☎ 32-953 317) goes to within about 1km of the Granizo entrance, slightly farther from Cajón Grande, every 30 minutes in season; the easiest place to catch the bus is on 1 Norte in Viña. Local transportation (Agdabus) leaves every 20 minutes from Limache and Olmué.

Direct access to Sector Ocoa is more problematic. Most any northbound bus from Santiago will drop you at Hijuelas (there is a sharp and poorly marked turnoff to the park just before the bridge across the Río Aconcagua), but from there you will have to hitch or walk 12km to the park entrance, or else hire a taxi.

From October to April, Altué Active Travel (☎ 02-232 1103, fax 02-233 6799), Encomenderos 83 in Las Condes (Map 9), runs full-day tours to La Campana for US$155 per person for a minimum of two persons, climbing Cerro La Campana and including lunch and all transfers. Larger parties pay substantially less per person.

LOS ANDES
☎ 34

Founded in 1791 by Ambrosio O'Higgins, Los Andes is a friendly foothills town on the international highway to the legendary ski resort at Portillo, near the Argentine border, and the Argentine city of Mendoza.

Orientation & Information

Los Andes is 77km directly north of Santiago via the congested, two-lane Ruta 57 through Colina, or slightly farther (but faster) via a combination of the Panamericana, Ruta 71 and Ruta 57. It is 145km northeast of Viña del Mar via Ruta 60, the international highway to Mendoza.

The helpful municipal Quiosco Turístico (☎ 421 121), Avenida Santa Teresa 333, is open 10 am to 2 pm and 4 to 8 pm weekdays, 10 am to 6 pm weekends. Correos de Chile (post office) is at the corner of Santa Rosa and Esmeralda. Entel is at Esmeralda 463, Chilesat at Esmeralda 399. Hospital San Juan de Dios (☎ 421 121, 421 666) is on Avenida Argentina at Avenida Hermanos Clark.

Things to See & Do

For a small provincial museum, Los Andes' **Museo Arqueológico**, Avenida Santa Teresa 398, features surprisingly good presentations on pre-Hispanic local cultures, but also includes material on forensic anthropology, colonial times, and Inka, Mapuche and Rapa Nui peoples. The curator, who once lived in Ann Arbor, Michigan, has also translated the exhibit captions into English. The museum (☎ 420 115) is open 10 am to 8 pm daily except Monday (US$1).

Across the street at Avenida Santa Teresa 389, dating from the early 19th century but reconstructed in the 1920s, the **Museo Antiguo Monasterio del Espíritu Santo** formerly served as the Convento Carmelitas Descalzas del Espíritu Santo de los Andes, a retreat for Carmelite nuns. It was home to Santa Teresa de los Andes, beatified in 1993; it also includes materials on Laura Vicuña, who legend says willed herself to die at the age of 12, in 1906, in atonement for her widowed mother's taking a married lover.

Facing the nicely landscaped Plaza de Armas, the **Gobernación Provincial** dates from 1850. From 1912 to 1918, Gabriela Mistral taught classes at the former **Colegio de Niñas** (Girls' School, now the Círculo Italiano, see Places to Stay & Eat, below), Esmeralda 246.

Los Andes' aging Terminal Rodoviario is on Membrillar between Esmeralda and O'Higgins, one block east of the Plaza de Armas, but it's due to move to the old train station at the end of Avenida Carlos Díaz,

the northern extension of Avenida Santa Teresa. There are many buses to and from Santiago and Valparaíso/Viña del Mar; buses from Santiago to Mendoza, Argentina, stop here but it's a good idea to buy tickets in advance. Pullman Bus (☎ 421 262) is the main Santiago carrier.

Places to Stay & Eat

Residencial Susi *(☎ 428 600, Santa Rosa 151)* charges only US$5 per person, but it's pretty basic. *Hotel Central* *(☎ 421 275, Esmeralda 278)* is friendly and passable, but for US$8 per person with shared bath, US$16 with private bath, it's not unreasonable – though some rooms lack windows.

A better but more expensive choice is *Hotel Plaza* *(☎ 421 169, fax 426 029, Rodríguez 370)*, facing the north side of the Plaza de Armas at Esmeralda 353 despite its formal street address. Rates are US$39/42 singles/doubles for comfortable, heated rooms with cable TV, and its café is a good breakfast choice. New on the scene are *Hotel Los Andes* *(☎ 428 484, Avenida Argentina 1100)*, charging US$32/36 with breakfast, and *Hotel Don Ambrosio* *(☎ 420 441, Freire 472)*, which costs US$32/45.

Half a block from the museum, the *Centro Español* *(O'Higgins 674)* has a good daily fixed-price lunch. Another good choice for lunch and dinner is the historic *Círculo Italiano* *(Esmeralda 246)*. Try also *El Guatón* *(☎ 423 596, Avenida Santa Teresa 240)*.

Southern Heartland

RANCAGUA
☎ 72

Founded in 1743 on lands 'ceded' by Picunche cacique Tomás Guaglén, Rancagua played an important role in Chilean independence. In 1814, it was the site of the Desastre de Rancagua (Disaster of Rancagua), when Spanish Royalist troops vanquished Chilean patriots, many of whom were exiled to the Juan Fernández archipelago. Chilean liberator Bernardo O'Higgins went into exile in Mendoza, Argentina, but the battle was only a temporary setback for criollo self-determination.

Capital of Region VI, Rancagua is partly an agricultural service center, but the regional economy mostly relies on the huge El Teniente copper mine in the Andes to the east. The presence of 10,000 mining families and the orientation of many Rancaguans toward Santiago (where they both work and shop because of easy rail connections) has made the city a cultural wasteland – it's the only regional capital without a university. The presence of many single male laborers has in turn fomented an economy that includes prostitution.

Still, for all these shortcomings Rancagua is the capital of Chilean rodeo and is close to the hot springs resort of Termas de Cauquenes, and to Conaf's Reserva Nacional Río de los Cipreses, a popular Andean retreat.

Orientation
On the north bank of the Río Cachapoal, Rancagua (population about 180,000) is

86km south of Santiago; the Panamericana passes east of the city. Like most cities of colonial origin, it has a standard grid pattern, centered on Plaza de los Héroes. Surrounded by the major public buildings, the plaza features an equestrian statue of Bernardo O'Higgins, while its northeastern corner has a carved-wood statue of Tomás Guaglén. Between Avenida San Martín and the plaza, the commercial street of Independencia is a pedestrian mall; street names change on each side of San Martín, but street numbering does not.

Information
Sernatur (☎ 230 413, fax 232 297), at Germán Riesco 277, 1st floor, is open 8:30 am to 5:15 pm weekdays. Try also the Automóvil Club de Chile (Acchi, ☎ 239 930), Ibieta 09. The municipal Kiosco de Turismo on Paseo Independencia, opposite Plaza de los Héroes, is marginally helpful.

Forex (☎ 235 273), Campos 363, is the only place to cash traveler's checks, but Banco Sudamericano has an ATM at the corner of Independencia and Bueras.

The post office (Correos de Chile) is on Campos between Cuevas and Independencia. Telefónica has long-distance offices at San Martín 440, Entel at Independencia 468.

Conaf (☎ 297 505) is at Cuevas 480.

For laundry, Lava Express (☎ 241 738) is at Avenida San Martín 270.

Rancagua's Hospital Regional is on O'Higgins between Astorga and Campos.

Things to See & Do
At the corner of Estado and Cuevas, the **Iglesia de la Merced** is a national monument dating from the mid-18th century, when it served as the Convento y Templo de la Merced de Rancagua. During the battle of Rancagua, it was headquarters for O'Higgins' patriots. Another religious landmark, the **Iglesia Catedral** at the corner of Estado and Plaza de los Héroes, dates from 1861.

At Estado and Ibieta, the late-colonial **Casa del Pilar de Esquina** (☎ 221 254) belonged to Fernando Errázuriz Aldunate, a key figure in the independence movement

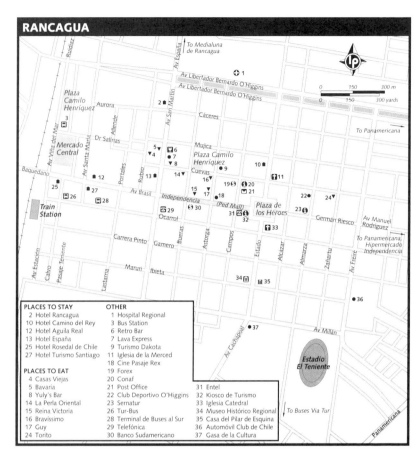

RANCAGUA

PLACES TO STAY
2 Hotel Rancagua
10 Hotel Camino del Rey
12 Hotel Aguila Real
13 Hotel España
25 Hotel Rosedal de Chile
27 Hotel Turismo Santiago

PLACES TO EAT
4 Casas Viejas
5 Bavaria
8 Yuly's Bar
14 La Perla Oriental
15 Reina Victoria
16 Bravíssimo
17 Guy
24 Torito

OTHER
1 Hospital Regional
3 Bus Station
6 Retro Bar
7 Lava Express
9 Turismo Dakota
11 Iglesia de la Merced
18 Cine Pasaje Rex
19 Forex
20 Conaf
21 Post Office
22 Club Deportivo O'Higgins
23 Sernatur
26 Tur-Bus
28 Terminal de Buses al Sur
29 Telefónica
30 Banco Sudamericano
31 Entel
32 Kiosco de Turismo
33 Iglesia Catedral
34 Museo Histórico Regional
35 Casa del Pilar de Esquina
36 Automóvil Club de Chile
37 Gasa de la Cultura

and one of the creators of the constitution of 1833. It's open to the public 10 am to 6 pm weekdays except Monday, 9 am to 1 pm weekends and holidays (US$1 adults, US$0.50 children, free Tuesday).

In another colonial house, across Estado from the Casa del Pilar de Esquina, the **Museo Histórico Regional** (also ☎ 221 254) focuses on O'Higgins' role in Chilean independence and also contains a selection of colonial religious artwork. It's open 10 am to 4 pm Tuesday to Friday, 9 am to 1 pm weekends and holidays (US$1 adults, US$0.50 children, free Tuesday).

At Millán and Cachapoal, four blocks south of Plaza de los Héroes, Rancagua's Casa de la Cultura was the headquarters of royalist Colonel Mariano de Osorio during the battle for the city. Administered by the Municipalidad, it now offers regular exhibitions of paintings and photographs. It's open 8:30 am to noon and 3 to 8 pm weekdays only.

National Rodeo Championship
In early autumn (late March), the Campeonato Nacional de Rodeo takes place at the Medialuna de Rancagua, on Avenida España,

the northward extension of Avenida San Martín. If planning to stay in Rancagua at this time, make hotel reservations early; otherwise, make it a day trip from Santiago.

Places to Stay

Easily the cheapest in town is bare-bones *Hotel Rosedal de Chile (Calvo 435)*, near the train station, for about US$8 per person. Several travelers have recommended *Hotel España (☎ 230 141, Avenida San Martín 367)* which has singles/doubles for US$26/40 with private bath. *Hotel Turismo Santiago (☎ 230 855, fax 230 822, Avenida Brasil 1036)* charges US$39/59 with cable TV and breakfast.

Family-oriented *Hotel Rancagua (☎ 228 158, fax 241 155, Avenida San Martín 85)* charges US$35 for doubles, but discounts IVA for foreign visitors. The new, three-star *Hotel Aguila Real (☎ 233 823, Avenida Brasil 1045)* charges US$38/50. Despite its aging façade, *Hotel Camino del Rey (☎ 239 765, fax 232 314, Estado 275)* features a tastefully modernized interior; rates are US$52/77.

Places to Eat

Yuly's Bar (Cuevas 745) has simple, inexpensive, well-prepared lunches, as does *Casas Viejas (☎ 230 006, Rubio 216)*. The local branch of the country-wide chain, *Bavaria (☎ 241 241, Avenida San Martín 255)* is reliable but uninspiring. *La Perla Oriental (☎ 235 447, Cuevas 714)* serves Chinese food.

Torito (Zañartu 323) is a *parrilla* with good atmosphere. *Guy (☎ 226 053, Astorga 319)*, an upscale French/continental restaurant, is probably the classiest in town.

Reina Victoria (Independencia 667) has good lunches for about US$4 and excellent ice cream. *Bravíssimo (☎ 230 596, Astorga 307)* is a branch of the popular Santiago ice creamery.

Entertainment

The *Cine Pasaje Rex*, Independencia at Astorga, at the back of a gallery, occasionally shows good movies. For drinks, try the *Retro Bar (☎ 243 556, Avenida San Martín 226)*.

Spectator Sports

Club Deportivo O'Higgins (☎ 225 630), Cuevas 226, is the perpetual cellar-dweller in Chile's first-division soccer league. They play at Estadio El Teniente, at the corner of Avenida Freire and Avenida Millán.

Getting There & Away

Rancagua's bus station (Terminal Rodoviario), at Dr Salinas 1165, is just north of the Mercado Central, but some bus companies continue to use their own terminals and the focus here is mostly on regional services. Carriers operating out of the Rodoviario include Via Tur (☎ 234 502) to Los Angeles, Puerto Montt and intermediates, and Andimar (☎ 237 818), which goes to coastal destinations like Pichilemu.

There are frequent buses to Santiago from the Terminal de Buses al Sur (☎ 230 340), Ocarrol 1039. Tur-Bus (☎ 241 117), at Calvo and Ocarrol, also has frequent service to Santiago and extensive long-distance routes.

Rancagua's train station (Estación de Ferrocarril, ☎ 225 239) is on Avenida Estación between Ocarrol and Carrera Pinto. Metrotrén runs frequent commuter trains to the capital, while EFE's infrequent long-distance passenger services, connecting Santiago with Temuco and Concepción, also stop at Rancagua.

AROUND RANCAGUA
Centro de Esqui Chapa Verde

Some 50km northeast of Rancagua via a mostly paved highway, Chapa Verde (☎ 294 255) is lesser known than more prestigious ski centers like Portillo and Valle Nevado, but has four lifts and eight runs, 2870m above sea level. Created for Codelco workers but open to the public, its facilities include a ski school, rental equipment, a café and a restaurant.

Since the road to Chapa Verde is not open to the public, visitors must take Codelco buses from the Hipermercado Independencia, Avenida Manuel Ramírez 665, at 9 am weekdays or between 8 and 9:30 am weekends

El Teniente

At Sewell, 55km northeast of Rancagua, El Teniente belonged to Braden Copper Company and then Kennecott Copper Corporation until its expropriation under the Unidad Popular, and is now part of the state-owned Codelco mining enterprise. Dating from 1904, the world's largest sub-surface copper mine has more than 1500km of tunnels. Sewell itself is now both a ghost town and a monument to 20th-century-company town architecture.

El Teniente and Sewell are open to the public for organized tours only. If you want to visit, contact Turismo Dakota (☎ 72-228 166), Astorga 270, Rancagua, or Across Travel (☎ 02-639 8813), Alameda 108, Local 208, Santiago. Including a country club lunch and transportation, the full-day trip costs US$125 per person from Santiago, with regular Friday departures with a minimum of four persons.

Termas de Cauquenes

In the Andean foothills east of Rancagua, Cauquenes' thermal baths have received such celebrated visitors as Bernardo O'Higgins and Charles Darwin, who observed that the buildings consisted of 'a square of miserable little hovels, each with a single table and bench.' Improvements since Darwin's day now allow *Hotel Termas de Cauquenes* (☎/fax 072-297 226, ☎ 02-638 1610 and fax 02-632 2365 in Santiago) to charge from US$72/100 for B&B to US$107/200 singles/doubles with full board, in an area that Darwin acknowledged as 'a quiet, solitary spot with a good deal of wild beauty.'

Overlooking the river, the dining room offers a popular Sunday lunch whose quality doesn't quite match the US$17 price tag. Non-guests can use the thermal baths, lined in Carrara marble, for US$6.50 per person, slightly more with Jacuzzi. The lodgings themselves are comfortable and the surrounding gardens professionally landscaped. For more information or reservations, write to Termas de Cauquenes, Casilla 106, Rancagua, Chile.

If you can't afford staying at Cauquenes, only 28km east of Rancagua, you can still spend the afternoon by taking Buses Coya (US$1.50) from Andén 13 of Rancagua's Terminal Rodoviario; buses leave daily at 9:30 am and 1:30 pm, returning at 11 am and 5:15 pm.

RESERVA NACIONAL RÍO DE LOS CIPRESES

Fifty kilometers southeast of Rancagua and set among the Andean foothills and cordillera, ranging from 900m to the 4900m summit of Volcán El Palomo in the upper drainage of its namesake river, 37,000-hectare Los Cipreses contains a variety of volcanic landforms, hanging glacial valleys with waterfalls, and fluvial landscapes. Just south of the park boundary, an Uruguayan air force plane carrying the national rugby team crashed in the winter of 1972, resulting in the notorious tale of survival by cannibalism told in Piers Paul Reid's book *Alive!*, later turned into an English-language film by director Frank Marshall (1993).

The reserve's flora includes extensive forests of cypress, olivillo and other native tree species, while the wildlife includes guanaco, fox, vizcacha, condor and many other birds. But the reintroduction of pumas a few years back has upset nearby ranchers who graze goats, sheep and cattle in the area, and there is also significant poaching of rabbits and other mammals – though not necessarily by locals.

At the park entrance at the north end of the reserve, Conaf's congenial and dedicated staff has a well-organized **Centro de Visitantes**, with a scale model of the park for orientation and fine natural history displays, including a full guanaco skeleton (there is also a bone lab here).

There are petroglyphs at several sites; ask Conaf for directions. It's possible to rent horses from local people, and one long trail ascends the valley of the Río de los Cipreses to Uriarte, where Conaf has a simple refugio.

Camping Ranchillos, 6km south of the park entrance, has grassy campsites for US$8, and also has a swimming pool.

No direct public transportation exists, but visitors can take a bus as far as Termas de Cauquenes (see above) and walk or hitch another 15km to the park entrance. With luck and persuasion, it may be possible to arrange transportation with Conaf's Rancagua office.

HACIENDA LOS LINGUES

Probably no other single site can match Hacienda Los Lingues, midway between Rancagua and San Fernando, in providing a glimpse into the life of colonial Chilean landowners. Dating from the 17th century, it now offers luxury hotel accommodations and is one of a handful of South American affiliates of the prestigious Relais & Châteaux group, with a reputation for outstanding but unobtrusive service in extraordinary surroundings.

The accommodations consist of 10 rooms, all furnished with antiques, in a 17th-century building with thick adobe walls. It was modified by 18th- and early 19th-century additions, plus modern amenities like private baths. Also a working farm, Los Lingues provides much of its own produce and breeds thoroughbred horses. Riding, mountain biking, hiking, tennis, swimming and fly-fishing are all possible on its extensive grounds.

For reservations, contact Hacienda Los Lingues (☎ 02-235 5446, 02-235 2458, fax 02-235 7604, loslingues@entelchile.net), Avenida Providencia 1100, Torre C de Tajamar, Oficina 205, Providencia. Rates are US$186 single or double, US$406 per suite. Breakfast costs an additional US$19, lunch US$46 and dinner US$62.

Hacienda Los Lingues is about 32km south of Rancagua, reached by a short graveled lateral just south of the town of Pelequén on the Panamericana. It's possible to get a cab from the turnoff, but Los Lingues provides roundtrip transportation from central Santiago or the international airport for US$320 for up to 11 persons. Day visits (US$46 per person with lunch including wine, pool access, a tour of the main house and a rodeo) are also possible, but usually as part of large groups to whom parts of the grounds are closed for privacy of overnight guests.

RUTA DEL VINO

The first credible attempt to organize Chilean wine tourism, centered on the town of Santa Cruz west of San Fernando, the Ruta del Vino is the creation of half a dozen wineries in the Colchagua valley. Full-day excursions, starting around 11 am, usually visit two of these wineries for guided tours and tasting, followed by a substantial lunch (with wine, of course) and then a visit to Santa Cruz's outstanding but controversial Museo de Colchagua (see below).

Most of the best wines in this area are reds and the wineries themselves are relatively new, but there is nevertheless great diversity among them. Some tours take in the baronial **Casa de Huique**, the only remaining original *casco* (main house) from any of the area's original haciendas; open Wednesday to Sunday 11 am to 6 pm, it now belongs to the Chilean army. Admission costs US$2.

Wine tours can be arranged for as few as two people, for around US$50 per person, through Ruta del Vino (☎/fax 072-823 199, rutadelvino@chilevinos.cl), Plaza de Armas 140, Oficina 6, Santa Cruz. Larger groups pay slightly less per person and the largest can lunch on the vineyard's grounds, while smaller groups usually eat at Santa Cruz's *Club Social* on the Plaza de Armas. Guides are available in both English and French.

Ruta del Vino tours are possible as day trips from Santiago, but this involves a three-hour bus ride with either Andimar or Nilahue from the Terminal de Buses Santiago, Alameda 3750. An 8 am bus arrives in plenty of time for a full-day tour (which usually requires 48 hours advance notice).

Museo de Colchagua

Part of most guided visits, this museum is the work of Chilean arms dealer Carlos Cardoen, wanted by the US government for illegal arms deals during the Gulf War (Interpol warrants limit Cardoen's travels to Chile and, ironically enough for an associate of the ferociously anti-Communist Pinochet regime, Cuba). Whatsoever their origins, the archaeological and historical artifacts in this state-of-the-art museum have few equals anywhere else in the country, with the possible exception of Santiago's Museo Precolombino. Open 10 am to 6 pm daily except Monday, the museum charges US$4 admission, though this is usually included in tour prices. Cardoen is also building a new hotel alongside the museum.

PICHILEMU & AROUND
☎ 072

Pichilemu has been Region VI's most popular beach resort since the turn of the 19th century. In summer, the Campeonato Nacional de Surf (national surfing championship) takes place at Punta de Lobos, 6km south of town, with perhaps the best left break in Chile.

There's an Oficina de Información Turística (☎ 841 017) in the Municipalidad, Angel Gaete 365.

The area is most easily accessible by bus from the city of San Fernando (55km south of Rancagua), though there are also direct buses from Santiago. Buses Andimar (☎ 841 081), Avenida Ortúzar 483, connects Pichilemu with San Fernando and Santiago.

For camping, try *Pequeño Bosque* (☎ 841 601, Santa Teresa s/n), where shady sites costs US$14 for up to four persons (try bargaining for a discount). At Punta de Lobos, *Nalu Surf Club* is cheap (charging per person rather than per site) but lacks shade; however, most guests here worry more about the waves.

Pichilemu gets crowded in high season, but reasonable accommodations are available. Try *Residencial Las Salinas* (☎ 841 071, Aníbal Pinto 51), which has singles with

Surf champs head for Punta de Lobos.

shared bath for US$12, or *Residencial San Luis* (☎ 841 040, Angel Gaete 237), charging US$10 per person with shared bath, US$20 with private bath, including breakfast; the latter also has restaurant facilities. Highly praised *Hotel Chile España* (☎ 841 270, Avenida Ortúzar 255) caters to surfers; rates are normally US$19 per person with breakfast, US$30 with full board at its recommended restaurant. Prices with shared bath are about 20% less, and there are also substantial off-season discounts.

About 20km south of Pichilemu is the smaller beach resort and fishing village of Bucalemu, where several residenciales have singles for about US$10 – try *Hotel Casablanca* (☎ 342 335, Avenida Celedonio Pastene s/n). From Bucalemu, it's possible to make a two- to four-day beach trek to the seaside village of Llico, a popular windsurfing spot with bus connections to Curicó.

Mendoza (Argentina)

☎ 54 country code

Settled from and originally part of colonial Chile, Argentina's Andean provinces of Mendoza and San Juan, plus adjacent San Luis, comprise the region known as Cuyo, which still retains a strong regional identity. The formidable barrier of the Andes is the backdrop for one of Argentina's key agricultural regions, which produces grapes for wine mostly for the internal market, rather than beef and grain for export; the term 'Cuyo' derives from the Huarpe Indian term *cuyum*, meaning 'sandy earth.'

Cuyo lies in the rain shadow of the massive Andean crest, where 6962m Cerro Aconcagua is the Americas' highest peak, but enough snowfall accumulates on the eastern slopes to sustain rivers that irrigate the extensive lowland vineyards, despite the dry climate. Because of these advantages, *mendocinos*, inhabitants of the province of Mendoza, call their home La Tierra de Sol y Buen Vino (Land of Sunshine and Good Wine).

The province's location on a major international transit route has encouraged the tourist economy. Besides the towering Andean landscape and its poplar-lined vineyards and orchards, Mendoza offers several provincial nature parks and reserves and important thermal baths. It's a popular destination for both summer and winter holidays.

With its varied terrain and gentle climate, Cuyo also offers outdoor recreation year-round. Possible summer activities include climbing, trekking, horseback riding, rafting, kayaking, canoeing, fishing, waterskiing, hang gliding, windsurfing and sailing. Downhill skiing is a popular, if costly, winter pastime. Many travelers visit Mendoza to renew their Chilean visas, but those who stay a few days or more will get a sample of the best the country can offer.

MENDOZA (CITY)
☎ 0261

Founded in 1561 and named for Chilean governor García Hurtado de Mendoza, the provincial capital sits 761m above sea level at the foot of the Andes in the valley of its namesake river. With a population of 880,000, it's the region's most important administrative and commercial center, with a major state university and a growing industrial base supported by nearby oil fields. Earthquakes have often shaken the city, most recently in October 1997.

Except during long siesta hours, Mendoza is a lively city. Its bustling downtown, where locals congregate to read the latest headlines on the chalkboards in front of the daily *Los Andes*, is surrounded by tranquil neighborhoods, where, every morning, meticulous shopkeepers and housekeepers swab the sidewalks with kerosene to keep them shining. The *acequias* (irrigation canals) along its tree-lined streets are palpable evidence of the city's indigenous and colonial past, even where modern quake-proof construction has replaced fallen historic buildings. Its wide downtown sidewalks contribute to an active street life, while numerous trees on the streets alleviate the summer heat.

History

When Vásquez de Espinosa visited Mendoza in the early 17th century, he found it a modest place with only '40 Spanish residents and over 1500 Indians to convert and civilize,' under the supervision of Franciscan, Mercederian and Jesuit convents. The Governor of Chile appointed a Mendoza-based *corregidor* (magistrate) as his representative in Cuyo, but creation of the Viceroyalty of the River Plate in 1777, which eventually subjected the province to the Intendencia of Córdoba, began a reorientation toward Buenos Aires.

In 1814, Mendoza played a major role in the Spanish American wars of independence, as General José de San Martín chose the city to train his Ejército de los Andes prior to crossing the Andes to liberate Chile. Only a few years later, though, Darwin found post-independence Mendoza depressing:

To my mind the town had a stupid, forlorn aspect. Neither the boasted alameda, nor the scenery, is at all comparable with that of Santiago; but to those who, coming from Buenos Aires, have just crossed the unvaried Pampas, the gardens and orchards must appear delightful.

Arrival of the railroad, along with the modernization of provincial irrigation works, returned Mendoza to prosperity. Today 80% of Argentina's wine comes from bodegas in and around the city, but construction of oil-fired and hydroelectric power plants has encouraged the development of petrochemicals and light industry, diversifying the city's economic base and related services, and thus promoting population growth. This has not been without cost: Expansion of the Universidad Nacional de Cuyo, for example, displaced squatters from the western outskirts of the city, north of Parque San Martín.

Orientation

Mendoza is 340km northwest of Santiago via the Los Libertadores border complex, whose trans-Andean tunnel has supplanted the higher Uspallata route. Strictly speaking, the provincial capital proper is a relatively small area with a population of only about 130,000, but inclusion of the adjacent suburbs of Gran Mendoza (Greater Mendoza) in the departments of Las Heras (to the north), Guaymallén (to the east), and Godoy Cruz (to the south) plus nearby Maipú and Luján de Cuyo, swells the population to nearly 900,000.

Renovated Plaza Independencia occupies four square blocks in the city center; on its east side, the Cámara de Diputados (pro-

vincial legislature) is painted *celeste* (sky blue) and white, the Argentine national colors. On weekends open-air concerts and an artisans' market often take place on the plaza.

Two blocks from each of the corners of Plaza Independencia, four smaller plazas are arranged in a virtual orbit. Beautifully tiled, restored Plaza España deserves special mention.

Often on weekdays and zealously on Saturday, mendocinos socialize at the numerous

Visiting Argentina

Even travelers who don't plan to spend a lot of time in Argentina may want to pay some brief visits, particularly to nearby Mendoza, if only to renew their Chilean visas.

Visas Nationals of the USA, Canada and most Western European countries are not required to have visas. Australians no longer need visas, but New Zealanders, who do need them, must submit their passports with a payment of US$24 and may need to show a return or onward ticket; ordinarily, the visa will be ready the following day. Argentina's Santiago consulate is particularly efficient. Verify whether the visa is valid 90 days from date of issue, or 90 days from first entry.

Customs On entering Argentina, customs officers will probably check your bags only for fresh fruit. Officials generally defer to foreign visitors, but if you cross the border frequently and carry electronic equipment such as cameras or a laptop computer, it's helpful to have a typed list with serial numbers stamped by authorities.

Money In recent years, Argentina has controlled inflation with strict fiscal measures, including a fixed exchange rate placing the peso at par with the US dollar. Outside large cities, changing traveler's checks may be difficult or impossible without paying a very high commission, so carry a supply of cash dollars. Since the 'dollarization' of the Argentine economy, many merchants readily accept US dollars in lieu of Argentine pesos, thus avoiding many currency dilemmas – but expect to receive your change in pesos. Many Argentine ATMs conveniently dispense both pesos and cash dollars.

Health Argentina requires no vaccinations for visitors entering from any country and, in general, the country presents few serious health hazards.

Getting Around Argentina's two major airlines, Austral and Aerolíneas Argentinas, have extensive networks throughout the country, but their fares are generally higher than competitors like LAPA, Andesmar and Kaikén Líneas Aéreas. Almost all flights between major cities use Buenos Aires as a hub, resulting in slow connections and high fares because of the backtracking involved.

Argentine buses, resembling those in Chile, are modern, comfortable and fast. Most large towns have a central bus terminal, though some companies operate from their own private offices. In some more remote and less populated areas, buses are few or even nonexistent, so make sure a bus is scheduled to come your way and be patient.. Hitchhiking is relatively easy in Argentina, but traffic is sparse in some areas and there may be long waits between lifts, not to mention the risks involved.

sycamore-shaded *confiterías* (confectioner's shops) on Avenida San Martín, which crosses the city from north to south. The poplar-lined Alameda, beginning at the 1700 block of San Martín, was a traditional site for 19th-century promenades. Avenida Las Heras, also shaded by sycamores, is the principal commercial street.

A good place to orient yourself is the Terraza Mirador, the rooftop terrace of the Municipalidad, 9 de Julio 500, which offers panoramic views of the city and surroundings. It's open to the public 8 am to 8 pm daily. See Tourist Offices, below, for where to get maps.

Information

Tourist Offices The Dirección Municipal de Turismo (☎ 449 5185, fax 438 1387) in the Municipalidad at 9 de Julio 500, is open 8:30 am to 1:30 pm weekdays. For most purposes, though, the municipal Centro de Información y Asistencia al Turismo (☎ 420 1333), on the broad Garibaldi sidewalk near Avenida San Martín, is the most convenient information source; open 9 am to 9 pm daily, it has good maps and detailed handouts, and there's usually an English speaker on hand. The best available map, sold here for US$7, is Guía Roja's *Todo Mendoza – Planos Gran Mendoza y Provincia*, which includes the capital and all its surrounding suburbs and an index of street names. Another Centro de Información (☎ 429 6298) is at Las Heras and Mitre. There's also an Oficina de Informes (☎ 431 3001), open 7 am to 11 pm, in the bus terminal.

At Avenida San Martín 1143, the provincial Subsecretaría de Turismo (☎ 420 2800) is open 7 am to 9 pm weekdays. The friendly staff operates an excellent computerized information system, but most of them seem to be on automatic pilot and dealing with them is like a voicemail encounter. They have good maps, but no brochures.

The Automóvil Club Argentino (ACA, ☎ 420 2900) is at Avenida San Martín and Amigorena.

Migraciones (immigration, ☎ 438 0569) is at Avenida España 1425.

Money Cambio Santiago, Avenida San Martín 1199, is one of the few places open on Saturday (until 8 pm); it takes a 2% commission on traveler's checks. Cambio Exprinter, another large but efficient cambio, is at Avenida San Martín 1198. Remember, though, that the Argentine peso is at par with the US dollar, which is widely accepted as legal tender.

Two downtown banks are also architectural landmarks: the massive Banco Mendoza, at the corner of Gutiérrez and San Martín, and Banco de la Nación, at Necochea and 9 de Julio. There are many ATMs downtown that dispense US dollars as well as Argentine pesos.

Post & Communications Correo Argentino is at Avenida San Martín and Avenida Colón; central Mendoza's postal code is 5500. There are many *locutorios* (long-distance phone offices), such as Fonobar, Sarmiento 23 (where you can order a drink while you make your call).

Fifty, Colón 199, offers Internet access for US$6 per hour.

Travel Agencies The student travel agency Asatej (☎/fax 429 0087, tstudent@satlink.com) is at Avenida San Martín 1366, Local 16. The American Express representative is Isc Viajes (☎ 425 9259), Avenida España 1016.

Bookstores The English House Bookstore, 9 de Julio 916, has a good selection of reading material. García Santos Libros (☎ 429 2287), Avenida San Martín 921, has a good selection of Spanish language literature and books on Argentina, as does Y Libros (☎ 425 2822), Avenida San Martín 1252.

Libraries The English Lending Library (☎ 423 8396), Pedro Molina 61, loans English-language books on a fee basis depending on the number of books borrowed, starting at US$5 per month for one book per week; it's open 8 am to 8 pm daily. The Instituto Cultural Argentino Norteamericano (see Cultural Centers, below) also has a lending library.

MENDOZA (ARGENTINA)

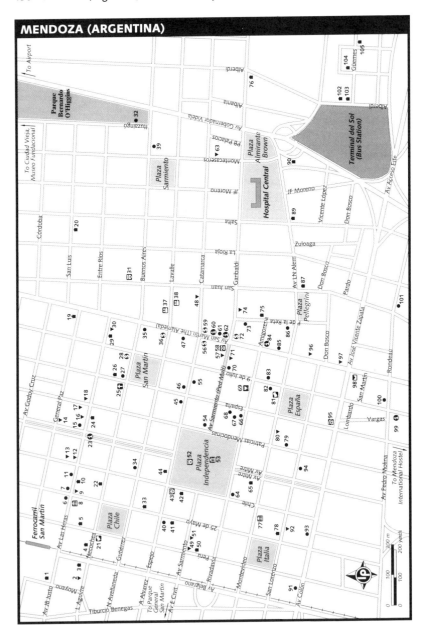

MENDOZA (ARGENTINA)

PLACES TO STAY
1 Hotel Margal
3 Hotel Laerte
4 Hotel Vigo
5 Hotel Petit
10 Hotel Rincón Vasco
19 Hotel City
20 Hotel Escorial
22 Hotel Necochea
24 Hotel Balbi
26 Hotel El Torreón
29 Imperial Hotel
33 Hospedaje Mayo
41 Hotel Princess
42 Plaza Hotel
44 Hotel Argentino
50 Hotel Crillón
65 Hotel Campo Base
75 Gran Hotel Huentala
76 Residencial Eben-Ezer
78 Hotel Aconcagua
87 Hotel Galicia
89 Hotel Center
90 Residencial Savigliano
102 Hotel Terminal
101 Residencial Alexander
104 Residencial 402
105 Hospedaje Carmen

PLACES TO EAT
2 Centro Andaluz
9 Café Mediterráneo
12 Rincón de La Boca
13 Arturito
14 Montecatini
16 Café La Avenida
17 La Marchigiana
18 Mercado Central
30 Trevi
48 Las Vías

49 La Florencia
51 Sarmiento
57 Soppelsa
63 Onda Verde
71 Il Tucco
74 La Nature
80 El Mesón Español
92 Línea Verde
96 Asia
97 Trattoria La Veneciana

OTHER
6 Expreso Jocolí
7 Esquí Mendoza Competición
8 Museo Popular Callejero
11 Turismo Mendoza
15 Las Viñas
21 Italian Consulate
23 Centro de Información y
   Asistencia al Turismo
25 Iglesia, Convento y Basílica
   de San Francisco
27 Migraciones
28 Banco de la Nación
31 Teatro Mendoza
32 Acuario Municipal
34 Localiza Rent A Car
35 Asatej
36 Banco Mendoza
37 Cine Opera
38 Cine Teatro Universidad
39 Hertz
40 Instituto Dante Alighieri
43 Teatro Independencia
45 Turismo Maipú
46 Andesmar
47 Y Libros
52 Teatro Quintanilla
53 Museo Municipal de Arte
   Moderno

54 Cámara de Diputados
55 LanChile
56 Cambio Exprinter
58 Fonobar
59 Cambio Santiago
60 Subsecretaría de Turismo
61 Mercado Artesanal
62 Centro de Información y
   Asistencia al Turismo
64 Instituto Cultural Argentino
   Norteamericano
66 Kaikén Líneas Aéreas
67 Lapa
68 Isc Viajes (AmEx)
69 Café Soul
70 Aerolíneas Argentinas;
   Austral
72 Citibank (ATM)
73 Turismo Sepean
77 Museo del Pasado Cuyano
79 Club Andino Italiano/Centro
   Italiano
81 German Consulate
82 English House Bookstore
83 Aymará Turismo
84 ACA
85 García Santos Libros
86 Avis
91 Extreme
93 Laverap
94 La Lavandería
95 Fifty
98 Post Office
99 Terraza Mirador/Dirección
   Municipal de Turismo;
   Microcine Municipal David
   Eisenchlas
100 English Lending Library
101 Iaim Instituto Cultural

Cultural Centers The Instituto Cultural Argentino Norteamericano (☎ 423 6367) is at Chile 987. The Alianza Francesa (☎ 423 4614) is at Chile 1754, the Instituto Dante Alighieri (☎ 425 7613) at Espejo 638.

Laundry Laverap (☎ 423 9706) is at Colón 547, La Lavandería (☎ 429 4782) at San Lorenzo 352.

Medical Services Mendoza's Hospital Central (☎ 420 0600) is at José F Moreno and Alem. For an ambulance, call the Servicio Coordinado de Emergencia (☎ 428 0000).

Ruinas de San Francisco
Occupying an entire block in the Ciudad Vieja (Old Town) at the corner of Ituzaingó and Fray Luis Beltrán, these misleadingly named ruins belong to a Jesuit-built church/school dating from 1638. After the Jesuits' expulsion in 1767, the Franciscans, whose church was eventually demolished in the 1782 earthquake, took over.

Museo Fundacional

One might call Mendoza's sparkling Museo Fundacional empty, but it would be more accurate to call it spacious. The high-ceilinged structure on Plaza Pedro del Castillo protects excavations of the colonial Cabildo, destroyed by an earthquake in 1861, and of the slaughterhouse then built on the Cabildo's foundations. From that time, the city's geographical focus shifted west and south to its present location.

The museum starts at the beginning – the Big Bang – and works through all of human evolution as if the city of Mendoza were the climax of the process. Nevertheless, for all the subtle pretensions it's one of few Argentine museums that acknowledges the indigenous Huarpes' role in the region's development and the region's contemporary mestizo culture. There are several good dioramas of the city at various stages of its development, a decent selection of historical photographs (most of them lamentably small), and ancient and modern artifacts.

Open 8 am to 8 pm Monday to Saturday, 3 to 10 pm Sunday, the air-conditioned facility (☎ 425 6927) at Alberdi and Videla Castillo has a small confitería and a shop selling decent reproductions of archaeological pieces. Admission is US$1.50 for adults, US$1 for students.

Museo Popular Callejero

This innovative outdoor museum along Avenida Las Heras, between 25 de Mayo and Perú, consists of a series of encased dioramas depicting changes in one of Mendoza's major avenues since its 1830 creation as Callejón de las Maruleilas, in a dry watercourse. The dioramas depict typical scenes as it became Calle de la Circunvalación (1863), Calle de las Carretas (an informal, common name dating from 1880), Calle Las Heras (1882, after San Martín's contemporary and colleague, Gregorio de Las Heras), Calle del Ferrocarril (1885, for obvious reasons), Boulevard de las Palmeras (1908, for the palm trees planted along it), and Calle de los Inmigrantes (1912).

Iglesia, Convento y Basílica de San Francisco

Many locals consider this church's image of the Virgin of Cuyo, patron of San Martín's Ejército de los Andes (Army of the Andes), miraculous because it survived Mendoza's devastating 1968 earthquake. In the Virgin's semicircular *camarín* (chamber), visitors leave tributes to her and to San Martín. A mausoleum within the building holds the remains of San Martín's daughter, son-in-law and granddaughter, which were repatriated from France in 1951. The church is at Necochea 201; public hours are 9 am to noon Monday to Saturday.

Museo Histórico General San Martín

José de San Martín's name graces parks, squares, and streets everywhere in Argentina, but the *libertador*, where he resided with his family and recruited and trained his army to cross into Chile, is especially dear to Mendoza. The museum (☎ 425 7947), at Remedios Escalada de San Martín 1843, is open 9 am to noon weekdays.

Museo de Bellas Artes Emiliano Guiñazú

Paintings and sculptures by Argentine artists, particularly mendocinos, add flavor to this art museum (☎ 496 0224), which is in a distinguished historical residence, the Casa de Fader, in the suburb of Luján de Cuyo. From downtown, take bus No 200 to San Martín 3651.

Other Museums

At Montevideo 544, the historical **Museo del Pasado Cuyano** (☎ 423 6031) has collections of documents and period furniture. It's open 9 am to noon weekdays, and Tuesday and Friday afternoon, with guided tours at 11 am.

The **Museo Municipal de Arte Moderno** (☎ 425 7279), underground at Plaza Independencia, is a relatively small but well-organized facility with rotating exhibits. It's open 9 am to 1 pm and 4 to 9 pm Tuesday to Saturday, 4 to 9 pm Sunday.

Acuario Municipal

Mendoza's municipal aquarium (☎ 425 3824), Ituzaingó at Buenos Aires, contains both local and exotic fish, the most interesting of which are species from the Río Paraná north of Buenos Aires. It's open 8:30 am to 8:30 pm daily (US$1.50).

Parque General San Martín

Originally forged for the Turkish Sultan Hamid II, the impressive gates to this 420-hectare park west of downtown came from England. Designed by architect Carlos Thays in 1897 and donated to the provincial government by two-time governor and later senator Emilio Civit, the park itself has 50,000 trees of about 700 different species and is popular for weekend family outings and other activities. The famous **Cerro de la Gloria** features a monument to San Martín's Ejército de los Andes for their liberation of Argentina, Chile and Peru from the Spaniards. On clear days, views of the valley make the climb especially rewarding.

Within the park, several museums focus on archaeology, mineralogy and natural history, including the **Museo de Ciencias Naturales y Antropológicas Juan Cornelio Moyano** (☎ 428 7666), the **Museo Domingo Faustino Sarmiento** (☎ 428 1133), and the **Museo Mineralógico Manuel Telechea** (☎ 424 1794). The **Museo Arqueológico de la Universidad Nacional de Cuyo** (☎ 449 4093), part of the Facultad de Filosofía y Letras, focuses on American archaeology.

Bus No 110 ('Favorita') from around Plaza Independencia or Plaza España goes to the park, continuing to the **Jardín Zoológico** (☎ 425 0130), in an impressive hillside setting. The zoo is open 9 am to 7 pm Tuesday to Sunday. From the park entrance, open-air buses called *bateas* carry visitors to the summit of Cerro de la Gloria.

Special Events

Mendoza's biggest annual event, the Fiesta Nacional de la Vendimia (Wine Harvest Festival), lasts about a week from late February to early March. It features a parade, with floats from each department of the province, on Avenida San Martín, as well as numerous concerts and folkloric events, terminating with the coronation of the festival's queen in the Parque General San Martín amphitheater.

In February, the provincial equivalent of the Tour de France is the Vuelta Ciclística de Mendoza. In July and August, the Festival de la Nieve features ski competitions.

Activities

Mendoza and its Andean hinterland constitute one of Argentina's major outdoor recreation areas, with several agencies organizing expeditions for climbers and trekkers, rafting trips on the Río Mendoza and other rivers, mule trips and the like. Among these agencies are the following with their specialties:

Andesport
(☎ 424 1003) Rufino Ortega 390 – climbing, trekking, mule trips

Aymará Turismo
(☎ 420 0607) 9 de Julio 933 – mule trips, trekking, rafting

Betancourt Rafting
(☎ 439 1949, betancourt@lanet.com.ar) Ruta Panamericana and Río Cuevas, Godoy Cruz – rafting, mountain biking, parasailing

Piuquén Viajes
(☎ 425 3984) Alvarez 332 – mule trips, trekking across the Andes

Rumbo al Horizonte
(☎ 452 0641) Caseros 1053, Godoy Cruz – climbing, skiing, expeditions, adventure courses

Travesía
(☎ 428 2677) Reconquista 1080, Godoy Cruz – rafting, trekking

Travesías Andinas
(☎ 429 0029, 424 0018) Avenida San Martín 1998 – mountain biking

Climbing & Mountaineering For the latest information, contact the Club Andinista Mendoza (☎ 431 9870), Fray Luis Beltrán 357, Guaymallén; the Club Andino Italiano (☎ 429 3973), in the Centro Italiano at Patricias Mendocinas 843; Fernando Grajales (☎/fax 429 3830), at José Francisco Mendoza 898, 5500 Mendoza; or Rudy

Parra at Aconcagua Trek (☎/fax 431 7003), Güiraldes 246, Dorrego.

For climbing and hiking equipment, both rental and purchase, try Orviz (☎ 425 1281), Avenida JB Justo 550.

Cycling & Mountain Biking Road cycling and, increasingly, mountain biking are popular activities in and around Mendoza. For bicycle-oriented events, see Special Events, earlier in this section.

Navegante EV&T (☎ 429 1615) runs 5½-hour, 25km mountain-bike tours every morning and afternoon in the *precordillera* (Andean foothills) of Mendoza (US$30), and also rents mountain bikes. Travesías Andinas (see list, above) runs full-day trips to Potrerillos (US$70) as well as shorter excursions.

Skiing For purchase and rental of ski equipment, try Esquí Mendoza Competición (☎ 425 2801), Las Heras 583; Extreme (☎ 429 0733), Colón 733; or Rezagos de Ejército (☎ 423 3791), Mitre 2002.

White-Water Rafting The major rivers are the Mendoza and the Diamante, near San Rafael, with trips ranging from half-day excursions (US$30) to overnight (US$190) and three-day expeditions (US$350). In addition to the agencies mentioned above, Ríos Andinos (☎ 02685-404 334), Adolfo Calle 965, Dorrego, Guaymallén, also comes recommended.

Language Courses

IAIM Instituto Intercultural (☎ 429 0269, fax 424 8840, info@iaimnet.com), Rondeau 277, offers Spanish-language instruction for foreigners.

Organized Tours

Get a route map of the Municipalidad's Bus Turístico (☎ 420 1333), whose well-versed guides (some of them English-speaking) offer the best possible orientation to the city for US$10. Good for 24 hours, the ticket allows you to board and reboard at any of several fixed stops throughout the city; the circuit begins at the corner of Garibaldi and Avenida San Martín and goes as far as the summit of Cerro de la Gloria. Hours are 10 am to 8 pm daily from January 1 to Semana Santa (Holy Week, early to mid-April).

Several conventional travel agencies organize trips in and around town, including Turismo Mendoza (☎ 429 2013), at Las Heras 543; Turismo Sepean (☎ 420 4162), at Primitivo de la Reta 1088; Expreso Jocolí (☎ 423 0466), at Avenida Las Heras 601; and Turismo Maipú (☎ 429 4996), at Espejo 207. Among the possibilities are tours of the city (US$12), the wineries and Dique Cipolleti (US$13), Villavicencio (US$17), and the high cordillera around Potrerillos, Vallecitos and Uspallata (US$28).

Places to Stay

Mendoza has abundant accommodations in all categories. The tourist booth at the bus terminal may help find good rooms at bargain prices, while the downtown office also keeps a list of casas de familia, offering accommodations from about US$10 to US$15 for a single. For March's Fiesta Nacional de la Vendimia, reservations are advisable.

Budget For camping, the recently renovated, convenient *Churrasqueras del Parque* (☎ 428 0511), in Parque General San Martín, has good facilities, but its popular restaurant means it can be noisy late at night, especially on weekends. Fees are US$2.50 per person, per tent and per vehicle. Take bus No 50, 100 or 110 from downtown.

Bus No 110 continues to *El Challao* (☎ 431 6085), a campground 6km north of downtown, which charges US$7 for two persons and US$1 for each additional person. Woodsy *Parque Suizo* (☎ 444 1991, 428 3915), 9km from downtown in Las Heras, charges US$12 per site for up to three persons. Each campground has clean, hot showers, laundry facilities, electricity and a grocery.

Mendoza has three Hostelling International affiliates. Reasonably close to the bus terminal, friendly *Hostel Campo Base* (☎/fax 155-696 036, info@campo-base.com.ar, Mitre 946), is most popular with climbers but draws a wider clientele as well and has good common spaces. Rates are US$8 per person; Internet access is available.

Equally friendly but more spacious and comfortable, the **Mendoza International Hostel** (☎/fax 424 0018, www.hostelmendoza .net, España 343) costs US$12 with breakfast. It also offers other meals, Internet access, entertainment and organized tours.

Mendoza's cheapest hotel accommodations are just north of the bus terminal, on Güemes and nearby streets. For around US$10 per person, these include funky, barely passable **Residencial 402** (Güemes 402) and **Residencial Alexander** (☎ 431 0859, Güemes 294). **Residencial Eben-Ezer** (☎ 431 2635, Alberdi 580) is another cheapie near the bus terminal, as is recommended **Hospedaje Carmen**, Güemes 519 (it has good hot water and friendly staff).

Across Avenida Videla from the bus terminal (take the pedestrian underpass), **Residencial Savigliano** (☎ 423 7746, savigliano@ hotmail.com, Pedro Palacios 944) has drawn enthusiastic commentary for its breakfast, shared bath, reasonable privacy, kitchen privileges and access to cable TV for US$10 per person. For about the same price in nearby Dorrego, try **Hotel Mariani** (☎ 431 9932, Lamadrid 121), with private bath and breakfast, and **Casa de Familia** (☎ 432 0645, Subremonte 1084), with breakfast plus kitchen and laundry privileges.

Recommended **Hotel Galicia** (☎ 420 2619, San Juan 881) is central, clean and friendly for US$12/20 singles/doubles with shared bath, US$30 for a double with private bath. Equally central **Hotel Vigo** (☎ 425 0208, Necochea 749) is perhaps one of the best budget hotels in town, a bit worn but with a nice garden; singles/doubles are US$15/26.

Mid-Range Mid-range hotels start around US$20/29, including clean, pleasant **Hotel Escorial** (☎ 425 4777, San Luis 263) and **Hotel San Remo** (☎ 423 4068, Avenida Godoy Cruz 477), north of downtown, for US$22/35. **Hotel Center** (☎ 423 8270, Alem 547), near the bus terminal, is basic though no longer really cheap, with rooms for US$23/35.

Similarly priced **Hotel Terminal** (☎ 431 3893, Alberdi 261) is tidy and comfortable but rooms are rather small. For US$25/35, enthusiastically recommended **Hotel Laerte** (☎ 423 0875, Leonidas Aguirre 19) is modern but homey. Comparable **Hotel Petit** (☎ 423 2099, Perú 1459) is clean and friendly for US$25/35. Also recommended, for the same price, are the downtown **Imperial Hotel** (☎ 423 4671, Las Heras 84) and **Hotel Margal** (☎ 425 2013, Avenida JB Justo 75). Slightly more at US$28/39, but still a good value, is **Hospedaje Mayo** (☎ 425 4424, 25 de Mayo 1265).

Though some travelers think **Hotel Rincón Vasco** (☎ 423 3033, Las Heras 590) is a bit run-down, it enjoys an excellent location. Rooms are US$30/40, but try negotiating a cheaper rate for longer stays. **Hotel City** (☎ 425 1343, General Paz 95) charges US$30/39.

Slightly costlier mid-range places include recommended **Hotel Argentino** (☎ 425 4000, Espejo 455) for US$39/55; central, comfy **Hotel Necochea** (☎ 425 3501, Necochea 541) for US$40/42; and **Hotel América** (☎ 425 6514, JB Justo 812) for US$45/60.

Top End Hotels in this category start at about US$50/65, including a continental breakfast at **Hotel El Torreón** (☎ 423 3900, España 1439). Two better values downtown, both close to Plaza Independencia and restaurants, are **Hotel Crillón** (☎ 423 8963, horcones@infovia.com.ar, Perú 1065) for US$60/75 and **Hotel Princess** (☎ 423 5669, 25 de Mayo 1168) for US$70/90. **Hotel Balbi** (☎ 438 0626, balbistahotel@arnet.com.ar, Las Heras 340) charges US$69/89.

In a stylish neocolonial building, the highly recommended **Plaza Hotel** (☎ 425 6300, Chile 1124) dates from 1925; it's a good value at US$85/100. Rates at **Gran Hotel Huentala** (☎ 420 0766, huentala@ lanet.com.ar, Primitivo de la Reta 1007) are US$94/142. **Hotel Aconcagua** (☎ 420 4455, San Lorenzo 545), charging US$98/130, has drawn criticism for noise, 'deferred maintenance' and glacially sluggish checkouts.

Places to Eat

Many of Mendoza's varied restaurants, pizzerias, cafés and snack bars are downtown, but diners should not hesitate to look elsewhere. Probably the best budget choice is the *Mercado Central*, at Avenida Las Heras and Patricias Mendocinas, where a variety of stalls offer inexpensive pizza, empanadas, sandwiches and groceries in general; its exceptional value and great atmosphere make it one of Mendoza's highlights.

Despite its Italian moniker, *Boccadoro* (☎ 425 5056, Mitre 1976) is a parrilla. Other possibilities include plain but cheap *Arturito* (☎ 425 1489, Chile 1515), *Sarmiento* (☎ 438 0824, Sarmiento 658), and *La Florencia*, at Sarmiento and Perú.

Several places specialize in pasta, however, including traditional favorite *Trattoria La Veneciana* (☎ 423 7737, Avenida San Martín 739), recommended *Montecatini* (☎ 425 2111, General Paz 370), and *Trevi* (☎ 423 3195, Las Heras 70), which has outstanding lasagna. The two locations of *Il Tucco*, Emilio Civit 556 near the entrance to Parque San Martín and Sarmiento 68 (☎ 420 2565), both have excellent food and moderate prices.

Mendoza's finest Italian restaurant is *La Marchigiana* (☎ 423 0751, Patricias Mendocinas 1550), which draws celebrities (Brad Pitt dined here while filming *Seven Years in Tibet*), but the gracious hostess welcomes everyone; though relatively expensive, it's worth the splurge. For inexpensive pizza, try *Rincón de La Boca* (Las Heras 485), with good *fugazzeta* (cheese and onion pizza), hard to find in Mendoza, and *chopp* (draft or lager), plus friendly service and sidewalk seating.

The *Centro Andaluz* (☎ 423 2971, Leonidas Aguirre 35) has tasty paella. *El Mesón Español* (☎ 429 5313, Montevideo 244) has typical Spanish food, with moderate fixed-price meals. *Café Mediterráneo* (Las Heras 596) has interesting, moderately priced lunch specials. *Praga* (Leonidas Aguirre 413) has drawn praise from local residents.

The popular *Asia* (Avenida San Martín 821) is one of few *tenedor libre* (all-you-can-eat) Chinese restaurants in town. For Middle Eastern cuisine, try *Café La Avenida* (Las Heras 341). For regional specialties, longtime residents recommend *El Retortuño* (☎ 431 6300), on Dorrego near Adolfo Calles in Guaymallén, which has live Latin American music on weekend evenings; take the 'Dorrego' trolley from downtown.

Vegetarians can find several choices, including wholesome, reasonably priced *Onda Verde* (Montecaseros 1177), *Línea Verde* (☎ 423 9806, San Lorenzo 550), which also has a takeaway rotisería, *La Nature* (☎ 420 0882, Garibaldi 63), and *Las Vías* (☎ 425 0053, Catamarca 76).

Café del Teatro, at the corner of Chile and Perú, is a hangout for the downtown theater crowd. For ice cream, try *Soppelsa* (Sarmiento 57).

Entertainment

Downtown discotheques include *La Luz* (San Martín 300), *Saudades* (☎ 438 0862), San Martín at Barraquero, and on the westward extension of Avenida Colón, *Epicentro* (☎ 429 8414, Aristides Villanueva 256), which has a karaoke bar. There are many others in the suburb of Chacras de Coria, on Mendoza's southern outskirts, such as *Aloha*, *Campo de Vuelo* and *Runner*.

The *Microcine Municipal Davíd Eisenchlas* (☎ 449 5100, 9 de Julio 500), in the basement of the Municipalidad, shows occasional art films. The only regular downtown cinema is *Cine Opera* (☎ 429 3120, Lavalle 54), though *Cine Teatro Universidad* (Lavalle 77), across the street, also shows films on occasion.

The remainder are suburban multiplexes: *Cine Village Mendoza* (☎ 421 0700), at Mendoza Plaza Shopping in Guaymallén (take the T-Red bus from 9 de Julio), and *Cinemark* (☎ 439 5245, Panamericana 2650), at the Palmares Open Mall (take bus No 43 from Plaza Independencia).

Mendoza also has a drive-in, *Autocine El Cerro* (☎ 425 2015), on Avenida Champagnat just north of the Ciudad Universitaria – Joe Bob sez check it out.

The **Teatro Quintanilla** (☎ 423 2310) is alongside the Museo Municipal de Arte Moderno, underground at Plaza Independencia. **Teatro Independencia** (☎ 438 0644) is nearby at the corner of Espejo and Chile. The Universidad Nacional del Cuyo runs **Teatro Mendoza** (☎ 429 7279, San Juan 1427).

The recommended **Café Soul** (☎ 429 9652, Rivadavia 135) is a bar with live music, including tango and flamenco from time to time. Another possibility is **El Rincón del Poeta** (Alberdi 456), in the Ciudad Vieja.

Shopping

Friday, Saturday and Sunday, the outdoor Plaza de las Artes market takes place on Plaza Independencia.

Open 8 am to 1 pm weekdays, the Mercado Artesanal (☎ 420 4239), downstairs at Avenida San Martín 1143, features provincial handicrafts, including vertical-loom weavings (Huarpe-style) from the northwest of the province and horizontal looms (Araucanian-style) from southern Argentina, woven baskets from Lagunas del Rosario, and braided, untanned-leather horse gear. Prices are reasonable, and the staff is knowledgeable and eager to talk about crafts and the artisans, who receive the proceeds directly.

Las Viñas (☎ 425 1520), Las Heras 399, has a wide selection of Argentine crafts.

Getting There & Away

When purchasing air or bus tickets, remember to distinguish between Santiago de Chile, on the Pacific side of the Andes, and the Argentine city of Santiago del Estero.

Air LanChile (☎ 420 2890), Espejo 128, flies twice daily to Santiago de Chile. The Chilean domestic airline Avant (☎ 420 0199), Espejo 285, flies twice weekly. Fares start around US$98 one-way, but discounted roundtrips can cost as little as US$90.

Aerolíneas Argentinas (☎ 420 4185) and Austral, sharing offices at Sarmiento 82, fly to Buenos Aires. Other Argentine airlines fly to Buenos Aires and to provincial destinations in generally smaller planes.

Bus Mendoza's sprawling Terminal del Sol (☎ 431 1299, 431 3001) is at Avenida Gobernador Videla and Avenida Acceso Este, in Guaymallén (really just across the street from downtown). Hot showers are available here for US$2.

Numerous companies cross the Andes to Santiago de Chile, Viña del Mar and Valparaíso (eight hours, US$20) every day. Among them are Tur-Bus (☎ 431 1008), Chile Bus (☎ 431 5596), El Rápido (☎ 431 4093), TAC (☎ 431 0518, 431 2687), Ahumada (☎ 431 6281), Tas Choapa (☎ 431 2140), O'Higgins (☎ 431 3199), Cata (☎ 431 0782), and Fénix (☎ 431 1800). Taxi colectivos with Coitram (☎ 431 1999) or Chiar (☎ 431 1736) take about seven hours (US$25, sometimes cheaper).

To Uspallata and Los Penitentes (four hours, US$9), for Parque Provincial Aconcagua, there are two buses daily with Expreso Uspallata (☎ 431 3309). Empresa Jocolí (☎ 431 4409) and Turismo Maipú (☎ 429 4976), at Espejo 207, each have a daily service, while several other companies have weekend service, including Turismo Mendoza (☎ 420 1701), at Las Heras 543; Mendoza Viajes (☎ 438 0480), at Paseo Sarmiento 129; and Turismo Luján (☎ 431 1685), at Las Heras 420.

Getting Around

Mendoza is more spread out than most Argentine cities, so you will need to walk or learn about the bus system to get around. Local buses and trolleys cost around US$0.55, more for longer distances such as the trip to the airport. A new system of magnetic fare cards, sold in multiples of this basic fare, has had a rocky beginning.

Aeropuerto Internacional Plumerillo (☎ 448 7128) is 6km north of downtown on RN 40. Bus No 60 ('Aeropuerto') from Salta goes straight to the terminal.

The enormous, modern and very busy Terminal del Sol (☎ 431 1299, 431 3001) is at Avenida Gobernador Videla and Avenida Acceso Oeste in Guaymallén, just beyond the Mendoza city limits. The 'Villa Nueva' trolley from Lavalle, between Avenida San Martín and San Juan, goes there, but it's walking distance for many people.

Rental cars can be difficult to get at the airport, a bit easier in town. Avis (☎ 429 6403) is at Primitivo de la Reta 914, Localiza Rent a Car (☎ 449 1492) at Gutiérrez 470, and Hertz (☎ 425 5666) at Buenos Aires 536.

AROUND MENDOZA

There are varied sights and recreational opportunities near Mendoza. Almost all of them are possible day trips, but some more distant ones would be more suitable for at least an overnight stay.

Wineries

Wineries in the province yield nearly 70% of the country's production; most of those near Mendoza offer tours and tasting. Southeast of downtown in Maipú, **Bodega La Colina de Oro** (☎ 0261-497 6777), Ozamis 1040, is open 9 am to 7 pm weekdays, 9 am to 11 pm weekends. Take bus No 150 or 151 from downtown.

In Coquimbito, Maipú, **Bodega Peñaflor** (☎ 0261-497 2388), on Mitre, is open 8 am to 4 pm weekdays. Bus Nos 170, 172 and 173 go there. Also in Coquimbito is **Bodega La Rural** (☎ 0261-497 2013), on Montecaseros, whose Museo Francisco Rutini displays wine-making tools used by 19th-century pioneers, as well as colonial religious sculptures from the Cuyo region. Open 9 am to 6 pm weekdays, 9 am to 11 am weekends, it produces the highly regarded San Felipe wines.

Bodega Santa Ana (☎ 0261-421 1000), at Roca and Urquiza, Villa Nueva, Guaymallén, is open 8:30 am to 5 pm weekdays; take bus No 200 ('Buena Nueva via Godoy Cruz'). **Bodega Escorihuela** (☎ 0261-424 2744), Belgrano 1188 in Godoy Cruz, is open 9:30 am to 4:30 pm weekdays. Take bus 'T.'

Bodega Chandon (☎ 0261-490 0040), at Km 29 of RN 40 in Luján de Cuyo, south of Mendoza, has five guided tours weekdays between 9:30 am and 3:30 pm from April to January. In February and March, there's an additional 5 pm tour weekdays and three tours Saturday morning.

Calvario de la Carrodilla

A national monument since 1975, this church in Carrodilla, Godoy Cruz, houses an image of the Virgin of Carrodilla, the patron of vineyards, brought from Spain in 1778. A center of pilgrimage for mendocinos and other Argentines, it also has samples of indigenous colonial sculpture. Reached by bus Nos 10 and 200, it's open 10 am to noon and 5 to 8 pm weekdays.

Cacheuta

About 40km west of Mendoza in the department of Luján de Cuyo, Cacheuta (altitude 1237m) is renowned for its medicinal thermal waters and agreeable microclimate. Since 1986, the facilities at **Hotel Termas Cacheuta** (☎ 02624-482 082, 0261-431 6085 and fax 0261-431 6089 in Mendoza) have undergone modernization, and singles/doubles now cost US$115/192 with full board. The rooms are pleasant but unexceptional for the price, which includes hot tubs, massage, mountain bikes and recreation programs. The local mailing address is Rodríguez Peña 1412, Godoy Cruz, Mendoza. Nonguests may use the baths for US$10.

Besides the hotel complex, there are also **Camping Termas de Cacheuta**, at Km 39 of RN 7, and the well-regarded restaurant **Mis Montañas**.

Potrerillos

Passing through a typical precordillera landscape along the Río Blanco (the main source of drinking water for the city of Mendoza), westbound RN 7 leads 45km to the Andean resort of Potrerillos (altitude 1351m). Bird-watching is excellent in summer, but the area is also becoming a mecca for white-water rafting.

Opposite the ACA campground (see below), Argentina Rafting Expediciones (☎/fax 02624-482 037, chemartin@cpsarg .com) does white-water rafting and kayaking on the Río Mendoza and the Diamante (south near San Rafael), as well as trekking and mountain biking. River trips range from a 5km, half-hour Class II float (US$10) to a 50km, five-hour Class III-IV descent over two days (US$120). Transfers from and to Mendoza cost an additional US$10.

Río Extremo Rafting (☎/fax 02624-482 007, cellular 02611-5563 0986, 02611-5563 6558, rioextremo@lanet.losandes.com.ar), Avenida Los Cóndores s/n, or Güemes 785, Dpto 9, Godoy Cruz in Mendoza, also descends the Río Mendoza.

Camping del ACA, on RN 7 at Km 50, costs US$10 per site for members, US$12 for nonmembers. There are two hotels: the modest *Hotel de Turismo* and the luxurious *Gran Hotel Potrerillos* (☎ 0261-423 3000), which charges US$78/84 with breakfast, US$96/120 with half board, and US$114/156 with full board. The town also contains the restaurant *Armando*.

Termas Villavicencio

Mineral water from Villavicencio is now sold throughout the country, though early travelers were unimpressed with the area. In the 1820s, Francis Bond Head wrote that 'the post of Villavicencio, which in all the maps of South America looks so respectable, now consists of a solitary hut without a window, with a bullock's hide for a door, and with very little roof,' while a few years later Darwin found it a 'solitary hovel.' Neither could have anticipated that the spectacular mountain setting would one day host the thermal baths resort of the Gran Hotel de Villavicencio, which has been closed for more than a decade because of legal entanglements. The hotel was due to reopen in 1995 but there's been no discernible movement since then.

Panoramic views make the *caracoles* (winding roads) to and beyond Villavicencio (altitude 1800m), 51km northwest of Mendoza on RP 52, an attraction in themselves. There's free camping alongside *Hostería Villavicencio*, which serves simple meals.

Expreso Jocolí (☎ 0261-431 4409 in Mendoza) runs buses to Villavicencio Wednesday, Saturday and Sunday.

Ski Resorts

While wine ages in the barrels, soil lies barren, poplars stand leafless, and the snow brings visitors to the province to ski. The two ski areas nearest to Mendoza are covered here.

Vallecitos Ranging between 2900m and 3200m in the Cordón del Plata, only 80km southwest of Mendoza, Vallecitos is the area's smallest (only 88 hectares with six downhill runs) and least expensive ski resort. It's open July to early October; for more information, contact Valles del Plata (☎ 0261-431 2713) in Mendoza.

Most skiers stay in Mendoza since the resort is so close, but *Hostería La Canaleta* (☎ 0261-431 2779) has four-bunk rooms with private bath, a restaurant and a snack bar. The cheapest accommodations are *Refugio San Antonio*, which has rooms with shared bath and a restaurant.

Los Penitentes Both scenery and snow cover are excellent at Los Penitentes (165km west of Mendoza via RN 7), which offers downhill and cross-country skiing at an altitude of 2580m. Lifts and accommodations are modern, and the maximum vertical drop on its 21 runs is more than 700m.

Hostería Los Penitentes has double and quadruple rooms with private bath, plus a restaurant and bar. Weekly rates during ski season range from US$617 to US$671 for singles, and US$499 to US$542 for doubles. For detailed information, contact the Los Penitentes office (☎ 0261-427 1641), Paso de los Andes 1615, Departamento C, Godoy Cruz.

Another resort hotel is four-star *Hostería Ayelén* (☎ 0261-427 1123, fax 0261-427 1283, ayelen@lanet.losandes.com.ar), which charges US$53/70 a night for singles/doubles in summer, US$88/114 in ski season. The postal address is Juan B Justo 1490, 5547 Godoy Cruz, Mendoza.

Five apart hotels (dormitory-style lodgings) in Los Penitentes also offer maid service, bar and reception. For more modest accommodations at nearby Puente del Inca, contact Gregorio Yapurai (☎ *0261-430 5118 in Mendoza*), who has *cabañas* with hot water, kitchen, and fridge for US$18 per person.

Confitería La Herradura is a skiers' hangout. A small *market* also keeps long hours.

Parque Provincial Volcán Tupungato

Serious climbers consider 6650m Tupungato a far more challenging and interesting climb than Aconcagua. The main approach is from the town of Tunuyán, 82km south of Mendoza via RN 40, where the Dirección de Turismo (☎ 02622-422 193), on República de Siria at Alem, can provide information. Many of the same outfitters who arrange Aconcagua treks can also handle Tupungato.

USPALLATA
☎ 02624

The polychrome mountains surrounding this crossroads village, 1751m above sea level and 105km west of Mendoza via RN 7, so resembles highland central Asia that director Jean-Jacques Annaud used it as the location for the Brad Pitt epic *Seven Years in Tibet*. Uspallata is an excellent base for exploring the scenic sierras, but in the long run, the prosperity of its 3000 inhabitants may rest more on its becoming a *zona franca* (duty-free zone) because of its proximity to Valparaíso, Chile.

Information

Uspallata's tourist office, a kiosk alongside the YPF gas station, was vacant at last pass. There's a post office (postal code 5545) and a branch of Banco de Mendoza, but no ATM. Comunicación Alta Montaña, just north of the highway junction, provides phone services.

Things to See & Do

A good rock-climbing area known as **Cerro Montura** is along RN 7 en route to Parque Provincial Aconcagua and Paso de los Libertadores, but farther up the valley the rock is too friable for safe climbing.

One kilometer north of the highway junction, a signed lateral leads to ruins and a museum at the **Bóvedas Históricas Uspallata**, a metallurgical site since pre-Columbian times. There are dioramas of battles on General Gregorio de Las Heras' campaign across the Andes in support of San Martín. About 4km northeast of Uspallata on the Villavicencio road, in a volcanic outcrop known as **Cerro Tunduqueral**, is a faded but still visible set of petroglyphs, near a small monument to San Ceferino Namuncurá.

Mendoza-bound motorists should consider taking the **Caracoles de Villavicencio**, a good gravel road even more scenic than paved RN 7. Ignore the sign at Uspallata that restricts the descent *(bajada)* to 2 to 8 pm and the ascent *(subida)* to 7 am to noon; it's now open to two-way traffic at all hours. About 3km past the entrance to the Caracoles is a memorial to Darwin, who discovered fossil *Araucaria* trees here; at present, their distribution is more southerly. At 3800m, 26km from Uspallata, the high point is the **Cruz del Paramillo**, a way station for the Virgin of Fátima, with expansive views of the Andean peaks to the west.

Places to Stay & Eat

Uspallata's poplar-shaded *Camping Municipal* (☎ *420 009*), 500m north of the Villavicencio junction on RP 52, charges US$5.60 per site. The north end of the facilities, near the wood-fire-stoked hot showers, is quieter and the best place to pitch a tent.

Hotel Viena (☎ *420 046, Avenida Las Heras 240*), east of the highway junction, is a bargain at US$15 per person, with private bath and cable TV. Closer to the junction, improved, friendly *Hostería Los Cóndores* (☎/*fax 420 002, 420 303*) costs US$25/35 singles/doubles; all rooms have cable TV, the bathrooms are huge, and it has a restaurant.

Built by the Confederación de Empleados de Comercio in the late 1940s, *Hotel Uspallata* (☎ *420 003*), about 1km west of the junction, looks a bit shopworn since its Peronist glory days but still offers spacious grounds, tennis courts, a huge swimming pool, a bar, a bowling alley, pool tables and a restaurant. For US$30/46 with breakfast, it remains one of the country's better values.

At the southern approach to town on RN 7, the highly recommended but still not outrageously expensive *Hotel Valle Andino* (☎ *420 033, 0261-425 8424 in Mendoza*) has an indoor pool. Rates are US$37 per person with breakfast, US$47 with half board, and US$74 with full board. Facilities also include tennis courts, a game room, a reading room and a TV lounge.

Several parrillas are the main dining alternatives. Behind the YPF station, *Parrilla San Cayetano* (☎ *420 049*) is a convenient stop offering decent food for travelers en route to and from Chile. South of the junction is *El Rancho de Olmedo*; another longtime favorite, *Dónde Pato* has moved to roomy new quarters nearby. *Café Tibet*, in a strip mall across the junction, capitalizes on Uspallata's cinematic notoriety.

Getting There & Away

From new offices just north of the junction, Expreso Uspallata runs three buses every weekday, four on weekends, between Mendoza (US$8) and Uspallata, as far as Puente del Inca. Buses between Mendoza and Santiago will carry passengers to and across the border, but are often full.

PARQUE PROVINCIAL ACONCAGUA

North of RN 7, nearly hugging the Chilean border, Parque Provincial Aconcagua protects 71,000 hectares of the wild high country surrounding South America's and the western hemisphere's highest summit, 6962m Cerro Aconcagua. Passing motorists can stop to enjoy the view of the peak from Laguna Horcones, a 2km walk from the parking lot just north of the highway, where there's a ranger available 8 am to 9 pm weekdays, 8 am to 8 pm Saturday. There are also rangers at the junction to Plaza Francia, about 5km north of Horcones; at Plaza de Mulas on the main route to the peak; at Las Leñas, on the Polish Glacier Route up the Río de las Vacas to the east; and at Plaza Argentina, the last major

camping area along the Polish Glacier Route.

Cerro Aconcagua

Often called the 'roof of the Americas,' the volcanic andesite summit of Aconcagua covers a base of uplifted marine sediments. The origin of the name is unclear; one possibility is the Quechua term *Ackon-Cahuac*, meaning 'stone sentinel,' while another is the Mapuche phrase *Acon-Hue*, signifying 'that which comes from the other side.'

Italian-Swiss climber Mathias Zurbriggen made the first recorded ascent in 1897. Since then, the peak has become a favorite destination for climbers from around the world, even though it is technically less challenging than other nearby peaks, most notably Tupungato to the south. In 1985, the Club Andinista Mendoza's discovery of an Inca mummy at 5300m on the mountain's southwest face proved that the high peaks were a pre-Columbian funerary site.

Reaching the summit requires a commitment of at least 13 to 15 days, including acclimatization time; some climbers prefer the longer but more scenic, less crowded but more technical Polish route. Potential climbers should acquire RJ Secor's climbing guide *Aconcagua* (1994). There's less detailed information in the 4th edition of Bradt Publications' *Chile & Argentina: Backpacking & Hiking*. There is also an informational Web page (www.aconcagua.com.ar).

Nonclimbers can trek to *base camps* and *refugios* beneath the permanent snow line; note that tour operators and climbing guides set up seasonal tents at the best campsites en route to and at the base camps, so independent climbers and trekkers usually get the leftover spots. On the Northwest Route there is also a rather luxurious and expensive *Hotel Plaza de Mulas* (☎ *radio-telephone 0261-425 7065*).

Permits From December to March, permits are obligatory for both trekking and climbing in Parque Provincial Aconcagua; park rangers at Laguna Horcones will not permit visitors to proceed up the Quebrada de los Horcones without one. These permits, which cost US$30 for trekkers (seven days), US$80 for climbers (20 days) in December and February, and US$120 for climbers in January, are available only in Mendoza, at the Dirección de Recursos Naturales Renovables (☎ 0261-425 2090), Avenida Boulogne Sur Mer s/n, in Parque San Martín. The process is routine, and the office is open 8 am to 8 pm weekdays, 8 am to noon weekends. A shorter, three-day trekking permit is available for US$15 (US$20 in January) to Plaza Francia only, but its lack of flexibility makes it a poorer deal than the permit for the longer period. Argentine nationals pay half price at all times.

Routes There are three main routes up Aconcagua. The most popular one, approached by a 40km trail from Los Horcones, is the **Ruta Noroeste** (Northwest Route) from Plaza de Mulas, 4230m above sea level. The **Pared Sur** (South Face), approached from the base camp at Plaza Francia via a 36km trail from Los Horcones, is a demanding technical climb.

From Punta de Vacas, 15km southeast of Puente del Inca, the longer but more scenic **Ruta Glaciar de los Polacos** (Polish Glacier Route) first ascends the Río de las Vacas to the base camp at Plaza Argentina, a distance of 76km. Wiktor Ostrowski and others pioneered this route in 1934. Climbers on this route must carry ropes, screws and ice axes, in addition to the usual tent, warm sleeping bag and clothing, and plastic boots. This route is more expensive because it requires the use of mules for a longer period.

Mules The cost of renting cargo mules, which can carry about 60kg each, has gone through the roof of the Americas – the standard fee among outfitters is US$120 for the first mule from Puente del Inca to Plaza de Mulas, though two mules cost only US$160. A party of three should pay about US$240 to get their gear to the Polish Glacier Route base camp and back.

For mules, one alternative is Ricardo Jatib's Aconcagua Express (☎ 0261-444 5987). Another reliable muleteer is Fernando Grajales, operating from Hostería Puente del Inca from December through February. One party recommended Carlos Cuesta, who lives next to the cemetery at Puente del Inca.

Puente del Inca

One of Argentina's most striking natural features, this stone bridge over the Río Mendoza is 2720m above sea level and 177km from Mendoza. (The Río de las Cuevas just south of the park becomes the Río Mendoza just beyond Punta de Vacas.) From here trekkers and climbers can head north to the base of Aconcagua, south to the pinnacles of **Los Penitentes** (so-named because they resemble a line of monks), or even farther south to 6650m **Tupungato**, an impressive volcano that is partly covered by snow fields and glaciers and is a more challenging technical climb than Aconcagua.

Camping Los Puquios is an inexpensive alternative for lodging, as is *Albergue El Refugio*. The pleasant *Hostería Puente del Inca* (☎ 02624-420 222, 0261-438 0480 in Mendoza) charges US$40/50 singles/doubles with breakfast, though posted prices may be higher. Multi-bed rooms may be as low as US$25 per person with breakfast. It has a *restaurant* and may help arrange trekking and mules. Dinner costs around US$15, but one visitor stated that the food there 'tastes better *after* the climb.'

Cristo Redentor

Pounded by chilly but exhilarating winds, nearly 4000m above sea level on the Argentine-Chilean border, the rugged high Andes make a fitting backdrop for this famous monument, erected after settlement of a territorial dispute between the two countries was settled in 1902. The view is a must-see either with a tour or by private car (since the hairpin road to the top is no longer a border crossing into Chile), but the first autumn snowfall closes the route. At Las Cuevas, 10km before the border, travelers can stay at *Hostería Las Cuevas*, or at the newly opened, 40-bed **Hostel Paco Ibáñez** (☎ *0261-429 0707 in Mendoza)*; reservations are made through the Campo Base hostel in the provincial capital.

Organized Tours

Many of the adventure-travel agencies in and around Mendoza arrange excursions into the high mountains; for their names and addresses see Activities in the Mendoza section, earlier in this chapter.

The most established operators are Fernando Grajales (☎/fax 0261-429 3830), José Francisco Mendoza 898, 5500 Mendoza, and Rudy Parra's Aconcagua Trek (☎/fax 0261-431 7003), Güiraldes 246, 5519 Dorrego, Mendoza.

Several guides from the Asociación de Guías de Montaña lead two-week trips to Aconcagua, among them Alejandro Randis (☎ 0261-496 3461), Daniel Pizarro (☎ 0261-423 0698), and Gabriel Cabrera of Rumbo al Horizonte (☎ 0261-452 0641). The trips leave from Mendoza by bus to Puente del Inca, then follow the Ruta Noroeste, partly on mule.

Operadores Mendoza (☎ 0261-425 3334, 0261-423 1883) at Las Heras 420, in Mendoza, has trips of three and six days from Puente del Inca, partly by horse or mule, usually contracted with Fernando Grajales (see above). Trips follow the route that climbers attempting the difficult south face of Aconcagua must traverse.

Language

Every visitor to Santiago should attempt to learn some Spanish, whose basic elements are easily acquired. If possible, take a short course before you go. Chileans are gracious hosts and will encourage your Spanish, so there is no need to feel self-conscious about vocabulary or pronunciation. There are many common cognates, so if you're stuck try Hispanicizing an English word – it is unlikely you'll make a truly embarrassing error. Do not, however, admit to being *embarazada* – unless you are in fact pregnant!

Note that in Latin American Spanish, the plural of the familiar 'tu' is *ustedes*, rather than *vosotros*, as in Spain. Chileans and other Latin Americans readily understand Castilian Spanish, but may find it either quaint or pretentious.

Phrasebooks & Dictionaries

Lonely Planet's *Latin American Spanish phrasebook*, edited by Sally Steward, is a worthwhile addition to your backpack. Another useful resource is the *University of Chicago Spanish-English, English-Spanish Dictionary*, whose small size, light weight and thorough entries make it ideal for travel.

Visitors confident of their Spanish (and judgment) can tackle John Brennan and Alvaro Taboada's *How to Survive in the Chilean Jungle*, jointly published by Dolmen Ediciones and the Instituto Chileno Norteamericano, an enormously popular book that has gone through many editions explaining Chilean slang to the naïve.

Chilean Spanish

Chileans relax terminal and even some internal consonants almost to the point of disappearance, so at times it can be difficult to distinguish plural from singular. For example, *las islas* (the islands) may sound more like 'la ila' to an English speaker. Chileans speak rather more rapidly than other South Americans, and rather less

clearly – the conventional *¿quieres?* (do you want?) sounds more like 'querí' on the tongue of a Chilean.

Other Chilean peculiarities include pronunciation of the second person familiar of 'ar' verbs as 'ai' rather than 'as,' so that, for instance, '*¿Adónde vas?*' (Where are you going?) will sound more like '*¿Adónde vai?*' Likewise, the common interjection *'pues'* (well . . .) at the end of a phrase becomes 'pueh' or 'po,' as in 'sí, po.'

There are many differences in vocabulary between Castilian and American Spanish, and among Spanish-speaking countries in the Americas. There are also considerable regional differences within these countries not attributable to accent alone – Chilean speech, for instance, contains many words adopted from Mapuche, while santiaguinos sometimes use *coa*, a working-class slang. Check the glossary for some of these terms.

Chileans and other South Americans normally refer to the Spanish language as *castellano* rather than *español*.

Pronunciation

Spanish pronunciation is, in general, consistently phonetic. Once you are aware of the basic rules, they should cause little difficulty. Speak slowly to avoid getting tongue-tied until you become confident of your ability.

Pronunciation of the letters f, k, l, n, p, q, s and t is virtually identical with English, and y is identical when used as a consonant; ll is a separate letter, pronounced as 'y' and coming after l in the alphabet. Ch and ñ are also separate letters; in the alphabet they come after c and n, respectively.

Vowels Spanish vowels are very consistent and have easy English equivalents:

a is like 'a' in 'father'

e is like the 'e' in 'met'; at the end of a word it's like the 'ey' in 'hey'

i is like 'ee' in 'feet'

o is like 'o' in 'for'

u is like 'oo' in 'boot'; after consonants other than 'q,' it is more like English 'w'

y is a consonant except when it stands alone or appears at the end of a word, in which case its pronunciation is identical to Spanish 'i'

Consonants Spanish consonants generally resemble their English equivalents, but there are some major exceptions:

b resembles its English equivalent, but is undistinguished from 'v'; for clarification, refer to the former as 'b larga,' the latter as 'b corta' (the word for the letter itself is pronounced like English 'bay')

c is like the 's' in 'see' before 'e' and 'i,' otherwise like English 'k'

d closely resembles 'th' in 'feather'

g before 'e' and 'i' is like a guttural English 'h'; otherwise like 'g' in 'go'

h is invariably silent; if your name begins with this letter, listen carefully when immigration officials summon you to pick up your passport

j most closely resembles English 'h,' but is slightly more guttural

ñ is like 'ni' in 'onion'

r is nearly identical to English except at the beginning of a word, when it is often rolled

rr is very strongly rolled

v resembles English, but see 'b,' above

x is like 'x' in 'taxi' except for very few words for which it follows Spanish or Mexican usage as 'j'

z is like 's' in 'sun'

Diphthongs Diphthongs are combinations of two vowels that form a single syllable. In Spanish, the formation of a diphthong depends on combinations of 'weak' vowels (i and u) or strong ones (a, e and o). Two weak vowels or a strong and a weak vowel make a diphthong, but two strong ones are separate syllables.

A good example of two weak vowels forming a diphthong is the word *diurno* (during the day). The final syllable of

obligatorio (obligatory) is a combination of weak and strong vowels.

Stress Stress, often indicated by visible accents, is very important, since it can change the meaning of words. In general, words ending in vowels or the letters n or s have stress on the next-to-last syllable, while those with other endings have stress on the last syllable. Thus *vaca* (cow) and *caballos* (horses) both have accents on their next-to-last syllables.

Visible accents, which can occur anywhere in a word, dictate stress over these general rules. Thus *sótano* (basement), *América* and *porción* (portion) all have the stress on the syllable with the accented vowel. When words are written all in capitals, the accent is often not shown, but it still affects the pronunciation.

Basic Grammar

Nouns in Spanish are masculine or feminine. The definite article ('the' in English) agrees with the noun in gender and number; for example, the Spanish word for 'train' is masculine, so 'the train' is *el tren*, and the plural is *los trenes*. The word for 'house' is feminine, so 'the house' is *la casa*, and the plural is *las casas*. The indefinite articles (a, an, some) work in the same way: *un libro* (a book) is masculine singular, while *una carta* (a letter) is feminine singular.

Most nouns ending in 'o' are masculine, and those ending in 'a' are generally feminine. Normally, nouns ending in a vowel add 's' to form the plural – unos libros (some books), las cartas (some letters) – while those ending in a consonant add 'es': los reyes (the kings) is the plural of el rey. Gender also affects demonstrative pronouns: este is the masculine form of 'this,' while esta is the feminine form and esto the neuter; 'these,' 'that' and 'those' are formed by adding 's.'

Adjectives also agree with the noun in gender and number and usually come after the noun. Possessive adjectives like *mi* (my), *tu* (your) and *su* (his/her/their) agree with the thing possessed, not with the possessor. For example 'his suitcase' is *su maleta*, while 'his suitcases' is *sus maletas*. A simple way to indicate possession is to use the preposition *de* (of). 'Juan's room,' for instance, would be *la habitación de Juan*, literally, 'the room of Juan.'

Personal pronouns are usually not used with verbs, except for clarification or emphasis. There are three main categories of verbs: those that end in 'ar,' such as *hablar* (to speak), those that end in 'er,' such as *comer* (to eat), and those that end in 'ir,' such as *reír* (to laugh); there are many irregular verbs, such as *ir* (to go) and *venir* (to come).

To form a comparative, add *más* (more) or *menos* (less) before the adjective. For example, *alto* is 'high,' *más alto* 'higher' and *lo más alto* 'the highest.'

Greetings & Civilities

In their public behavior, Chileans are exceptionally polite and expect others to reciprocate. Never, for example, approach a stranger for information without extending a greeting like *buenos días* or *buenas tardes*. Most young people use the informal 'tu' and its associated verb forms among themselves, but if in doubt you should use the more formal 'usted' and its forms.

hello	*hola*
good morning	*buenos días*
good afternoon	*buenas tardes*
good evening, night	*buenas noches*
goodbye	*adiós, chau*
please	*por favor*
thank you	*gracias*
you're welcome	*de nada*

Useful Words & Phrases

yes	*sí*
no	*no*
and	*y*
to/at	*a*
for	*por, para*
of/from	*de, desde*
in	*en*
with	*con*
without	*sin*

before	*antes*
after	*después*
soon	*pronto*
already	*ya*
now	*ahora*
right away	*en seguida, al tiro*
here	*aquí*
there	*allí*
I understand	*entiendo*
I don't understand	*no entiendo*

I don't speak much Spanish.
   No hablo mucho castellano.

Is there …? Are there …?
   ¿Hay …?

Where?	*¿Dónde?*
Where is … ?	*¿Dónde está … ?*
Where are … ?	*¿Dónde están … ?*
When?	*¿Cuando?*
How?	*¿Cómo?*

I would like …	*Me gustaría …*
coffee	*café*
tea	*té*
beer	*cerveza*

How much?	*¿Cuanto?*
How many?	*¿Cuantos?*
What does it cost?	*¿Cuanto cuesta?*

Getting Around

plane	*avión*
train	*tren*
bus	*ómnibus*, or just *bus*
small bus	*colectivo, micro, liebre*
ship	*barco, buque*
car	*auto*
taxi	*taxi*
truck	*camión*
pickup	*camioneta*
bicycle	*bicicleta*
motorcycle	*motocicleta*
hitchhike	*hacer dedo*
airport	*aeropuerto*
train station	*estación de ferrocarril*
bus terminal	*terminal de buses*

I would like a ticket to …
   Quiero un boleto/pasaje a …

What's the fare to …?
¿Cuanto cuesta el pasaje a …?
When does the next plane/
train/bus leave for …?
¿Cuando sale el próximo avión/tren/
ómnibus para ….?

student/university discount	*descuento estudiantil/ universitario*
first/last/next	*primero/último/ próximo*
first/second class	*primera/segunda clase*
one-way/roundtrip	*ida/ida y vuelta*
left luggage	*guardería, equipaje*
tourist office	*oficina de turismo*

Accommodations

hotel	*hotel, pensión, residencial*
single room	*habitación single*
double room	*habitación doble*
per night	*por noche*
full board	*pensión completa*
shared bath	*baño compartido*
private bath	*baño privado*
too expensive	*demasiado caro*
cheaper	*mas económico*
May I see it?	*¿Puedo verlo?*
I don't like it.	*No me gusta.*
the bill	*la cuenta*

Can you give me a deal?
¿Me puede hacer precio?

Toilets

The most common word for 'toilet' is *baño*, but *servicios sanitarios,* or just *servicios* (services), is a frequent alternative. Men's toilets will usually bear a descriptive term such as *hombres, caballeros* or *varones.* Women's toilets will say *señoras* or *damas.*

Post & Communications

post office	*correo*
letter	*carta*
parcel	*paquete*
postcard	*postal*
airmail	*correo aéreo*
registered mail	*certificado*
stamps	*estampillas*
person to person	*persona a persona*
collect call	*cobro revertido*

Geographical Terms

The words below are among the most common you will encounter in this book as well as in Spanish-language maps and guides.

bay	*bahía*
bridge	*puente*
farm	*fundo, hacienda*
glacier	*glaciar, ventisquero*
highway	*carretera, camino, ruta*
hill	*cerro*
lake	*lago*
marsh, estuary	*estero*
mount	*cerro*
mountain range	*cordillera*
national park	*parque nacional*
pass	*paso*
ranch	*estancia*
sound	*seno*
river	*río*
waterfall	*cascada, salto*

Countries

The list below includes only countries whose spelling differs in English and Spanish.

Canada	*Canadá*
Denmark	*Dinamarca*
England	*Inglaterra*
France	*Francia*
Germany	*Alemania*
Great Britain	*Gran Bretaña*
Ireland	*Irlanda*
Italy	*Italia*
Japan	*Japón*
Netherlands	*Holanda*
New Zealand	*Nueva Zelandia*
Peru	*Perú*
Scotland	*Escocia*
Spain	*España*
Sweden	*Suecia*
Switzerland	*Suiza*
United States	*Estados Unidos*
Wales	*Gales*

I am from …   *Soy de …*
Where are you from?
¿De dónde viene?
Where do you live?
¿Dónde vive?

Numbers

1	*uno*
2	*dos*
3	*tres*
4	*cuatro*
5	*cinco*
6	*seis*
7	*siete*
8	*ocho*
9	*nueve*
10	*diez*
11	*once*
12	*doce*
13	*trece*
14	*catorce*
15	*quince*
16	*dieciseis*
17	*diecisiete*
18	*dieciocho*
19	*diecinueve*
20	*veinte*
21	*veintiuno*
22	*veintidós*
23	*veintitrés*
24	*veinticuatro*
30	*treinta*
31	*treinta y uno*
32	*treinta y dos*
33	*treinta y tres*
40	*cuarenta*
41	*cuarenta y uno*
42	*cuarenta y dos*
50	*cincuenta*
60	*sesenta*
70	*setenta*
80	*ochenta*
90	*noventa*
100	*cien*
101	*ciento uno*
102	*ciento dos*
110	*ciento diez*
120	*ciento veinte*
130	*ciento treinta*
200	*doscientos*
300	*trescientos*
400	*cuatrocientos*
500	*quinientos*
600	*seiscientos*
700	*setecientos*
800	*ochocientos*
900	*novecientos*
1000	*mil*
1100	*mil cien*
1200	*mil doscientos*
2000	*dos mil*
5000	*cinco mil*
10,000	*diez mil*
50,000	*cincuenta mil*
100,000	*cien mil*
1,000,000	*un millón*

Ordinal Numbers

1st	*primero/a*
2nd	*segundo/a*
3rd	*tercero/a*
4th	*cuarto/a*
5th	*quinto/a*
6th	*sexto/a*
7th	*séptimo/a*
8th	*octavo/a*
9th	*noveno/a*
10th	*décimo/a*
11th	*undécimo/a*
12th	*duodécimo/a*

Days of the Week

Monday	*lunes*
Tuesday	*martes*
Wednesday	*miércoles*
Thursday	*jueves*
Friday	*viernes*
Saturday	*sábado*
Sunday	*domingo*

Time

Eight o'clock is *las ocho,* while 8:30 is *las ocho y treinta* (literally, 'eight and thirty') or *las ocho y media* (eight and a half). However, 7:45 is *las ocho menos quince* (literally, 'eight minus fifteen') or *las ocho menos cuarto* (eight minus one quarter).

Times are modified by morning *(de la mañana)* or afternoon *(de la tarde)* instead of am or pm. It is also common to use the 24-hour clock, especially with transportation schedules.

What time is it?	*¿Qué hora es?*
It is …	*Es la una …*
	or *Son las …*

Glossary

This list contains common words, including geographical and biological terms as well as slang terms from everyday speech.

aerosilla – chairlift
afuerino – casual farm laborer
aguas – herbal teas
alameda – avenue or boulevard lined with trees, particularly poplars
albergue juvenil – youth hostel
almuerzo – lunch
anexo – telephone extension
Araucanians – major grouping of indigenous peoples, including the Mapuche, Picunche and Pehuenche Indians
arroyo – watercourse
ascensores – picturesque funiculars that connect the center of Valparaíso with its hillside neighborhoods

bahía – bay
balneario – bathing resort or beach
barrio – neighborhood or borough
bencina – petrol or gasoline
bencina blanca – white gas used for camping stoves; usually available in hardware or chemical supply stores
bidón – spare fuel container
bodega – cellar or storage area for wine
boleto inteligente – multitrip ticket for Santiago metro; also known as *boleto valor*

cabildo – colonial town council
cacique – Indian chieftain
calefón – water heater; in some budget accommodations, travelers must ask to have the calefón turned on before taking a shower
caleta – small cove
callampas – shantytowns on the outskirts of Santiago, literally 'mushrooms' since they seemed to spring up overnight around the capital. Some former callampas have become well-established neighborhoods.
cama – bed; also a sleeper-class seat on a bus or train
camarote – sleeper class on a ship or ferry

caracoles – winding roads, usually in a mountainous area; literally 'snails' or 'spirals'
carretera – highway
casa de cambio – money exchange house, which usually buys foreign cash and traveler's checks
casa de familia – modest family accommodations, usually in tourist centers
casco – 'big house' on a *fundo* or *estancia*
casilla – post office box
cena – dinner
cerro – hill
certificado – registered, as in mail
cine arte – art cinema (in contrast to mass commercial cinema), generally available only in Santiago and at universities
ciudad – city
coa – working-class slang of Santiago
cobro revertido – collect (reverse charge) phone call
Codelco – Corporación del Cobre, the state-owned enterprise that oversees Chile's copper mining industry
colación – lunch
colectivo or **taxi colectivo** – shared taxi
comedor – inexpensive market restaurant; also, dining room of a hotel
comida corrida – a cheap set meal
comparsa – group of musicians or dancers
comuna – local governmental unit
confitería – confectioner's shop
con gas – 'with gas'; carbonated, as in soft drinks
congregación – in colonial Latin America, the concentration of dispersed native populations in settlements, usually for political control and/or religious instruction; see also *reducción*
congrio – conger eel, a popular and delicious Chilean seafood
cordillera – mountain range
costanera – coastal road; any road along a seacoast, riverside or lakeshore
criollo – in colonial times, a person of Spanish parentage born in the New World
curanto – Chilean seafood stew

desayuno – breakfast
duros – hard-boiled

elaboración artesanal – small-scale production, often by a family
encomendero – individual Spaniard or Spanish institution (such as the Catholic Church) exploiting Indian labor under the *encomienda* system
encomienda – colonial labor system, under which Indian communities were required to provide workers for encomenderos (see above), in exchange for which the encomendero was to provide religious and language instruction. In practice, the system benefited the encomendero far more than native peoples.
esquí en marcha – cross-country skiing
estancia – extensive cattle- or sheep-grazing establishment, with a dominant owner or manager and dependent resident labor force
estero – estuary

feria – artisans' market
fuerte – fort
fundo – Chilean term for hacienda, usually applied to a smaller irrigated unit in the country's central heartland

garúa – coastal desert fog
golpe de estado – coup d'etat, a sudden, illegal seizure of government
guanaco – police water cannon, so named after the spitting wild camelid

hacendado – owner of a *hacienda*, who was usually resident in the city and left day-to-day management of his estate to underlings
hacienda – throughout Latin America, a large but often underproductive rural landholding, with dependent labor force in residence, under a dominant owner. In Chile, the term fundo is more common, though it generally applies to a smaller irrigated unit.
hospedaje – budget accommodations, usually in a large family home with one or two extra bedrooms for guests and a shared bathroom
hostería – inn or guesthouse that serves meals, usually outside the main cities

hotel parejero – urban short-stay accommodations, normally patronized by young couples in search of privacy
huaso – horseman, a rough Chilean equivalent of the Argentine gaucho

IGM – Instituto Geográfico Militar; mapping organization whose products are available and useful to travelers but also rather expensive
inquilino – tenant farmer on a fundo
intendencia – Spanish colonial administrative unit
isla – island
islote – small island, islet
istmo – isthmus
IVA – *impuesto de valor agregado*, value-added tax (VAT) often added to restaurant or hotel bills

kuchen – sweet, German-style pastries

lago – lake
laguna – lagoon
latifundio – large landholding, such as a fundo, hacienda or estancia
lista de correos – poste restante
llano – plain, flat ground
local – a numbered addition to a street address indicating that a business occupies one of several offices at that address; for example, Maturana 227, Local 5

machista – male chauvinist (normally used as an adjective)
Mapuche – indigenous inhabitants of the area south of Chile's Río Biobío, but also numerous in Santiago
marisquería – seafood restaurant, usually reasonably priced with excellent quality, in family-oriented beach resorts
media pensión – half-board, in a hotel
mestizo – a person of mixed Indian and Spanish descent
micro – small bus, often traveling along the back roads
minifundio – small landholding, such as a peasant farm
mirador – lookout point, usually on a hill but sometimes in a building

momios – 'mummies,' pejorative term for upper-class Chileans resistant to social and political change
municipalidad – city hall
museo – museum
música funcional – elevator music

nevado – snow-capped mountain peak
Nueva Canción Chilena – the 'New Chilean Song' movement, which arose in the 1960s and combined traditional folk themes with contemporary political activism

oferta – promotional fare, often seasonal, for plane or bus travel
onces – 'elevenses,' Chilean afternoon tea

parada – bus stop
parque nacional – national park
parrilla – restaurant specializing in grilled meats
parrillada – grilled steak and other cuts of beef
peatonal – pedestrian mall, usually in the center of larger cities
pensión – family home offering short-term budget accommodations; may also take permanent lodgers
pensión completa – full board, in a hotel
peña – folk music and cultural club; many of these originated in the capital in the 1960s as venues for the New Chilean Song movement
picada – simple family restaurant, usually informal, that acquires a reputation for quality and often expands its operations. Common in resort towns, but not unusual in cities, the picada can be an excellent value. Chileans often abbreviate the term to *picá*.
playa – beach
porteño – a native or resident of the port city of Valparaíso
portezuelo – mountain pass
posta – clinic or first-aid station; these are often found in smaller towns that lack full-scale hospitals
postre – dessert
propina – a tip, for service at a restaurant or elsewhere

puente – bridge
puerto – port
pulpería – company store on a fundo, estancia or nitrate office
punta – point

quebrada – ravine

reducción – the concentration of Indians in towns modeled on the Spanish grid pattern, for purposes of political control or religious instruction; the term also refers to the settlement itself
refugio – a shelter, usually rustic, in a national park or other remote area
reserva nacional – national reserve
residencial – budget accommodations, sometimes seasonal; in general, residenciales occupy buildings designed expressly for short-stay lodging
río – river
rodeo – annual roundup of cattle on an estancia or hacienda
roto – 'ragged one,' a dependent laborer on a Chilean fundo
ruta – route, highway

SAG – *Servicio Agrícola Ganadero*, the Agriculture & Livestock Service; its officials inspect baggage and vehicles for prohibited fruit and meat imports at Chilean border crossings
salón cama – bus with reclining seats
salón de té – literally 'teahouse,' but more like an upscale cafetería
santiaguino – native or resident of Santiago
sierra – mountain range
siesta – afternoon nap during the extended midday break of traditional Chilean business hours
sin gas – 'without gas,' noncarbonated mineral water
s/n – 'sin número,' indicating a street address without a number
soroche – altitude sickness
Southern Cone – in political geography, the area comprising Argentina, Chile, Uruguay and parts of Brazil and Paraguay; so called after the area's shape on the map

tajamares – dikes built to control flooding of the Río Mapocho in late-colonial Santiago
teleférico – gondola cable car
tenedor libre – all-you-can-eat fare
todo terreno – mountain bike
toqui – Mapuche Indian chief
turismo aventura – nontraditional tourism, such as trekking and white-water rafting

Unidad Popular – 'Popular Unity,' a coalition of leftist political groups that supported Salvador Allende in the 1970 presidential election

Valle Central – 'Central Valley,' the Chilean heartland that extends south from the Río Aconcagua to near the city of Concepción; this area contains most of Chile's population and its industrial and agricultural wealth
ventisquero – glacier
volcán – volcano

Index

Text

A

accidents 47
accommodations 85-91. *See also individual locations*
   long-term rentals 91
Aconcagua 167-8
activities 81-4
Acuario Municipal 159
addresses 34-5
Aeropuerto Internacional Arturo Merino Benítez 52, 62
AIDS 42, 123
air travel 52-9
   glossary 55
   tickets 57
airlines 58-9
airports 52, 62
alcoholic drinks 95-6
Aldunate, Carmen 23
Allende, Isabel 19
Allende, Salvador 13, 19, 21, 22, 23, 39, 75, 77, 80
Almagro, Diego de 11, 122
Altar de la Patria 70
Ampuero, Roberto 22
amusement parks 77
antiques 109-10
apart hotels 91
aquariums 76, 159
Arancibia Clavel, Enrique 12-3
Araucanians 10, 11
archaeology 19
Argentina
   Mendoza (province) 152-69
   visiting 154
Arrau, Claudio 22
art. *See also* museums
   galleries 111, 127
   painting 23
   sculpture 23
ascensores 127-8

Bold indicates maps.

astronomy 19, 75
ATMs 33

B

Balmaceda, José Manuel 77
Baños Colina 120
Baños Morales 120
bargaining 34
Barrio Bellavista 69, 77, **Map 7**
   accommodations 87
   restaurants 98-100
Barrio Brasil 74-7, **Map 6**
   accommodations 86, 87
   restaurants 97-8
Barrio Ecológico 81
Barrio París Londres 70
bars & pubs 51, 104
Basílica del Salvador 74, 75
beaches 135, 141-2
beef 93
Bello, Andrés 19
Berríos, Eugenio 13
Biblioteca Nacional 70
Biblioteca William Mulloy 135
bicycling. *See* cycling
blues 106
Bolívar, Simón 19
Bolsa de Comercio 70
books 38-9
bookstores 111-2
Bóvedas Históricas Uspallata 166
buses
   domestic 59-60, 132
   international 59-60, 132
   local 62, 63
business
   doing 49-50
   hours 48

C

Cachagua 142
Cacheuta 164
Cajón del Maipo 117-20, **117**

Caleu 114
Calvario de la Carrodilla 164
Capilla La Ermita 74
carabineros 46
Caracoles de Villavicencio 166
carrier codes 36
cars 60-1, 63-6
   accidents 47
   documents 30, 64
   driver's licenses 29-30
   insurance 64
   renting 65-6
   restrictions 65
   road assistance 64
   road rules 64
   shipping 65
Casa Colorado 69
Casa de Huique 151
Casa de la Cultura 78
Casa del Pilar de Esquina 147-8
Casa Manso de Velasco 68
Cascada de las Animas 119
Catedral Metropolitana 68, 70
cell phones 37
Cementerio General 77
Centro Cultural Montecarmelo 77
Centro de Esqui Chapa Verde 149
Cerrillos 81
Cerro Aconcagua 167-8
Cerro La Campana 143, 144
Cerro Montura 166
Cerro San Cristóbal 78
Cerro Santa Lucía 69, 73-4
Cerro Tunduqueral 166
chambers of commerce 50
children, traveling with 44
cinemas 107. *See also* films
classical music 22, 107
climate 14-5
climbing 82-3, 159-60, 166, 167-8

Boxed Text

Bold indicates maps.

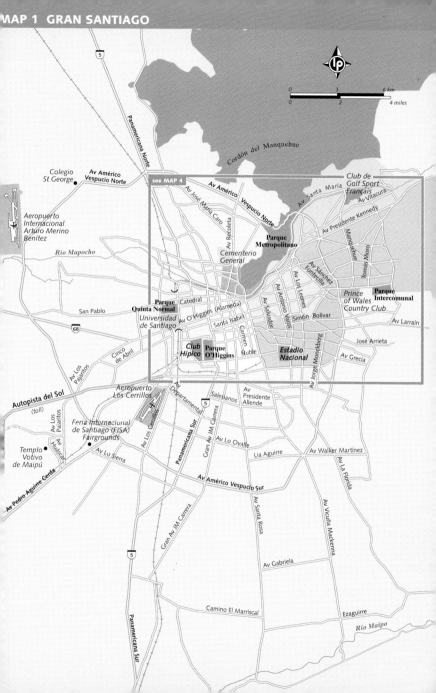

MAP 1 GRAN SANTIAGO

0   3   6 km
0   2   4 miles

Colegio
St George
Av Américo
Vespucio Norte
Aeropuerto
Internacional
Arturo Merino
Benítez
Río Mapocho
San Pablo
68
Cinco
de Abril
Av Los
Pajaritos

Club de
Golf Sport
Français
Av Santa María
Av Vitacura
Av Presidente Kennedy
Cordón del Manquehue
Manquehue
Tomás Moro
see MAP 4
Av Américo Vespucio Norte
Av José María Caro
Av Recoleta
Parque
Metropolitano
Av Sánchez
Fontecilla
Cementerio
General
Prince
of Wales
Country Club
Parque
Intercomunal
Av Los Leones
Av Salvador
Av Antonio Varas
Av Larraín
Parque
Quinta Normal
Catedral
Universidad
de Santiago
Av O'Higgins (Alameda)
Santa Isabel
Carmen
Simón
Bolívar
José Arrieta
Club
Hípico
Parque
O'Higgins
Ñuble
Estadio
Nacional
Av Jorge Montt
Av Grecia

Autopista del Sol
(toll)
Av Los
Pajaritos
Av Huscar
Aeropuerto
Los Cerrillos
Av Departamental
Av Los Cerrillos
Salesianos
Av
Presidente
Allende
Feria Internacional
de Santiago (FISA)
Fairgrounds
Panamericana Sur
Gran Av JM Carrera
Av Lo Ovalle
Lía Aguirre
Av Walker Martínez
Av La Florida
Templo
Votivo
de Maipú
Av Lo Sierra
Av Américo Vespucio Sur
Av Santa Rosa
Av Pedro Aguirre Cerda
Gran Av JM Carrera
Av Vicuña Mackenna
Av Gabriela
5
Camino El Marriscal
Ezaguirre
Panamericana Sur
Río Maipo
Panamericana Norte
5

MAP 2 COMUNAS DE SANTIAGO

QUILICURA

Panamericana Norte

5

LO BARNECHEA

HUECHURABA

Av Américo Vespucio Norte

Cordón del Manquehue

CONCHALÍ

RECOLETA

VITACURA
MAP 9

Parque
Metropolitano
MAP 7

LAS CONDES
MAP 9

Aeropuerto
Internacional
Arturo Merino
Benítez

RENCA

INDEPENDENCIA

Río Mapocho

CERRO NAVIA

Barrio
Bellavista
MAP 7

PROVIDENCIA
MAP 8

QUINTA
NORMAL

LA REINA

PUDAHUEL

68

LO PRADO

SANTIAGO

ÑUÑOA
MAP 10

Barrio Brasil
MAP 6

Santiago
Centro
MAP 5

ESTACIÓN CENTRAL

MACUL

PEÑALOLÉN

Aeropuerto
Los Cerrillos

PEDRO
AGUIRRE
CERDA

5

Autopista del Sol
(toll)

CERRILLOS

SAN
JOAQUÍN

SAN MIGUEL

MAIPÚ

LO
ESPEJO

Panamericana Sur

LA CISTERNA

LA GRANJA

LA FLORIDA

Av Américo Vespucio Sur

Av Pedro Aguirre Cerda

SAN
RAMÓN

EL BOSQUE

SAN BERNARDO

5

LA PINTANA

Panamericana Sur

Río Maipo

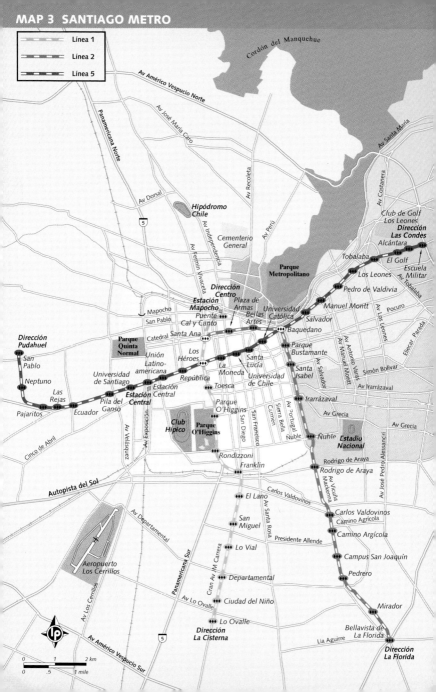

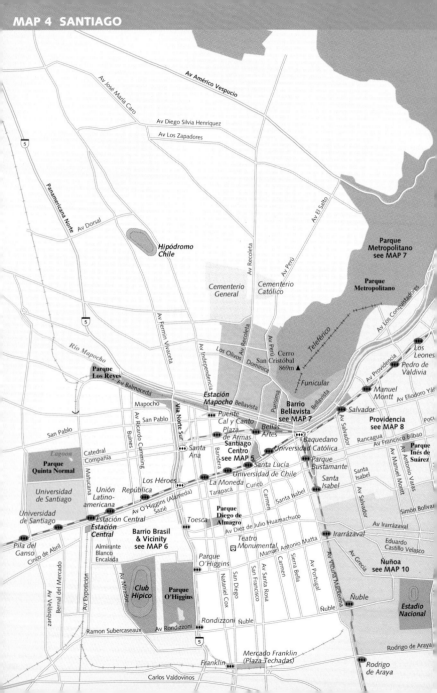

MAP 4 SANTIAGO

Av Américo Vespucio

Av José María Caro

Av Diego Silvia Henríquez

Av Los Zapadores

Panamericana Norte

Av Dorsal

5

Hipódromo
Chile

Av Fermín Vivaceta

Río Mapocho

5

Av El Salto

Parque
Metropolitano
see MAP 7

Cementerio
General

Cementerio
Católico

Parque
Metropolitano

Av Perú

Av Recoleta

Av Recoleta

Av Perú

Av Los Conquistadores

Teleférico

Los Olivos

Parque
Los Reyes

Av Independencia

Av Balmaceda

San Cristóbal
869m

Purísima

Funicular

Dominica

Av Providencia

Los
Leones

Providencia

Pedro de
Valdivia

Manuel
Montt

Av Eliodoro Yá

Estación
Mapocho

Mapocho

Av San Pablo

Vía Norte Sur

Bellavista

Puente
Cal y Canto

Bellavista

Bellavista

Salvador

Barrio
Bellavista
see MAP 7

Av Salvador

Providencia
see MAP 8

San Pablo

Av Ricardo Cumming

Bulnes

Catedral

Compañía

Santa
Ana

Bandera

Plaza
de Armas

Santiago
Centro
see MAP 5

Bellas
Artes

Baquedano

Universidad Católica

Rancagua

Av Francisco Bilbao

Parque
Inés de
Suárez

Lagoon

Parque
Quinta Normal

Matucana

Unión
Latino-
americana

República

Los Héroes

Universidad de Chile

Santa Lucía

Parque
Bustamante

Av Manuel Montt

Av Antonio Varas

Universidad
de Santiago

La Moneda

Curicó

Carmen

Santa Isabel

Santa
Isabel

Santa
Isabel

Simón Bolívar

Universidad
de Santiago

Estación Central

Estación
Central

Av O'Higgins (Alameda)

Sazié

Tarapacá

Av Salvador

Pila del
Ganso

Almirante
Blanco
Encalada

Toesca

Av Diez de Julio

Huamachuco

Irarrázaval

Av Irarrázaval

Cinco de Abril

Barrio Brasil
& Vicinity
see MAP 6

Parque
Diego de
Almagro

Av Vicuña Mackenna

Eduardo
Castillo Velasco

Bernal del Mercado

Av Exposición

Av Mirador

Parque
O'Higgins

Teatro
Monumental

Manuel Antonio Matta

San Diego

San Francisco

Carmen

Santa Rosa

Sierra Bella

Av Grecia

Ñuñoa
see MAP 10

Av Velásquez

Club
Hípico

Parque
O'Higgins

Natanel Cox

Av Portugal

Ñuble

Estadio
Nacional

Ramon Subercaseaux

Av Rondizzoni

Rondizzoni

Ñuble

5

Rodrigo de Araya

Franklin

Mercado Franklin
(Plaza Techadas)

Rodrigo
de Araya

Carlos Valdovinos

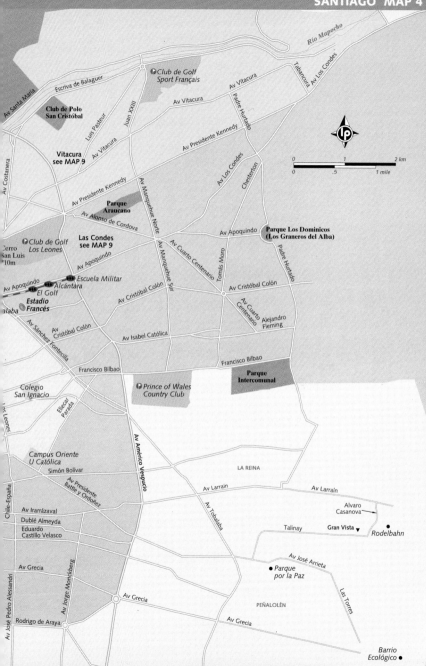

Río Mapocho

Escriva de Balaguer

Club de Golf
Sport Français

Av Vitacura

Av Vitacura

Tabancura

Av Los Condes

Av Santa María

Club de Polo
San Cristóbal

Luis Pasteur

Juan XXIII

Av Vitacura

Av Presidente Kennedy

Padre Hurtado

Vitacura
see MAP 9

Av Costanera

Av Presidente Kennedy

Av Los Condes

Chesterton

Parque
Araucano

Av Alonso de Cordova

Av Manquehue Norte

Av Apoquindo

Parque Los Dominicos
(Los Graneros del Alba)

Cerro
San Luis
²10m

Club de Golf
Los Leones

Las Condes
see MAP 9

Av Cuarto Centenario

Av Manquehue Sur

Tomás Moro

Padre Hurtado

Av Apoquindo

Escuela Militar

Alcántara

El Golf

Estadio
Francés

Av Apoquindo

Av Cristóbal Colón

Av Cristóbal Colón

Av Cuarto
Centenario

Alejandro
Fleming

alaba

Av Sánchez Fontecilla

Av Cristóbal Colón

Av Isabel Católica

Francisco Bilbao

Francisco Bilbao

Parque
Intercomunal

Colegio
San Ignacio

Eliecar
Parada

Prince of Wales
Country Club

Av Américo Vespucio

Campus Oriente
U Católica

Simón Bolívar

Av Presidente
Batlle y Ordóñez

LA REINA

Los Leones

Chile-España

Av Larrain

Av Larraín

Av Irarrázaval

Alvaro
Casanova

Dublé Almeyda

Av Tobalaba

Talinay

Gran Vista

Eduardo
Castillo Velasco

Rodelbahn

Av Grecia

Av Jorge Montckberg

Av José Arrieta

Parque
por la Paz

Av José Pedro Alessandri

Av Grecia

Las Torres

PEÑALOLÉN

Rodrigo de Araya

Av Grecia

Barrio
Ecológico

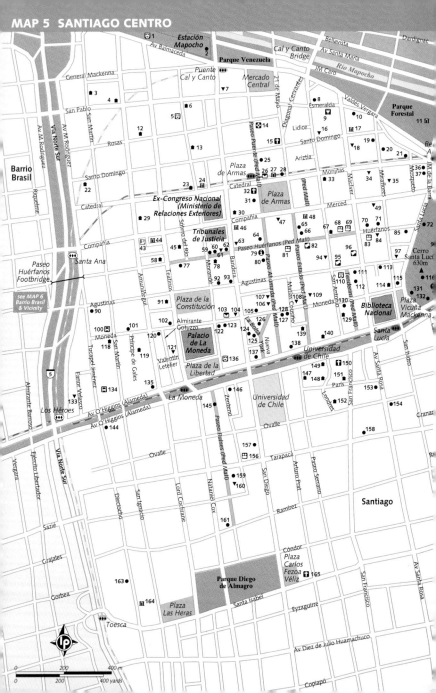

MAP 5 SANTIAGO CENTRO

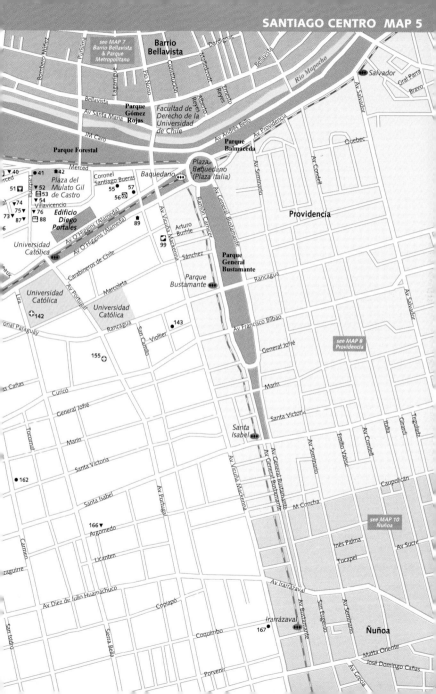

Barrio Bellavista

see MAP 7
Barrio Bellavista
& Parque
Metropolitano

Dardinac

Bellavista

Río Mapocho

Salvador

Gral Parra

Bravo

Bombero Núñez

Purísima

Pío Nono

Constitución

Mallinkrodt

Ernesto Reyes

Alberto Reyes

Av Salvador

Bellavista

Av Santa María

Parque Gómez Rojas

Facultad de Derecho de la Universidad de Chile

JM Caro

Av Andrés Bello

Av Providencia

Quebec

Parque Forestal

Parque Balmaceda

Av Condell

Av Salvador

Merced

Coronel

Baquedano

Plaza Baquedano (Plaza Italia)

Av Vicuña Mackenna

Providencia

▼40

●41

■42

Plaza del Mulato Gil de Castro

Santiago Bueras

55 ●

57

Av Condell

51 ⊡

▼52

53

▼54

Villavicencio

56

Av General Bustamante

▼74

▼75▼

▼76

Edificio Diego Portales

89

Ramón Carnicer

73 ▼

87▼

88

Av O'Higgins (Alameda)

Arturo Burhle

Universidad Católica

Av O'Higgins (Alameda)

99

Sánchez

Carabineros de Chile

Av Portugal

Marcoleta

Parque General Bustamante

Rancagua

Universidad Católica

Parque Bustamante

Av Salvador

⊕142

Universidad Católica

Rancagua

San Camilo

Viollier

143

Av Francisco Bilbao

General Jofré

see MAP 8
Providencia

nal Paraguay

Lia

155 ⊕

Marín

as Cañas

Curicó

General Jofré

Santa Victoria

Marín

Santa Victoria

Italia

Girardi

Tegualda

Santa Isabel

● 162

Santa Isabel

Av Portugal

Av Vicuña Mackenna

Av General Bustamante

Av General Bustamante

Av Seminario

Emilio Vaïsse

Av Condell

Caupolicán

see MAP 10
Ñuñoa

166▼

Argomedo

M Concha

Inés Palma

Av Sucre

Licantén

Tucapel

Carmen

zaguirre

San isidro

Av Diez de Julio Huamachuco

Copiapó

Av Irarrázaval

Av Bustamante

San Eugenio

Av Seminario

Sierra Bella

Coquimbo

Irarrázaval

167 ●

Ñuñoa

Porvenir

Matta Oriente

José Domingo Cañas

Av Vicuña Mackenna

Av Urcia

MAP 5 SANTIAGO CENTRO

PLACES TO STAY

3 Hotel Caribe
4 Hotel Pudahuel
6 Nuevo Hotel Valparaíso
12 Hotel Indiana
13 Hotel Cervantes
22 Majestic Hotel
23 Hotel España
29 Hotel Europa
30 City Hotel
33 Hotel Tupahue
42 Hostal del Parque
45 Hotel Metrópoli
50 Hotel Foresta
58 Hotel Panamericano
67 Hotel Santa Lucía
78 Hotel Gran Palace
86 Hotel Montecarlo
89 Holiday Inn Crowne Plaza
91 Hotel Carrera
114 Hotel Riviera
118 Hotel di Maurier
119 Residencial Tabita
129 Hotel Galerías
139 Hotel El Conquistador
140 Hotel El Libertador
147 Hotel Fundador
148 Hotel Las Vegas
149 Hotel Plaza San Francisco
151 Hotel París
152 Residencial Londres

PLACES TO EAT

7 Bar Central
16 Kam-Thu
18 Da Carla
34 Kintaro
35 El Puente de Bórquez
40 Les Assassins
47 Chez Henry
49 Izakaya Yoko
52 Pérgola de la Plaza
54 Cocoa
61 Bar Nacional 2
63 Bar Nacional 1
73 Rincón Español
74 Squadritto
75 Gatopardo
76 Café del Biógrafo
84 San Marcos
87 Don Victorino
94 Le Due Torri
97 Au Bon Pain
104 El Novillero
106 Café Caribe
107 Café Haití
108 Café Cousiño
109 Pizza Napoli
121 100% Natural
133 El Mesón de Fanor
160 Bavaria
166 Los Adobes de Argomedo

OTHER

1 Teatro Casa Amarilla; Teatro
  Estación Mapocho
2 Centro Cultural Estación Mapocho
5 Sala Agustín Sire
8 Posada del Corregidor
9 Bar Excéntrico
10 Instituto Goethe
11 Palacio de Bellas Artes
12 South Central American
  Information Club
14 Bar del Centro
15 Templo de Santo Domingo
17 Casa Manso de Velasco
19 Instituto Chileno de la Lengua
20 Lys Rent a Car
21 Lavandería Autoservicio
24 Palacio Edwards
25 Cuerpo de Bomberos
26 Correo Central (Main Post Office)
27 Palacio de la Real Audiencia;
  Museo Histórico Nacional
28 Municipalidad de Santiago
31 Librería Manantial
32 Catedral Metropolitana
36 Antigüedades Haddad
37 Antigüedades Mujala
38 Librería El Cid
39 Teatro La Comedia
41 Instituto Chileno-Francés
43 Asociación Cristiana de Jóvenes
  (YMCA)
44 Palacio La Alhambra
46 Real Casa de Aduana; Museo
  Chileno de Arte Precolombino
48 Casa Colorada; Municipal Tourist
  Office
51 Bar Berri
53 Museo Arqueológico de
  Santiago; Ricardo Bravo Murúa
55 Queen
56 Café Virtual; Cine Alameda
57 Avant Airlines
59 American Airlines; Canadian
  Airlines International
60 Ladeco
62 DHL Express
64 Harry Müller Thierfelder
65 Librería Francesa
66 Avant Airlines
68 Cine Huelén
69 Cine Hoyts; Cine Rex
70 Librería Inglesa
71 Feria Chilena del Libro
72 Ascensor (Elevator)
77 Codelco
78 Gran Palace; Libro's
79 Municipal Tourist Kiosk
80 Feria del Disco
81 Cine Central, Cine Huérfanos
82 Paraguayan Consulate
83 Cine Lido
85 Galería Enrico Bucci
88 Cine El Biógrafo

90 Instituto Nacional de la Juventud
92 Huimpalay
93 Iberia
95 German Embassy
96 Brazilian Consulate
98 Jardín Japonés
99 Argentine Consulate
100 Tour Express (Airport Buses)
101 Instituto Chileno-
  Norteamericano de Cultura
102 Ministerio de Hacienda
103 Post Office
105 Chile Típico
110 Teatro Municipal
111 Sociedad Nacional de Agricultura
112 United Airlines
113 LanChile
115 Instituto Chileno-Británico
116 Capilla La Ermita
117 Municipal Tourist Office
120 Departamento de Extranjería
122 Intendencia de Santiago
123 Ecuatoriana; Lloyd Aéreo
  Boliviano; Sportstour Chile
124 Dirección de Fronteras y Límites
  del Estado
125 Bolsa de Comercio
126 Tec-Fo
127 Ultramar
128 Casimires Castrodonoso
129 Galería R
130 Aerolíneas Argentinas
131 Grutas del Cerro Welen; Centro
  de Exposición de Arte Indígena
132 Plaza Neptuno
134 Terminal Los Héroes
135 Torre Entel
136 Teatro Nacional Chileno
137 Club de La Unión
138 Alitalia; Lufthansa
140 Galería Libertador; Venta de
  Pasajes
141 Centro Artesanal Santa Lucía
142 Clínica Universidad Católica
143 Movimiento Unificado de
  Minorías Sexuales (MUMS)
144 Confitería Las Torres
145 Altar de la Patria
146 Edificio de las Fuerzas Armadas
150 Iglesia de San Francisco; Museo
  de Arte Colonial
153 Servicio de Impuestos Internos (SII)
154 DHL Express
155 Posta Central
156 Cine Normandie
157 Librería Rivano
158 La Habana Vieja
159 Fondo de Cultura Económica
161 Conaf
162 Centro Cultural Carmen
163 IGM
164 Palacio Cousiño
165 Iglesia Santísimo Sacramento
167 Laberinto

Monument to Pedro de Valdivia (& bird perch)

Date of Pinochet's coup, Providencia

Changing of the guard at Palacio de la Moneda

Monument to the indigenous people

Salvador Allende's tomb at Cementerio General

MAP 6 BARRIO BRASIL & VICINITY

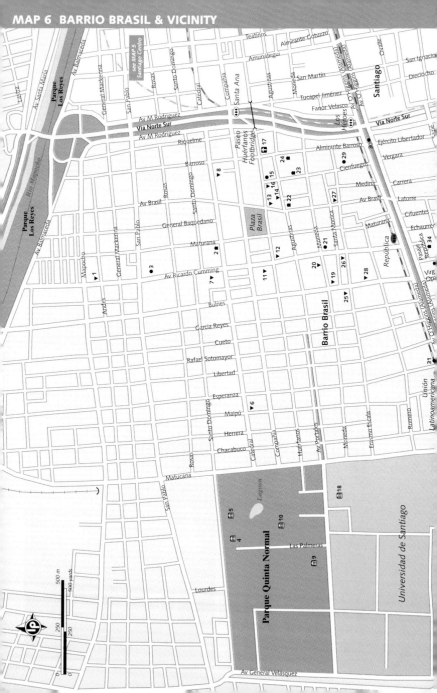

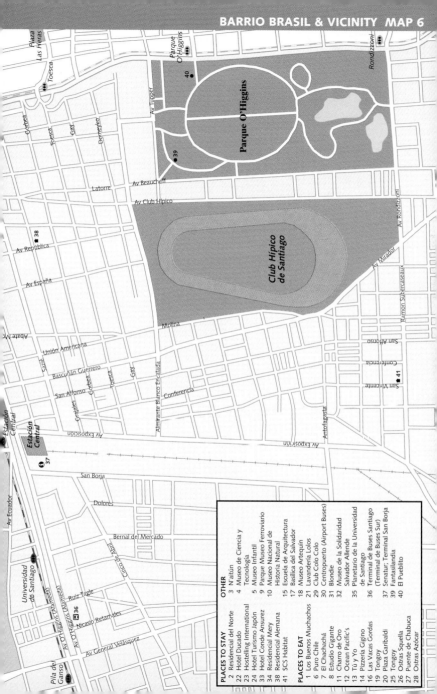

Parque O'Higgins

Parque O'Higgins

Rondizzoni

Av Tupper

Av Beaucheff

Av Club Hípico

Club Hípico
de Santiago

Av República

Av España

Molina

Abate M

Unión Americana

Bascuñán Guerrero

San Alfonso

San Alfonso

Conferencia

Conferencia

Confluencia

Almirante Blanco Encalada

Av Exposición

Av Exposición

Estación Central

Estación Central

San Borja

Dolores

Bernal del Mercado

Cinco de Abril

Universidad de Santiago

Ruiz Tagle

Nicasio Retamales

Av General Velásquez

Pila del Ganso

Av Ecuador

Av O'Higgins (Alameda)

Av O'Higgins (Alameda)

Plaza Las Heras

Toesca

Toesca

Gorbea

Gay

Domeyko

Latorre

Toesca

Gorbea

Grajales

Toesca

Gay

Av Rondizzoni

Av Mirador

Ramón Subercaseaux

San Alfonso

Confidencia

San Vicente

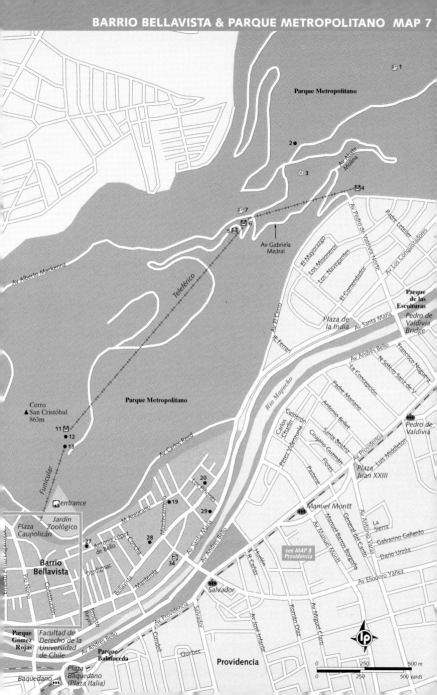

Parque Metropolitano

Av Alinte Molina

Parque Metropolitano

Cerro
▲ San Cristóbal
863m

Av Alberto Mackenna

Teleférico

Av El Cerro

Av J F Ferrari

El Mayorazgo

Los Misioneros

Los Navegantes

El Comendador

Plaza de
la India

Av Santa María

Parque
de las
Esculturas

Pedro de
Valdivia
Bridge

Av Pedro de Valdivia Norte

Padre Letelier

Av Los Conquistadores

Av Gabriela
Mistral

Rio Mapocho

Av Andrés Bello

Francisco Noguera

N Sótero Sanz de V.

La Concepción

Padre Mariano

Antonio Bello

Carlos Chaitin

Calderón

Cirujano Guzmán

Santa Beatriz

Pérez Valenzuela

Pedro de
Valdivia

Plaza
Juan XXIII

Av Providencia

Luis Middleton

Manuel Montt

La
Sierra

Av Antonio Varas

Galvarino Gallardo

Darío Urzúa

General del Canto

Manuel Barros Borgoño

Av Manuel Montt

Huelén

R Cañas

see MAP 8
Providencia

Funicular

entrance

Jardín
Zoológico

Plaza
Caupolicán

Barrio
Bellavista

Antonia López
de Bello

Dardignac

Constitución

Pío Nono

M Araucano

Montecarmelo

Bellavista

Mallinkrodt

Ernesto
Reyes

Av Andrés Bello

Av Santa María

Av Andrés Bello

Salvador

Salvador

Av Providencia

Román Díaz

Av José Infante

Av Miguel Claro

Av Eliodoro Yáñez

Parque
Gómez
Rojas

Facultad de
Derecho de la
Universidad
de Chile

Parque
Balmaceda

Plaza
Baquedano
(Plaza Italia)

Providencia

Baquedano

Condell

Quebec

0   250   500 m

250   500 yards

2 ●

※ 3

☐ 4

☐ 7

☐ 6

5 ☐

11 ☐
● 12
● 13

20 ●

● 19

29 ●

27 ●

28 ●

34 ☐

Los Pinones

Av Carlos Reed

MAP 7 BARRIO BELLAVISTA & PARQUE METROPOLITANO

PLACES TO STAY
- 30 Hotel Parlamento
- 70 Apart Hotel Monteverde

PLACES TO EAT
- 8 El Amir Issa
- 9 Club Palestino
- 10 Omar Khayyam
- 15 El Rinconcito
- 16 Acapela
- 18 Rodizio
- 22 Di Simoncelli
- 42 Tasca Mediterránea
- 44 El Tallarín Gordo
- 45 El Caramaño
- 48 Cristóforo
- 49 Eladio
- 54 La Flor de la Canela
- 55 Las Mañanitas
- 58 El Otro Sitio
- 59 Le Coq au Vin
- 62 Café de la Dulcería Las Palmas
- 63 El Viejo Verde
- 64 El Rinconcito Peruano
- 65 Cocoa
- 67 Eneldo
- 69 La Venezia
- 77 Muñeca Brava
- 78 Al Karim
- 79 Etniko
- 80 Galindo
- 81 Azul Profundo
- 82 Il Siciliano
- 84 Pizzas Gloria
- 85 Tasca Mediterránea
- 89 Armandita

- 90 Como Agua para Chocolate
- 91 Kilomètre 11,680
- 92 Sommelier
- 93 Zen
- 94 Cava Dardignac
- 97 El Antojo de Gauguin

OTHER
- 1 Piscina Antilén
- 2 Enoteca
- 3 Jardín Botánico Mapulemu
- 4 Teleférico Station
- 5 Casa de la Cultura
- 6 Estación Tupahue
- 7 Piscina Tupahue
- 11 Estación Cumbre
- 12 Santuario Inmaculada Concepción
- 13 Terraza Bellavista
- 14 Clínica Dávila
- 17 Havana Salsa
- 19 Greenpeace Pacífico Sur
- 20 Blue Mountain
- 21 Policia Internacional
- 23 Clan Destino
- 24 Bar Dionisio
- 25 Bunker
- 26 Sala Shakespeare's
- 27 Centro de Idiomas Bellavista
- 28 Centro Cultural Montecarmelo
- 29 Fausto
- 31 Chip Day Tours
- 32 International Sporting Club
- 33 Teatro El Conventillo
- 34 Bivouac Café
- 35 Il Rittorno
- 36 El Rincón Habanero

- 37 Cooperativa Almacén Campesina
- 38 Club 4-40
- 39 Escuela Violeta Parra
- 40 Vox Populi
- 41 Galería Ziebold
- 43 Bokhara
- 46 Tadeo's
- 47 Salsoteca Maestra Vida
- 50 La Chascona (Museo Neruda)
- 51 Oz
- 52 Teatro Galpón 7
- 53 Teatro La Feria
- 56 Máscara's
- 57 Jammin' Club
- 60 Da Lua
- 61 Rase
- 66 Zoom
- 68 Discotheque Puerto Bellavista
- 71 La Barra de Mamil
- 72 Plazuela Camilo Mori
- 73 La Casa en el Aire
- 74 Galería del Cerro
- 75 Altazor
- 76 Don Mario Gutiérrez
- 83 Teatro Bellavista
- 86 Arte del Mundo
- 87 Artesanía Nehuen
- 88 Teatro Taller
- 95 Capricho Español
- 96 Peña Nano Parra
- 98 Lapiz Lazuli
- 99 Lapiz Lazuli House
- 101 Tomm
- 100 Callfücura
- 102 Chilean Rent a Car

KRZYSZTOF DYDYNSKI

One of Santiago's trendy spots on Avenida Suecia in Providencia

MAP 8 PROVIDENCIA

PLACES TO STAY
3 Hotel Los Españoles
6 Hotel Santa María
9 Sheraton San Cristóbal
15 Hotel Aloha
23 Hotel Diego de Velásquez
25 Santiago Park Plaza
32 Hotel Neruda
33 Eurotel
34 Hotel Torremayor
36 Hostal Thayer
64 Hotel Flores
66 Hotel Posada del Salvador
67 Hotel María Angola
70 Hotel Bonaparte
72 Hotel Embassy Suites
74 Residencial Salvador
75 Hotel Lyon
79 Hotel Principado
100 Hotel Holley
114 Tempo Rent Apart Hotel
133 Hotel Orly

PLACES TO EAT
5 La Vera Pizza
13 Aquí Está Coco
14 Mare Nostrum
17 Au Bon Pain
18 La Pizza Nostra
21 Der Münchner Hof
30 Pizza Napoli
40 Phone Box Pub; Café del Patio
41 La Escarcha
44 Peters
56 Bravíssimo
57 Liguria
58 Rincón Brasileiro
63 Dos Cuates
90 Puerto Perú
92 Casa de la Cultura de México
95 Pizzería Morena
110 Freddo
113 Trattoria Rivoli
117 Sbarro
121 Le Flaubert
123 Sebastián
125 Eladio
128 El Huerto; La Huerta

OTHER
1 Bolivian Embassy
2 Morita Gil
4 Cámara de Comercio Italiana de
 Chile
7 Cine Tobalaba
8 Belgian Consulate
9 Avis
10 United Rent a Car
11 Peruvian Embassy
12 Centro de Ski La Parva
16 Hostelling International
19 Librería Inglesa
20 Silber Editores
22 Aeroflot
24 Tango Bar Siglo XX
26 Linguatec Language Center
27 Hertz
28 Alameda Rent a Car
29 Federal Express
31 Instituto Cultural de Providencia
35 Cámara Oficial Española de
 Comercio de Chile
37 News Review
38 Sernatur; Mercado Providencia
39 Nautigift
40 Librería Chile Ilustrado; Books; Lila
42 Dity Office
43 Automóvil Club Chileno (Acchi)
45 Copa; Juan Alarcón Rojas
 (Customs Agent)
46 Cubana de Aviación
47 Costanera Rent a Car
48 Post Office
49 Parroquia Nuestra Señora de la
 Divina Providencia
50 Laverap
51 Cámara de Comercio e Industria
 Franco-Chilena
52 Swissair
53 Austrian Embassy
54 Japanese Embassy
55 Atal Rent a Car
59 Líneas Aéreas de Costa Rica
 (Lacsa)
60 JLM Cartografía
61 Centro Cultural de España
62 Cine Arte Aiep
65 Uruguayan Embassy
68 Ansa Rent a Car
69 Artesanías de Chile
71 Netherlands Embassy
73 French Embassy
76 Natalis Language Center
77 Teatro Universidad de Chile
78 Torre Telefónica CTC Chile;
 Internet Access; Sala de Arte
 Telefónica
80 Federación de Andinismo
81 Museo del Deporte
82 Museo Nacional y Biblioteca
 Histórica Benjamín Vicuña
 Mackenna
83 La Mitad del Mundo
84 First Rent a Car
85 Codeff (Comité Pro Defensa de
 la Fauna y Flora)
86 Italian Embassy & Consulate
87 Corporación Chilena de
 Prevención del Sida
88 Lacroce Rent a Car
89 La Casa en el Aire
91 Antigüedades Eliecer Miranda
 Sánchez
93 Galería Praxis
94 Mister Ed
96 Kasbba
97 Casimires Castrodonoso
98 CyberCenter
99 Wall Street
101 Brannigan's
102 Los Pájaros
103 El Deseo
104 Joyas LA Cano
105 DHL Express
106 Saeta
107 Boomerang
108 Old Boston Pub
109 Ladeco
111 Feria del Disco
112 Spanish Consulate; Swedish
 Consulate
114 Avianca
115 Transportes Aéreos Mercosur
 (TAM)
116 Photo von Stowasser
118 Photo Service
119 SAS
120 LanChile
122 American Airlines
124 Air New Zealand
126 Cámara Chileno-Británica de
 Comercio
127 Teatro Oriente
129 Avant Airlines
130 Cascada Expediciones
131 Turismo Tajamar
132 Disquería Fusión
134 Libro's
135 Electric Cowboy
136 Mall Panorámico; Northwest
 Airlines, Alamo Rent a Car
137 Alamo Rent a Car

MAP 8 PROVIDENCIA

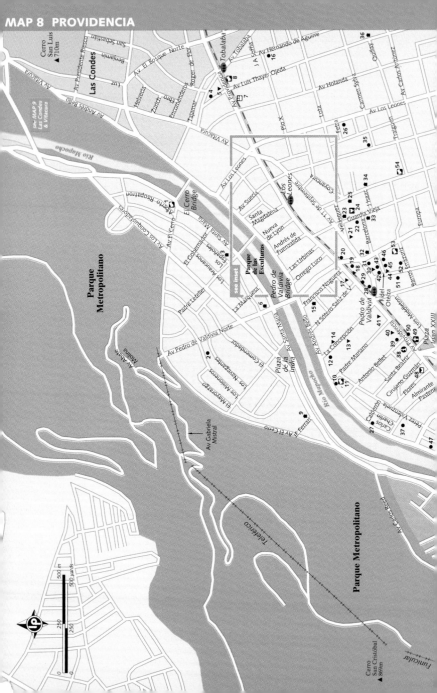

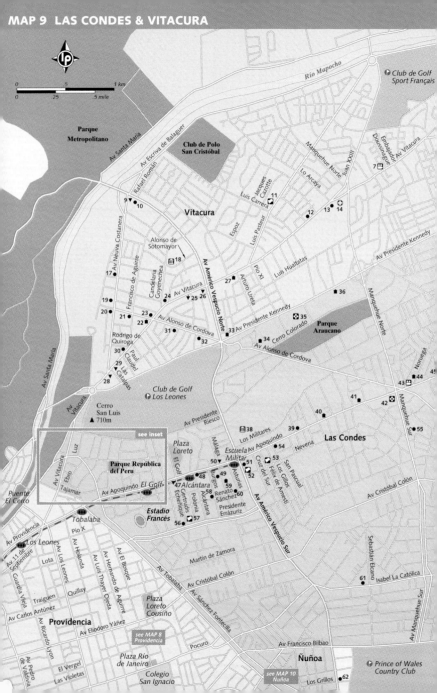

MAP 9 LAS CONDES & VITACURA

0   5   1 km
0   25   .5 mile

Parque
Metropolitano

Río Mapocho

Club de Golf
Sport Français

Club de Polo
San Cristóbal

Embajador Doussinague

Av Vitacura

7

Av Santa María

Av Escriva de Balaguer

Rafael Román

Av Nueva Costanera

9   10

Vitacura

Lo Arcaya

Manquehue Norte

Juan XXIII

Luis Jacques Cazotte
Carrera   11

Espoz

Luis Pasteur

12   13   14

Alonso de
Sotomayor

18

Av Vitacura

Pio XI

Luis Hualtatas

Av Presidente Kennedy

17

Francisco de Aguirre

Candelaria
Goyenechea

24   23

19

20   21   22

25 26

27

Arturo Ureta

36

Rodrigo de
Quiroga

31

Av Alonso de Cordova

33   Av Presidente Kennedy

35

Parque
Araucano

Cerro Colorado

Manquehue Norte

30

32

34

Av Alonso de Cordova

Paul
Claudel

29   Las
Cásalas

28

Av Santa María

Club de Golf
Los Leones

43   44

Noruega

Manquehue Sur

Av Vitacura

Cerro
San Luis
▲ 710m

Av Presidente
Riesco

41

42

40

39

55

Los Militares

38

Las Condes

see inset

Plaza
Loreto

Av Apoquindo

54

Neveria

El Golf

Malaga

Escuela
Militar

51

53

Luz

Parque República
del Peru

50

Los Gillos

San Pascual

Félix de Amesti

Ebro

Av Vitacura

48

Burgos

49

52

Cruz del Sur

Tajamar

Av Apoquindo   El Golf

47 Alcántara

58

59

Polonia

Alcántara

Renato
Sánchez 60

Av Cristóbal Colón

Puente
El Cerro

Gertrudis
Echenique

Presidente
Errázuriz

Av Américo Vespucio Sur

Estadio
Francés

56   57

Tobalaba

Av Providencia

Pio X

Los Leones

Av 11 de Septiembre

Guardia Vieja

Lota

Av Los Leones

Av Holanda

Av El Bosque

Av Luis Thayer Ojeda

Av Hernando de Aguirre

Martín de Zamora

Sebastián Elcano

61

Isabel La Católica

Quillay

Traiguen

Av Carlos Antúnez

Providencia

Av Eliodoro Yáñez

Av Ricardo Lyon

Plaza
Loreto
Cousiño

Av Tobalaba

Av Cristóbal Colón

Av Sánchez Fontecilla

Av Manquehue Sur

El Vergel

Av Pedro de Valdivia

Las Violetas

Plaza Río
de Janeiro

Colegio
San Ignacio

see MAP 8
Providencia

Pocuro

Av Francisco Bilbao

Ñuñoa

Prince of Wales
Country Club

see MAP 10
Ñuñoa

Los Grillos

62

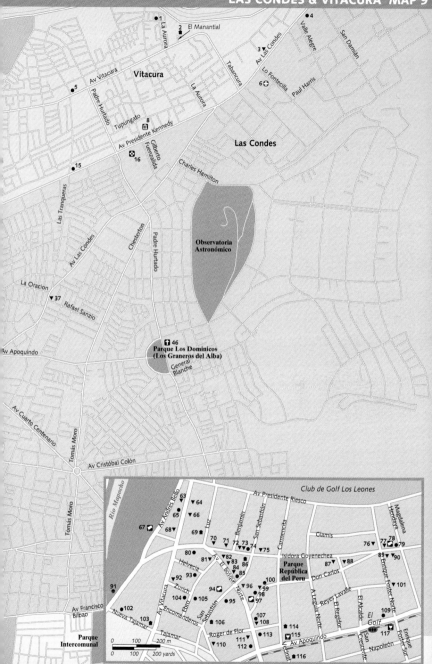

1
2 El Manantial
La Aurora
4
3 Av Las Condes
Av Vitacura
Vitacura
5
Padre Hurtado
Tupungato
La Aurora
Tabancura
Lo Fontecilla
6
Valle Alegre
San Damián
Paul Harris
8
Av Presidente Kennedy
Gilberto Fuenzalida
16
Las Condes
15
Charles Hamilton
Las Tranqueras
Chesterton
Padre Hurtado
Av Las Condes
Observatoria
Astronómico
La Oracion
37 Rafael Sanzio
46
Parque Los Dominicos
(Los Graneros del Alba)
General Blanche
Av Apoquindo
Av Cuarto Centenario
Tomás Moro
Av Cristóbal Colón
Tomás Moro
Parque
Intercomunal
Rio Mapocho
Av Andrés Bello
Av Vitacura
Nueva Tajamar
Av Francisco Bilbao
Club de Golf Los Leones
Av Presidente Riesco
Luz
63
64
65 66
67 68
69
70
71 72 73 74 75
80
81 82 83 84 85 86
Helvecia
79 93
91
92
Zurich
94
104 105
102
103
111
110
112
95
96 97 98 99 100
113
114 115
116
Benjamín
San Sebastián
Carmencita
Isidora Goyenechea
Parque República del Perú
Clamis
Don Carlos
A Leguia Norte
El Regidor
Reyes Lavalle
El Alcalde
San Crescente
El Golf
San Napoleón
Enrique Foster Norte
Enrique Foster Sur
Magdalena
Hendaya
76 77 78
87 88 89 90
101
109
117
Av Apoquindo
Tajamar
Roger de Flor
El Bosque Norte
San Sebastián
A El Bosque
Encomenderos
0   100   200 m
0   100   200 yards

MAP 9 LAS CONDES & VITACURA

PLACES TO STAY
2 Hotel Acacias de Vitacura
22 Hotel Director
27 Hotel Río Bidasoa
33 Hotel Kennedy
34 Hyatt Regency Santiago
36 Marriott Hotel
40 Hotel Parinacota
41 Hotel Regal Pacific
44 Hotel Irazú
59 Hotel Leonardo da Vinci
69 Hotel Intercontinental Santiago
86 Hotel Montebianco
103 Radisson Royal Santiago Hotel
106 Apart Hotel La Sebastiana
114 Apart Hotel Director
116 Hotel Tarapacá

PLACES TO EAT
3 Santa Fe
9 Benyarong
25 Sakura
26 Wok House
28 El Suizo
29 Delmónico
34 Anakena
37 Chang Cheng
47 Au Bon Pain
50 Da Dino
63 El Mexicano
64 El Madroñal
66 Ginza Teppanyaki
68 Taberna de Papagayo
70 Pinpilinpausha
71 Puerto Marisko
72 Le Due Torri
73 La Cascade
75 Ruby Tuesday
76 Shoogun
77 Gioia
81 München
82 Coco Loco
83 Hereford Grill
84 Au Bon Pain
87 Jaipur
88 TGIFriday's
89 Cangrejo Loco; La Cocina Peruana
90 Da Renato

92 El Naturista
96 PubLicity
99 Café Melba
101 Asador del Golf
108 New York Bagel Bakery
110 Flannery's Irish Geo Pub
111 Food Garden

OTHER
1 Cámara Chileno Canadiense de Comercio
4 Skuba
5 Automovil Club Chileno
6 Clínica Las Condes
7 Cine Arte Vitacura
8 Museo de Artes Decorativas Casas de lo Matta
10 Club de Amantes del Vino
11 Danish Embassy
12 Librería Eduardo Albers
13 Deutsch-Chilenischer Bund
14 Clínica Alemana
15 Automóvil Club Chileno (Acchi)
16 Alto Las Condes
17 Mará Inés Matte
18 Museo Ralli
19 Galería Isabél Aninat
20 Galería Tomás Andreu
21 Galería Artespacio
23 Rincón Chileno
24 Cine Lo Castillo; Anfiteatro Lo Castillo
30 Escuela de Vino
31 Chile Típico
32 Faba
35 Parque Arauco; Showcase Cinemas
38 Museo Histórico de la Escuela Militar
39 Centro de Ski El Colorado
42 Cosmocentro Apumanque
43 Cine Las Condes
45 Instituto Cultural de Las Condes
46 Iglesia los Dominicos
48 Air France
49 Dollar Rent a Car
51 Cámara Chileno-Norteamericana de Comercio (AmCham)

52 Swiss Embassy
53 Mexican Embassy
54 Servicio de Impuestos Internos (SII)
55 Budget Rent a Car
56 Valle Nevado
57 Australian Embassy
58 Colomba
60 Centro de Ski Portillo
61 Toluka Rent a Car
62 New Rent a Car
65 The Wine House
67 US Embassy
74 British Airways; Qantas; Japan Airlines
78 New Zealand Embassy
79 Vinoteca
80 Cámara Chileno Alemana de Comercio e Industria; Turismo Cocha
85 Pluna; Varig; United Airlines
91 Universidad Católica (Soccer Offices)
93 Just Rent a Car
94 Israeli Embassy
95 Cámara Chileno-Neozelandesa de Comercio; Norwegian Embassy & Consulate
97 British Embassy
98 Cámara Chileno Australiana de Comercio
100 A Touch of Home
102 Continental Airlines; Canadian Consulate
104 Aeroméxico
105 TAME (Ecuador)
107 American Airlines
109 Centro Cultural Las Condes
110 Altué Active Travel
112 Vinópolis
113 Centro Cultural del Vino
115 Los Andes
117 Nichola's Pub

Restored palace, Barrio Brasil

Façade of historic building, Calle Lastarría

Colorful neighbors on Avenida Pío Nono in Barrio Bellavista

MAP 10 ÑUÑOA

Providencia

Marin

see MAP 8
Providencia

Santa Victoria

Santa Isabel

Santa
Isabel

Av Seminario

Emilia Vásse

Girardi

Tegualda

Av Salvador

Santa Isabel

Av José Infante

Av Miguel Claro

Diagonal Oriente ● 1

Av Condell

Av Italia

Caupolicán

M Concha

Rengo

Av Sucre

Plaza
Francke

Mujica

▼ 3

6 ▼

Inés Palma ● 4

Av Sucre
▼ 5

Av Condell

Av Italia

Tegualda

Julio Prado

Luis Beltrand

Av José Infante

Av Manuel Montt

Av Sucre

Simón Bolívar

Av Antonio Varas

Tucapel

Av Irarrázaval

San Eugenio

Av General
Bustamante

Av Seminario

Av Irarrázaval
▼ 16

Av General Baquedano

Irarrázaval

Manuel Antonio Matta

Matta Oriente

José Domingo Cañas

23 ▼

Capitán Fuentes

Monseñor Eyzaguirre

Carmen Covarrubias

Campos de Deportes

Duble Almeyd

Av Grecia

Eduardo Castillo Velasco

▼ 25

26 ●

24
▼

27 ▼

28 ▼

29
▼

Av Vicuña Mackenna

Av Salvador

Obispo Orrego

Av José Infante

Av República de Israel

Eduardo Castillo Velasco

Crescente Errázuriz

Ñuñoa

31 ●

Miranda

Suárez Mujica

Presidente Mazfor

see MAP 5
Santiago
Centro

Av Grecia

Av Marathon

Estadio
Nacional

Av Pedro de Valdivia

Santiago

Ñuble ●●●

Av Carlos Dittborn

Ñuble

San Eugenio

Guillermo Mann

Av Vicuña Mackenna

Av Zañartu

Williams Rebolledo

Av Marathon

Rodrigo de Araya

●●● Rodrigo de Araya

● 33